In Defence of the Russian Revolution

In memoriam, Francis Ambrose Ridley (1897-1994)

συναγαγετε τα περισσευσαντα
κλασματα ινα μη τι αποληται

Nikolai Bukharin, Lev Kamenev, Vladimir Lenin, Karl Radek, Leon Trotsky, Mikhail Tukhachevsky and Grigory Zinoviev

In Defence of the Russian Revolution

A Selection of Bolshevik Writings, 1917-1923

Edited and Introduced by Al Richardson

Porcupine Press

Published by Porcupine Press, 10 Woburn Walk, London WC1H 0JL

Copyright © 1995 Socialist Platform Ltd
Translation Chapter 12 Copyright © 1995 Porcupine Press

Production by Paul Flewers
Cover design by Catlin Harrison
Illustrations courtesy of the Socialist Platform Library
Printed in Britain by TJ Press (Padstow) Ltd

ISBN 1 89 943801 7 (cloth), 1 89 943802 5 (paper)

Contents

Introduction

WHOEVER REGARDED the Russian Revolution of 1917 as a change for the better in world affairs cannot but be dismayed by the collapse of the Soviet Union and its replacement by the Commonwealth of Independent States and a number of other bourgeois nation states. That this should be accompanied by the disappearance of all the regimes akin to it in the rest of Europe shows that we are witnessing the fall of an entire system dependent on the Soviet Union, even in Albania, Yugoslavia and Romania, which were outside its direct control. Its immediate effects on the international arena have been profound. A united Germany at the heart of Europe seems set to dominate the new superpower envisaged by the European Union, and the removal of the constraints upon American imperialism appear to have given it for the time being unlimited capacity to intervene all over the globe, unchallenged as it is in its domination of the United Nations.

However hollow its claims to a planned economy (and here the journal *Critique* should take all the credit for exposing them), the fall of the Soviet Union has had a demoralising effect upon the labour movement elsewhere. The complete internal collapse of the system, naturally linked in the minds of the workers with the unpleasant functioning of capitalist nationalisation, has all but discredited the very concept of public ownership. So not only has Stalinism entered into predictable crisis, but there can be little doubt that it has also had a dispiriting effect upon Social Democracy, which everywhere in Europe has weakened and moved to the right, advocating a 'mixed economy' with as little state admixture as possible.

These profound material changes have thrown the thinking left into confusion. The largest part of the Communist Party of Great Britain and important spokesmen of the New Left have repudiated Leninism completely, some of them going so far as to advocate voting in elections for the Liberal Democrats. Of course, it could be argued that since *The British Road to Socialism* the former could not even make a formal claim to revolutionary politics, and the latter's advertisement of one aberrant (and abhorrent) non-Russian form of Stalinism after another was bound to end in an impasse. They were, after all, fair weather friends, drawn to Marxism when it was the fashionable culture of the hour, and we are well rid of them. As Trotsky remarks below, 'the ethical-aesthetic standard by which is guided a considerable, and not the worst, part of the intellectuals, is entirely unfit for the grasping of great historical events'.[1]

But what of those who are not what Trotsky described as 'worshippers of the accomplished fact', the genuine left, which still remains loyal to the heritage of October? It has to be said that the collapse of the Soviet Union caught them all napping. In spite of their claims to scientific Socialism, possession of this science gave them no predictive powers whatever, and apart from the above-mentioned *Critique* magazine, you can scan their journals right up to the event in vain for any suggestion of what was coming. Nor has any coherent explanation emerged since.

Those who had always argued that the Soviet Union was a transitional regime seemed to have had no inkling that transitions can go back as well as forwards. What was worse, for those of us who envisaged it at all, the circumstances attending the disintegration of the Soviet state in no way accorded with our expectations.[2] Trotskyists always expected that the workers would fiercely resist any counter-revolution, and a Marxist party would be present to lead the struggle to restore working class control over social property. The bureaucracy, so we believed, not being politically homogeneous, would divide, one faction — the 'Butenko faction' — would be quasi-fascist supporters of capitalist restoration, and the other, the 'Reiss faction', would ally with the workers.[3] The Butenko faction is certainly in evidence in the former Soviet Union, but the Reiss faction is nowhere to be seen. Nor did the expected soviet forms emerge, and the new-born trade unions proved to be enthusiastic supporters of free market capitalism. Although a real bourgeoisie had not existed in these countries for over a generation, bourgeois nationalism emerged all over the place. And what was not at all expected was that these states would collapse without an armed counter-revolutionary overturn accompanied by a civil war. Can one property form really change into another with so little dislocation in its state apparatus, no visible destruction of it caused by revolution or counter-revolution? Is not this phenomenon a direct challenge to the class theory of the state?

Those who held to a state capitalist analysis came up with the illuminating suggestion that a state capitalist class had slimmed down its bankrupt concern into smaller private firms, oblivious of the observation that whilst many a small shopkeeper dreams of being a monopoly capitalist, few monopoly capitalists dream of being small shopkeepers. Their agitational literature even made use of the fashionable language about 'the collapse of Communism', uncomfortably reminding us of the people handled so severely by Radek in one of our texts below.[4] A feature this analysis shared with the 'new class' theories was that nothing in its structure indicated whether the property forms of the Soviet Union were regressive as regards private capitalism or a mirror of the future, so that they can both be said to have had it both ways, though neither tendency predicted its imminent collapse in any case.

No overall theory has emerged about the structure of this state form that explains its birth, its mechanism of decline and its subsequent collapse, and it should be added that no theory can be counted as adequate unless it explains the whole process from start to finish. We may well take Radek out of context and say that 'the question of the fall of Communism in Russia is still a matter for further discussion'.[5]

Such a theory is a most pressing need, for a whole new consensus is emerging about these events in the mass media, aided by the failure of the left to challenge it in any coherent way. The Bolsheviks, so we are told, were impractical fanatics who seized power in a conspiratorial coup in a country quite unfitted for utopian experiments, during a period in which capitalism had by no means exhausted its creative potential, and their project was bound to fail. This book is an attempt to allow the Bolsheviks to answer these charges for themselves, by reproducing speeches and articles in which they explain what they were doing and describe the difficulties and dangers they encountered, as well as their projections for the future. This makes it an untimely or a timely publication — depending on your point of view — or at any rate an unfashionable one. But that does not make it a mere work of apologetic, for we have included such pieces as Trotsky's arguments for the militarisation of the trade unions, Radek's contribution to the personality cult in his eulogy of Lenin, Lenin's own refusal to repudiate the 'contrary-to-nature' alliance with German reaction, and Zinoviev's first manoeuvres against Trotsky, which by no means reflect favourably on their authors 70 years afterwards. As far as we are aware none of these texts is still in print, and others appear here in English for the first time.

Let us see if there is anything in these statements that throws light upon present-day understanding.

We may as well begin with the charge of utopianism. Radek gives a most interesting answer; whilst pointing out that 'Marxist theory laid down that the reorganisation of society on a Socialist basis was impossible in Russia',[6] and while emphasising that all their measures were not taken 'in a doctrinaire fashion', but as 'the result of necessity', he explains how 'the necessities of the war and the necessities of the struggle were transformed in the heads of the masses into the religion of Communism', and that 'ideology, which had taken on its own dynamic, very often transformed provisional, transitional measures into a system'.[7] Of course, every revolution there has ever been outruns its material base in an ideological sense, as the examples of the Levellers, Babeuf and the Equals, the Paris Communards, etc, abundantly prove, for 'revolution not only gives rise to coolness of judgement, but also to illusions, which are not 'mistakes', but which give wings to the offensive, give it strength and lead it to ends that are historically put before it'.[8]

Some of the remarks made here contain considerable foresight. All the Bolsheviks at that time believed that the revolution would either spread and transform the world, or that left to its own devices in backward Russia it would be overthrown. Lenin puts the matter of the future of the state quite plainly: 'We say that the revolution can be brought about only through the efforts of the advanced workers of the advanced countries. On that point no conscious Communist has ever had a shadow of doubt.'[9] Tukhachevsky draws the further conclusion that not only was a Cold War inevitable from this time forward, but many hot wars as well: 'What is impossible and untenable is the supposition that this world, shaken to its foundations by the Great War, might quite peacefully divide itself into two halves, one Socialist and the other capitalist, which could now live together in peace and good neighbourliness.'[10] .

Of course, it may be objected, the revolution did expand, in Eastern Europe and elsewhere, but that still did not save it. But here our material allows us to explore the connection between this expansion and the Stalinist national degeneration of the revolution. Ever since Marx, Socialists have understood that the working class cannot come to power except by its own efforts, consciously creating the new society by its understanding of historical necessity. This belief is well reflected in the words of *The Internationale*, 'no saviour from on high deliver'. But what happens if this class is placed in 'power' by armed conquest from an already victorious revolution elsewhere? Lenin's speeches show that spreading the revolution by armed conquest was certainly not ruled out in principle from the very start.[11] Tukhachevsky develops this by saying, 'if anywhere a Socialist revolution reaches power, then it has the self-evident right to expand, it will strive with elemental force to spread by direct action to all neighbouring countries to involve the whole world. Its most important instrument will naturally be its military power.'[12] Of course, this was at a time when he still believed that the Soviet army should have 'forgotten of what nationality it was in its majority composed', and that it 'must be aware that it is the army of the world proletariat, and nothing else'.[13] But what would be the result if this army **became** something else — the instrument of a national state?

Tukhachevsky's comment calls to mind the connection between military conflict and the rise of Stalinism in the first place. Whenever the Whites captured a town during the Civil War, they eliminated the soviet, the trade unions, the Bolshevik Party cell, and whatever other working class organisations existed there. When the Bolsheviks recaptured it, these institutions were reconstructed from above by personnel sent out from the centre at the request of the military authorities. The working class had already lost any direct control it may ever have had over this centre by the breakdown of industry in the Civil War and the atomisation of the class. By the very nature of the war, these new cadres placed in control of the local organisations were drawn from the Russian heartland, from Moscow and Petrograd. In these circumstances it is not at all surprising that Zinoviev warns against 'allowing the appearance of even the least trace of colonialism',[14] and speaking already about the conquest of Transcaucasia, Trotsky notes that if Great Russian chauvinist tendencies 'were to get the upper hand, the contradiction between our programme and our actual policy would inevitably lead to catastrophe',[15] a remark Armenians and Azerbaijanis may well be pondering at the moment. Lenin, at least, was keenly aware of these dangers, and traced Stalin's hand in the affair of the treatment of the Georgian Bolsheviks. This great Russian brutality masquerading as Socialist internationalism was imposed upon entire nations in Eastern Europe at the end of the Second World War by the same method of armed conquest, and has made the very name of Marxism an abomination in these lands.

Nor can the Bolsheviks be accused of a doctrinaire attitude as regards the economy. Trotsky calls an orientation to the market an 'absolute necessity of the transitional stage',[16] and Radek points out repeatedly that the New Economic Policy, in affording scope to private enterprise, was actually a return to the plans they had formulated in 1917.[17] Trotsky shows that there was never any intention to nationalise the whole of the economy at that time.[18] It was a measure forced upon the Bolsheviks by the requirements of the Civil War. Moreover, they talk quite frankly of the mechanisms of capitalism they are employing. 'The question of creating surplus value in state industry is the fateful question for the soviet power', says Trotsky, calling for 'an expanded reproduction of state industry, which is unthinkable without the accumulation of surplus value by the state.' He even considers that 'measures which retain poorly-furnished enterprises in operation, or employ in a mill a number of workers not proportionate to the actual productivity of the enterprise, constitute the most expensive and irrational form of social insurance, and are therefore against the interests of the future of the working class'.[19] Radek adds that 'we knew that the captains of industry would be necessary to us and that state cartelisation of industry with state participation, but under the practical management of capitalists controlled by the state, would for the moment be the form of industrial organisation most favourable to us'. 'So long as the proletariat has not triumphed in the principal capitalist states', he writes, 'so long as it will not be in a position to utilise all the productive forces of the world for Socialist construction, so long as capitalist states exist alongside proletarian states, the proletarian states will be forced to conclude compromises with them, and there will be neither pure Socialism nor pure capitalism.'[20] So the Soviet state was a battleground between capitalism and the revolution from the very beginning: 'if the tendencies of capitalist growth gain the upper hand over the tendencies to improve large industry', notes Bukharin, 'then we are doomed'.[21]

If we have here a true workers' revolution, how are we to explain these obvious remarks about capitalism, the law of value, etc, and similar comments about the desirability of Taylorism in Soviet industry made by Lenin and Trotsky, referring not only to firms in private hands during the NEP, but to the state-owned industry itself?[22]

It is at this point in the argument that we have to say that the tools of analysis used by the thinkers of the left are quite inadequate for a true appreciation of the problem. The debate on the class nature of the Soviet state has hitherto been conducted as a clash of set definitions, of workers' state versus state capitalism, as if each excluded the other, an arid encounter between fixed Aristotelian categories bereft of dialectical content. But if we follow the indications left us by the classical thinkers of Marxism, we can discover a far more fruitful working model. We shall see that they lead back like an Ariadne's thread through Trotsky to Lenin, and then to Engels and Marx himself.

Let us begin, as do Lenin and Trotsky, with Marx's *Critique of the Gotha Programme*:

'Such defects [inequality, the wages system, etc — ed], however, are inevitable in the first phase of Communist society, given the specific form in which it has emerged after prolonged birth-pangs from capitalist society. Right can never rise above the economic structure of a society and its contingent cultural development.'[23]

Lenin adds the following comment on this passage in his notebooks: 'This NB! With (semi-bourgeois) rights the (semi-bourgeois) state obviously does not fully disappear either. This is a Nota Bene!!'[24]

He expands the point in his famous *State and Revolution*:

'In its first place, or first stage, Communism cannot as yet be fully mature economically and entirely free from traditions or vestiges of capitalism. Hence the interesting phenomenon that Communism in its first phase retains the narrow horizon of **bourgeois** right. Of course, bourgeois right in regard to the distribution of **consumer** goods inevitably presupposes the existence of the **bourgeois state**, for right is nothing without an apparatus of **enforcing** the observance of the standard of right.

'It follows that under Communism there remains for a time not only bourgeois right, but even the bourgeois state, without the bourgeoisie!

'This may sound like a paradox or simply a dialectical conundrum, of which Marxism is often accused by people who have not taken the slightest trouble to study its extraordinarily profound content.'[25]

Trotsky adds the following remarks about this startling definition of a workers' state being 'a bourgeois state without a bourgeoisie' in his classic investigation of the causes of the degeneration of the Soviet state:

'This highly significant conclusion, completely ignored by the present official theoreticians, has a decisive significance for the understanding of the nature of the Soviet state — or more accurately, for a first approach to such an understanding. Insofar as the state which assumes the task of Socialist transformation is compelled to defend inequality — that is, the material privileges of a minority — by methods of compulsion, insofar does it also remain a "bourgeois" state, even without a bourgeoisie. These words contain neither praise nor blame; they merely name things with their real names.

'The bourgeois norms of distribution, by hastening the growth of material power, ought to serve Socialist aims — but only in the last analysis. The state assumes directly and from the beginning a dual character: socialistic, insofar as it defends social property in the means of production; bourgeois, insofar as the distribution of life's goods is carried out with a capitalistic measure of value and all the consequences ensuing therefrom. Such a contradictory characterisation may horrify dogmatists and scholastics; we can only offer them our condolences...

'For the defence of "bourgeois law" the workers' state was compelled to create a "bourgeois" type of instrument — that is, the same old gendarme, although in a new uniform.'[26]

Let us pause for a minute to unravel some of these concepts. The state is, as Marxists have always maintained, essentially armed men standing in defence of property.[27] The first act of a Socialist revolution is that the state takes control of production, converting private into public property. Exploitation by private capitals is replaced by exploitation by one, state capital. But **property remains**, and exploitation remains, until the higher development of the productive forces enables property to wither away, and with it the state itself. Now a state which defends property in the means of production and perpetuates the wages system is still, in that sense, **bourgeois**, however much it may be under the control of the working class. The ultimate goal of Marxism is the abolition of all property, the wages system, and all classes. In that sense **there is no such thing as a healthy workers' state**. It is a necessary, temporary, social evil. As Trotsky adds:

'A Socialist state, even in America, on the basis of the most advanced capitalism, could not immediately provide everyone with as much as he needs, and would therefore be compelled to spur everyone to produce as much as possible. The duty of a **stimulator** in these circumstances naturally falls to the state, which in its turn cannot but resort, with various changes and mitigations, to the method of labour payment worked out by capitalism.'[28]

This 'method' is, of course, the wages system, that essential component of a capitalist economy.

These may be upsetting and paradoxical conclusions, but on second sight they are perfectly logical, and even predictable. No society replacing another ever immediately obliterates even the basic institutions of the previous society. Even after many centuries of bourgeois development Britain still has the monarchy, the church, and the House of Lords, not to mention far older institutions such as the family which predate feudalism by thousands of years. Because the system replaced by the Socialist revolution is capitalist, it is obvious that the institutions it will inherit will have a bourgeois stamp — not only the wages system, money, the family, etc, but the **state itself**. In this sense Trotsky's comparison of the Soviet state with a trade union in power is an apt one, for trade unions, whilst 'owned' by the workers, are thoroughly bourgeois institutions, dependent on the existence of the wages system and the capitalist mode of production.

Another conclusion that follows is that state capitalism exists and functions both **before** and **after** the Socialist revolution. Let us first see how Engels explains the relationship between the two:

'In the trusts, free competition changes into monopoly and the planless production of capitalist society capitulates before the planned production of the invading Socialist society. Of course, this is initially still to the benefit of the capitalists. But the exploitation becomes so palpable here that it must break down. No nation would put up with production directed by trusts, with such a barefaced exploitation of the community by a small band of coupon-clippers.

'In one way or another, with trusts or without, the state, the official representative of capitalist society, is finally constrained to take over the direction of production...

'All the social functions of the capitalist are now conducted by salaried employees. The capitalist no longer has any social activity save the pocketing of revenues, the clipping of coupons and gambling on the stock exchange, where the different capitalists fleece each other of their capital. Just as at first the capitalist mode of production displaced the workers, so now it is displacing the capitalists, relegating them, just as it did the workers, to the superfluous population, although not immediately to the industrial reserve army.

'But neither conversion into joint-stock companies and trusts nor conversion into state property deprives the productive forces of their character as capital. This is obvious in the case of joint-stock companies and trusts. But the modern state, too, is only the organisation with which bourgeois society provides itself in order to maintain the general external conditions of the capitalist mode of production against encroachments either by the workers or by individual capitalists. The modern state, whatever its form, is an essentially capitalist machine, the state of the capitalists, the ideal aggregate capitalist. The more productive forces it takes over into its possession, the more it becomes a real aggregate capitalist, the more citizens it exploits. The workers remain wage-workers, proletarians. The capitalist relationship is not abolished, rather it is pushed to the limit. But at this limit it changes into its opposite. State ownership of the productive forces is not the solution of the conflict, but it contains within itself the formal means, the handle to the solution.

'This solution can only consist in actually reorganising the social nature of the modern productive forces and in therefore bringing the mode of production, appropriation and exchange into harmony with the social character of the means of production. This can only be brought about by society's openly and straightforwardly taking possession of the productive forces, which have outgrown all guidance other than that of society itself. Thus the social character of the means of production and of the products, which today reacts against the producers themselves, periodically ruptures the mode of production and exchange, and enforces itself only as a law of nature working blindly, violently and destructively, will be quite consciously asserted by the producers, and instead of being a source of disorder and periodical collapse will change into the most powerful lever of production itself...

'By increasingly transforming the great majority of the population into proletarians, the capitalist mode of production creates the force which, under penalty of its own destruction, is compelled to accomplish this revolution. By increasingly driving towards the transformation of the vast socialised means of production into state property, it itself points the way to the accomplishment of this revolution. **The proletariat seizes state power and to begin with transforms the means of production into state property.**'[29]

The important point to notice here is that to begin with the Socialist revolution does not abolish property. It converts all property into state property. But in the nature of things, while that property subsists it **remains capitalist**.

The historic function of state capitalism under the bourgeois order as a necessary preparation for the Socialist revolution was analysed concretely in the case of Russia by Lenin. Before we set out what he has to say, it is wise to bear in mind that here the capitalist class was historically so weak that the state had to play a predominant rôle in the development of the economy in the first place, and that this already huge state sector was swollen during the First World War when firms had to be taken out of private hands in order to prevent their breakdown from impeding the war effort. Our first illustrations are taken from the very eve of the revolution:

'Given a really revolutionary-democratic state, state monopoly capitalism inevitably and unavoidably implies a step, and more than one step, towards Socialism...

'For Socialism is merely the next step forward from state-capitalist monopoly. Or, in other words, Socialism is merely state-capitalist monopoly which is made to serve the interests of the whole people and has to that extent ceased to be capitalist monopoly...

'It is impossible to advance from monopolies... without advancing towards Socialism...

'The dialectics of history is such that the war, by extraordinarily expediting the transformation of monopoly capitalism into state-monopoly capitalism, has thereby extraordinarily advanced mankind towards Socialism.

'Imperialist war is the eve of Socialist revolution. And this is not only because the horrors of the war give rise to proletarian revolt — no revolt can bring about Socialism unless the economic conditions for Socialism are ripe — but because state-monopoly capitalism is a complete material preparation for Socialism...'[30]

Well, we may add, so state capitalism, capitalism pushed to its limits, as Engels would have put it, is a necessary foundation for the Socialist revolution. But does that mean that it will continue to operate after it? What is actually taken over in real terms into the new order? Lenin's answer is that this is none other than some of the essential mechanisms of the bourgeois state!

'In addition to the "chiefly oppressive" apparatus — the standing army, the police and the bureaucracy — the modern state possesses an apparatus which has extremely close connections with the banks and syndicates, an apparatus which performs an enormous amount of accounting and registration work, if it may be expressed this way. This apparatus must not, and should not, be smashed. It must be wrested from the control of the capitalists; the capitalists and the wires they pull must be cut off, lopped off, chopped away from this apparatus; it must be subordinated to the proletarian soviets; it must be expanded, made more comprehensive, and nation-wide. And this can be done by utilising the achievements already made by large-scale capitalism (in the same way as the proletarian revolution can, in general, reach its goal only by utilising these achievements.)

'Capitalism has created an accounting apparatus in the shape of the banks, syndicates, postal service, consumers' societies, and office employees' unions. Without big banks Socialism would be impossible.

'The big banks are the state apparatus which we need to bring about Socialism, and which we take ready-made from capitalism...'[31]

Let us take note that Lenin's final words here show that what is being envisaged is not the mere appropriation of individual capitalist institutions, but their adoption as essential adjuncts of the state apparatus, which is a further illustration of his argument that a workers' state is a bourgeois state without a bourgeoisie. And not only did Lenin freely admit that state capitalism was the economic and political mechanism of this state, he argued that it was all the more necessary in the case of backward Russia:

'State capitalism would be a gigantic step forward even if we paid more than we are paying at present... because it is worth paying for "tuition" because it is useful for the workers, because victory over disorder, economic ruin and laxity is the most important thing, because the continuation of the anarchy of small ownership is the greatest, the most serious danger, and it will certainly be our ruin (unless we overcome it), whereas not only will the payment of a heavier tribute to state capitalism not ruin us, it will lead us to Socialism by the surest road. When the working class has learned how to defend the state system against the anarchy of small ownership, when it has learned to organise large-scale production on a national scale along state-capitalist lines, it will hold, if I may use the expression, all the trump cards, and the consolidation of Socialism will be assured.

'In the first place economically state capitalism is immeasurably superior to our present economic system.

'In the second place there is nothing terrible in it for the Soviet power, for the Soviet state is a state in which the power of the workers and the poor is assured.'[32]

This evidence shows quite clearly that Lenin believed that a workers' state and state capitalism were not, as our modern epigones believe, opposites which exclude each other on an either-or basis, but dialectical opposites depending upon each other for their existence. In other words, this simple logical demonstration alone is enough to condemn the present debate between supporters of the workers' state theory and the proponents of state capitalism as a puerile exercise, unworthy of the attention of serious Marxists, as well as being a waste of time and effort. Even more counter-productive is the argument about when one of these 'states' was replaced by the other (we will leave for the moment the problem of the last few years to the end of our argument, where it belongs). The cheap jibes that the workers could not be an oppressed class and a ruling class at one and the same time, or about the impossibility of the existence of a counter-revolutionary workers' state also fall into dust in these words. The tortuous discussions as to whether the law of value did or did not apply in the Soviet Union show themselves to be equally light-minded. Obviously, from the demonstration here, it did, and this was freely admitted by those who were directing the economy of the country, as the material collected for this book shows.

Of course, there must have been a logical point at issue here for so much energy to have been expended on it. The whole dispute obviously arose because not enough attention was given to the possibility that the functioning of state capitalism would continue (in an altered form) after the revolution, as well as before it. Marx and Engels had indicated as much, but no more than that. Here again Lenin locates the problem more precisely:

'Not a single book has been written about state capitalism under Communism. It did not even occur to Marx to write a word on this subject; and he died without leaving a single precise statement or definite instruction on it...

'The state capitalism discussed in all books on economics is that which exists under the capitalist system, where the state brings under its direct control capitalist enterprises. But ours is a proletarian state... That is why very many people are misled by the term state capitalism. To avoid this we must remember the fundamental thing that state capitalism in the form we have here is not dealt with in any theory, or in any books, for the simple reason that all the usual concepts associated with this term are associated with bourgeois rule in capitalist society. Our society is one which has left the rails of capitalism, but has not yet got on to the new rails. The state in this society is not ruled by the bourgeoisie, but by the proletariat. We refuse to understand that when we say "state" we mean ourselves, the proletariat, the vanguard of the working class. State capitalism is capitalism which we shall be able to restrain, and the limits of which we shall be able to fix. This state capitalism is connected with the state, and the state is the workers, the vanguard. We are the state.

'State capitalism is capitalism that we must confine within certain bounds; but we have not yet learned to confine it within those bounds. That is the whole point. And it rests with us to determine what this state capitalism is to be...

'Never before in history has there been a situation in which the proletariat, the revolutionary vanguard, possessed sufficient political power and had state capitalism existing alongside it. The whole question turns on our understanding that this is the capitalism that we can and must permit, that we can and must confine within certain bounds; for this capitalism is essential for the broad masses of the peasantry and for private capital, which must trade in such a way as to satisfy the needs of the peasantry. We must organise things in such a way as to make possible the customary operation of capitalist economy and capitalist exchange, because this is essential for the people. Without it, existence is impossible.'[33]

This remarkable speech, one of the last full expositions Lenin's health permitted him, also contains the key to understanding the further degeneration of the Soviet Union. The whole conflict between the proletarian and capitalist aspects of this state, a conflict that could only in the end be resolved in one way or the other, came down to the problem of the control of the working class over the state, and hence over state capitalism. 'If we take Moscow with its 4700 Communists in responsible positions, and if we take that huge bureaucratic machine, we must ask: who is directing whom?', said Lenin. And he answered his own question: 'I doubt very much whether it can be truthfully said that the Communists are directing that heap. To tell the truth, they are not directing, they are being directed.'[34] For by the time he spoke the workers no longer had any direct political control over this state. The whole lively ferment of democracy in the local soviets and the workers' control in industry that accompanied the revolution had ended by the winter of 1918; one-man management had replaced it everywhere in industry; the state had become militarised, had absorbed many of the best worker-militants, and was largely staffed and directed by the personnel of the old Tsarist bureaucracy, hostile to the revolution and to workers' rule. By the end of the Civil War, in fact, the Soviet working class hardly existed any more, as the figures for industrial production painfully show. Workers' democracy, both as regards the other parties, and in the Workers' and Democratic Centralist Oppositions within the Communist Party, had been choked off. History was presented with the unprecedented phenomenon of a class that had successfully accomplished a revolution and erected a state, but which no longer existed, except in embryo. It takes generations for a working class to create (or in this case, recreate) its institutions, painfully from the bottom up. Moreover, this was the class that above all needed to be conscious of its historic tasks in taking and wielding power by the fullest exercise of democratic debate and activity.

The working class never regained political control of the state in the Soviet Union. Since it was in essence a 'bourgeois' state from the very first, surrounded by economically far more advanced capitalist states and a dynamic and expanding capitalist world market, the degeneration could only proceed in one direction, unless further proletarian revolutions succeeded elsewhere. The introduction of the NEP itself was a step backwards in the direction of capitalism, in circumstances in which the largest and most productive part of the economy, agriculture, was in private hands, apart from the question of who controlled the state itself. Here again we have the benefit of Lenin's extraordinary foresight when drawing attention to the opinions of one of the regime's opponents in an emigré journal:

'Ustryalov... says: "You can think what you like about Communism, but I maintain that it is not a matter of tactics, but of evolution." I think that being straightforward like this, Ustryalov is rendering us a great service... *Smena Vekh...* says quite plainly: "Things are by no means what you imagine them to be. As a matter of fact, you are slipping into the ordinary bourgeois morass with Communist flags inscribed with catchwords stuck all over the place..." This is very useful. It is not a repetition of what we are constantly hearing about us, but the plain class truth uttered by the class enemy. "I am in favour of supporting the Soviet government", says Ustryalov... "I am in favour of supporting Soviet power because it has taken the road that will lead it to the ordinary bourgeois state..." We must say frankly that such candid enemies are useful. We must say frankly that the things Ustryalov speaks about are possible. History knows all sorts of metamorphoses... The enemy is speaking the class truth and is pointing to the danger that confronts us, and which the enemy is striving to make inevitable. *Smena Vekh* adherents express the sentiments of thousands and tens of thousands of bourgeois, or of Soviet employees whose function it is to operate our New Economic Policy.'[35]

It is a simple matter using these basic guidelines to determine the capitalist direction of this degeneration in a thumb-nail sketch of the events that followed.

The revolution sustained defeat after defeat elsewhere, and became more isolated in Russia than ever before. First came the destruction of the Left, the Left-Centre and the Right Oppositions, leaving the state a monolith, and ridding the working class of its last voice. It goes without saying that a precondition for the existence of the fully-fledged Stalinism of the period of the terror was the prior annihilation of any autonomous expression or organisation of the working class. And the forced industrialisation and collectivisation generalised wage labour and expanded state capitalism to an extraordinary degree. This was certainly a decisive turning point, if not a qualitative one. For there can be little doubt that there is more than an atom of truth in Tony Cliff's argument that the capitalist tendencies within the Soviet Union received an enormous boost at this time, even if they had been there all along, and the actual state and economic structure did not change in its essentials, as he would have it.

After the Second World War this already warped state form exported its 'revolution' into Eastern Europe at bayonet point, where Hitler had already annihilated the vestigial native bourgeois classes on its behalf. True to its counter-revolutionary character, to begin with it tried to recreate these states as bourgeois states of the normal sort, but failing in this, it created mini 'Socialisms in One Country' after its own model. It had itself, of course, already degenerated from being a federal international state of the working class to the far inferior level of a nation state, and a nationally oppressive one at that. It might be argued that if the state of Lenin and Trotsky had still been in existence at the time, the Soviet Union would not have set up separate states in these countries at all. For was it not in its origins an international state, representing an international class? Would it not simply have added to itself further Soviet republics and fixed its new capital in Prague, where the working class was far more advanced than in the USSR, both materially and in consciousness, since they had only recently lost their autonomous institutions?[36] For in creating these new states Stalin took great care to sharpen the national antagonisms between them by means of border adjustments and population expulsions. Here again, *Lutte ouvrière* have considerable truth on their side when they deny the same sort of workers' state character to the countries of Eastern Europe as they ascribe to the Soviet Union. After all, the workers had once actually wielded state power in Russia directly through their own democratic institutions, but apart from (to a slight extent) in Czechoslovakia, the workers played no part in the creation of 'the Peoples' Democracies' at all. Direct military force created them, and when it could sustain them no longer they crashed, along with the Soviet Union itself.

These new states also experienced development, partly in imitation of the Soviet Union, but also along the lines of the material basis of their own existence. This can be illustrated by a study of the changes in consciousness expressed by the workers in revolt against them. For example, the programmes put forward by the insurrection of the East Berlin workers in 1953 and the Hungarian revolutionaries of 1956 were suffused with genuine Socialist aspirations and radical working class content.[37] They contrast quite markedly with the market-oriented programme of the Prague Spring of 1968[38] and the openly pro-capitalist and clerical demands of Solidarnosc in the 1970s, a clear indication of the extent and direction of the process. We need not go on to describe the further stage of bourgeois and anti-working class degeneration involved in the creation of even more alienated state forms by means of guerrilla war waged by military cliques basing themselves on the peasantry.

Whether the reader accepts all the details of the above analysis or not, the important thing to establish is that this degeneration is a **process in the direction of purely bourgeois norms**, not a fixed entity. And here we encounter a paradox, that those who above all should have been in a position to understand this, the Trotskyists, demonstrated their utter theoretical ineptitude. The supposed supporters of Trotsky's theory have done him a grave disservice. One tendency, taking its cue from the International Committee of the Fourth International, simply took *The Revolution Betrayed* as a Bible and tried to use it to explain everything. For that amazing book described the process of degeneration up to when it was written, and indeed is a sort of measurement of the extent of the process of decline reached at that date. Those who regarded Trotsky's work as a fixed entity, valid for all time, did not bear in mind that it was the last of a series of analyses he made of the Soviet Union, grappling successively with the definitions of Thermidor, Bonapartism, Bureaucratic Centrism, etc, and changing his perspectives from reform to revolution as the state degenerated further. His last thoughts on the problem were that if Stalinism survived the Second World War a further assessment of its nature was called for.[39] Trotsky's thought was thus thoroughly dialectical, and attuned to the rate of change he observed in the Russian state. The assumption that no further change had taken place since made by some of his epigones left them incapable of analysing the direction and extent of the development. They repeated endlessly the one-sided definition of the Soviet Union as a workers' state, neglecting totally its dialectical opposite, that it was a bourgeois state as well, and so landed themselves in hopeless contradictions. The most laughable must surely be the plight of the American Spartacists, who after many years of extreme Stalinophobia, sprang to the defence of the workers' state with renewed vigour when it had practically no working class content left in it at all. The fact that the workers themselves felt and showed this by their refusal to defend that state makes the pretensions of such people to Marxism even more ludicrous.

Yet it should be said that the opposing tendency which drew its inspiration from the United Secretariat of the Fourth International fared no better. The best that could be said for it is that at least it realised that movement was taking place, but it interpreted the Khrushchev-Brezhnev period as a progressive development, when decentralisation of the economy and a further shift to market relations were rapidly ridding the USSR of the last echoes of 1917. So neither of the major schools of Trotsky's thought was capable of predicting the collapse of the Soviet system, or of working out a viable policy for the revolutionaries caught up in it.

At a certain observable point of development the dialectic dictates that quantity turns into quality. In this case that point was reached in the Brezhnev era, when it was found that Soviet planning was a sham, that the national income had fallen, and that the state no longer controlled the economy at all. At this stage the state was poised to topple over into its opposite. State capital then began to convert itself into private capital. Sections of the political bureaucracy and the technical and managerial strata aspired to convert their control into ownership, as Lenin and Trotsky feared they would. Trotsky's contention that it was not Socialism, but a transitional form, a crisis state, was finally vindicated, though not in a way he would have hoped. The workers' state had become a corpse. Stalinism was, after all, not a sound and healthy organism, but a terminal illness, the syphilis of the international labour movement, as he so trenchantly put it.

The end of the road that began in 1917 leaves many historical questions unresolved, in particular that of the nature of the epoch, as Trotsky pointed out in *In Defence of Marxism*. This preface is not the place to go any further into them, except to say that discussion should now focus upon whether the revolution was premature, a false start like the Anabaptist uprisings at the end of the Middle Ages or the Paris Commune, a revolution whose time had not yet come, or whether the state set up by it was simply one of those bastard and anomalous forms history produces during its turning points. For example, Byzantium was neither a slave nor a feudal state. The Imperial German cities and the autonomous cities of the Italian Renaissance proved to be inadequate state forms for the further development of bourgeois power. Enlightened despotism had abandoned the feudal state, but was far from adopting bourgeois methods of rule. History is full of transitional forms, false starts, and blind alleys. It is not at all a preoccupation for those who like their thoughts in neat and tidy packages. And history's periods of transition can go on for centuries.

Yet the revolution was young once, and held out a real hope for a war-torn world, as we intend to show in what follows. The pieces we present have been chosen to show its bright and its dark sides, its mixture of soaring idealism and hard-headed practicality, the range of its theoretical sweep and the obstacles placed in its path by harsh material reality. State building, economy, working class organisation, nationalism and internationalism, war and peace, ideas and personalities, jostle each other untidily in these pages. But the book will only be faithful to its subject if it appears untidy, for revolutions are far from tidy affairs. Some of the pieces we include, like Lenin's speeches, are startling in the daring of their realpolitik, whilst others, such as Radek's two articles, show a bold and imaginative sweep. For here we find a statement of the theory of Permanent Revolution developed along very different lines from those of Trotsky, showing that it has a real scientific basis, and is not dependent on the personal gifts of any individual. Some of Radek's conclusions are quite startling, for example that the theory had deep roots in the thought of Plekhanov, Luxemburg and Kautsky, who in 1905 is shown to have seen far further than Lenin himself. Even the future degeneration of the revolution is quite clearly forecast, should the world revolution fail to materialise. It is no historical accident that with the sole exception of Lenin, all our writers fell victim to Stalin's executioners.

∞   ∞   ∞

It only remains for me to thank our translators, Guy Desolre and Brian Pearce, and Harry Ratner and Bruce Robinson, whose expert surveillance over my own work prevented many a gaffe. We are equally in the debt of Ken Tarbuck and the Workers International League for their permission to reprint articles that appeared in the *New Interventions* pamphlet series and *Workers News*. Malcolm Pratt, Ray Challinor and Sebastian Budgen have also given us valuable material. All their contributions are indicated at the appropriate point in the footnotes. The splendid format of this book is due to our production manager, Paul Flewers, whose skills have for some time delighted his readers, and the staff of Porcupine Press, whose patience has been sorely tested during its long gestation period. Last in line, but certainly not least, come the comrades of Socialist Platform, whose warmth and solidarity provided the inspiration for this book's appearance in the first place.

We hope that our readers will learn from it that the Russian Revolution left a theoretical legacy it will take generations to assimilate. If, like the Paris Commune, it was a false start, we can still salute its spokesmen, who have now joined the heroes of the Commune in the memory of the working class.

Al Richardson
25 October 1994

Notes

1. Below, p116.
2. The extent to which living experience refuted all such expectations has been touched upon by myself in an article in *New Interventions*, Volume 2, no 4, January 1992, p27, and by Walter Kendall in *Revolutionary History*, Volume 4, no 4, Spring 1993, pp207-8.
3. This is the well-known analysis developed in *The Transitional Programme* (LD Trotsky, *The Transitional Program for Socialist Revolution*, New York, 1977, p143). But cf also the far more accurate assessment in 'Discussions with Trotsky: The Russian Question', 25 March 1938, *Writings of Leon Trotsky 1937-38*, New York, 1976, p304.
4. Below, p49.
5. Below, p49.
6. Below, p47.
7. Below, p65.
8. Below, p65.
9. Below, p153.
10. Below, p169.
11. Below, pp140-2.
12. Below, p164.
13. Below, p173.
14. Below, p244.
15. Below, p180.
16. Below, p240.
17. Below, pp60, 62.
18. Below, p185.
19. Below, p196.
20. Below, pp52, 63. The final remark made by Radek about the absence of 'pure capitalism' in its confrontation with the Soviet Union, although not part of our discussion here, is most interesting in view of the development of nationalisation and the welfare state, and of étatism in general, in capitalist countries since 1917. The best general investigation of this phenomenon is undoubtedly that conducted by Sam Levy, *The Étatist Stage of Capitalist Development*, *Socialist Current*, Volume 9, no 10, December 1964
21. Below, p193.
22. Cf those appearing in VI Lenin, *Collected Works*, Volume 27, Moscow, 1965, pp258 and 316, etc, and LD Trotsky below, p187.
23. K Marx, *The First International and After*, Harmondsworth, 1974, p347.
24. VI Lenin, *Marxism and the State*, Moscow, 1972, p32.
25. VI Lenin, 'State and Revolution', *Collected Works*, Volume 25, Moscow, 1964, p471.
26. LD Trotsky, *The Revolution Betrayed*, London, 1973, pp53-5.
27. Cf F Engels, *The Origin of the Family, Private Property and the State*, Moscow edition, pp281ff.
28. LD Trotsky, *The Revolution Betrayed*, p53.
29. F Engels, *Anti-Dühring*, Peking, 1976, pp358-62. Cf also p369, where Engels lists as the final contradictions of capitalism: 'Partial recognition of the social character of the productive forces imposed upon the capitalists themselves. Appropriation of the large production and communication organisations, first by joint-stock companies, later by trusts, then by the state. The bourgeoisie proves itself a superfluous class; all its social functions are now performed by salaried employees.' (Cf Radek, below, p10)
30. VI Lenin, 'The Impending Catastrophe and How to Combat It', 10-14 September 1917, *Collected Works*, Volume 25, Moscow, 1964, pp357-9. Cf Bukharin, below, p91.
31. VI Lenin, 'Can the Bolsheviks Retain State Power?', 1 October 1917, *Collected Works*, Volume 26, Moscow, 1964, pp105-6.

32. VI Lenin, 'The Tax in Kind', 21 April 1921, *Collected Works*, Volume 32, Moscow, 1965, p333.
33. VI Lenin, 'Political Report of the Central Committee to the Eleventh Congress of the RCP(B)', 27 March 1922, *Collected Works*, Volume 33, Moscow, 1966, pp278-9.
34. Op cit, p288. Other translations render the word 'heap' as 'mess', which is probably more idiomatic, and sharpens the point of it.
35. Op cit, pp286-7. For *Smena Vekh*, cf below, p246, n5, p248. These remarks by Lenin make it clear that he was not at all taken in by the complacent tone adopted at this time by official Soviet pronouncements, considered the attacks of the regime's enemies a necessary corrective to it, and followed them with careful attention. The scepticism expressed by Robin Blick when it was pointed out that there is considerable proof that Lenin helped finance Martov's paper in exile thus shows more about his views of Lenin than it does about the man himself. Cf Nils Dahl, 'With Trotsky in Norway', *Revolutionary History*, Volume 2, no 2, Summer 1989, p37 and n11, p42; Robin Blick, 'Lenin and Martov', *Revolutionary History*, Volume 2, no 3, Autumn 1989, p51.
36. This is not quite so fantastic a scenario as it may seem. Marx maintained that each successive revolution serves to perfect the state apparatus (*The Eighteenth Brumaire of Louis Bonaparte*, Moscow, 1977, p105). The highest expression of the organisation of bourgeois politics so far is the nation state. The working class is an international class, and unless we accept right from the start the premises of the argument for 'socialism in one country', we should expect it in the epoch of revolution to create state forms transcending this nation state. This is in fact what happened with the USSR in 1917, and even to a certain extent with Tito's Yugoslavia. Moreover, since the basic interests of the working class are the same worldwide, it is arguable that the state set up by Lenin and Trotsky in some way represented the workers of the whole world, not just those placed geographically under its rule.
37. Cf Peter Brandt, 'The German Question in the Light of the Insurrection of 17 June 1953', *International Bulletin* of the RCL, no 2, Winter 1970, pp15-8; Balacz Nagy, 'The Present Day Relevance of the *Transitional Programme*', *Revolutionary History*, Volume 3, no 1, Summer 1990, pp27-9. At the time this document was printed I was unaware of the fact that a translation had already appeared in *International Correspondence*, Volume 1, no 7, 25 May 1967, pp93-5.
38. That is, the *Two Thousand Words*. Cf V Karalasingham, *Czechoslovakia 1968*, Colombo, pp18-29.
39. LD Trotsky, *In Defence of Marxism*, London, 1966, pp10-11. Cf Jean Van Heijenoort, *With Trotsky in Exile*, Cambridge Massachusetts, 1978, p141: 'In June or July 1939, Trotsky asked me to do research in Mexico City's National Library and try to find some texts on the sixteenth century wars of religion and on the end of the Roman Empire. According to him, these two epochs of historical fracture were the ones to compare with ours... An echo of these preoccupations of Trotsky's are found in the last articles that he wrote, during the polemics of the American Trotskyite group, in which he touches the theme of Socialism or barbarism. But I have the impression that his thoughts had advanced further than what he was then ready to put on paper.'

Book One

Karl Radek

The Revolution and Marxist Theory

The items that make up this section were selected to show how the Russian Socialists placed their revolution within the context of the general development of Marxist theory between 1871 and 1923. They consist of only a small selection from the innumerable short articles written at the time by Karl Radek, one of the more neglected figures of Russian Marxism.

Karl Bernhardovich Sobelsohn (1885-1939) took the pseudonym 'K Radek' from the fact that he had been expelled from the German Social Democratic Party, allegedly for theft. He began his career as a revolutionary in Poland and then moved to Germany, where he early earned the censure of Rosa Luxemburg. He was an accomplished linguist, equally at home in the Marxist movements of Poland, Germany and Russia, and drew close to the positions of Lenin in Switzerland, returning to the Soviet Union after the October Revolution to join the Bolsheviks. In 1918 he was one of the leaders of the Left Communist faction within the party, and until 1923 played a prominent part as representative of the Communist International in the affairs of the German Communist Party, where he was famous for the 'Schlageter speech' approving of a Freikorps saboteur killed by the French troops occupying the Ruhr. On his return to the USSR he became a member of the Left Opposition, and was Principal of the Sun Yat-Sen University specialising in Chinese affairs. He was expelled from the Communist Party and banished to Siberia at the end of 1927, but in 1929 he broke with the Left Opposition and placed his pen at the service of Stalin. The only full-length collection of his articles in English, *Portraits and Pamphlets* (1935), dates from this time. It is a pale shadow of his output during the 1920s, some of which we include here. Trotsky's *Permanent Revolution* (1929) was written as a reply to him, for he had formerly espoused this theory with some conviction, as the second and third of our items show. Although he revised the Stalin Constitution of 1936, his past did not endear him to Stalin, and he was one of the main defendants in the Trial of the Seventeen in January 1937.

Radek's writings during this time argue that during the period of the slow organic development of Social Democracy in Europe during the last quarter of the nineteenth century, Marxism had become systematised at the expense of its revolutionary thrust and its programmatic flexibility. Karl

Kautsky had popularised Marxism and applied it to the range of human thought, but his ideas were evolutionary rather than revolutionary, owing more to Darwin than to Hegel's dialectical leaps and discontinuities. Ideas are themselves, of course, a reflection of material reality, and we should not forget that new insights in Marxism are inevitably connected with revolutionary upheavals, *The Communist Manifesto* coinciding with the great year of the European revolutions (1848), and the adoption of the concept of the dictatorship of the proletariat with the Paris Commune (1871). Radek shows that the Russian revolutions of 1905 and 1917 had a similar impact upon the development of Marxism, restoring to it much of its original revolutionary thrust, as well as making its application a practical question for the first time. He demonstrates the incomparable superiority of the theory of Permanent Revolution over all others as a forecast and an explanation of this process, and although he obviously owes a considerable debt to Trotsky for his basic analysis, his own application of the theory both before (Chapter 2) and after the events (Chapter 3) indicates that it is a significant scientific addition to the arsenal of Marxism, and not a personal aberration on the part of Trotsky himself. Radek's 1922 essay in Chapter 3 has a keen awareness of the limitations of the revolution within the framework of the USSR alone, and forecasts that it would fail to survive unless it spread to the countries of developed capitalism. He incidentally shows that the well-worn Stalinist argument that Trotsky's theory had no impact among the Bolsheviks at the time of the revolution and after is quite fallacious. Moreover, he reveals how deeply rooted it was in the thought of Plekhanov, Rosa Luxemburg, and especially Kautsky, who moved leftwards in 1905 under the impact of the Russian events and the German strike wave — so far leftwards, in fact, that Radek suggests that he understood the potential impact of the Russian Revolution in Europe far better at the time than did Lenin himself (below, pp36-9). But the final short piece included here draws our attention to the superb flexibility of Lenin's tactical approach, and his tremendous sense of the concrete in his application of Marxist theory.

Karl Radek

The Development of Socialism from Science into Action[1]

The Development of Socialism from Utopianism into a Science

W HAT IS Communism? This question is answered by the Young Friedrich Engels in a sketch for the *Communist Manifesto* in the year 1847: 'Communism is the doctrine of the conditions for the emancipation of the proletariat.'[2] According to this definition, which in itself contains the whole spirit of scientific Socialism, the whole work of Marx and Engels consisted in seeking in the development of capitalistic society the development of the conditions of the final victory of the working class, in order to make of it a starting point for Communist activity. In this manner the development from utopia into science was accomplished.

The predecessors of Marx and Engels, the Utopian Socialists, have accomplished much in the characterisation of bourgeois society. The grim Fourier,[3] who scourged himself and divested himself of all masks; the Faust-like gifted Saint-Simon,[4] who illuminated whole epochs of human history in a few words; Owen,[5] who penetrated deeply into the nature of man, and exhibited his dependence on economic conditions in his writings and his speeches — all of them contributed building blocks for the mighty edifice of scientific Socialism. Without them, Marx would have been impossible. But in spite of their deeply penetrating criticism of capitalist society, the predecessors of Marx did not understand how this very society could furnish those mass forces which would overthrow it. For this reason, they had to play the rôle of historic prophecy, and to work out a plan for the rescue of humanity from the claws of capitalism, a plan the only weakness of which was that the architect was missing who could by means of it erect that temple of humanity to heaven. Marx and Engels showed how the development of the powers of production under the rule of capitalism would result in ever-increasing anarchy and enslavement of the masses, but also how by means of the concentration of industry, the formation of a strong working class and the realisation by them intellectually and emotionally of the coming of a new order, and the iron will to attain it, the foundations of Socialism would also be created. Marx and Engels showed the international proletariat the historic necessity of its victory — the victory of Socialism. At the same time they showed it also that this victory of the disinherited and the enslaved was not going to fall mechanically into their lap when a certain stage of historic development had been reached, but that they must prepare themselves for this victory in the sweat of their brows, by the uninterrupted struggle of their brains, fighting day by day against the bourgeoisie in all spheres of social life, in order then in the direct revolutionary struggle, class against class, to win it. This final revolutionary struggle which will result in the iron dictatorship of the proletariat, this alone will guide the workers into the promised land of Socialism.

The theory of Marx and Engels as to the conditions of the victory of the proletariat remains true, it has been untouched by the tooth of time, it stands like a granite boulder. The 70 years which separate us from the day on which the magnificent young men saw the future of mankind sharply illumined and pointed it out to us in the unforgettable *Communist Manifesto*, have caused many changes in the capitalist structure, to comprehend which has been the not always well-performed task of the successors of Marx. But the outlines of the development have not changed, and only at the present time, during the first Socialist revolution which the world has ever experienced, do we really comprehend the theory of Communism. Through the first Socialist revolution, through its stern necessities, we can see the splendid proof of the prophetic power of the intellect of our masters. Communism is a theory of revolution, and therefore it can only be understood in its entire significance during a period of revolution. On this account we can see that in the long period of quiet development which preceded the era of revolution only a few keen intellects were in a position to comprehend the theory of Communism so completely and clearly as when, during the revolutionary epoch of rising capitalism, it was born in the brains of those children of the period of storm and stress, in the brains of Karl Marx and Friedrich Engels.

In the epoch of quiet development the **most diverse non-Communistic elements were mixed with it**, and so under the name **Social Democratic conception**, different **substitutes for Communism** were created which the international working class must discard if it wishes to be equal to its duty. It is the diluted and false Communism from which the living spirit has been purged, which makes it difficult for the workers to understand and take to heart the theories of the Russian Revolution. On that account, one of the first duties in the proletarian struggle for freedom is to free the teachings of Communism from all impurities. This can be done very easily if we learn to understand historically the development of the separate forgeries of Communism, if we learn to know the conditions under which they arose.

The Falsification of Communism

The theory of Marx, the outlines of which were created in the 1850s, was not disseminated among wide circles until the 1880s. When in the 1860s and 1870s the German working class movement was started under the leadership of Ferdinand Lassalle,[6] the workers were not acquainted with a single one of Marx's writings. The ideas of Communism became familiar to them through the small, inflammatory pamphlets of Lassalle, in which the theory of Communism, if not entirely falsified, was yet very peculiarly presented. Ferdinand Lassalle wanted to stir up the working class at a time when an epoch of capitalist prosperity had strengthened the counter-revolutionary forces in all Europe and made it possible for them to solve all the problems with which at the time they were confronted.

In Germany the junkers,[7] together with the grand bourgeoisie, were occupied with the at that time important problem of creating a unified capitalist state. The powers which tried in the year 1848 by revolutionary means to found a united

Germany proved themselves too weak, and what they were not in a position to accomplish — the founding of the German state as an organ of the German bourgeoisie — was accomplished by the bourgeoisie and the junkers. They executed this task by rearing the reactionary structure of a bureaucratic-capitalistic federation of states, in which a clique of big capitalists, together with the junkers and the generals, with the Hohenzollerns[8] at the head, guided the destiny of the German Empire. At such a time, Lassalle was trying to make the working class into a power, which, even though it had not the power to guide the destinies of the German people, could still be in a position to wring concessions from the governing class. The Communist propaganda was directed to this narrow object, as Lassalle disseminated it among the workers. In order to be able to get across as much of his propaganda as possible in spite of the oppression from the reactionary period of Bismarck,[9] he attempted to give Communism as innocent a look as possible. The young lion, whose paws were not yet in a state to deal death to the enemy, was to be led upon the meadows disguised as a lamb. Lassalle tried to present Communism as a movement which could succeed by peaceful means. By means of the popular vote, the workers were to gain the influence over the state and were to use it to organise cooperative societies which gradually would change a capitalist society into a Socialistic one. This propaganda developed in the workers a respect for the idea of the state regardless of whether the state was in the hands of the capitalists or of the victorious workers. This idea was indeed put to a severe test insofar as the relations with the Bismarck government were concerned during the era of the fierce persecutions of the workers' movement in the period from 1878 to 1880, when the violent pressure from above, and the baiting of the workers' movement, created intense hatred against the capitalist state in the front ranks of the workers' movement, and a hope nourished by this hatred that it would crumble as a result of the blows of the social revolution. This mood of the working class was increased by the long-drawn-out crisis which existed in the economic life of Europe during the 1880s. But this was only an interruption in the process of the reformistic falsifying of Communism which had been going on since the establishment of the capitalistic states in the 1870s. As soon as the workers had somewhat recovered from the blows dealt them, as soon as they were a little stronger and the fiercest storms of capitalist persecution disappeared, the process of diluting and falsifying Communism took on the widest range. The rapid economic development, the period of prosperity of capitalism, as it everywhere in the last 10 years of the preceding century gained a foothold, especially in the domain of the electric and the metal industry, contributed to this. Since the 1880s, thanks to the development of American agriculture, the prices of grain fell, and now wages began to rise under the influence of the lively movement of business. The front ranks of the workers saw before them a path strewn with roses. The governments were obliged to cease their persecutions, and they began to promise social reforms. The workers everywhere won representation in the parliaments; the aristocracy of the working class earned good wages, and so the idea became a fixed one to them: the revolution is a superseded phase in bourgeois development. The working class will force the bourgeoisie to make more and more concessions, which will finally change the economic system of capitalism into a system which shall exist for the advantage of the workers. This decision found expression first in opportunistic parliamentary practice, in the policy of the parliamentary labour leaders, who hoped by flirting with the bourgeoisie, by limiting their demands, by giving up revolutionary propaganda, to be able gradually to better the condition of the workers. Then this tendency found its theoretical expression in the **doctrine of reformism** (revisionism), as coined by **Bernstein**[10] in Germany, **Sarante**[11] and **Jaurès**[12] in France, and **Treves**[13] and **Turati**[14] in Italy.

To reduce the doctrines of reformism to a formula, they consisted in the attempt to prove that the evolution of capitalism **does not render the differences between the proletariat and the bourgeoisie more acute but tends to soften them**, and that therefore **not revolution** but the **cooperation of the proletariat with the sensible strata of the bourgeoisie is the true path to the liberation of the proletariat**. Reformism denied the **practical possibility of the Socialist revolution** and set up in its stead **evolution through social reform**. It was a **counter-revolutionary doctrine**, attempting to represent the revolution of the workers as an infant disease of the labour movement, in order to yoke the workers to the cart of the bourgeoisie. This tendency of reformism is most glaringly reflected in a series of articles by Bernstein's disciple, Eduard David[15] on the dictatorship of the proletariat, published in the year 1903 in the *Sozialistische Monatshefte*, the chief organ of international reformism. Not revolution but parliamentary action, the organisation of unions and brotherhoods, this was the course which reformism preached to the working class.

The Collapse of Reformist Illusions

But the same evolution which, according to the conviction of the reformists, was to do away with the necessity for a revolution, again showed the workers the utter absurdity of the reformistic illusions. The junkers defended themselves against the growing competition of the young agrarian nations by raising the price of food by means of agrarian tariffs. The development of capitalism led to the forming of trusts and cartels, big capitalist organisations, which pushed aside and conquered not only the crafts but also the middle bourgeoisie. For the protection of the cartels they demanded for industry also a high tariff. They united with the junkers to rob and plunder the people; at the same time the growing trustification of industry meant an enormous extension of power for the capitalists — against the unions. The same unions which could without much trouble force the small textile baron to yield to their demands, were powerless against the iron and coal kings, who commanded more than ten thousands of workmen. If the worker in a textile factory was dissatisfied with his wages, he could find work in some other factory. The trustified coal and iron barons did not recognise the unions, they held fast together against each demand of their workers, and understood how to guard themselves against the workers by means of blacklists. The aggravation of the friction between proletariat and bourgeoisie, in the factory as well as in the consumers' market, was still further intensified by the imperialist policy, which threatened to turn the struggle of the trustified industries in the world, the struggle of wares and of capital, into a war. The growing burden of taxation, caused by the growth of militarism and navalism, the growing danger of war which became ever more intense, and conflicts with the unions, led the possessing classes to adopt a sharper policy against the working class. **Because exploitation grew, oppressive measures had to be intensified also.** The growing political reaction had the effect on the working class of a **storm signal**, and showed them in all countries that not revolutionary Communism, but, on the contrary, the so-called **'real' reformism was a utopia**: not, to be sure, one that would give wings to the soul, that would stimulate the energies of the workers, that would make the journey of humanity seem shorter in the visions it presents, so that the sluggish ones might be encouraged to hasten their steps, but on the contrary one that would lame their stride, transforming them into creeping beasts.

Since the great strike in the Ruhr district,[16] since the great fights of the electric workers of Berlin, and the violent agitation of the French workers for the attainment of the eight-hour day, the great faith of the workers in the peaceful evolution to Socialism had disappeared. They saw now how the forces of capitalism had been uniting against the proletariat in economic life as well as in political life, they saw how the bourgeois parties were solidifying more and more into a reactionary mass, they saw how the entire bourgeois society was moving toward the abyss of war, they saw how parliaments were becoming constantly less able to cope with the development, if for no other reason than because they were themselves being forced in all countries to resign their powers in favour of secret cabinets in which the bureaucracy in combination with the sharks of capital settled the most vital affairs of the people.

The fires of the Russian revolution of the year 1905 showed the masses of Europe what latent power can be summoned by the working class when it arises, and when it is disposed to throw its personality into the fight for the cause. Since the year 1905 the problem of **the struggle for power, that is, the problems of the Socialist revolution**, which were brought up in a theoretical way in the discussion of reformism (Kautsky's pamphlet *The Social Revolution*, published in 1903),[17] were present in the consciousness of the masses of the people.

In Search of the Way to Power

An anxious search began for the exit out of the blind alley into which capitalistic evolution had blundered. The first question before the toiling masses was: **'Where are we going?'** The question was answered by developments as clearly and precisely as one could wish. In France the attempt to better the condition of the workers through cooperation with the bourgeoisie turned out a complete failure. Millerand's[18] entrance into the bourgeois government was of no advantage to the working class, and led to the compromising of the Social Democracy in the eyes of the masses of workers. The results of the elections of 1907[19] showed the workers that the bourgeois parties would unite into a solid wall against them as soon as it became a question of imperialism, that is, a question of the extension of capitalist power over weaker peoples, and of the armed competitive struggle between the capitalist states. The facts of the economic crisis of 1900 spoke so plainly that as well known a reformist as Max Schippel[20] could not end his investigation of the course of the economic crisis in any other way than by the assertion of the intensification of the class struggle in the entire world. Karl Kautsky summed up the entire development in the year 1908 in his work *The Road to Power*,[21] in which he proved that the whole capitalist world was moving in the direction of a frightful Socialistic world crisis, that we were on the eve of the Socialist revolution. This conviction, which became more and more rooted in the minds of the foremost ranks of the workers, faced them with this second question: 'What means will the workers use to defend themselves when the new situation arises, and what means will they use when they launch the attack on the fortresses of capital?' Already in 1905 the German and Austrian proletariat had worked its way through to the idea of the mass strike. Regardless of the complete ossification of the intellectual life of the leaders of the party, whose quiet, petit-bourgeois lives reflected the mood of the working class very faintly, the workers had recognised in the mass strike a means of defence against the attacks on the fundamental rights of the working class (the German Social Democracy in Jena, 1905),[22] or even a means of attack by the proletariat against particularly obstinate opponents (the Austrian Social Democracy). The mass strike as a general strike was exalted by the French Syndicalists as a means of winning complete liberty. The working class, which, up to this time, had battled only politically in parliaments, began to reflect on its rôle in the process of production, in the words of Freiligrath:[23] 'Every wheel shall stop, at the will of your mighty arm.'

For years the leaders of the left wing of the workers discussed the conditions that would make practicable the use of the general strike. Should the leaders of the workers' organisations decide upon the strike if parliamentary action should fail, if the enemy through his reckless policy should drive the masses to despair — should it be a pistol, then, held in readiness to back up the parliamentary struggle, or should it be the actual mode of the struggle itself, emerging spontaneously out of the increasingly acute class conflicts, prepared not in the conference chambers of the leaders, but preparing every hour in the shops and in the factory prisons — and not only through the growing agitation, but the **stimulated action** of the proletariat? These were the questions to which the left wing of the international labour movement devoted itself most intensively during the years preceding the World War. And right at this point it appeared that even in this simple question the Socialist ranks, the ranks that fought under the banner of Marx were divided, the one section under the leadership of Karl Kautsky outwardly embracing the approaching Socialist revolution, it is true, yet anxiously avoiding the intensifying of the class struggle, although the internal and external situation of the proletariat positively demanded it.

In this struggle to find the way to power the question came up here and there: **'Wherein shall the power of the victorious workers express itself?'** For nowhere was the question given a positive hearing, and for very simple reasons. First upon the order of business of history came the question of the mobilisation of the battalions of workers, the question of their general objective, and not of the halting-places to be passed through on the way. In order to prove the necessity for the general strike, the radical Socialists pointed to the collapse of parliamentarism. They showed how it was more and more becoming a stronghold of the capitalistic highwaymen; they criticised very sharply the sham republicanism and the sham democracy of the republican countries, and frequently the question arose: 'How shall capitalistic democracy and its parliamentary agencies be converted into agencies of power of the victorious proletariat?' When Anton Pannekoek,[24] the clearest head of West European Socialism, answered the question by saying that one must destroy the democratic forms of the capitalist state and must create new organs of power of the working people in the fires of the proletarian revolution, he was accused by Karl Kautsky, the most authoritative Marxian theoretician, of being an Anarchist. However correct the answer of Pannekoek may have been, it was only half an answer. It pointed to the fact that the organs of compulsion used by the capitalist state must be destroyed, but it did not show what organs of control the proletariat must build in order to carry on and assure its victory.

While the majority of even the revolutionary Socialists saw in democracy the means by which Socialists would gain the victory, the Syndicalists, representing the revolutionary theory of those countries in which the bankruptcy of democracy had brought about the complete disillusionment of the masses of the people, pointed to the labour unions as the agency which should win the power and become the wielders of the power of the masses.

This problem, as has been said, was put only sporadically by those intellects who were able to see beyond the confines of the present time, and could not be answered by them. The historic solutions are never found by the theoreticians of the working class, they can only be discovered by the revolutionary struggle of the masses; to the theoretician is left only the duty to grasp the practical measures of the proletariat, to make them common knowledge, and to make them the universal object of the struggle of the proletariat, the solution of its struggle.

The Lessons of the World War

Before the working class could be confronted with the problem of its organs of power, they were first compelled to experience all the consequences of their powerlessness in the literal sense physically. They had to wade through the horrors of war, to be torn in pieces by grenades; they had to bleed to death for the interests of the capitalists; they had to heap up mountains of corpses, in order that the lesson that capitalism leads to the bloodiest anarchy, to the destruction of the few cultural achievements which have been created, to the deepest misery of the masses, to their literal enslavement, so that this lesson might be converted out of a theoretical thesis into a crying and burning certainty, at least in the minds of the front ranks of the working class.

In the theoretical propaganda of the revolutionary Social Democrats, experience, the defeats which capital had inflicted upon the workers since the end of the last century, did not suffice to encourage the workers to aspire to more activity than the first timid steps forward. The opportunistic policy of the leaders of the workers' movement lulled the front ranks of the workers' aristocracy to sleep, a sleep which proved that the élite of the workers found themselves in a very favourable condition. The lower strata of the working class, though, were too ignorant, too helpless, to be in a position to throw themselves into a revolution without the bureaucracy of the party and the unions, or against its will. So there came the long-awaited beast of war, and it began to teach the proletariat with its claws the lesson which it had not understood when revolutionary Socialism was preaching it.

The Russian people is the first which has understood this lesson and has drawn from it the consequences, and this it accomplished by means of the revolution. The Russian Revolution is the first response of the proletariat to the World War, it is the advocate and the forerunner of the international revolution, it gives the answer to the riddles which the sphinx of the revolution has been giving Socialism to solve for the last century, to the question which the working class must answer, if it does not wish to be torn to pieces by it.[25] The fact that the Russian proletariat through its revolution is making the first steps on the road of the development of

Socialism from science into action means that at the same time that révolution marks a mighty stride in the development of the science of Communism. 'Communism is the doctrine of the conditions of the liberation of the proletariat.'[26] These conditions become clearest in the process of victory, so on that account the comprehension of the Russian Revolution is a preliminary condition for the development of Communism from a science into action.

The Lessons of the Russian Revolution: The Ripening of Capitalism and the Socialist Revolution

The first question of the Socialist revolution which confronts the working class is this: '**When can the social revolution come?**' As Marxism showed the workers that the victory of Socialism is dependent on the forces of production, a perverted conception became rooted in the ranks of the Marxists that the social revolution would only then become possible when capitalism had the entire economic life of the nation in its grasp, when, so to say, it had divided it relentlessly into a small group of capitalists and an oppressed proletariat. Yes, those who were the most consistent in their falsification of Communism, the revisionists, declared that Socialism could not come in Europe until capital had subjugated the entire world: on that fact they based — as is well known — the necessity of having the working class support the colonial policy. The whole argument of the pseudo-Socialist parties of Russia, which rallied to the support of the bourgeoisie during the revolution, and since the workers' revolution have fought in the ranks of the counter-revolutionaries — the Mensheviki — consists of this fact: Socialism in Russia is impossible because the proletariat does not constitute a majority of the Russian nation. This argument won much approbation in Europe from those who had made out of Marxism a mechanical arithmetical problem. But to show the absurdity of this attitude to the question, it will suffice to point out that in Germany, the European state most highly developed economically, men as scientifically important as Heinrich Cunow[27] are of the opinion that this is still the case, not so much due to the few per cent more or less of proletarians in relation to non-proletarians, but rather to a **completely nebulous conception of the transition from capitalism to Socialism**. The hypothesis of a conception such as Cunow gives on the question of the stage of ripeness of capitalism, gives rise to the idea that capitalism will in fact do the work of socialisation itself, and that Socialism will simply be invited to a table already set. When Cunow explains that Germany is not yet ripe for Socialism, he supports this theory by referring to the fact that the capitalist state must first take over all industry before the proletariat could receive it by seizing the reins of the government. But why should not the proletariat be in a position to take the cartelised and trustified industries directly out of the hands of the capitalised trusts and industries? Of course, if the proletariat is going to seize power only when, as Bernard Shaw[28] says, a brainless, ape-like, degenerate capitalist master by pressing on a button can set in motion millions of men who have become slaves, it will have a very easy task to chase away the brainless monkey-master from the keys of the central apparatus and dash in his brains. But this simplification of its task the proletariat would have to pay for with all those sufferings which a policy of watchful waiting would impose upon them, watching how capitalism strides mechanically over the bodies of millions. To the honour of mankind be it said that the idea of a mechanical transition from capitalism to Socialism is contradicted by all hitherto existing historical conceptions, as also does every sensible theory of the possibility of capitalist evolution. The earlier forms of economic life did not collapse only after they had prepared the way for an entirely new order, but as soon as they became an oppressive hindrance to the new order.

The transition from capitalism to Socialism begins when capitalist society causes so much suffering to the people that they are ready to break with the even tenor of life and rise up against the domination of capital, when the masses can no longer endure the conditions created by a capitalist society. **When capitalist development in a country has reached a point where the most important branches of industry, those of credit and transportation, are controlled by a concentrated, capitalistic group, then the proletariat which has rebelled not only can but must try to take over industry into its own hands, into the hands of the victorious proletariat, a proletariat organised into a governing power.** The proletariat will model the economic life of the country to a greater or lesser extent for its own benefit, according to the degree of capitalist penetration of the economic life of that country, or it will perhaps have temporarily to restrict itself to the socialisation of the already concentrated branches of the administration, while it gradually may take over the others, for instance, the administration of land (thanks to its lack of dependence on the socialised centres of industry, thanks to its independence of the city), and socialise them. This is the state of things in Russia. In Russia the proletariat is certainly the minority of the population, but the Russian iron industry, the coal mines, the naphtha production, the railroads and the telegraphs are concentrated in a few hands, they are directed by a small number of banks, and they dictate the economic laws of the entire agrarian population.

The unbearable situation which capitalism created in the World War brought the masses of the people into the struggle against the Tsaristic capitalistic state. With the help of the peasants, who bled to death for capitalism during three years, the workers succeeded in gaining the power in the government. What should they do with this power? The advocates of the mechanical idea that Socialism is possible only after nine-tenths of the people have become proletarians tried to make it clear to the people that it was impossible to establish Socialism. Back to capitalism, that was the solution of the Mensheviki. But the workers could not return to capitalism without throwing the country into the greatest misery. Should the capitalists return to power, they would impose the expenses of the war upon the workers, forcing them to work 12 hours a day in order to liquidate these burdens and raise the expenses of rearmament for the next year. They would not put an end to the confusion of the economic life of the country, but only shift the consequences of this confusion upon the workers. The Communistic system of economy is the utilisation of all the forces of production according to a distinct plan, in the interest of the mass of the people. **Just because the country has been unbelievably shattered through the war, Communism is the only way by which the workers can hope to emerge from the want and misery of the shattered capitalistic society.** To forego beforehand the chance to organise this economic life in its own interest would mean to rush into capitalistic misery for fear that the inexperienced proletariat would be incapable of directing the main forces of national economic life concentrated by capitalism. This would not only be historical suicide, but is furthermore **impossible practically**. What does the return to capitalism mean? It means in the first place giving back the power of the state to the capitalists, for naturally a proletarian state could not undertake to protect capitalist profits. The purpose of showing this is **to reveal the whole utopianism of the solution 'back to capitalism'**. It was certainly not by chance that the proletariat took the power into its hands in October 1917. The proletariat won the power because the capitalistic regime had lost all confidence, not only in the eyes of the proletarian, but also of the bourgeois masses. The first representatives of Russian capital, the Guchkovs,[29] Milyukovs,[30] Tereshchen-kos,[31] and their Socialist fig-leaves, the Tseretelis,[32] Kerenskys[33] and Chernovs,[34] were so hateful to the masses of the people that the people drove them away. Had the workers not seized the reins of power, the representatives of capitalism would not have been one whit more able to master the situation. Russia would have sailed without a rudder into the sea of anarchy, headed for a chaos, out of which the star of Socialism could not have crystallised, but also not a capitalist regime either. Russia was simply the **prey of foreign capital**, which is certainly not 'riper', or more called upon to 'set in order' the disrupted country in the interests of the masses of the people than is the young, but energetic, Russian proletariat itself.

Austria and Italy find themselves in the same situation as Russia, and the experience of the Russian Revolution teaches that the **Socialistic revolution by no means will begin in the place where capitalism is at its highest stage of development.** Even the strongest capitalistic organisation is not able to protect the masses from the unspeakable sufferings which capitalist anarchy creates; it is much better suited, as the government of the young capitalist countries, to hold the masses down.

The Socialist revolution starts first in those countries in which the capitalist organisation is not so strong. Those capitalist countries with the most unsettled organs for oppression are the **breaches where Socialism may break through**, where the social revolution will begin. It is difficult for it to break through within national boundaries, because after crushing its own bourgeoisie, it is threatened by the bourgeoisie of the remaining capitalist countries. The Socialistic revolution can only be successful if it breaks out on the entire continent; but the Socialistic revolution cannot wait until the proletariat of the whole world rises to one single call; on the contrary, as national, Socialistic revolutions are themselves a product of international capitalist disintegration, they furnish the accelerating element. In this way the answer is given to the first question which confronts the international proletariat: 'When can the Socialist revolution begin?' **It can and will begin in every country in which the conditions created by capital for the working class become unbearable.** The sufferings of the people jeer at the statistics of Cunow & Co, and the volcanoes of revolution are not waiting until the scholastic statisticians of would-be Marxism give them the signal. Whoever proves to the masses of the people by means of tables of statistics the impossibility of the Socialistic revolution shows that he understands Marx not at all. Friedrich Engels may have made a mistake when he thought in the 1880s that the end of capitalism was at hand.[35] But the possibility of such a mistake shows that he had nothing to do with this statistical conception of his and Marx's theory. This ossification of Marx was an offence easily explained during the peaceful evolution of capitalism; after the experience of the Russian workers' revolution it is not only a product of a counter-revolutionary state of mind, but it is also, as the experience of the

Russians shows, a counter-revolutionary utopia. All the adjurations with the falsified spirit of Marx could not save the political necks of the Tseretelis and Dans.[36] They were cast on the manure heap of history by the same proletariat which is 'still unripe for the social revolution', and from this place they may spit upon the revolution of the Russian working class, but cannot impede its progress. The revolution may temporarily be conquered by European capital if the European proletariat does not make use of the same weapons which the Russian proletariat made use of, within a reasonable time. But that it is a proletarian revolution, and that it is trying to overcome heroically the anarchistic-capitalistic economic methods through the Socialist organisation, that it is, therefore, a Socialist revolution, which can only be put down by the Attilas of imperialism,[37] neither the Mensheviki nor their European parrots can deny, just as little as they can disclaim its Socialist character: for its Socialist character shines above it like its star of destiny, it was created with iron necessity out of the imperial character of the war.

The Dictatorship of the Proletariat

The Socialist workers' revolution in Russia shows the European proletariat the way which leads to power. The press of world capital is crying that this is bloody, and is yelling about the rough, violent character of the revolution. It has every right to do so. It was created by capital to be an organ of the battle against the working class, and it is its duty to throw dirt upon and to spit upon the first workers' revolution, in order to frighten the workers of the other countries with its Medusa head.[38] But how comes it that the Axelrods,[39] Martovs,[40] and the — **risum teneatis!** — Kautskys use the violence of the revolution as a ground of complaint against it? **They used to defend the idea of the dictatorship of the proletariat against the reformists.**

What does the dictatorship mean? **Dictatorship is the form of government by which one class forces its will ruthlessly on the other class.** During the period of social evolution, in which one class is preparing itself for the struggle for power, it foregoes the use of force because it is too weak to use force. It is only gathering together and concentrating its powers, and on this account it is not necessary for the ruling class to use open force against it. The ruling class only holds its forces in readiness, but it gives the class which is striving upward a certain room for development, as long as it does not consider this class dangerous. From the moment when the ruling class lays burdens on the oppressed class, which are so heavy that the ruling class fears a possible uprising of the oppressed, it puts into play the machinery of force. The war laid burdens such as these on the masses of the workers, and on that account it brought with it the suspension of the few scanty rights enjoyed by the working class in the time of peace, that is, it brought the **dictatorship of imperialism,** which cost the workers millions of lives. In order to break the dictatorship of imperialism, the working class must employ force: force brings about the revolution. But no hitherto existing ruling class can be conquered at one blow. Beaten once, it attempts to rise again, and it can do so because the victory of the revolution is by no means able to alter the economic system of society in an instant, and to tear out by the roots the power of the deposed class. **The social revolution is a lengthy process**, which begins with the dethronement of the capitalist class, but ends only in the transformation of the capitalist system into a workers' community. This process will require at least **a generation** in every country, **and this space of time is precisely the period of the proletarian dictatorship**, the period during which the proletariat must keep the capitalists in subjection with the one hand, while it can use only the other for the work of Socialist construction.

Everything that is being said, on the ground of principle, against the rule of force of the Russian working class, means nothing else than the disavowal, not only of the teachings of Marx, but of the plainest facts of the past. When Renner[41] does not blush to assert with scientific mien that the political revolution, that is, the employment of brute force, contradicts the character of the Socialist revolution, because the Socialist revolution demands the organisation of a new economic system and not force, that only means that this former Marxist with a Lassallean enthusiasm for the state is not a worshipper of the state idea after the manner of Lassalle, as he has been characterised, but an ordinary **capitalistic sophist**. Just because the social revolution must transform the entire economic system of capitalism, which gave to one class unheard-of privileges, it must necessarily arouse the strongest opposition of this class, an opposition that can only be broken by the use of guns. **And the stronger capitalism is developed in a country, just so much more ruthless, just so much wilder will the defensive struggle be, just so much bloodier the proletarian revolution, and just so much more ruthless the measures by means of which the victorious working class will hold down the defeated capitalist class.** But the molluscs from the 'also-Marxist camp', the opponents of the Russian workers' revolution, answer us that it is not a question of refusing to recognise the principle of proletarian dictatorship, **but that they decline to recognise the dictatorship in a country where the proletariat is in a minority, and where the dictatorship degenerates into a rule of the minority over the majority**, as is supposed by them to be the case in Russia. This argument is a cowardly evasion.

Never, in any country, will the revolution begin as an act of the majority of the population. Capitalism never signifies the mere physical control of the means of production, everywhere it signifies simultaneously the intellectual control of the masses of the people, even in the most highly developed capitalist countries. Under the pressure of misery and want, under the convulsing of the masses by such means as the war, all the oppressed and the exploited do not rise at once. The most active, a minority, rises, accomplishes the revolution, and its success depends on whether this revolution follows the line of historic development, that is, whether it responds to the needs of the masses, who can then sever themselves from the former ruling class. The creative and dynamic force of the revolution was necessary to arouse the masses of the people, to free them from the intellectual slavery of capitalism, and to bring them into that camp which was defending their interests.

One might say: **every revolution is begun by the minority; the majority rallies to its aid while the revolution is going on,** and so determines its victory. Were it not so, the dictatorship in a country like Russia, which possesses a proletarian minority, would not only be harmful, as the Kautskys maintain, but in a country with a proletarian majority, to which the Kautskys graciously permit the dictatorship, it would be unnecessary. The capitalist class forms in these countries such a very small minority that it would not be able to use weapons against the proletariat. **The Marxian theory of the unavoidability of the** proletarian dictatorship as a way to Socialism is, therefore, either superannuated, or this dictatorship is as much justified in Russia as in another country.

Revolution and Counter-Revolution

The Russian Revolution has shown us not only the dictatorship of the proletariat, but also the concrete forms which the resistance of the bourgeoisie takes; in fact, it shows us in general the typical features of a workers' revolution. Friedrich Engels, in his *Anti-Dühring*, has pointed out the process by which capitalism breeds militarism, militarises the entire population (that is, puts it at the mercy of the drill-master), simultaneously, however, creating those elements that destroy militarism by means of the class opposition in the army.[42] This opposition, at a certain point in the historical process, causes the army, which is the sword of capital, to go to pieces in the latter's hand, by dividing the army into its proletarian and bourgeois components, into a Red Army and a White Army.

This the pupils of Marx and Engels forget when they continually recite the remark which Engels made in his introduction to *The Class Struggles in France*, in which Engels draws attention to the wide streets, etc, which make an uprising so much more difficult.[43] The Russian Revolution showed how the rising may occur on the field of battle, as well as in the trenches, not to speak of the streets; for the revolutionary idea may grip the hearts of the soldiers and form them into mass columns which march against the capitalistic elements of the army and of society. The Russian Revolution showed also how the attempt to organise new armies out of the capitalistic and the undecided elements is one of the **principal methods adopted by the bourgeois counter-revolutionists**. In the more highly developed capitalistic countries, with a well-fed, strongly capitalistic peasantry, this tendency of the counter-revolutionary bourgeoisie will result directly in the struggle between the regiments from the peasant-capitalist localities and the proletarian regiments. **The civil war between the revolution and the counter-revolution will be a war in the literal sense of the word. The development of the proletarian revolution will change the imperialist fronts into revolutionary and counter-revolutionary fronts.** The German attack on the Ukraine and the French-English-Japanese attack on Russia is an indication of this evolution. The development of the revolution and counter-revolution will bring up the problem of the **strategy of the Socialist revolution**. The Russian Revolution shows in what way this question will develop. If the Russian Revolution suffers from the fact that it has no corps of officers, that it is compelled to educate the workers to be army administratives as well as factory administrators, that is not merely a Russian problem. **De te fabula narratur** — so speak the experiences of the Russian Revolution to the European proletariat, but at the same time these experiences show that, eventually, the revolution is unconquerable from a military standpoint also. It conquers by the fact that **the bourgeoisie, being a small minority, cannot get together a counter-revolutionary army out of purely bourgeois elements**, that it is compelled to take deluded proletarian elements also, elements which, while the battle with the armies of the revolution is going on, will deteriorate, and sooner or later will rally to the side of the revolution.

Just as it was not only power on which the rule of the bourgeoisie was based, but also on its function as the administrator of production, just so it does not try to overcome the proletariat by armed power alone, but also by the **sabotage of the bourgeoisie and the bourgeois intelligentsia**. This sabotage, which in Russia reached its highest point in the period from the November uprising to March 1918, is not a Russian product. From it the European proletariat may take a hint. And when the eunuchs of Marxism point to the fact that up to the present time the Russian proletariat has not been able to organise production on a Socialistic basis, they are only mocking themselves without knowing it. Everywhere the bourgeoisie and the bourgeois intelligentsia place the greatest hindrance in the way of the proletariat in its work of organisation, and nowhere will the proletariat, even the most highly developed, be in a position, within a short time, to find the abilities in its own ranks which will be necessary to accomplish the work of Socialist organisation. In the much-praised land of organisation, in Germany, the number of workers who would be able today to guide whole branches of production is extraordinarily small, and even the number of workers who would be able, as technicians, to administer the production of a factory, is very small. Everyone knows this who has ever been active in the German workers' movement. The working class of every country will only be able to educate itself for the task of managing and administering production through thousands of mistakes, and nowhere will it be able to do without the services of bourgeois specialists. They will be forced, just as the Russian working class was forced, to adopt the measures of an iron dictatorship, in order to drive the bourgeois elements into the service of the workers.

No proletariat will be spared the struggle which has forced the Russian working class to take the sharpest measures of a dictatorship: the **struggle for bread**. Nowhere will the peasants range themselves on the side of the revolution; less in capitalist countries than they did in Russia, where the revolution gave them land and soil. **As the revolution develops from a military standpoint into a struggle between the workers' regiments and the regiments of the peasants, so also from the social standpoint it will be fought out between the workers and peasants for bread**, until the conquered peasantry learn that a Socialist society can offer them a life more worthy of a human being than a capitalist society can.

Democracy or the Rule of the Working Class

And this in a word indicates clearly enough what a mighty obstinacy, or what an enormous lack of sense one must have in order to accuse the Russian Revolution of harming poor democracy. Concretely considered, democracy is the rule of capital, and it is so strong, so fixed in the minds of the masses that it can allow itself the luxury of permitting the masses the liberty of discussing the affairs of state. There is, in modern history, no democracy which goes any further than that, for as soon as the masses make the slightest attempt to convert the liberty of speech into a right to decide any question of government, democracy goes flying. **Modern democracy is the camouflage of the autocracy of capital.** As the feeble proletariat is interested in free speech, in free voting, in order to collect its forces, we have recognised democracy as a way to Socialism; that means that it was necessary for us to enjoy and to participate freely in the affairs of state. But abstractly considered, democracy signifies the rule of the majority of the people. The idea that the proletariat will not begin the revolution until it has proofs that the majority of the people are behind it is absurd, if only for the fact that capitalist democracy will never remain unchanged long enough for the proletariat to assure itself that the majority of the people is behind it. Nowhere do the highly exploited young men and women workers enjoy full rights. If they did, the bourgeoisie would sooner turn out the parliament long before the workers reached the point where they could perform the will of the people by peaceful means. But it is really silly to imagine that one could, by peaceful means, through agitation only, without revolution, overcome the lack of confidence which the masses have in their own powers. Only in the revolution can the front ranks of the workers carry the masses along with them.

But a revolution means that one class dictates its will to the other class. The conditions which Kautsky & Co set for a revolution are these: **the revolution, to be sure, has the right to dictate its will to the bourgeoisie, but it is its duty, at the same time, to give the bourgeoisie the possibility, by means of the freedom of the press, and from the vantage of the Constituent Assembly, of airing its accusations.** This intellectual demand of a professional kicker, who is not so much concerned with gaining his point as with registering his kick, could be abstractly complied with without harming the revolution; but the revolution is a civil war, and classes, who fight each other with cannon and machine guns, forego the Homeric battle of words. The revolution does not argue with its enemies, it crushes them: the counter-revolution does the same, and both of them will know how to bear the reproach of not having followed the order of business of the German Reichstag.

The Soviets: The Token by Which the International Proletariat Will Conquer

The harsh face which the Russian Revolution shows to the international proletariat is the same face which, blackened with powder, the international proletariat will itself proudly wear in the near future. **He who is frightened at this face or turns away from it, as from a Medusa's head, will turn away from the proletarian revolution, and away from Socialism.** But the Russian Revolution not only shows the European proletariat the battles which it must fight its way through, if it does not want to rot away in the trenches, but also the forms, **the symbol, in which it will conquer. What form will the dictatorship of the proletariat take in Europe? The form of soviets, that is, the representation of the workers in the factory, in the city, in the country, and in the nation.** That is the form in which the workers of Europe will establish their rule. The idea of soviets is as simple as one can imagine it to be. Only history creates such splendid crystallisations. In the factory, the slaves of capital worked. The factory is bound by a thousand threads with the other factories, with the whole economic life of the locality. It is dependent on the transportation of the locality, on the factories which work up its semi-manufactured goods, or from which it receives them. It depends also on all the factories in the same branch of industry, and, in the last analysis, on the economic life of the entire country. The representation of the factory is, consequently, political and economic, the cell of the state mechanism. The representatives of the proletariat of the locality are, simultaneously, the economic administrators of the locality. But just as the representatives of the workers of the whole country have their policy prescribed for them by the workers of the different localities, but generalise it and make it into laws for the local units of government, in this way having their roots in the local soviets, but at the same time representing to the local soviets the general proletarian interests, just so the General Economic Council, formed from the representatives of the workers, is a body which prevents the local economic councils from considering merely local interests, but to make them subsidiary to the interests of the whole country. The experiences of the Russian Revolution have shown what was strong and creative in Syndicalism and what was petit-bourgeois and sectarian.

The workers of a factory as masters of a factory might easily begin to work for their own particular interests, and in this way might become petit-bourgeois. The Economic Soviet of Industry represents in each factory the interests and the needs for expansion of every branch of industry. But it, too, might favour the interests of a certain branch of industry as against the general interests of the working class. The General Economic Soviet, which designs the whole economic plan and carries it out, equalises the interests of the workers, and makes the general interest the law. In this manner the sectarian tendencies of Syndicalism are done away with, and simultaneously the problem is solved which Syndicalism disowned, and on which it turned its back. The Congress of the Workers' Soviets, the Executive Committee of the Workers' Soviets — that is the proletarian governing power; not the means of capitalist oppression, but the fighting arm of the proletariat. **The Soviet government is not a democratic form of government, it is the form of government of the workers**, it shows its class character clearly and does not veil it with democratic phrases, but it is at the same time the form of government in which the will of the revolutionary working class can express itself clearly, unmistakably and ruthlessly. In this way the problem which was insoluble in bourgeois democracy is solved: the problem of the bureaucracy.

Syndicalism turned away from this problem with disgust. It wanted to do away with bureaucracy and its organisation — but it could not do away with it; it negated it only in words. In capitalist society the proletariat is doomed to catch only the crumbs which fall from the table of capitalistic science. In capitalist society there had to be even in the workers' movement bureaucrats who alone had the time and leisure to learn the technique of the workers' movement. After capitalism is shaken off, in the process of the Socialist revolution, which rouses the proletariat to the very depths, and which brings out all its capabilities, the possibility arises for the first time for the proletariat to manage its own affairs.

The form of the worker-delegate councils, which can always be re-elected, which always return to their native soil, the factory — this form will be the one with which the proletariat will conquer capitalism, and with which it will become capable of accomplishing Socialism. And it is more than significant that all the 'Marxists' who carp at the Russian Revolution have not been able up to the present time to attack the idea of the Soviet government. In order to do that, they would be compelled to defend the secret chambers in which the bureaucracy, together with the representatives of financial capital, manage the affairs of state. The parliament is a debating society, a club for gossip. Parliament does not manage any factories, nor build any railroads. **The government machine, which is growing more and more from a police machine into a business office, could have become a bureaucratic, capitalist association, with parliament as camouflage, otherwise bodies of workers had to be created, who, together with**

professionals, could set economic life in motion and guide it. While this alternative was clear to everyone who had the least conception of the actual mechanism of the so-called democratic states, the opponents of the Soviet government had to confine themselves to defending the right of the nation, that is, the bourgeoisie, to have its say, but they did not dare to defend the **very kernel of the system (the actual rule of the united clique of the bureaucracy and the sharks of finance). That is, they had to leave the cardinal question of the form of the workers' revolution completely untouched.** And that is the best proof of the fact that the learned gentlemen were not only not able really to attack the Russian Revolution, but were unable even to grasp it.

The European proletariat will, without doubt, march forward so quickly in the near future that it will not have the time to learn the experiences of the Russian Revolution out of learned books, but it will learn them practically, before it is in a position to learn them out of the documents of the revolution. We, who have the immeasurable good fortune after four years of horror, the horror of the world war, to be living, that is, to be fighting, in the midst of a newly created society, do not flatter ourselves that we can be the teachers of the European proletariat. Insofar, however, as history gives it a little spare time in which to study the whole scheme of the Russian Revolution, before it uses this scheme practically on its own account and surpasses it, it is our duty to describe the strivings and doings of the Russian proletariat to the international proletariat. The facts will then speak to the longing heart of the proletariat and to its brain, which believes that facts are facts, and need no apology. The Russian Revolution does not need to defend itself before the tribunal of the European proletariat. When Socialism has really fulfilled the longings and strivings of the best proletarians, as we are sure that it has, they will recognise that fact in the Russian Revolution, because it is the first step in the development of Socialism from a theory into action. And they have already recognised in the Russian Revolution the fulfilment of their dreams. From San Francisco to Vladivostok, whether one goes by way of the Atlantic or the Pacific, from all points of the world we are receiving proofs daily of the fact that, in spite of the lies of the bourgeois press, in spite of the cowardice of the traitors to Socialism, the workers of all countries, when they are just beginning to stir, or just feeling the desire for the struggle, turn their eyes to blood-drenched Russia, to that Russia in which the working class is battling with a world of foes, and, as we hope, to conquer.

May this little book of my friend Bukharin,[44] of which three millions of copies were scattered over the wide plains of Russia in three months in order to make clear to the proletariat the object of its activities, may it present to the proletariat of the world, whose blood is still being shed in streams by the capitalists, a picture of something that is worth fighting for, and to die for which is the greatest happiness for one to whom Socialism is not an empty sound.

Moscow
September 1918

Notes

1. K Radek, 'The Development of Socialism from Science into Action', September 1918, in *The Class Struggle*, Volume 3, no 3, August 1919, pp272-95. Another English translation was published in pamphlet form by the Socialist Labour Press in Glasgow, but it is usually less

skilfully rendered than in the American edition which we have mainly followed here, although we have chosen the readings of the English edition where the sense of the American version is not apparent. We would like to offer our thanks to Sebastian Budgen and Ray Challinor for the loan of these original texts.

2. F Engels, 'Principles of Communism', October 1847, K Marx and F Engels, *Collected Works*, Volume 6, London, 1976, p341.

3. François Marie Charles Fourier (1772-1837), the founder of a French school of utopian Socialism, was famous for his asceticism and sensitivity to human suffering.

4. Claude Henri de Rouvry, Comte de Saint-Simon (1760-1875), was a famous French thinker who pioneered a number of schemes for a utopian society.

5. Robert Owen (1771-1858) was a philanthropic cotton manufacturer in New Lanark whose utopian Socialist thinking led him to the fundamental insight that conditions determine consciousness.

6. Ferdinand Lassalle (1825-1864) was the founder of the General Association of German Workers, one of the groups that later came together to form the German Social Democratic Party.

7. The Junkers were the landowning aristocracy of the Prussian state and later of the German Empire, who dominated the administration and the army until the German revolution of 1918-19.

8. The Hohenzollerns, previously Margraves of Brandenburg and kings of Prussia, were the royal family of Imperial Germany.

9. Following an attempt on the life of the Kaiser, Otto, Prince von Bismarck-Schönhausen (1815-1898), the 'Iron Chancellor', attempted to suppress the German working class movement with an Anti-Socialist Law in 1878.

10. Eduard Bernstein (1850-1952), one of the main thinkers of the German Social Democratic Party, began the 'Revisionist' controversy with his article 'Probleme des Sozialismus' in *Die Neue Zeit* in October 1896.

11. We have been unable to trace any reference to Sarante.

12. Jean Jaurès (1859-1914) was the foremost spokesman for the French Socialist Party in the chamber, and the hero of the Dreyfus affair. He was assassinated on the eve of the First World War.

13. Claudio Treves (1869-1933) was a parliamentary deputy for the Italian Socialist Party, and editor of *Avanti!* from 1909 to 1912. He stood on the party's right wing.

14. Filippo Turati (1857-1932) had voted against the war credits of the Italian government, but was opposed to the Italian Socialist Party's adherence to the Communist International.

15. Eduard David (1863-1930) was a leader of the trade unions and a supporter of the right wing of the German Social Democratic Party.

16. A great strike of the Ruhr miners shook Germany from 7 January to 19 February 1905, triggering off further strikes involving half a million workers altogether in that year.

17. The English version can be consulted in Karl Kautsky, *The Social Revolution and On the Morrow of the Social Revolution*, London, 1909.

18. Alexandre Millerand (1859-1943) was the first French Socialist to enter a bourgeois government, that of Waldeck-Rousseau in 1899, where he sat alongside Gallifet, the butcher of the Paris Commune. From this time onwards Socialist participation in such governments was known as 'Millerandism'.

19. The number of seats of the German Social Democrats in the Reichstag dropped from 81 to 43 as a result of the January 1907 election.

20. Max Schippel (1859-1928) was one of the leaders of the right wing of German Social Democracy.

21. The English version can be consulted in Karl Kautsky, *The Road to Power*, Chicago, 1909.

22. The Jena Congress of the German Social Democratic Party (17-23 September 1905) passed a resolution declaring that the mass political strike was 'one of the most effective means' to defend universal suffrage and trade union rights, and that propaganda had to be carried out for the use of it.

23. Ferdinand Freiligrath (1810-1876) was a revolutionary poet and a close friend of Karl Marx.

24. Anton Pannekoek (1873-1960) was a Dutch astronomer and revolutionary Socialist. His polemic against Kautsky, 'Marxist Theory and Revolutionary Tactics' was published in *Die Neue Zeit* in 1912 (Volume 31/1, pp272-81 and 365-73), and can be consulted in an English translation in DA Smart (ed), *Pannekoek and Gorter's Marxism*, London, 1978, pp50-73.

25. The sphinx referred to is not the well-known figure of Egyptian royal iconography, but a monster of Greek fable, which punished with death those who failed to answer its riddle.

26. F Engels, 'Principles of Communism', October 1847, K Marx and F Engels, *Collected Works*, Volume 6, London, 1976, p341.

27. Heinrich Cunow (1862-1936) was a leader of the German Social Democratic Party and editor of *Die Neue Zeit* in 1917-23. Marx formed a very low opinion of him. He supported the German government in the First World War and opposed the Russian Revolution.

28. George Bernard Shaw (1856-1950), the famous playwright, was a reformist and a supporter of the Fabian Society.

29. Aleksandr Ivanovich Guchkov (1862-1936), a leader of the right wing Octobrist Party, was Minister of War under the Provisional Government of Prince Lvov.

30. Pavel Nikolayevich Milyukov (1859-1943), the leader of the Cadets, was Minister for Foreign Affairs in Prince Lvov's government.

31. Mikhail Ivanovich Tereshchenko (1888-1958), a sugar magnate, was Minister of Finance and later for Foreign Affairs in the Provisional Government.

32. Irakli Georgevich Tsereteli (1881-1960) was a prominent Menshevik and member of the Provisional Government.

33. Aleksandr Fyodorovich Kerensky (1881-1970) was the last Prime Minister of the Provisional Government overthrown by the Bolshevik Revolution.

34. Vladimir Mikhailovich Chernov (1876-1952), the leader of the Socialist Revolutionaries, was Minister for Agriculture in Kerensky's government.

35. For Engels' expectations of a collapse of capitalism and a revolution in Germany at this time, cf Gustav Mayer, *Friedrich Engels*, London, 1936, pp236-42.

36. Fyodor Ilyich Dan (Gurvich, 1871-1947) was a leading Menshevik.

37. Attila, the king of the Huns (434-453), led a mixed army of barbarian tribes against the Roman Empire spreading fear and devastation.

38. Medusa the Gorgon, a figure from Greek mythology, was supposed to be able to turn those who looked upon her face to stone.

39. Pavel Borisovich Axelrod (1850-1928) was one of the pioneers of Russian Marxism, and a supporter of the Menshevik right.

40. Julius Ossipovich Martov (Tsederbaum, 1873-1923) was the main theorist of Menshevism and leader of its internationalist wing.

41. Karl Renner (1870-1950) was a leader of Austrian Social Democracy, and later Chancellor (1919-20) and President (1931-33) of Austria.

42. Cf F Engels, *Anti-Dühring*, Peking, 1976, p218.

43. F Engels, Introduction to K Marx, *The Class Struggles in France*, 6 March 1895, Russian edition, Moscow, 1972, pp18-21.

44. The reference here is probably to Bukharin's *Programme of the World Revolution*, published in May 1918 (English edition by the Socialist Labour Press, 1920).

Karl Radek

The Driving Forces of the Russian Revolution[1]

The Soldiers' Revolution

No REVOLUTION resembles those that preceded it. Each has a particular identity. This is why we ask every time a revolution breaks out: is it indeed one? We evaluate it with reference to old schemas and we shake our heads with amazement as regards its 'abnormalities'. When on 9 January 1905 some hundreds of thousands of workers marched in St Petersburg on the palace of the Tsar led by a priest, many turned up their noses: What, a revolution led by a priest?

Equally the revolution which reared its head on 23 February 1917 has now to be evaluated in a critical fashion. What was the significance of the soldiers, who so tumultuously took centre stage in the revolution? The Russian revolution of 1905-07 superficially collapsed because it did not succeed in involving the army on the side of the insurgent population.

Even if the underlying reasons for the collapse of the 1905 revolution were diverse, the main reason is the fact that the bourgeoisie passed over to the side of Tsarism; it also resulted from the help that foreign capital provided to the bourgeoisie. Superficially the revolution was thrown back by the bayonets of the peasants in uniform. But in the revolution of 1917 the soldiers of the St Petersburg garrison attacked the arsenals, distributed the arms to the people, and exerted the most lively pressure upon the Duma.[2] Even the younger generation of the officers was not opposed to it, and moreover, for the time being at least, resistance from the heads of the army, Brusilov, Ruzky and Evert,[3] was not noticeable. Are we not led to believe that the coming over of the masses of the soldiers to the workers took place with the approval of the generals, and that it was a military revolution, a repetition on a larger scale of the revolution of the Young Turks of 1908?[4] But it was nothing of the sort. It is first of all necessary to establish one indisputable fact right from the start: namely, that the revolution began with the agitation of the working class, mass strikes and demonstrations. To begin with, the soldiers fired on them in many places. It was only later that a few regiments came over to the popular masses who were demonstrating, until at last the fire engulfed the whole of the garrison of St Petersburg.

The soldiers' uprising followed on from the workers' revolution; but between the two and a so-called military revolution there was no similarity. A so-called military revolution, such as the Decembrists had envisaged[5] and such as has since occurred in the histories of Spain, Portugal, Greece and finally Turkey, were coups d'état carried out by the officer corps, the only organised force in these under-developed countries. The mass of the soldiers was normally not at all drawn into the struggle, and whenever this was the case it was only as a brute and passive force, commanded by its officers. But in the revolution of 1917 it was the masses of the soldiers who appeared in the first instance, and not the generals. And what did these masses of soldiers represent? The peasants and the workers who had lived through the history of the last 12 years, the years of revolution and counter-revolution, the two and a half years of war, and who had been shaken by it to the depths of their being. The workers who already before the war had recovered from the blows of the counter-revolution, who just before the unleashing of the war had erected barricades in St Petersburg, peasants who had been proletarianised by Stolypin's reforms,[6] and peasants whom the war had snatched from their homes and their fields — that was the soldiers' revolution. The war may have given a uniform to the majority of the popular masses, but it only strengthened the revolutionary tendencies within them. The opposition between the people and the army was suppressed in that the people became the army during the war. From another point of view, the war also made easier the passing over of a part of the army to the side of the working class. The great losses of officers forced the government to enlist university youth and teachers, etc, into the officer corps. Naturally, these democratic elements could not form a barrier against revolutionary tendencies in the army. It is not necessary to show in detail and at great length that the generals were opposed to these tendencies. Every revolutionary agitation was suppressed in the Russian army by a means as Draconian as in every other army. Naturally the Brusilovs and the Everts were not opposed to a renewal of the government by the liberals which could contribute to strengthening the conduct of the war. But the generals understood perfectly that a revolution is not a means that would strengthen the conduct of imperialism's war. And if they were not able to send troops against the rebellious St Petersburg soldiers it is because they took into account — as General Ruzky told the Tsar, according to an account in *The Times* — the fact that every regiment they sent to St Petersburg would pass over to the side of the revolution. The part played by the soldiers in the revolution, which seemed to contradict its popular proletarian character, on the contrary bears testimony to its depth and breadth.

It was not by a command from on high, but by the spark which spread from the street into the barracks that the army was set in motion. And it was this which also determined the character of the insurrection. Even if revolutionary-patriotic elements had influence in the army and had cherished the hope of being able to gain victory over Prussian militarism at the head of revolutionary troops, a proletarian and peasant army would not rise up at the end of 32 months of war in order to go on with it for yet another 32 months. The part played by the army in the revolution, which seemed to give the revolution a warlike character, was to reinforce the tendencies of the revolution which worked towards a peace. So now we come to the bearers of the imperialist tendencies, those who wished to use the revolution as a means of gaining victory, the imperialist bourgeoisie whose participation in the revolution makes up the second characteristic that distinguishes the year 1917 from the year 1905.

The Imperialist Revolutionaries

The National-Liberal Muscovite capitalist Guchkov and the conservative Shulgin,[7] representing the great landowners, graciously invited the Tsar to abdicate at Pskov. Capitalists trod on each other's toes in the new revolutionary government. Was this a repetition of the events of January to December 1905, when the capitalists paid the workers their wages for the days of the mass political strike, those selfsame capitalists who flung themselves into the arms of Tsarism when it transpired that the proletariat was beginning to struggle for the eight-hour day after its victory over Tsarism? Or did the bourgeoisie understand that its interests were irreconcilable with those of Tsarism and decide to make a radical revolution? Were not the opportunists within the Russian Social Democracy perhaps right in reaffirming that the revolution would only triumph when the bourgeoisie placed itself at its head? The facts themselves answer these questions.

At the beginning of the 1905 revolution, the bourgeoisie was not fully conscious of its antagonism towards the proletariat. It hoped that the proletariat would pull its chestnuts out of the fire. But during the war years it no longer returned to the follies of its youth. It did not for an instant forget the decade of struggle with the proletariat, and at each stage it anxiously turned round to see if it had not set the proletariat in motion by its conflicts with Tsarism. No, the joys, mistakes and aberrations of its adolescent love remained totally forbidden to a bourgeoisie now 10 or more years older. Did it therefore conclude a marriage of convenience with the proletarian revolution? Did it therefore perhaps estimate that it would certainly have to make concessions to the proletariat, but that it would obtain power in return? This was not the case either. The bourgeoisie had organised itself powerfully in the course of these last 10 years. It had given birth to cartels, joint stock companies and employers' associations; in the course of the war it had organised itself into committees of industry and war, and it had put not merely humanitarian work, but also a large part of the provisioning of the army into the hands of the confederation of cities.[8] And it occupied itself with this work, not to support the Tsarist war policy, but because it saw in the world war a means of satisfying its own interests.

We do not find a faction as large as the bourgeoisie of Britain or of Germany behind Russia's imperialist policy, but it is a greater capitalist faction than that which supported the war with Japan. The conquest of Constantinople and of Armenia, which would also put an end to Persia's independence, would not only open up new markets, but thanks to the strengthening of Russia's position in the world, would also provide the Russian bourgeoisie with favourable conditions for borrowing the capital which it needs. Victory over Germany would allow a more advantageous trade agreement to be snatched, in other words, an agreement that would guarantee an even higher monopoly charge under the protection of a strengthened industrial tariff control. The bourgeoisie has been in agreement with Tsarist imperial policy since 1907. Insofar as this involved the state apparatus it saw this as a means of forcing concessions from Tsarism on internal policy.

The unfolding of the world war showed that if Russian militarism had made much more progress since the Russo-Japanese war[9] than one might have thought possible, the bureaucracy was also still utterly corrupt and incapable of fulfilling the enormous tasks of supplying the front and of organising the rear. In fact, it was the bourgeoisie and its organisations which fulfilled these tasks, as we have already said. Consequently, the bourgeoisie hoped that this state of affairs would also find its political expression. It sought to persuade the bureaucracy as you persuade an unruly horse, but it received kicks in return. It protested, and received kicks once again. Then it decided to take the stubborn animal by the bit. It tried first of all with the help of the Allies, who saw that the Russian bourgeoisie could organise the conduct of the war far better than the Tsarist bandits, and could resist far longer in the struggle against Germany. Buchanan, the British ambassador,[10] ostentatiously supported the bourgeois imperialist opposition. According to a public statement in the *Manchester Guardian*, Lord Milner[11] saw the Tsar to persuade him to make concessions to the bourgeoisie. When this step also failed, the bourgeoisie tried to reach an understanding with the liberal admirals and generals to put joint pressure on the Tsar to obtain the nomination of a liberal government. The bourgeoisie did not dream of going any further. A little threat of a little putsch, and His Majesty would return to reason and the war could calmly follow its course, that was the plan. They did not dream of revolution, they did not want it, and they even feared it. Nor did they make one.

On 25 February the bourgeoisie still sought to make peace with the Tsar. To its great disappointment the Tsar did not want any compromise. To this was added yet another factor which outflanked the bourgeoisie: the proletariat and the soldiers, who were fighting Tsarism on the streets on 23 February. These put the bourgeoisie in a completely new situation. There was an armed people in St Petersburg, and the Tsar had fled, in other words, declared war on the bourgeoisie. Should it therefore also reject the help of the people? That would be suicide. The bourgeoisie had a little family chat with the Tsar and entered the revolution.

The proletariat made the revolution in overalls. 'The revolution seemed to begin as a soldiers' uprising supported by the working class, but the Duma firmly and rapidly took the power into its hands', wrote *The Times* of 16 March.[12] This judgement of the great British Conservative journal, written very freshly under the impact of events, rings true and gives the lie to *The Times* which now condemns the Russian working class by saying that it was not it which had taken power and that therefore it must keep quiet and help the bourgeoisie win. The poor *Times* was deceived when on 16 March[13] it expressed the hope that the most dangerous days had passed, in other words that the revolution had ended. It has only just begun, and the working class will play the decisive rôle in it. That is why it is important to see what it has done to date. From this also will flow the principles of its future policy.

The Rôle of the Working Class

The driving force of this revolution, like that of 1905, is represented by the working class. The ferment among the petit-bourgeoisie, and the aspirations of the bourgeoisie for power, only formed favourable conditions in which the revolutionary advance of the proletariat could transform itself rapidly into a revolution and straightaway deliver Tsarism a crushing blow. Without the support of the petit-bourgeoisie in town and country the proletariat will not accomplish the revolution victoriously, and should it defeat the bourgeoisie it could not maintain itself in an agrarian country like Russia for a long period without the aid of the peasants. We are not emphasising these events in order to set out a perspective of development — that will be the task of other articles — but to show that our conception of the rôle of the proletariat does not derive from an overestimation of its strength. We know its limits, but that does not prevent the bourgeoisie in 1917 from being as little a driving force of the revolution as it was in 1905, or to deny that today, as previously, this motor force is the working class.

The revolution began in 1905 with the 'petition' of the proletariat before the Tsar on 9 January, and ended with its defeat in the Moscow uprising of December

1905. In 1906 the proletariat sought to keep the positions conquered in its bloody hands, but the blows with which capital struck it and the Tsarist shootings brought it down. Yet again the working class arose in St Petersburg when the Social Democratic deputies of the Second Duma were dragged before the Tsarist courts.[14] The St Petersburg proletarians fired their last bullets to tell their trusted representatives: 'We are here.' But then the darkness of counter-revolution fell over the proletariat, and it was only from the prisons that news came about the fighters who had been snatched from its ranks.

And even though a part of the Social Democracy, the Liquidators,[15] had capitulated, left the ranks of the party, or rather had admitted that the only task of the Social Democracy was to create all sorts of legal organisations that would gradually allow the working class to take over positions in a Russia which had already completely abandoned the road of bourgeois revolution to take the road of a long bourgeois development, the radical elements in the party, the Bolsheviks, had maintained their revolutionary aims: so long as Tsarism and the bourgeoisie had not satisfied the demands of the peasants it was necessary to maintain the objective of the violent overthrow of Tsarism, to direct the party's struggle towards this aim and not towards reforms, and only to make use of all legal positions with a view to this end. Between these two points of view, that of the Liquidators who considered that the revolution had ended, and that reforms were the next task, and that of the Bolsheviks, there was a middle position essentially represented by Trotsky. This tendency obviously did not renounce the revolution, but saw the struggle for partial reforms as the means of getting there. When the working class, which had been vanquished in 1905-07, began to lift up its head again in 1912 thanks to the cyclical economic improvement, when after the Lena massacres[16] it took on an insurrectionary character, then the real course of events cut short the struggle within the party. The majority of the proletariat that really began to struggle did not adopt as its aim the reform of Tsarism, but its overthrow. It did not even wish to take the struggle for reforms as its point of departure, but went for the throat of Tsarism. In July 1914, in the course of the month preceding the war, Poincaré[17] was able to witness barricades and mass demonstrations in St Petersburg. Perhaps the result of these struggles might only have been to obtain reforms and not victory over Tsarism if the war had not enormously sharpened all the contradictions. But then history will also teach all those who see the way to revolution in the struggle for reforms that it knows also another dialectic: reforms as a result of the yearning for revolution. History has already proved the Bolsheviks to be completely right against the Liquidators and Conciliators.[18] The transformation of the majority of the Liquidators into social patriots showed the extent to which the Bolsheviks had been right in their policy of splitting with the Liquidators.

To begin with, the war inhibited the struggle of the working class. The Bolsheviks' anti-war attitude and their propaganda for revolutionary mass struggle were represented as insignificant by the social patriots abroad: small groups of ideologists embittered against Tsarism who had nothing to lose. But when the news arrived from Russia about the struggles of a ceaselessly growing fraction of the working class, about munition strikes, and about demonstrations, they took them to be symptomatic but in reality insignificant. The Bolshevik slogan, 'Not social peace, but civil war!', yet again appeared to the centrist **realpolitiker** as an exaggeration that life would correct of itself: it would be sufficient for Social

Democracy to keep its hands clean and not to assume responsibility. At present Russia is in a civil war in the literal sense of the word. It was unleashed against the will of the bourgeoisie. Under the pressure of the proletariat, the Tsar has been deposed and imprisoned, the policemen of reaction arrested, and the supreme command has been withdrawn from the Grand Duke Nicholas.[19] The proletariat immediately brought to life the soviet of workers' deputies, the instrument of struggle born of the masses in 1905, the direct representation of the class, and armed itself. Against whom? Against the still living forces of the old regime and against the new regime of the bourgeoisie. The new regime was not yet secure against a reactionary conspiracy. In the meantime only the Tsar was vanquished, but democracy had not yet been achieved. Wasn't it too soon, then, when from that moment on radical Social Democracy armed the people for future struggle, when it put forward other demands which went further, not only within the sphere of a democratic republic, but in the social sphere; when it demanded the eight-hour day for the working class and land for the peasants? Given that these demands were directed not only against the rulers of the past, but also against the present men in power, the Entente[20] press spoke of the counter-revolutionary activity of the Bolsheviks and of the working class in general. But one look at the forces of reaction and the external situation of the revolution will show that the revolution would have taken place in vain for the working class and the peasants if it had been declared finished by the Social Democracy.

The Tactic of the Working Class

'Given that Russia has greeted the new regime with joy, it is ridiculous to speak at present of the possibility of the restoration of the domination of reaction; but the extremists [that means the revolutionary Social Democrats — KR] maintain that it is dangerous for the workers to return to the factories and the soldiers to their duty', *The Times* correspondent telegraphed on 20 March,[21] whose dispatches, despite their craftiness, provide the best understanding of the contradictory currents of the revolution. And in an officious note in the Paris *Temps* of 27 March[22] we read: 'The present government has little to fear from a return to reaction. But it seems that it does have to fear the Socialists, who have revealed themselves to be revolutionaries in the fullest sense of the word.' It is not the old regime but the proletariat that is the danger; such is the slogan that British and French finance capital has given to the Russian bourgeoisie. And this is also its point of view. But too weak to settle accounts so soon with the proletariat, the bourgeoisie seeks to lull it to sleep with the first part of the counter-revolutionary slogan, with the joyful shout: 'The old regime is dead!' Reactionary forces have never laid down their arms without the most desperate resistance. The Russian junkers[23] and bureaucrats would be the last to do this; for years economic development as well as their own carelessness have undermined their basis as large semi-feudal landowners; state power is their last lifebelt. To the great consolation of the exploiters and bureaucratic brigands, the state is the sole source of money and power. If they do not want to disappear they must fight to the death. They have been shaken by events, but they do not yet see very clearly what they can expect from certain bodies of soldiers. They want to wait until the bourgeoisie, frightened by the growth of the proletarian movement, throws itself into their arms.

Can the proletariat defend itself against this by 'level-headedness'? If it now gives up the struggle for bread, peace and liberty, whilst the present bourgeoisie confers upon it crowns of laurel and is able to maintain itself against the Nikolaievs,[24] then the workers will continue to bleed for imperialism and come out at the end empty-handed. There exists only one way to ensure the new regime against the old. It consists of deepening and strengthening the revolution, both socially and politically. The social revolution consists in this: that the proletariat should immediately arm itself, immediately force local city elections, take over the apparatus of administration, put the homeless in the apartments of the rich, and take Draconian measures against war profiteers. The city administrations must straightaway encourage the creation of administrations in the rural areas, incite the peasants to take over the great landed estates, and place at their disposal the means necessary to cultivate the land. It should be the task of great commissions and of the soviets of workers' deputies to raise openly the following demands: that the factories provide agricultural implements, and that the peasant soldiers are given leave of absence to go home and cultivate their fields. But this is impossible without a halt in any offensive which is supposed to guarantee Persia, Armenia and the Dardanelles[25] to Russian imperialism, and without any defensive action on the German front.

And that leads on to political demands: an immediate armistice, peace negotiations, an eight-hour day, elections for the Constituent Assembly on the basis of universal suffrage, equal for both men and women, and the arraignment of the Romanovs[26] before the courts. Can you imagine any more powerful demands? And in the same way that the struggle for these objectives will advance the combativity of the working class, it will tie the Russian workers and peasants to the revolution's fortunes to such an extent that reaction would no longer be able to rely on either the backwardness of the peasants or the tiredness of the workers.

But isn't this the 'plan' of those revolutionary alchemists who elaborate recipes in their studies? Anyone who pays close attention to the chaos of telegrams reported from St Petersburg by the big newspapers will notice that we have only systematised what the radicalised working class had already realised on the spot under the pressure of necessity. Even the soldiers' demand for the demobilisation of the oldest men to allow them to go and cultivate the fields had been reported by *The Times* on 24 March.[27]

It cannot be otherwise. The proletariat must attempt to exploit the success to its own advantage. And this exploitation of the victory by the proletariat in its own interests is the 'anarchy' of 'fanaticism', of 'extremism' on the part of 'unknown orators' in the soviet of workers' deputies against whom *The Times* and *Le Temps* rail so much. Like Antaeus,[28] it returns to mother earth to gain strength! And so the retrenchment work of the proletariat will sooner or later lead to a clash with 'the new government' of the imperialist bourgeoisie which on this occasion will find itself in the same position as the men of the old regime. At the moment the proletariat does not aspire to the overthrow of the new government, it only seeks to defend itself against those greedy hands who wish to take away from it all the fruits of its victory. But because it does not wish to deliver itself over to the old exploitation which the new government would exercise over it at will, we can surely foresee that the struggle between the proletariat and the new government will be a fight to the death. On its issue depends the consequences unleashed by the Russian Revolution.

The Struggle for Peace

The question of war and peace stands at the centre of all the problems of the revolution. Even if the historic roots of this revolution lie much deeper — it is not only the result of the war, but also of a long process of decomposition in Russia, as well as prolonged revolutionary struggles — the revolution was unleashed by the war. The bourgeoisie went into opposition to Tsarism because it believed that it could direct the war in a more energetic manner, whereas the popular masses arose because they wished to struggle against the terrible consequences of the war. But it is not just because the revolution was born (to begin with) as a result of the war that the problem of the war was placed at the centre of all questions. Tsarism has been overthrown, but a new regime has not yet been built. Therefore this question is posed: what will be the effect of the continuation of the war and its outcome upon Russia's internal structure? Hence all the contradictions and all the antagonisms of the revolution are concentrated upon this one question — peace or war? The imperialist bourgeoisie desires war until victory. It was on account of this hoped-for victory that it revolted against Tsarism, and contributed to the creation of a situation thanks to which the victory of the revolution became possible. And by making propaganda for a war to the finish, it asserts that it is helping the work of democratising Russia. It is only when Russia will have achieved its imperialist objectives, in the first instance by seizing Constantinople and obtaining a free passage through the Dardanelles, that it will have the perspective of a prosperous economic development without which internal reconstruction is impossible. Only the annihilation of Austria, the defeat of Germany, and the general victory of the Entente would allow the creation of a democratic Europe in which Russia would be protected against the counter-revolutionary attacks of Germany. This is why all those who refuse to associate themselves with Messrs Guchkov and Milyukov's imperialist war are traitors to the revolution. The Russian workers will not allow themselves to be taken in by these snake charmers. To begin with they know Messrs Guchkov and Milyukov, the great liberal capitalist junkers and professors, all too well. The revolution of 1917 has not experienced a honeymoon. All its protagonists came so closely into contact with each other in the course of the period 1907-16 that none of them surprise each other. It is true that bourgeois liberals of the Milyukov type denounced Tsarism at the time, but they were always ready to conspire with it against democracy; they did not struggle for Tsarism's overthrow, but for its reform and its modernisation. Even on 28 February, after the triumph of the revolution, Milyukov declared in favour of a constitutional monarchy, as against a republic. And if in the end the Central Committee of his party, the Cadets[29] declared in favour of a republic, it was only under the growing pressure of the masses; therefore absolutely no reliance can be placed on them. Things are even clearer as regards Guchkov and his party, the Octobrists.[30] There is not a single infamy committed by Tsarism after 1905 for which this party of big capitalists, the sworn enemies of the proletariat, is not responsible. And these are the defenders of democracy, people capable of directing a war which has as its aim to ensure a republic in Russia? It is only by a mortal struggle with them, a struggle that has the aim of overthrowing them, that democracy can be ensured in Russia. This struggle equally applies to their war aims. Far from forming the conditions for Russia's prosperous economic development, these war aims represent an obstacle to it; if they are realised they will make Russia bear the heaviest burdens. Constantinople and a free passage through the Dardanelles are valueless for the peaceful development of Russia. If Russia were at peace with Turkey, it could send its ships loaded with cereals throughout the world as far as it wished. The Dardanelles are only necessary to Russia if it is dreaming of a policy of imperialist brigandage, and if it wishes to embark upon adventures in the Mediterranean. But that would mean a gigantic rearmament policy all over again, and new entanglements for the resolution of which millions of Russian workers and peasants would have to give up their lives.

The war aims of the Cadets, like those of the Octobrists, require a war until Europe is bled white, a war which will cause its costs to grow until they become an insufferable burden. And even if this objective should be attained, the Russian workers and peasants will have to prepare themselves for fresh wars. It is obvious that the interests of the Russian Revolution require a mortal struggle against the Cadets and the Octobrists, and against the Provisional Government[31] which pursues their aims. However good his subjective intentions, he who sits in this government, as does the petit-bourgeois democrat Kerensky, betrays the revolution: 'Obviously we must therefore struggle against imperialist war aims, but we cannot lay down our arms, however, before Prussian militarism and the Hohenzollerns have been defeated. If they emerge from this war unscathed there would be no place for a Russian republic. We will have to defend Russia's youthful liberty with bayonets until the danger threatening it from outside has been overcome by the victory of the Entente.'

Not only open social patriots, the Plekhanovs abroad and the Potresovs and Chkhenkelis[32] inside Russia, declare this, but even centrists such as the deputy Chkeidze, Skobelev[33] and his supporters who formally accept the Zimmerwald[34] resolutions. The majority of the St Petersburg soviet of workers' and soldiers' deputies, representing the popular masses of St Petersburg, is of that opinion. The Entente press reports triumphantly: 'with the exception of the "extremist" Bolsheviks, who are paid German agents or fanatical fools, all the Russian Socialists are for the continuation of the war which they take to be a defensive war'. And if the social patriots and the centrists could hold on to the majority that they hold for the moment in the soviet of workers' deputies, the Entente would be right to embrace them; for by their efforts these social patriotic gentlemen along with the centrists not only support the aims of the Entente and of their own imperialism, but also play the game of the Milyukovs and Guchkovs, and consequently of the adversaries of the victory of the revolution and the enemies of the republic.

These social patriotic and centrist gentlemen declare: 'Yes, we are against the war aims of imperialism, we are against shedding the blood of Russian workers and peasants for the conquest of the Dardanelles and Constantinople. We only wish to defend the Russian republic against Prussian bayonets.' All this is very fine. But if the imperialist bourgeoisie remains in power, if the Guchkovs and the Milyukovs maintain the government in their hands, it will not be the wishes of the social patriots and centrists that will prevail, but the war aims of Russian imperialism and of the Entente. If the Entente should win with the help of the Russian social patriots and centrists, it would be imperialism's victory, and not the peace without annexations and indemnities which the soviet of workers' deputies proclaims as its aims. But if the Russian workers and peasants were to overthrow the Provisional Government of the imperialist bourgeoisie, were to cancel all the imperialist obligations and alliances that Tsarism has agreed to and the Provisional Government has recognised, then they could say: 'We have guaranteed the republic which wants no conquests, and he who is against us is carrying on a war of conquest'; then they could launch an appeal to the proletariat of the entire world for the conclusion of a peace between all peoples. Then the Russian Revolution could say: 'A peace of all peoples against imperialism, or rather the year 1793 of the Russian proletariat and peasantry,[35] the struggle of the Russian revolution against all the reactionary forces in the world.' We would then see if the conditions for such a revolutionary war existed — we only wish to state that it is really ridiculous to see Chkeidze and Skobelev pretending to be Danton.[36] Meanwhile, they are assisting the enemies of the Russian revolution, not only the Girondins[37] but even the monarchists of the Russian Revolution, not only the Cadets but the Octobrists as well. For what in practice does the slogan mean that 'we are continuing a defensive war'? It only means that the Russian soldiers will continue to pour out their blood for imperialist objectives, and social peace within. The soviet of workers' deputies may well quarrel every day with the Provisional Government, just as the newspapers report. But it is not allowed to tell the workers: 'Struggle for your proletarian rights, as in December 1905!' For if the social patriots and centrists did this, they would considerably damage the conduct of the war, given that munitions production would be disorganised and weakened. If the social patriots and centrists wish to defend the fatherland 'for the time being', they must not push for the immediate democratisation of the army and the abolition of the officers' privileges, for in struggling for these objectives they would weaken the army's fighting capacity. If the social patriots wish to retain the generals whose elimination would doubtless weaken the present power of the army, they must not say to the peasants: 'Take over big feudal landed property immediately.' If they did this, these gentlemen generals, who are closely related to the junkers, would straightaway begin to ask if it was worthwhile defending so ungrateful a fatherland. Let us sum up briefly: the social patriots and the centrists want to defend the republic provisionally under the leadership of the Guchkovs and Milyukovs, so that youthful Russian liberty may not be vanquished by Prussian militarism. But that liberty can only be assured — as the history of every revolution shows — if the working class and peasantry, without waiting for the Constituent Assembly, build democracy from below, take effective power, and root it socially. The social patriots and centrists must abandon this effective protection of the revolution if they wish to continue the war under the leadership of the imperialist bourgeoisie. The revolution that they want to protect is handed over to the enemies of the revolution. There therefore remains but one thing: the struggle for imperialist objectives. But fortunately for the revolution, its logic is stronger than that of the social patriots and centrists. In spite of the efforts of the liberal bourgeoisie and its social patriotic and centrist lackeys, the Titan[38] does not allow itself to be tamed. As the big press of the Entente reports whilst grinding its teeth, the struggle of the working class to realise democracy, for the eight-hour day and for the land continues. But this struggle is directed against the prosecution of the war. And it finds its agents in the Sansculottes,[39] the vanguard of the Russian Revolution, in the Russian revolutionary internationalist Social Democracy, the Bolsheviks, who are opposed to the momentary wave of republican-revolutionary illusions. And nothing shows better the growth of their power than the peevishness with which they are combated by *The Times* and *Le Temps*, the avowed organs of European finance capital.

The fate of the Russian Revolution, of the European upheaval and of peace in the following period depends upon the fortunes of this proletarian party. The question of its position and its struggle with which we are going to deal now, coincides with the problem of the perspectives of the Russian Revolution.

The Attitude of the Bolsheviks

The Russian revolutionary Social Democrats, the Bolsheviks, who out of all the factions of Russian Socialism have carried out the most energetic and the most effective struggle against Tsarism, who during the period of the unleashing of the counter-revolution continued to work unceasingly for the overthrow of Tsarism, do not have to prove that they wish to defend the revolution against all its enemies, and that they are its most faithful guardians. The Russian revolutionary Social Democrats, who ever since the war was unleashed have demonstrated its imperialist character in the sharpest manner, and who consistently sought at Zimmerwald and Kienthal[40] to engage in a generalised struggle against imperialist governments, stick to this view. The Central Powers[41] do not have the slightest illusion on this score. However, in politics it is not a question of intentions, but of results, whether they be intended or no. What are the premises of the politics of the Bolsheviks, and what consequences do they have? This question, which is wholly justified, has to be answered.

Internally, the Bolsheviks start off from the principle that the supporters of the Russian Revolution are only to be found in the working class, the poor peasantry and the poor and dissatisfied petit-bourgeoisie — the working class having been and remaining the only truly consistent and conscious vanguard of the revolution — therefore democracy can only be created in Russia in the struggle against big capital. At the stage of development in which Russia finds herself today, when enormous proletarian masses are opposed to concentrated capital, when dissatisfaction reigns in the villages, when young nations are awakening along Russia's frontiers, Russian capital will attempt to concentrate the maximum power in its hands and slow down the development of democracy.

No confidence can be placed in the parties of the Cadets and the Octobrists. The proletariat must create democracy from now on. It will come up against the most determined resistance, not only from Russian capital, but from foreign capital as well. The press of the Entente tries to frighten the Russian revolutionaries with the spectre of Prussian bayonets. But its own press is already insisting upon the fact — see the editions of *Figaro* — that the providers of foreign funds have the right to insist that order reigns in Russia. There is no need to search far for the reasons: in a capitalist country where a working class exists that is powerful and conscious of its own class interests, democracy means the greatest struggles for the eight-hour day, for decent labour laws, and for political control. All this is already immediately directed against capitalism's unfettered power — also that of foreign capital, which plays an important rôle in the Russian economy — and if we take into consideration the fact that Russian capital wishes to conduct an imperialist policy, and that foreign capital is pushing Russia in the same direction, it is clear that the one, like the other, must resist the victory of the revolution. Consequently, the struggle even if only for democracy signifies for the Russian working class a break not only with its own capital, but also the most determined struggle against world capital.

It is a matter of conducting this struggle in a situation where, viewed superficially, there does not exist a united front of world capital, and where the struggle between the capital of the Central Powers and that of the Entente has reached its highest stage. A glance at the situation shows that the next enemy which will prevent and hold back the development of democracy with all its strength will be Russian capitalism itself. It has power at the moment. It is supported by British and French capital. It 'needs' the 'German danger' to postpone the process of Russia's democratisation in order ultimately to check it. Whoever allies with it is killing the revolution. If the Russian working class submits to the rule of its capitalists, if it limits its proletarian objectives in order to protect the revolution from outside threats, then it will surrender to its internal enemies. If it shows its strength, it will overthrow its internal enemy.

The perspective of a proletarian 1793 provides a reply to the question of the social patriots and the centrists: 'Do you want to deliver the Russian Revolution to the foreign enemy?' The Bolsheviks reply: 'Neither to the foreign enemy nor to the enemy within!' But just as it is not possible to defeat the revolution's internal enemy, Russian capital, by allying with the enemy abroad, world capital, it is also not possible to overthrow the enemy abroad by allying with the enemy within. If we were to make common cause with the Guchkovs and Milyukovs for the defeat of Germany, we would not only be helping Anglo-Saxon capital — the strongest part of world capital — to exploit the world, but also to ransack Russia as well. The proletariat can only directly struggle against its own bourgeoisie.

Notes

1. Article published under the title 'Die Triebkräft der Russischen Revolution' in *Arbeiterpolitik*, II, Jahrgang no 13 18 (1917), and in K Radek, *In den Reihen der Deutschen Revolution 1909-1919*, Kurt Wolff Verlag, München, 1921, pp437-55. Together with the following article by Radek, it was translated by the editor, with the assistance of Harry Ratner and Bruce Robinson.
2. The Duma was a constitutional assembly to be elected along the lines of differential class voting granted by the Tsar in October 1905 to defuse the demand for a democratic parliament.
3. General Alexei Alexeyevich Brusilov (1853-1926) was Commander-in-Chief of the South-Western Front in 1916-17; General NV Ruzky (1854-1918) was Commander-in-Chief of the Northern Front; General AE Evert (1857-1917) was Commander-in-Chief on the Western Front in 1915-17.
4. The movement of opposition to the autocracy by the Young Turks, important in the Turkish army, provoked a rebellion of the troops in July 1908 under Enver Pasha, and forced the Turkish government to grant a constitution.
5. The Decembrists were young officers who initiated an attempted coup d'état in 1825, encouraged by the Tsar's brother with the promise of a constitution.
6. Count Pyotr Arkadyevich Stolypin (1862-1911) was the Tsar's Chief Minister and Minister of Finance. By this reform between 1906 and 1910 he neutralised a part of the peasantry by 'breaking up' the rural commune to the advantage of a minority.
7. Vassily Vitalyevich Shulgin (1878-1945) was a right wing Tsarist statesman and writer.
8. The Confederation of Cities, called the Zemstvos, was a system of provincial and county self-government set up in 1864 and administered by the local gentry. During the war it played an important rôle in supplying the Russian army.
9. During the Russo-Japanese War (1904-06) the Russian army and navy sustained a series of humiliating defeats in the Far East.
10. Sir George William Buchanan (1854-1924) was British ambassador to Russia, 1910-24.
11. Alfred, Viscount Milner (1854-1925) was a representative of the Allied Military Mission in Russia.
12. This date in the Gregorian Calendar corresponds to 3 March in Russia. Until 1917 Russia still adhered to the old Julian Calendar, which by then was 13 days behind the modern Gregorian one.
13. 3 March in Russia.
14. The members of the Bolshevik fraction in the Duma were arrested during the night of 4-5 November 1914 and were later tried and exiled for their opposition to the First World War.
15. The Liquidators were a group of Mensheviks led by AN Potresov after 1907 who argued for the liquidation of the illegal organs of the party in order to function solely within the limits of Tsarist legality.

16. The Tsarist gendarmerie fired upon an unarmed demonstration of strikers at the Lena Goldfield in Siberia on 4 April 1912, triggering off a wave of strikes and protests in Russia.

17. Raymond Nicholas Landry Poincaré (1860-1934), a noted chauvinist and right winger, had been Prime Minister and was later President of France.

18. The Conciliators, or 'Party Bolsheviks', were a group led by Rykov, Lozovsky and Sokolnikov who argued for a restoration of party unity with the Mensheviks in 1910.

19. The Grand Duke Nicholas Nikolayevich (1850-1929) was Supreme Commander-in-Chief of the Russian armies from 1914 to August 1915.

20. The Entente Cordiale entered into by Britain and France in 1904 gave its name to the alliance of Britain, France, Russia, Serbia, Japan, Belgium, Italy, Romania, the USA and Greece which fought in the First World War.

21. 7 March in Russia.

22. 14 March in Russia.

23. The Junkers were the noble class which provided officers for the German army and bureaucrats for the state administration. Radek is using this phrase for the Russian nobility to make his account intelligible to a German readership. It should not in this instance be confused with the use of the term junker in Russia for officer cadets.

24. Nikolayevichs? cf n19 above.

25. The Dardanelles, also called the Bosphorus, was the passage out from the Black Sea into the Mediterranean past Istanbul, the Turkish capital, which had long been coveted by the Tsarist state as a means of expanding in the Near East at the expense of the Turkish empire.

26. The Romanovs were the dynasty which had ruled Russia since the seventeenth century.

27. 11 March in Russia.

28. Antaeus was the giant in Greek mythology who wrestled with Heracles. He drew strength from his mother, the earth, every time he was thrown down.

29. The Constitutional Democrat Party (KD, Cadets) was a bourgeois 'liberal' party created in 1905.

30. A party created by the supporters of the Tsar's manifesto of October 1906 envisaging a constitutional regime.

31. The Provisional Government was a committee set up by the Duma after the fall of the Tsar to rule Russia until the convening of an All-Russian Constituent Assembly to decide on a future constitution for the country.

32. Georgi Valentinovich Plekhanov (1856-1918) was the pioneer of Marxism in Russia. He adopted a policy of support for the Russian war effort in the First World War, and of support to the Provisional Government in 1917. Alexander Nikolayevich Potresov (Starover, 1869-1934) was a leading Menshevik who supported the Provisional Government. Arkady Ivanovich Chkhenkeli (1874-1959) was a Menshevik deputy in the Fourth Duma and later a minister in the Menshevik Georgian republic.

33. Nikolai Semyonovich Chkeidze (1864-1926) and Matvei Ivanovich Skobelev (1885-1939) were leaders of the Menshevik right wing.

34. The Zimmerwald Conference (September 1915) was a gathering of left wing Socialist internationalists in Switzerland opposed to the First World War. Its manifesto was written by LD Trotsky.

35. In 1793 the French revolutionaries, already at war with much of Europe, received requests from the people of some of the neighbouring countries to help them overthrow their feudal rulers. In these circumstances was born the famous slogan: 'War to the castle, peace to the cottage!'

36. Georges-Jacques Danton (1759-94) was the revolutionary leader who galvanised the resistance of France against foreign invasion after the defeat at Valmy.

37. The Girondins were the moderate faction during the French Revolution which attempted to put a brake upon its progress. Several of them came from the area of Bordeaux, hence their name.

38. The Titans were the giants of Greek mythology, overthrown by the gods when they began their rule.

39. The Sansculottes were the Parisian lower classes who played a leading rôle in the French Revolution.

40. A second international Socialist conference against the First World War was held at Kienthal in Switzerland in April 1916.

41. The Central Powers, so-called because of their position in the middle of Europe, is the name of the alliance of Germany, Austria-Hungary, Turkey and Bulgaria which fought in the First World War.

Karl Radek

The Paths of the Russian Revolution[1]

I

Russian Marxism, which prepared the ground for the activity of the Russian working class by clearly setting forth the tendencies of Russia's development at the end of the nineteenth century and by defining the rôle of the different social classes in the struggles to come, began by destroying the illusions of the petit-bourgeois Socialists about the driving forces and nature of the Russian Revolution. Already in his first works, Plekhanov showed that Russia also had to pass along the road of capitalism and that it was doing so. He destroyed the dreams of the possibility of leaping from the yoke of Tsarism into the rule of Socialism as a damaging illusion. The working class, he said, must put every effort into gaining democracy for Russia, and that only after having become informed, organised and enlightened, would it, within the framework of capitalism and democracy, be able to conclude successfully the struggle for Socialism. In his pamphlet *Socialism and the Political Struggle* which appeared in 1881, Plekhanov wrote:

'To bind together in one two so fundamentally different matters as the overthrow of absolutism and the Socialist revolution, to wage revolutionary struggle in the belief that these elements of social development will **coincide** in the history of our country means **to put off the advent of both**.'[2]

By thus establishing the **bourgeois** content of the coming Russian Revolution, he nonetheless at the same time explained that the **revolution itself would in the first place be the work of the working class.** 'Political liberty will be conquered by the working class, or it will not be conquered at all', Plekhanov explained in the *Sozialdemokrat* in 1888. The arguments of the pioneers of Russian Marxism on the Russian Revolution thus make evident the **objective bourgeois limits** of that revolution, but also ascribe to the proletariat **the rôle of the leading agent, the executor of the revolution**.

The years that preceded the start of the great revolutionary movements in Russia were full of struggles concerning the methods of work of the revolutionary Social Democratic Party, the tactics of the young working class party that was in the process of formation, and by the struggles of *Iskra* against the 'Economists',[3] which were only indirectly linked to the great historical questions. But the question of the social content of the Russian Revolution was to pose itself again to the party in the broadest manner when the birth of the petit-bourgeois peasant Socialism of the Socialist Revolutionaries[4] and the rise of the liberal movement required the taking up of clear positions. In the course of the year 1904-05 the

Menshevik and Bolshevik tendencies crystallised within the Russian Social Democracy, arising precisely around these questions. What were **the differences between the two tendencies in their analysis of the character of the Russian Revolution and of its motor forces?** In Lenin's pamphlet *Two Tactics of Social Democracy in the Democratic Revolution* (Summer 1905) we read this:

'Finally, we will note that the resolution, by making implementation of the minimum programme the provisional revolutionary government's task, eliminates the absurd and semi-Anarchist ideas of giving immediate effect to the maximum programme, and the conquest of power for a Socialist revolution. **The degree of Russia's economic development (an objective condition), and the degree of class-consciousness and organisation of the broad masses of the proletariat (a subjective condition inseparably bound up with the objective condition) make the immediate and complete emancipation of the working class impossible. Only the most ignorant people can close their eyes to the bourgeois nature of the democratic revolution which is now taking place;** only the most naive optimists can forget how little as yet the masses of the workers are informed about the aims of Socialism and the methods of achieving it. We are all convinced that the emancipation of the working classes must be won by the working classes themselves; a Socialist revolution is out of the question unless the masses become class-conscious and organised, trained, and educated in an open class struggle against the entire bourgeoisie. Replying to the Anarchists' objections that we are putting off the Socialist revolution, we say: we are not putting it off, but are taking the first step towards it in the only possible way, along the only correct path, namely, **the path of a democratic republic.** Whoever wants to reach Socialism by any other path than that of **political democracy** will inevitably arrive at conclusions that are absurd and reactionary both in the economic and the political sense. If any workers ask us at the appropriate moment why we should not go ahead and carry out our maximum programme we shall answer by pointing out how far from Socialism the masses of the democratically-minded people still are, how undeveloped class antagonisms still are, and how unorganised the proletarians still are. Organise hundreds of thousands of workers all over Russia; get the millions to sympathise with our programme! Try to do this without confining yourselves to high-sounding but hollow Anarchist phrases — and you will see at once that achievement of this organisation and the spread of this Socialist enlightenment depend on the fullest possible achievement of democratic transformations.'[5]

This was not just a passing thought, but **the theoretical foundation of the entire position of Lenin and the Bolsheviks during the first revolution.** How, therefore, did it differ from that of the Mensheviks?

The differences did not begin to show until it was a question of determining the rôle of the non-proletarian classes in the revolution and relationships with them. Starting off from the fact that the Russian Revolution would to begin with prepare the ground for the free development of capitalism — this concept was common to both Mensheviks and Bolsheviks — the Mensheviks concluded from it that **leadership in the revolution must fall to the bourgeoisie.** The Mensheviks combated in the most resolute manner the idea that the working class along with the peasantry must take power for the revolution to achieve its bourgeois democratic aims — if nothing more. According to the Menshevik conception, the rôle of the revolutionary working class and its party had to be the rôle of a **left opposition**. The Mensheviks compared the efforts of the working class to conquer power along with the peasantry to Millerandism, to the participation of the Social Democracy in bourgeois governments towards the end of the nineteenth century, and prophesied that any attempt to participate in government would be a disaster for the Social Democracy. On their side, the Bolsheviks demonstrated that, firstly, the Menshevik conception was completely schematic, and, secondly, that it was renouncing the radical victory of the bourgeois revolution. From the fact that the Russian Revolution was bourgeois in content it did not absolutely follow, they said, that the industrial bourgeoisie had to be its agent. The industrial bourgeoisie was too allied to Tsarism and feared the working class too much to be able to place itself at the head of the popular masses in the struggle against Tsarism. The entire history of the nineteenth century had already rendered it too conscious of its antagonism with the working class. But there was outside of the industrial bourgeoisie a bourgeois class whose interests cried out for the victory of the revolution. This was the **peasantry**. The Bolsheviks explained that the peasantry had to struggle against Tsarism up to the final victory if it wished to obtain the land. The peasantry is a bourgeois class. But is it a class which must destroy the edifice of Tsarism in order to achieve its bourgeois aims? This class is uneducated, and is beginning to take its first steps. The task of the Social Democracy must be to lead in struggle, not only the working class, but the peasantry as well. If the work of the Social Democracy were to be successful, if the masses of the people were to rise up against Tsarism, then the creation of a **revolutionary government** would be necessary, whose job it would be to lead the bourgeois revolution to its conclusion by a struggle against the forces of the old regime who could not be annihilated by a single blow. The Bolsheviks saw in participation in this common revolutionary proletarian government a guarantee of the achievement of the revolution; they reproached the Mensheviks with wanting to limit themselves to an oppositional rôle, and abandoning the leadership a priori to elements who did not want the final victory of the revolution, but sought for a compromise with Tsarism. The controversies between the Mensheviks and the Bolsheviks just before and during the revolution consequently involved different relations with the peasantry on the one side and with the liberal bourgeoisie on the other. These differences also posed the question of **the rôle of the working class in the revolution**, the question of knowing if the working class should take the leadership during the revolution, or if it should leave the leadership to the bourgeoisie.

Trotsky and Parvus[6] on the one side, and Kautsky[7] and Rosa Luxemburg[8] on the other, were already at this time expressing concepts differing from those of both tendencies of Russian Social Democracy. Beginning with Kautsky, who is now calling absurd and utopian all those who dare to express a doubt about the correctness of Menshevik concepts, this is what he declared in reply to an inquiry from Plekhanov:

'The questionnaire includes the following three questions:
' 1. What would seem to be the **general character** of the Russian Revolution? Are we confronted with a **bourgeois** revolution or a **proletarian** revolution?
' 2. Given the futile attempts of the Russian government to suppress the

revolutionary movement, what attitude should the Social Democratic Party adopt with regard to the **bourgeois democracy** which after its own fashion is fighting for political freedom?

'3. What tactic should the Social Democratic Party follow in the elections for the Duma, in order to exploit, without breaking the Amsterdam resolutions,[9] the forces of the bourgeois oppositional parties in the struggle against our ancien régime?

'It does not seem to me that we can reply to the first of these questions simply in one sense or the other. **The era of bourgeois revolutions, in other words, revolutions whose motor force is made up of the bourgeoisie, is over, even for Russia.** Equally, in Russia the proletariat no longer represents an appendix and an instrument of the bourgeoisie as was the case in the bourgeois revolutions, but an autonomous class with its own revolutionary aims. But where the proletariat has appeared in this way, the bourgeoisie ceases to be a revolutionary class. The Russian bourgeoisie, to the extent to which it generally follows an autonomous class policy and is liberal, obviously detests absolutism, but it detests the revolution even more, and it detests absolutism above all because it sees in it the basic cause of the revolution; and to the extent to which it calls for political freedom, it does so above all because it hopes thereby to find the sole means of putting an end to the revolution.

'**Consequently the bourgeoisie does not make up part of the motor forces of the actual revolutionary movement in Russia, and to this extent we cannot describe the revolution as bourgeois.**

'**But we cannot therefore conclude that it is a Socialist movement. It can in no way in fact lead the proletariat to sole power, to dictatorship.** The Russian proletariat is too weak and insufficiently developed for that. Nonetheless, it is very possible that in the development of the revolution **victory could be achieved by the Social Democratic Party**, and it would do well to give its supporters confidence in this victory, because you cannot struggle successfully if you renounce victory beforehand. **But it will be impossible for the Social Democracy to carry off the victory with the proletariat alone, without the help of another class. This is why, as a victorious party, it will not be able to go further in carrying out its programme than the interests of the class which is supporting the proletariat would allow.**

'**Upon what class, however, can the Russian proletariat lean in its revolutionary struggle?** If we only look at the surface of politics, we may perhaps consider that all classes and all parties who aspire to political freedom must simply cooperate to obtain it, and argue out their differences only after political freedom has been achieved. But any political struggle is basically a class struggle, and consequently also an economic struggle. Political interests are the result of economic interests; it is to defend these interests that the popular masses are rising, and not to attain abstract political ideas. Whoever desires to inspire the popular masses for the political struggle must show them at what point it is directly linked to their economic interests. Therefore these must not at any time pass into the background if the struggle for freedom is not to be halted. The alliance of the proletariat with other classes in the revolutionary struggle must therefore rest upon a community of economic interests if it wishes to be lasting and triumphant. The tactic of the Russian Social Democracy must also be founded upon such a community of interests.

'But a solid community of interests for the entire period of the revolutionary struggle **only exists between the proletariat and the peasantry. This must therefore provide us with the basis for the entire revolutionary tactic of Russian Social Democracy.** Cooperation with liberalism can only be envisaged when it does not impede cooperation with the peasantry.

'The revolutionary strength of Russian Social Democracy is based upon the existing community of interests between the industrial proletariat and the peasantry, as are also its chances of victory, as well as **the limits of its possibilities for exploiting it.**

'We will not be able to win so soon in Russia without the peasants. But we must not wait for the peasants to become Socialists. Socialism can only be built upon the basis of big industry, and of large enterprises; it is too inconsistent with the conditions of small industry and small economic units for it to be born and maintain itself in the midst of a population whose majority is peasant. **Once Socialism has become preponderant in big industry and in extensive agricultural exploitation, it can eventually by force of example convince the small peasants and induce them to imitate it, but it cannot originate from them.** And the intellectual and material conditions for this are lacking in Russia even more than elsewhere. The Communism of the Russian village is completely linked with the land, and in no way means production in common. That is why it is impossible for modern exchange production to pass over to a superior mode of production on the basis of the rural commune. This requires at least the context of a great city, but Russian agricultural producers are absolutely incapable of production upon a national basis.

'The present revolution would only lead in the countryside to the creation of a powerful peasantry on the basis of private ownership of the land, and consequently would widen the gulf between the proletariat and the possessing part of the rural population, such as already exists in Western Europe. **It would therefore appear to be unthinkable that the present Russian Revolution would straightaway lead to the introduction of a Socialist mode of production, even if it did temporarily bring the Social Democracy to power.**

'**But of course we could well see many surprises. We do not know how long the Russian Revolution will last**, and from the forms it has now assumed, it does not seem to want to stop very quickly. We also do not know **what influence it will exert over Western Europe and how it will fertilise the proletarian movement there.** Finally, we do not know at all **how the success of the Western European proletariat that would result from this would rebound upon the Russian proletariat.** We would do well to familiarise ourselves with the idea that here we are touching upon **entirely new problems and situations** which do not correspond to any of the models already laid down so far.

'We would best do justice to the Russian Revolution and the tasks that it sets us **by considering it neither as a bourgeois revolution in the traditional sense of the word, nor equally as a Socialist revolution, but as an entirely unique process which would develop as far as the boundary which delimits bourgeois society from Socialist society, which would accelerate the dissolution of the one and prepare the formation of the other**, and which would **in any case** make the whole of humanity of capitalist civilisation take a great leap forward in its development.'[10]

We should compare these declarations of Kautsky's with what he confidently wrote in his latest elaboration: *Von der Demokratie zur staatssklaverei*:

'We are not blaming Lenin and his companions for considering capitalism as inevitable given the level of Russia's development, but for **only now** recognising this after almost four years of having proceeded in the opposite direction with brutal energy, and having branded as traitors and renegades all those who already had a real understanding of affairs; but this was not difficult for those who had a Socialist training, **since the Marxists had recognised and sketched out 10 years earlier the coming Russian Revolution as a bourgeois revolution.**

'Four years of blood, tears and ruins would have been spared Russia if the Bolsheviks had possessed **the sense of the Mensheviks to limit themselves to what was possible**, thus revealing their mastery.'[11]

This honest fellow here seeks to create the impression that he had been a Menshevik, so to speak, from birth. But as the quotation above shows, he was not only solidly with the Bolsheviks on the **decisive question of the understanding of the rôle of the bourgeoisie in the Russian Revolution**, but where he departed from the Bolsheviks **he went even further than they did by estimating as possible the passing over of the Russian Revolution to a direct struggle for Socialism.** The respected Karl Kautsky can plead in his defence that his present ideas are the echo of Martov's, and that in 1905-06 he had echoed Rosa Luxemburg.

Kautsky's arguments of 1906 were the reflection of a tendency which had its representatives at the time of the first revolution in Trotsky, Parvus and Rosa Luxemburg, a tendency which, as we have said, was outside both of the factions of Russian Social Democracy. The representatives of this tendency pointed out that even if the peasantry represented a great revolutionary force which the working class must by all means attempt to develop and on whom it had to rely, it was not capable of carrying out an independent policy because of its social atomisation, its dispersion, and the low level of its development.

Whereas Lenin and the Bolsheviks **talked about the dictatorship of the proletariat and the peasantry**, the above-named Marxists laid down the formula of **the dictatorship of the proletariat supported by the peasantry.** From 1905 onwards Trotsky posed the following questions in his article 'The Perspectives of the Russian Revolution':[12]

'The whole problem consists in this: **who will determine the content of the government's policy, who will form within it a solid majority?** It is one thing when representatives of the democratic strata of the people enter a government with a **workers'** majority, but it is quite another thing when representatives of the proletariat participate in a definitely **bourgeois-democratic** government in the capacity of more or less honoured hostages... It is sufficient to try to imagine a revolutionary democratic government without representatives of the proletariat to see immediately the senselessness of such a conception. The refusal of the Social Democrats to participate in a revolutionary government would render such a government quite impossible, and would thus be equivalent to a betrayal of the revolution. But the participation of the proletariat in a government is also objectively most probable, and permissible in principle, only as **a dominating**

and leading participation. One may, of course, describe such a government as the dictatorship of the proletariat and peasantry, a dictatorship of the proletariat, peasantry and intelligentsia, or even a coalition government of the working class and the petit-bourgeoisie, but the question nevertheless remains: **who is to wield the hegemony in the government itself, and through it in the country?**'[13]

Trotsky came down in favour of **the hegemony of the proletariat in the government**, and sought to show that in spite of the backwardness of social conditions, in spite of the low level of capitalist development in Russia, the revolutionary government would be forced to take **transitional measures** leading to Socialism:

'**The political domination of the proletariat is incompatible with its economic enslavement. No matter under what political flag the proletariat has come to power, it is obliged to take the path of Socialist policy.** It would be the greatest utopianism to think that the proletariat, having been raised to political domination by the internal mechanism of a bourgeois revolution, can, even if it so desires, **limit its mission** to the creation of republican-democratic conditions for the social domination of the bourgeoisie. The political domination of the proletariat, even if it is only temporary, will weaken to an extreme degree the resistance of capital, which always stands in need of the support of the state, and will give the economic struggle of the proletariat tremendous scope. The workers cannot but demand maintenance for strikers from the revolutionary government, and a government relying upon the workers cannot refuse this demand. But this means paralysing the effect of the reserve army of labour and making the workers dominant not only in the political but also in the economic field, and converting **private property in the means of production into a fiction.** These inevitable social-economic consequences of proletarian dictatorship will reveal themselves very quickly, long before the democratisation of the political system has been completed. **The barrier between the "minimum" and the "maximum" programme disappears immediately the proletariat comes to power.**'[14]

Trotsky is thus faced with the question of the relations existing between the political necessity which he describes and the state of the Russian economy. He replies to this by referring to **the very high degree of Russia's industrial concentration**, to the concentration and very strong cohesion of the young Russian capitalism imported from abroad, and to the influence of the Russian Revolution upon the European proletariat:

'**Without the direct state support of the European proletariat the working class of Russia cannot remain in power and convert its temporary domination into a lasting Socialist dictatorship.** Of this there cannot for one moment be any doubt. But on the other hand, there cannot be any doubt that **a Socialist revolution in the West will enable us directly to convert the temporary domination of the working class into a Socialist dictatorship.**'[15]

Thus for him the Russian Revolution is the point of departure for the European proletarian revolution. He conceives of **the Russian Revolution as one element of the permanent European revolution.**

We will refrain from quoting in detail the concepts of Rosa Luxemburg, which hardly differ from those of Trotsky. We shall only add one more point to the construction of this picture. Rosa Luxemburg already occupied herself with the perspectives of the Russian revolution just after the defeat of the revolution of 1905-06 in an article in which she polemicised against a book of the celebrated Menshevik publicist Cherevanin.[16] In this article, which appeared in 1908 in the Polish Marxist journal *Przeglad socjaldemokratyczny*, she defended the thesis that even bourgeois revolutions such as those of the French Revolution, **in order to attain even their limited bourgeois aims, had to go beyond them**, and that the more a revolution deepened its development, the less could it be forced back by counter-revolution.

We have sketched out here the basic questions which already before and during the first Russian Revolution were posed to the vanguard of the Russian proletariat. As can be seen, these are **the decisive questions of the destiny of the present Russian Revolution.** The revolution of 1905-06 was the prologue to the revolution of 1917. All the classes which were to measure their strength 12 years later in other circumstances were already in struggle, and that is why all the questions to which we are in practice replying at present by the actions and the history of the Russian Revolution were already posed. The revolution of 1905-06 could not provide an answer to all the questions posed, since Tsarism succeeded, with the aid of European capital, in defeating the young proletariat and peasantry before the first Russian Revolution could spread its international influence sufficiently. The first Russian Revolution stimulated the international proletarian movement in an extraordinary manner. It placed the mass strike on the order of the day, and it is no accident that Rosa Luxemburg's pamphlet *The Mass Strike*,[17] which was written on the basis of the experiences of the Russian Revolution, is the first international document of the modern Communist movement, the point of departure for the revolutionary tendency of the German far left.

But the first Russian Revolution in many ways gave a clear and unequivocal response to those 'accursed questions' of our time. It showed in fact that, whatever the limits of the Russian Revolution, the bourgeoisie was already in Russia a counter-revolutionary factor at the time of the first revolution. From the first revolution, in fact, it contented itself with verbal concessions from Tsarism, and sought to conclude a compromise with it. When Tsarism succeeded in strangling the revolution only with the aid of European capital, whose attitude was determined, amongst other things, by the following fact: it knew that the Russian bourgeoisie did not want the fall of Tsarism, in spite of a show of opposition. However the Mensheviks, by linking their perspectives for revolution to a new upsurge of bourgeois opposition,[18] even after the defeat of the first revolution, showed that they were suffering from congenital political blindness. The Russian bourgeoisie carried on a show of struggle against Tsarism in the Duma. But at the same time it was again seeking agreement with Tsarism on the terrain of Russian imperialism. Peter Struve,[19] the foremost ideologist of Russian liberalism, became the prophet of the Greater Russia, and Paul Milyukov, the political leader of Russian liberalism, became the promoter of Russian policy in the Balkans, which along with the German policy in Turkey led to the 1914 war.

The war also buried under its ruins liberalism's shows of struggle. During the war of 1914-17 the liberals were to make up the bulk of the patriotic forces of the Russian war. The revolution of 1917, which was no more than the uprising of the

Russian popular masses against the devastating consequences of the Tsarist participation in the world war, had, from the start, also to be against the bourgeoisie.

However, the counter-revolutionary rôle of the bourgeoisie meant that the working class had to conduct a very hard struggle against the industrial bourgeoisie in order to fight Tsarism. The working class had to struggle against it step by step in order to assert its influence over the semi-proletarian and petit-bourgeois masses. At the same time it appeared that the struggle of the proletariat against the bourgeoisie corresponded not only with its attitude towards democracy, but that the struggle for democracy also developed from the social rôle of the proletariat, its struggle against capitalist exploitation. The proletariat didn't even need to venture beyond the limit of the minimum programme to enter into struggle with the bourgeoisie. From the moment it began to struggle against the methods of primitive accumulation, which were then practised in Russia by capitalism, it came right up against the bourgeoisie. The struggle for the eight-hour day (bourgeois democracy is a nonsense if this demand is not satisfied, for a beast of burden, who is welded from dawn till late at night to the machine, obviously cannot take part in political life) led after the October Manifesto to the great struggle between the proletariat and the bourgeoisie, a struggle in which the bourgeoisie as a class was openly, clearly and unequivocally ranged on the side of Tsarism, from which it sought help against the proletariat. The antagonism between the proletariat and the bourgeoisie was shown as one of the most important driving forces of the Russian Revolution.

The revolution did not definitely impose itself on the village, but there it undermined the foundations of Tsarism as much as in the town. Over a large part of Russia it drove the peasantry to engage in an armed struggle against the nobility. The red cockerel made its cry resound over the lands of the nobles who had mobilised all the scorpions of the government against the peasants. Even though the class consciousness of the peasantry in the army was still too little developed to prevent the peasants from playing the rôle of executioner as regards their own brethren, the punitive military expeditions into the villages nonetheless undermined the old mentality in the army, just as in the village. Tsarism understood better than the Mensheviks the danger threatening it from the side of the peasantry. The Tsarist government, after having hoped at the time of the elections for the first duma in 1906 that the ignorant mass of peasants would form a counterweight to the city vote, sought after the first revolution to split them up in order to rely upon the rich peasants against the poor, and thus to be able, thanks to this new antagonism inside the peasant mass itself, to weaken and paralyse the force of its blows against the Tsarist state.

The new factor, which the Marxist analysis had not foreseen, was the form by which the working class organised itself as a revolutionary agent. Alongside political parties and alongside trade unions, soviets instinctively arose. During the days of October 1905, at the time of the great shaking of Tsarism by the general strike, in some cities the soviets were the organs of power, and the bourgeoisie had to capitulate before them in many places. They showed themselves in an embryonic way as organs of the struggle for power. Marxists explained their appearance by the absence of old trade unions solidly implanted in the working class, from which sprang the need for loose proletarian organisations. Even the Russian Marxists, not to speak of the European Marxists, did not then see that they were not only organisations of struggle against the bourgeois government, but also the embryos of the future organisation of proletarian power. It is entirely characteristic that the idea of soviets had absolutely not penetrated the intellectual universe of the European Socialist movement, which was enlivened in so many things by the first Russian Revolution.

II

The revolution of February 1917 picked up again the thread of the first revolution of 1905. A rapid victory was only possible in February 1917 because the revolution of 1905 had already profoundly worked the terrain in Russia. The opportunists of the Second International who had explained after the defeat of 1907 that the Russian Revolution had been futile (Karl Leutner,[20] the animator of the *Wiener Arbeiterzeitung*, explained in 1908 that the 'remarkably organised' revolution of the Young Turks impressed him far more than the Russian revolutionary chaos) once more appeared in the light of the events of 1917 to be short-sighted. Thanks to the experiences accumulated in the course of the revolution of 1905-06, the Russian popular masses were to begin the revolution of 1917 with a store of political concepts which had been reinforced and sharpened by two and a half years of experience of war; they were therefore to push the revolution straightaway much further than the bourgeoisie wished to tolerate. The arrest of the Tsar, the checkmating of the installation of the regency,[21] and the proclamation of the republic were not the least important results of the work of the first revolution. At the same time, the worker and soldier masses spontaneously began to form soviets of workers and soldiers. The peasants imitated them in the countryside, and these mass organisations, formed spontaneously, became, before even being conscious of the fact that they were the constituent organs of proletarian power, the organs which would take power. The governmental power fell into the hands of the bourgeoisie, and it only later invited the petit-bourgeois proletarian and peasant parties of the Mensheviks and the Socialist Revolutionaries to participate in government. But the bourgeois Provisional Government from the first day of its existence had to complain about 'double government', for the soviets of workers and soldiers not only grabbed control over the bourgeois Provisional Government, but even part of the executive power. Perhaps I might be permitted to recall here a fact that is little known, but which casts a glaring light upon the creative power of the popular masses during the revolution. When during the first days of the February Revolution — at the time when the news of the St Petersburg events was still very vague — a group of Bolsheviks who were in Norway asked Comrade Lenin a question about the attitude to be adopted towards the slogan of a Constituent Assembly. Lenin replied in the following manner: The Constituent Assembly, he said, will certainly not be rapidly convoked by the Provisional Government; parliament, moreover, in general is of highly doubtful importance as a central focus for the revolution. He advised the passing over of the local administration, everywhere, or wherever possible, into the hands of the working class, in order to make of it strongholds for the revolution. Lenin had therefore already recognised in a penetrating manner that it would not be the bourgeois democratic republic that would maintain the power of the revolution, but a republic of the type of the Paris Commune,[22] in which the revolutionary people at the same time concentrated into one hand legislative, executive and judicial power. But he could not discover the concrete form of this republic of the type of the Paris Commune. It was created by the masses of the workers and soldiers by their obscure impulses towards struggle.

But what was the content of the February Revolution? It was a revolution where the peasants in uniform and the workers, crushed by the burden of the war, arose not only against the war itself and its continuation, but against the government which had conducted it so badly and had imposed all its burdens upon them. Only a small minority of the proletarians and soldiers were then opposed to the war in general. But the masses mature very quickly in a revolution. The February Revolution therefore very quickly became a revolution against the war. It turned against the imperialist bourgeoisie and the nobility who more and more openly and recklessly opposed the revolution. The workers and peasants were the bearers of the revolution. Their positive aims stemmed from their social position. The peasants aspired to take over the land. Neither Stolypin's punitive expeditions nor his agrarian reform had killed the revolutionary tendencies of the peasants; no more could they create a rich peasantry strong enough to form a rampart against the revolutionary tendencies in the village. The workers aspired to an immediate improvement in their situation, and since this aim was unobtainable by the usual ways in the economic collapse provoked by the war, they spontaneously began to take in hand the control of production by factory committees, with the aim of overcoming the anarchy of production and so improving their situation.

What were the positions taken up by the parties of the revolution? The Socialist Revolutionaries and the Mensheviks set themselves the task of holding back the struggle of the workers against the capitalists, and of preventing the peasants from taking possession of the lands of the nobility, since this 'disorder' would be prejudicial to the conduct of the war. They justified their social patriotism by saying that the revolution had triumphed in Russia, and that consequently it was not a question of defending the fatherland, but of defending the revolution. Even Tsereteli and Chernov, who were Zimmerwaldists, took the road to Damascus and united themselves politically with the most vulgar social patriots of the type of Plekhanov and Alexinsky.[23] By wanting to hold back the social aims of the revolution — even of the bourgeois-democratic revolution — until the convening of the Constituent Assembly, they were applying their concept of the Russian Revolution which they had developed in the course of the first revolution; they were handing over power to the bourgeoisie as the class whose interests made up the objective limit of the revolution, and to whom the leadership of the revolution therefore belonged. Their antiquated verbiage about the rôle of Social Democracy as an extreme opposition vanished like vapour into thin air. They were not an extreme opposition to the bourgeoisie, but the only supporters of the bourgeois government within the masses of peasants, soldiers and workers.

On its part the Bolshevik Party explained that you cannot envisage the immediate victory of Communism given Russia's degree of social development. 'It is not our immediate task to "introduce" Socialism, but only to bring social production and the distribution of products at once under the **control** of the Soviets of workers' deputies.'[24] This is how Lenin formulated the social tasks of the revolution on his arrival in Petrograd on 3 April. In his polemic against Kamenev,[25] who was defending the old concept of the Bolsheviks on the bourgeois content of the revolution, Lenin referred to what he had already written in 1905 in one of his pamphlets on the two tactical lines which we have already quoted:

'Like everything else in the world, the revolutionary-democratic dictatorship of the proletariat and the peasantry has a past and a future. Its past is autocracy, serfdom, monarchy and privilege... Its future is the struggle against private property, the struggle of the wage-worker against the employer, the struggle for Socialism.'[26]

And he went on:

'Comrade Kamenev's mistake is that even in 1917 he sees only **the past** of the revolutionary-democratic dictatorship of the proletariat and the peasantry. As a matter of fact its **future** has already begun, for the interests and policies of the wage-worker and the petty proprietor have **actually** diverged already, even in such an important question as that of "defencism", that of the attitude towards the imperialist war.'[27]

This reference to the war constitutes the crucial point for understanding the differences that exist between the policy of the Bolsheviks at the time of the first and the second revolution. The simple fact that the second revolution happened at a far higher level of Russian economic development increased the weight of the proletarian elements in this revolution. The conditions of war in which it broke out confronted these elements with new tasks, and created a new international context for revolutionary politics in Russia. The first question with which the revolution was confronted — and it was a life and death question — was that of its attitude as regards the war. **The revolution that was born from the failure of Tsarism during the war and the misery of the masses engendered by it struck at the very roots of the war. If it had not been capable of killing off the war, the war would have struck it down.** Because the revolution threatened Russia's military potential, of necessity it had to provoke the most determined resistance of the classes who were interested in pursuing the war: finance capital, the nobility, and the officer caste. To undermine the power of these classes it was not enough to install a parliamentary republic whilst everywhere else keeping the old repressive organs of the Tsarist state. It was necessary to replace the police and gendarmerie with a popular militia. The soviets had to try to take over local power; but it was insufficient and impossible to limit the revolutionary overthrow to the political sphere, because the millions of peasant soldiers — after the unheard-of sacrifices of the war and at the very moment when they were smashing the armed violence of the nobility — also wanted to take over the land for which they had fought during the war. The workers, whom the revolution had armed and enthused with confidence in themselves, would naturally not content themselves with standing guard over the cash boxes of the bourgeoisie. Everywhere in the factories they began to interfere with management. But when the owners closed the factories, in order to subdue the workers with a lockout, they occupied the factories and sold the products. This was not only the **logic of the revolution**, it was also **revolutionary necessity** if we wished to break the power of the classes whose interests were to prosecute the war. To break the power of the nobility it was necessary to incite the peasants and not to wait for the convening of the Constituent Assembly in order to take over the land. To break the power of the capitalists it was necessary to show how the employers' syndicates and the banks were coining the blood of the Russian workers and peasants into gold. The proletariat had to break open the cash boxes and vaults that were guarding the business secrets of the bourgeoisie. Marxist theory laid down that the reorganisation of society on a Socialist basis was impossible in Russia; but at the same time it asserted that it was also impossible, without workers' control over heavy industry and finance, not only to improve the ever-deteriorating position of the working class, but also to put an end to the war. The war therefore confronted the revolution with new social tasks:

'Under no circumstances can the party of the proletariat set itself the aim of "introducing" Socialism in a country of small peasants so long as the overwhelming majority of the population has not come to realise the need for a Socialist revolution.

'But only bourgeois sophists, hiding behind "near-Marxist" catchwords, can deduce from this truth a justification of the policy of postponing immediate revolutionary measures, the time for which is fully ripe; measures which **have been frequently resorted to during the war by a number of bourgeois states**, and which are absolutely indispensable in order to combat impending total economic disorganisation and famine.

'Such measures as the nationalisation of the land, of all the banks and capitalist syndicates, or, at least, the **immediate** establishment of the **control** of the Soviets of Workers' Deputies, etc, over them — measures which do not in any way constitute the "introduction" of Socialism must be absolutely insisted on, and, whenever possible, carried out in a revolutionary way. Without such measures, which are only steps towards Socialism, and which are perfectly feasible economically, it will be impossible to heal the wounds caused by the war and to avert the impending collapse; and the party of the revolutionary proletariat will never hesitate to lay hands on the fabulous profits of the capitalists and bankers, who are enriching themselves on the war in a particularly scandalous manner.'[28]

This is how Lenin formulated the tasks of the Bolshevik Party and of the revolution in a draft platform for the party which he wrote in 1917. This programme, which objectively went beyond the limits of Social Democracy's minimum programme, already constituted a **transitional programme towards Socialism**. It was not aimed at establishing measures to **achieve** Socialism. But whereas the minimum programme of Social Democracy contained reforms for improving the condition of the working class within the limits of a capitalist society in which the bourgeoisie held power, here the Bolshevik Party was setting in motion a programme which was placing the bourgeoisie and capitalist production under the control of the working class. The development of events had necessarily to lead to the struggle of the soviets of workers and peasants against the bourgeois Provisional Government, if they in their turn took up this programme; consequently, it had to lead to the **revolutionary dictatorship of the proletariat and peasantry**.

Could such a dictatorship last, could it realise this programme which in fact only constituted the vital necessities of the revolution? It is clear that this was impossible so long as Russia was surrounded by a normal capitalist world. But Russia was not surrounded by a normal capitalist world, but by the ocean of flames of the world war. The February Revolution had already threatened the war and shaken the ruling classes in all the capitalist countries. Even though censorship had everywhere suppressed the news of the February revolution, its echo was undoubtedly very powerful. In Germany Bethmann-Hollweg[29] rushed to the Prussian landtag, the bastion of German reaction, before the news of the revolution had even been made public, and announced an era of reform. In Britain the strike wave increased. The French government was sitting on a powder barrel. The revolution shook the equilibrium that had been formed during the war, and threatened not only to provoke the defeat of the Entente but also to spread the revolution throughout all Europe. Without a doubt the seizure of power by the proletariat and peasantry in Russia as well as their resolute policy of peace had to make a **revolutionary breach in the war front** through which other detachments of the proletariat would penetrate. The predictions of the revolutionary Marxists that the imperialist war would be transformed into a civil war and would open up the era of world revolution were beginning to be realised. **The Russian Revolution was the signal for the European revolution**, and it had the chance of not being left isolated to the destructive attack of world capital. **In an international revolutionary situation, the programme of the world proletarian revolution developed in a backward petit-bourgeois country.**

The programme of the Bolsheviks corresponded to the necessities of the Russian Revolution, and this is why it became the programme of the revolution. The peasant masses were struggling for peace and land. The working masses were struggling for peace and for measures of transition towards Socialism. Thanks to the war, which had enlisted millions of peasants into the army and had thus overcome their dispersion and atomisation, the peasant mass had acquired a powerful centralised thrust that it had never previously possessed in history. Thanks to the young revolutionary working class which controlled the centres of industry and communications, the peasant mass received a political leadership which it had heretofore lacked in history. The Bolshevik Party, the result of a 25 year history of revolutionary struggles, understood how to appreciate the situation coldly and lucidly, and to concentrate the spontaneous movements of the masses on the decisive objectives of the political struggle. **That is how the victory of the October Revolution came about as an historic fact** which can only be denied either by blind doctrinaires or by emigrés led astray by class hatred. Even that limited and stupefied individual who is Karl Kautsky had to recognise in his latest work against the Russian Revolution:

'The question is not to know whether the seizure of political power by the proletariat in Russia should be approved of or not; the revolution of 1917 was like any great revolution, an elemental event which it was impossible either to prevent or to provoke at will.'

And Kautsky then adds:

'But this still does not reply to the question of the attitude to be adopted by Socialists. This reply is obvious for a Marxist: they had to take into consideration the level of maturity of economic relations as well as of the proletariat, and to determine from there the tasks of the victorious proletariat.

'Before the appearance of the Marxist conception of history, which makes the evolution of history depend upon economic development and which shows that this develops according to laws and cannot leap over any stage, before this Marxist conception of history therefore, revolutionaries in periods of revolutionary up-heaval saw no limit to their will. In one leap they tried to attain the highest ends. But they therefore always failed; that is why every revolution, in spite of the real progress it produced, always ended with the downfall of the revolutionaries. Marx taught the method of only setting feasible ends, including during periods of revolution, which could be attained with the means and forces at our disposal, and in this way avoiding defeats. The Mensheviks recommended this method in Russia and successfully applied it in Georgia.[30] The Bolsheviks, on the other hand, set for the Russian proletariat tasks which it was impossible for it to resolve given that circumstances were not ripe. It is therefore not surprising that their Communism has collapsed.'[31]

The question of the fall of Communism in Russia is still a matter for further discussion. Let us note in the meantime that Kautsky — who represents the seizure of power by the proletariat in Russia as an elemental event which it was as impossible to prevent as to provoke at will — is condemning the methods of 'limitation' envisaged by the Mensheviks as an attempt to hold back historical necessity. For all that, by placing himself in sympathy on the side of the Mensheviks, he is pronouncing as an historian his own condemnation as a politician. The question of knowing what the Bolsheviks, coming to power in a country in which the great majority of the population was petit-bourgeois, should have done, forms the crucial point of the **nature** of the policy of the proletarian state in Russia from the seizure of power up to the change of course in the March of this year.[32]

III

The period from October 1917 to March 1921 is described by our opponents as the period of the realisation of Communism in Russia. For this then allows them to talk about the bankruptcy of Communism starting from the beginning of 1921. To refute this legend I will first of all quote a long extract from an article on the general situation in Russia which I wrote in **December 1919** in prison in Berlin, which was then published in the Berlin edition of *The Communist International* under the pseudonym of 'Struthan'. This quotation is worth more than a description after the event of this chapter in the history of the Russian Revolution, for we well know that we are always wiser after the event. This is what I wrote in December 1919:

'When the Russian working class took power in October 1917, neither the bourgeois nor the Socialist world thought that it would be able to hold on to state power for two months, let alone for two years. If German imperialism negotiated with Soviet Russia this is because it was forced to do so by the situation in which it found itself as a result of the war; it wanted to conclude peace in the East, even with so provisional a government, convinced, and moreover correctly, that even if the Bolsheviks disappeared, no party and government could mobilise the peasants in the foreseeable future. But Soviet Russia had to conclude peace, not only because it no longer had any army, but also because it could only become a reality by obtaining a momentary respite; at the time of the Brest negotiations[33] the Soviet government only represented a programme, it only existed in the declarations of the decrees of the people's commissars. Even Tsarist absolutism had not been completely destroyed in its lower organs, and feudal landed property had not been eliminated. Soviet forms of government in country and state still appeared to be an experiment, and not an organic reality. The Bolshevik government had a choice: either to conduct as a government a revolutionary partisan struggle, a guerrilla war beginning from the Urals with the help of the Allies against German imperialism and allow the restoration of Russian capital under the protection of German bayonets; or to climb the path of Golgotha to Brest, and at the cost of national humiliation to give priority to the task of overthrowing the bourgeoisie and organising the proletariat.

'As for the "Independent"[34] German imbeciles who now talk about the illusory foreign policy of the Soviet government, after having accused the Bolsheviks of "disorganising" the Russian army and that after their own November experience,[35] there is naturally nothing to do for these bankrupt Wilsonians.[36] The correctness of the policy of the Soviet government, which was convinced that the process of the decomposition of world imperialism would not be halted, but accelerated by the Brest peace, is proved by the reality of its success; the Brest-Litovsk torturers are lying helpless in the ditch, and the Soviet Union has succeeded in getting itself together and reorganising itself between two rocks, between the devil and the deep blue sea, as the English put it; and by the fact that only a year after the fall of German imperialism it extracted from the representatives of the imperialism of the victorious Entente the admission that Bolshevism cannot be beaten by weapons. The Brest peace, which in spite of its robber character, had a positive significance for the Soviet Union because it put an end to the Great War, was not imposed by the Soviet Union thanks to its own strength; nor was it the German workers who imposed it; the Brest peace was achieved by the pressure of the armies of the Entente in the West. Even if the imperialism of the victorious Entente now concluded a yet more rapacious peace with Soviet Russia, this peace, by allowing the Soviet Union the possibility of existing, would be a rupture, a breach in the system of capitalist states; this peace would then in fact be the result of the resistance effected by the Soviet Union thanks to its own strength, the result of the help afforded it by the world proletariat. **But why should the Soviet Union, which cannot be destroyed by weapons, have to conclude a compromise peace with the Entente?** Why should it not await, arms in hand, the time when the decomposition of Entente capitalism would be so far advanced that it would be obliged to assure it an honourable peace?

'The reply to this question is simple: **During the world war, whilst the criminal policy of all the imperialist states was making it drag on at length, we could count upon a rapid catastrophe of world capitalism, on the uprising of the popular masses in several countries, if the slaughter did not allow them any other way out.** At the time of the conclusion of the Brest peace, the Soviet government estimated that the pause that this peace allowed it would be of short duration; we thought then either that the world revolution would soon break out and save Soviet Russia, or that it would rapidly go under in an unequal struggle. The conception of the Bolsheviks corresponded to the then situation.

'The collapse of German imperialism, the inability of the Allies to overthrow Soviet Russia militarily, as well as the fact that the world war has provisionally ended, that the crisis of demobilisation has been overcome, the fact that the world revolution has triumphed over capitalism not in the form of an explosion, but by disorganisation, in other words as a long drawn out process, all this completely changes the situation and conditions of the foreign policy of the Soviet government. **It cannot count mechanically upon a rapid liberation, by means of a spontaneous mass movement that will once and for all send to the devil all the Clemenceaus, Lloyd Georges and Wilsons**[37] **and all that hides behind them, but it can have the mathematical certitude that the process of capitalist decomposition will continue and will ease its position.** But because this will be a **long drawn out process** which it is necessary to take into account, Soviet Russia must seek to find a **modus vivendi with the still capitalist states.** If the proletarian revolution is triumphant tomorrow in Germany or France, the position of Soviet Russia will be made easier, because two proletarian states, by their economic and armed force, will exercise a far greater pressure upon the capitalist world; they would nevertheless still be interested in concluding peace with the still capitalist states, if only to ensure their economic recovery.

'Soviet Russia has not allowed itself to be struck down. And we are sure that if the Entente states do not now offer it an acceptable peace, it will continue the struggle, it will undergo hunger, and in the end they will be forced to grant it a more advantageous peace. The overthrow by blockade of a country that has resources like Russia requires a lapse of time which imperialist policy in the Entente countries will not outlive. But it is clear that if Soviet Russia has to prolong the struggle, it could not begin its economic reconstruction. **War demands that its weakened forces of production be devoted to arms production, that its best forces be used in war industry, and that its ruined railways be used to transport troops. The necessities of war force the concentrated strength of the state to be centralised into the hands of the executive; they therefore threaten the Soviet system, and a far more important thing, they are threatening in the long run to swallow up the best elements of the working class.** The Soviet government has made superhuman efforts to struggle against this. Its achievements in the field of education, in spite of all the obstacles and difficulties, are already astonishing its honest bourgeois opponents — as you can read in Goode's account in the *Manchester Guardian* — and in two or three years Soviet Russia will have thousands of new organisational and cultural forces.

'The March Congress of the Bolshevik Party, whose minutes — a very interesting document — have now appeared, shows to what extent its leaders are taking seriously the dangers of the restoration of the bureaucracy of functionaries and of corruption under new forms. But war is war; it is a source of barbaric destruction, and if you can stop it with sacrifices, it must be stopped. **Obviously it is serious if the Russian people must grant mining concessions to English, American and French capitalists, because it would be far better to use these mines itself than to pay tribute.** But for as long as it is forced to prosecute the war, it cannot exploit its mines, and it must even throw its miners into the furnace of war. If the only choice was between Socialist economic construction or war against world capital which sets limits to Socialist construction, the only correct decision would be war. But things are not posed in this way. The question to be resolved expresses itself in this way: **Socialist construction within the limits of a temporary compromise or war without any economic construction at all.**

'Already in the spring of 1918 the Soviet government had been confronted with the question of economic compromise. When the American Colonel Raymond Robins[38] left Moscow for Washington on 3 May 1918, he carried with him a concrete proposal from the Soviet government laying down conditions for economic concessions.[39] The Assistant People's Commissar for Commerce and Industry, Bronsky,[40] in the course of his first session with the representatives of the German government, presented practical proposals for the collaboration of the Soviet government with German capital. The essentials of the negotiations were confidentially transmitted to Bruce Lockhart (the British representative).[41] In the midst of a world war we could have hoped that an approaching revolutionary explosion would have removed the necessity for such concessions, but basically the policy of concessions had already then been decided upon, and it was largely justified. **So long as the proletariat has not triumphed in the principal capitalist states, so long as it is not in a position to utilise all the productive forces of the world for Socialist construction, so long as capitalist states exist alongside proletarian states, the proletarian states will be forced to conclude compromises with them, and there will be neither pure Socialism nor pure capitalism; geographically limited, they would in effect be forced to make reciprocal concessions within their own national territories. The extent of concessions that it is necessary to make to capitalism will depend on the strength and number of the proletarian states.** It is impossible to deny the necessity for concessions, unless at the same time you indicate the method that would permit the proletariat to attain victory at one blow in every country.

'But by recognising the necessity for compromise between the proletarian states and the capitalist states, are we not also recognising the possibility and **the necessity for a compromise with capitalism within each state**, and consequently does that not mean renouncing the revolution and the dictatorship of the proletariat as ways to Socialism? Were not Renner, Bauer,[42] Cunow and Kautsky right all the time? Isn't agreement with capitalism on the basis of democracy definitely the only correct method? Isn't Communism with its programme of a soviet dictatorship bankrupt? These questions, which have to be thought out and gone into in all frankness and clarity, must first of all be examined historically within the context of the experience of the Russian Revolution; after that it is necessary to see to what extent they can lay claim to international validity.

'The enemies of Communism, who have come out of the camp of the tottering elements of the defunct Second International, are holding in reserve **two stories** that are mutually contradictory. According to the first, the whole "soviet theory" has come about only as the **product of necessity**; it came into existence when it transpired that the elections for the national assembly had not given a majority to the Bolsheviks; this fact therefore forced the Bolsheviks to appear as the proud champions of the proletarian dictatorship. According to the second story, the Bolsheviks came to power as **savage representatives of a dictatorship**, but then, made wise by their own experiences, they were more and more forced to pour water into their wine. But what do the facts say? Before the revolution of 1905 the Bolsheviks saw in the dictatorship of the proletariat and peasantry the historic path that Russia was to follow. Rosa Luxemburg and Trotsky sought to correct this formula by speaking of the dictatorship of the proletariat supported by the peasantry. By this correction they wished to affirm the concept, also admitted by the Bolsheviks, that the urban proletariat would have the leadership in the revolution. The entire camp of which Russian Communism is now made up was in agreement on the fact that in an essentially agrarian country such as Russia, the proletariat must take into consideration the interests of the peasantry, and cannot exclude the peasants from power. When in 1917 the Bolsheviks resolutely engaged in struggle against the peasant party of the Socialist Revolutionaries led by Chernov, they did so not to oppose the interests of the peasants, but on the contrary, to defend them. In fact, by their coalition with the capitalist Cadet party, the leaders of the Socialist Revolutionaries were betraying the interests of the peasants, were holding back the solution of the agrarian problem, and were sacrificing the peasant masses to the war carried on by Russian imperialism. When as a result of this policy the mass of soldiers and peasants went over to the side of the working class and helped the Bolsheviks take power on 25 October 1917, the Bolsheviks offered to share power with their vanquished adversaries; they not only negotiated with the Mensheviks but also with the Socialist Revolutionaries for two weeks after the defeat of Kerensky with a view to forming a coalition government which would form the dictatorship of the proletariat and peasantry. The negotiations broke down because the Mensheviks and the Right Socialist Revolutionaries still believed in the victory of the bourgeoisie. The Bolsheviks nonetheless attracted into the government the left wing of the Socialist Revolutionaries, which had separated from its party and was ready to resolve the question of the land and peace by means of a revolutionary dictatorship.[43] The split with this party took place when it transpired that nationalist elements had also taken over in it, and that its intellectual elements, subject to a nationalism with a revolutionary coloration, could not decide for the policy of peace. It was again in defence of the interests of the peasants that the split took place with this peasant party, which more and more lost contact with real life, and was developing into a party of intellectual revolutionary nationalism. The split of the Bolsheviks with the parties that aspired to represent the peasants, but which for the most part were only the intellectual ideologists of the peasantry, never interfered with their insight into the real relationship of forces. On the one hand they tried to gather together an organisation of the village poor, not only the workers who had taken refuge in the villages on account of the famine in the towns and the decay of industry, but also the rural proletarians and the small peasants, in order to allow proletarian interests to break through in the village; and on the other hand they tried more and more to attract the middle peasants onto the side of the proletarian dictatorship through concessions (for example, as regards agricultural cooperatives). He who sees opportunism in this does not understand the ABC of Socialism. Given that capitalism in the form of factory concentrations has nowhere in the world occurred in such a way, and given that there are everywhere millions of small and medium agricultural enterprises, the socialisation of agriculture will everywhere be a very slow process, which will take generations; Socialism will not be instituted there by means of expropriations, but only by the nationalisation of mortgage loans, of trade in cereals and animal feed, of transport and the sale of agricultural machinery, and by all the cultural assistance that the Socialist state could provide for the peasants. **The proletariat will everywhere, after its victory over the bourgeoisie, be obliged to compromise with the peasants, because it could only conclude this compromise precisely when it had vanquished the bourgeoisie and the peasants were obliged to consent to this compromise.**

'But was the victory of the working class over the bourgeoisie possible other than by civil war and dictatorship? Was it not possible by means of democracy? The entire history of the Russian Revolution, however, provides a negative answer to this question. The Menshevik policy collapsed because it was impossible by means of peaceful methods not only to expropriate the bourgeoisie, but even to save the popular masses from the jaws of the world war in which only the top section of the bourgeoisie — finance capital and its beneficiaries — was interested. It was necessary to overthrow the bourgeoisie and construct the dictatorship of the popular masses whose interests were concerned with peace before even being able to satisfy the most vital of the elementary interests of the toiling masses. The attempts, whether direct or indirect, of the bourgeoisie and its accomplices to overthrow Soviet power determined with iron necessity the form and content of the measures of the dictatorship. It was necessary to respond by the persecution of the bourgeois press and the saboteurs, etc, to the attempts of the bourgeois intelligentsia supported by the banks to sabotage economic life and the functioning of the machinery of state. This, however, for a certain time involved far more primitive forms of control over production and management until the bourgeois intelligentsia ceased its resistance. In order to smash the attempts of the bourgeoisie to deprive the people of its property by a crime of high treason, to counter the manufacturers, merchants and bankers who sought to shelter behind German protection after the Brest Peace, and place their property in hiding by trying to pass it off as "German" by means of all sorts of fraudulent transactions, it was necessary on the one hand to proceed by methods of intimidation, **and on the other hand by measures of rapid nationalisation. To avoid large numbers of industries being sold off to German capital, it was necessary to nationalise them rapidly at the time of the negotiations over the clauses annexed to the Brest Peace, without being able to prepare these radical measures with sufficient care.** When the bourgeoisie went over to the side of the Entente once more and began to support all the Entente's conspiracies — from individual terror to the organisation of revolts — it was necessary to resort to the Red Terror, which only became extensive when the armies of Kolchak and Denikin[44] — equipped by the Entente, but supported by all the capitalist elements in Russia — began open war against Soviet Russia.

'In the course of the two years' history of the dictatorship of the proletariat in Russia there has basically not been a single important measure taken in a doctrinaire fashion, and which has not been the result of necessity. The fall of the Kerensky government stemmed from its utter inability to get Russia out of the bloody deadlock. In fact it was impossible to carry out the most elementary popular interests against the resistance of the bourgeoisie by methods other than dictatorial ones; dictatorship also became a necessity.

'The Bolsheviks understood this necessity right from the start, and demanded all power to the soviets from April 1917 onwards. But it was clear that the popular masses could only lose their confidence in the national assembly in the course of a process of struggle against its capitalist policy; moreover, compared with the uncontrolled clique activity of the Kerensky government, the parliamentary tribunal represented a step forward. Because the Kerensky government had adjourned the calling of the national assembly, the Constituent Assembly met at the time when the dictatorship of the proletariat had already been created. What came into the world was a corpse. Nonetheless, it was necessary to allow it to bury itself. If, however, the Soviet government attempted to hasten its burial, this was because it threatened, as the corpse of the Kerensky government, to suck the blood of the people.[45] The Soviet government was engaged in peace negotiations with an unscrupulous enemy; that is why any trifling with the idea of peace in the

National Assembly could assist the German military party to break off negotiations for peace, and overthrow the young Soviet Russia that was coming into being. The indifference with which all layers of the population witnessed the burial of the Constituent Assembly showed that it did not have the support of the popular forces. It was a shadow from the past.

'All those who follow the history of the Russian Revolution as historians and not as moralists cannot avoid recognising that the policy of the Bolsheviks was a consistent policy, adapted to necessity. All those who study it as revolutionaries cannot avoid recognising it as the only possible revolutionary policy. The Mensheviks themselves recognised it in their declaration on the occasion of the first anniversary of the October Revolution. But there is something more important than this! The only force that could replace the proletarian dictatorship would be the dictatorship of the Russian feudal-capitalist cliques, which could only maintain itself with the aid of the world dictatorship of finance capital. The Russian Revolution can be defeated; the dictatorship of the White generals would then replace the dictatorship of the proletariat. But the Russian Revolution can only triumph as a dictatorship of the proletariat which would lead the popular masses in an assault on capital.

'Even dying, the Russian proletarian revolution would broadcast to the world proletariat the proclamation of its testament: the dictatorship of the proletariat! And so we come to the final question: will the dictatorship of the proletariat maintain itself by a compromise with world capitalism? We are therefore touching on the question of the limits of the compromise that a workers' state can make in its foreign policy.'[46]

'What are the limits of the economic concessions that Soviet Russia can make?', I asked in my article:

'Just as Soviet Russia did not demean itself by becoming a vassal of German imperialism at Brest, **so it cannot now demean itself by playing the rôle of the vassal of Anglo-Saxon imperialism.** All through the negotiations carried on by Soviet Russia with the British and German representatives of the imperialist cartel, it did not cease explaining this: the world has been so impoverished by war that any one of the belligerent parties is utterly incapable of satisfying the enormous economic needs of Soviet Russia. Russia must take machines, forces and organisational assistance from wherever it finds them, and at the lowest price. Has the end of the war changed this situation? Germany has collapsed, but its apparatus and its technological knowledge are at a very high level. The Anglo-Saxon countries are victorious, but their economic disorganisation is nonetheless so deep that they are completely incapable of supplying sufficient aid to France and Italy. The tendency to exploit the economic resources of Germany to the maximum is growing in French capitalist circles; this tendency is accentuated still further by the continual lowering of the franc[47] with relation to the shilling and the dollar (a good example of the use of victory and the "solidarity of the victors"). Poland and Czechoslovakia, Entente vassals, are being forced to conclude economic agreements with Germany, to begin with because the aid they are receiving from the Entente is insufficient, and also because no victory can rub out economic links that stem from geographical closeness.

'To this is added a very important economic fact. The crushing disorganisation of the world capitalist economy means that even if Russia wanted to carry out a short term policy, for example, to acquire goods to begin with, instead of thinking about mobilising its economic forces, it would not obtain these goods in sufficient quantities. It must first of all apply itself to the organisation of its economy with what few means of production it receives from the foreign capitalist. It will then soon have to manufacture on its own soil the necessary machines. If it understands the necessity for this, it must therefore as a priority import from abroad the qualified technical forces that it lacks. Following the ruin of its external relations and the collapse of its economy, Germany disposes of thousands of engineers, chemists and skilled workers wandering about with neither bread nor work who would render considerable service to Soviet Russia in its reconstruction. Naturally Entente journalists will cry out when reading this: "So the Bolsheviks therefore want to help the Germans to rebuild the power of German capital on Russian territory." These outcries on the new German-Bolshevik link up are as deceitful as the old hue and cry. We are not even offering German capitalism the concessions we are offering Entente capitalism. This is not only because it does not have the strength to extort them from us, but also because it would not know what to do with them. The export of capital is necessary for its expansion. Now Germany has come out of the war a miserable and impoverished country. In vain it begs for credits from America, but it cannot itself go in for any expansion. The German-Russian economic relations that we think necessary, independently of the concessions that Soviet Russia must make to Britain, absolutely cannot be built up on the old capitalist basis. It is not the exchange of goods nor the export of capital, but assistance through labour which forms the new basis of German-Russian economic relations. These will not give the Germans the possibility of dominating Russia; but by helping Russia rebuild its economic strength, they will give to thousands of German intellectual and manual workers bread and work; they will also create the basis for an exchange of goods in the future between Russia and Germany. Russia would have had to follow this policy even if it had been a bourgeois state. It is a policy dictated by Russian interests. But it coincides with the principles which a proletarian state must not set aside, even when confronted with necessity: it must not make itself the instrument of a policy which consists in impoverishing and isolating other peoples. Naturally, it needs two for political as well as personal relationships. If the German government continues stupidly to fear Bolshevism as well as the Entente, if it continues to remain completely passive, hoping that the Devil will finally carry off Soviet Russia and deliver it into the arms of Denikin, then it will have to take the blame for its own self-imposed blockade.

'The limits of the economic concessions that Soviet Russia can make to Entente capital are far more of a social nature. It cannot allow imperialist colonies to be born on its soil in which the Russian proletariat will play the part of white slaves. Even if Soviet Russia is obliged to provide a certain amount of wealth to foreign capital, **this could only take place on the basis of conditions which would be concretely fixed between the contracting states.** It is first of all a question of **working conditions**, which must not be worse than those of the rest of the Russian proletariat — allowing that Russian workers have to be employed at all. **Then it is a question of the relationship between the production of the concessionary enterprises and the overall economic plan of the Soviet republic.** The agreements must define that part of production that must benefit the organised Russian economy. If Russia desires to be reborn economically, it must draw immediate benefit from the development of the concessionary enterprises by buying from them at cost price **a share of the production** which would then be used to provide it with the means of production. It is only thus that the tribute that it is necessary to pay to foreign capital would not amount to bleeding Russia dry. We cannot enter into detail upon this question here, because that would take us too far. Nonetheless, last year there were very deep and concrete consultations on this subject in the circles that direct the economic policy of Soviet Russia. If it was doubtful last year whether capitalist circles, used to an individualistic method of economic production, would accept that their private initiative had to be limited by social controls, the situation has become visibly modified in the meantime. In fact, they are confronted with the same problems in their own countries, and however much they may be opposed to all attempts at social control, it is obvious that without a doubt the pressure of the working class movement and the necessity of overcoming economic anarchy in one way or another has forced them to give up their old unlimited individualism. What they have been forced to concede to the British and American workers, even before they had conquered political power, they must also concede to the Russian workers who are supported by the Russian workers' state.

'We do not wish to exaggerate things here, or paint them up in rosy colours. In spite of the importance of the concessions that foreign capital will be obliged to make to the Russian proletariat if it desires to make profits in Russia, the fact is that the Russian workers **will have to work for foreign capitalist profit, that Russia's natural wealth will be exploited by a foreign capitalist economy**, and that a **foreign body** will consequently come into existence in Soviet Russia. But so long as Soviet Russia itself forms a foreign body inside the system of capitalist states, it cannot avoid such dangers.

'**It is clear that there is in fact a danger here.** For independently of the difficulties that the proletarian government will encounter in the event of conflicts between the Russian proletarians and the foreign capitalist concessionaires, the danger also exists that the **remnants of the defeated Russian bourgeoisie will reform around the foreign private enterprises.** This danger will increase to the extent to which the Soviet government would be obliged to make more and more concessions to foreign capital if the present transitional stage were to be prolonged. This is precisely what Lloyd George and the other Entente leaders who are inclined to conclude peace with Soviet Russia are counting on. The realisation of their hopes or no depends upon the probable length of this collaboration; the influence that peace with Entente capitalism would have upon the development of the Russian proletarian state also depends upon it. **If this collaboration were to go on for many years, the Soviet Republic would at best become a state like those of New Zealand or Australia, a capitalist state governed by the workers and farmers, in which finance capital has made great concessions to the proletariat as regards their living standards...** Obviously this is a better position than in Europe or America, but it is not the dictatorship of the proletariat intended to bring about Communism. **However, if as is likely, the world revolution spreads slowly but surely, these arrangements with regard to foreign capitalist interests will be neither so important nor so prolonged as to threaten the real power of the proletariat.** By giving Soviet Russia peace and the possibility of proceeding with the reconstruction of its economy, these arrangements might even allow the effective power of the proletariat to be strengthened. For it is clear that this power will be all the stronger if transport conditions improve, if industries are provided with raw materials and fuel, and if the peasants can buy goods in exchange for bread, even if we have to renounce many objectives and fall back for a while.

'The stronger the Soviet Union becomes, the more it will be possible to give up the terror, which is only a means of defence, and **the more it will be able to apply the dictatorship gently.** The dictatorship must not be terminated so long as there are threats to the domination of the proletariat. **But the severity of the dictatorship depends upon the extent of the threats; insofar as they grow smaller we can enlarge the circle of those hesitant layers to whom we can allow the exercise of political rights.** Paragraph 2 of the political part of the programme of the Russian Communist Party (March 1919) says this: "Contrary to bourgeois democracy, which conceals the class nature of the state, the Soviet government openly recognises the historic necessity of the class nature of any state up to the disappearance of the class division of society, and therefore all state power. The Soviet state is essentially aimed at suppressing the resistance of the exploiters. The Soviet Constitution, which recognises that freedom is only a fraud if it forms an obstacle to the emancipation of labour from capitalist oppression, does not hesitate to deprive social groups of the enjoyment of political rights. The task of the proletarian party is to suppress unhesitantly the resistance of the exploiters, and to lead the ideological struggle against deep-rooted superstition about the absolute nature of bourgeois laws and freedoms; but it also consists in explaining that **the withdrawal of political rights and other measures restricting freedom are only temporary measures in the struggle against the exploiters** who are defending their privileges or who hope to re-establish them. To the extent to which the objective possibility of the exploitation of man by man disappears, the necessity for temporary repressive measures also disappears, measures which the party will do its utmost to limit and finally bring completely to an end."[48]

'To the extent to which the victories of the Red Army over the counter-revolutionary armies weaken the hopes of the Russian nobility and exploiters of seeing their rule re-established, the possibilities of softening the proletarian dictatorship in Russia also increase. For the first time in world history, this dictatorship has given to large masses of people the real possibility of taking part in intellectual life and in directing the state, and of creating as a result a real democracy such as does not exist in any state. But at the same time this dictatorship has deprived the bourgeoisie and those intellectuals who support it of political rights because they were using them to hold back the emancipation of the popular masses. The armed struggle of the Russian proletariat against the counter-revolution would have been over long ago if the capitalist states (Germany to begin with, and then the Entente) had not supported the Russian counter-revolution by all means, and so forced Soviet Russia to strengthen its measures of defence. Counter-revolution has suffered great defeats in this struggle. If Entente imperialism finally ceases to stir up the Russian Civil War, if it lifts its deadly blockade, then the victorious working class could renounce its military measures as a result of the end of the Civil War. This does not mean that it would give up directing the state in conformity with the workers' interests, but that it would on the contrary really develop the proletarian state from the victory of the proletariat over bourgeois oppression towards democracy. This development will happen gradually. Any attempt by the pressure of Entente capital to accelerate this development will hamper it. Any interference to the advantage of the members of the old bourgeoisie will awaken a deep distrust within the proletariat and drag out the civil war, whether the Soviet government wishes it or not.

'We have described the concessions that Soviet Russia can make. Many revolutionaries will regard this as a deep humiliation. **What? Proud Soviet Russia, which repudiated its war debts, will in the end pay them? Soviet Russia, which has defeated the Russian bourgeoisie, will make concessions to private capital? Yes, precisely because Soviet Russia alone cannot vanquish world capital — only the world proletariat can do that — it has to pay tribute to the world bourgeoisie. It is futile to get angry about this. This situation will go on until the overwhelming capitalist decomposition brings about the world revolution.** One section of the capitalist press and the press of the so-called Socialist traitors to the working class will talk about the Soviet Republic's road to Damascus, and of the surrender of Communism. Let them continue to chatter, they have already said all that after Brest-Litovsk; but we survive whilst the victors of Brest Litovsk are broken on the wheel of history. We take back nothing. All that we taught about the dictatorship of the proletariat remains completely valid, in whatever way it is exercised, and the Russian Soviet government will always be the representative of the power of the proletariat or it will not exist. Let both enemies and friends understand one thing: there will not be a pretence of a Soviet republic. If the Soviet republic did not have the strength to defend real power, it would not defend the shadow of an existence, but would openly capitulate or go down fighting. The result of the autumn attack upon the main cities shows that it has no need to do this. Why did it fight if it was at the end of its strength? Since it did fight and overcame a severe military test, it will also be able to overcome the severe economic test of a harsh winter. Amongst the Denikins and the Kolchaks the economic conditions are even worse; it is also necessary to note the following fact: whilst in Soviet Russia the working class is convinced that the proletarian government has done its utmost to help it, it could not while hungry help looking beyond the doings of the Kolchak and Denikin cliques at how the rich were feasting. This winter half of Europe will suffer infernal torment, and no part of the Entente will give any help. It will not do so because it cannot do it. Aid requires millions and millions, and France and Britain are themselves on the verge of bankruptcy. The Soviet government has no need to surrender, either openly or surreptitiously. To remedy the appalling misery it is obliged, in the name of peace, to make concessions. The coming months will decide if the Entente is capable of having any rational idea on the Russian question. If it fails, Soviet Russia will have to prevail through great sacrifices; but the collapse of Entente imperialism will be all the more rapid because it will be once more forced to make unheard of efforts to defeat Soviet Russia. The difference between our opponent and ourselves is that time is on our side. We came to the decision to make concessions because we knew that we would be victorious in the end; the policy of gambling everything on one throw of the dice may predominate. What will happen depends on the attitude of the Entente workers this winter, and upon political developments in all parts of the world. But one thing is certain in all this jumble of tendencies: the continuation of capitalist disintegration and the extension of the proletarian revolution. We, who are its advance guard, will suffer more hard times. But in any case it is certain to win!'[49]

These lines were written, as I said, **in December 1919 at the time of the decisive victories of Soviet Russia over the Whites**, at the time when Kolchak and Yudenich[50] were liquidated and Denikin was thrown back to the Caucasus. And what do these lines say? They say that at the time of the greatest victories we did not for a moment abandon the following points of view: that to begin with Russia is a country whose **population is essentially petit-bourgeois**, and that for this reason Communist policy has to mark time in the village, and that the socialisation of agriculture is a problem that will require the work of generations; moreover, that the Soviet government must for the moment work with a view to a compromise with the peasants. In short, it was laid down that the greater part of the Russian economy within the near future would be oriented towards petit-bourgeois commodity production. It was then established that the **world revolution** would develop slowly after the overcoming of the demobilisation crisis, and that consequently for the time being the Soviet government had to aim for a modus vivendi with the capitalist states, and to this end, to be prepared to make concessions to capital:

'So long as the proletariat has not triumphed in the principal capitalist states, so long as it will not be in a position to utilise all the productive forces of the world for Socialist construction, so long as capitalist states exist alongside proletarian states, the proletarian states will be forced to conclude compromises with them, and there would neither be pure Socialism nor pure capitalism; geographically limited, they would in effect be forced to make reciprocal concessions upon their own national territories.'

This concept was not my own, it was the common concept of the leading authorities of the Russian Communist Party and of the Soviet government. And this concept was not just the result of the experiences of 1919. In fact Lenin not only defended this concept at the time of the conflicts relating to the signing of the Brest Peace, but also he defended it in April 1918, during his speech on the immediate tasks of Soviet power. This speech was delivered on 29 April 1918 to the Central Executive Committee of the Soviets. In it Lenin developed the following ideas: in the sphere of foreign policy, it was on the one hand necessary to create the Red Army, and on the other hand to make concessions to international capital for so long as the world revolution had not triumphed. In the sphere of the organisation of the economy, he supported not only the necessity to call in bourgeois specialists by offering them higher wages, the necessity to make a compromise not only with the petit-bourgeois cooperatives, but even also with capitalist cartels who were to organise heavy industry under the control of the state with participation in the profits. In April 1918 Lenin declared that it was necessary to learn how to organise Socialism from the magnates of the capitalist trusts, and he demanded a temporary halt to attacks upon capital because he thought that the Soviet government had already expropriated much more than it was capable of controlling.[51] The following question is posed at present: **why did the Soviet government carry out the opposite policy during the period between the autumn of 1918 and March 1921, the policy of requisitions in the village, the policy of the nationalisation of all the means of production in**

the town, the policy of even the total suppression of internal trade attacked as speculation, why then did the Soviet government not follow the policy defended by Lenin in April 1918, and often defended theoretically in 1919 by the leaders of the Soviet republic? (Cf Lenin's speech on relations with the middle peasantry in April 1919;[52] cf the unceasing peace proposals and offers of concessions that the Soviet government addressed to foreign capital in 1919.) In his speech to the Congress of Popular Political Education Departments in October 1921, Lenin explained that the policy of these three years had been a **mistake** and proclaimed a return to the policy of 1918.[53] This explanation was interpreted by the enemies of Communism as a confession of bankruptcy by Russian Communism, as a confirmation of the correctness of all that the press, not only Menshevik but world capitalist as well, had developed at such great length on the policy of Russian Communism. Obviously Lenin is without doubt a man of exemplary political rectitude, a trustworthy man who is never afraid of admitting errors committed. It is, however, clear that he did not pronounce this speech, as the leader of a great government, to pour out his heart in front of the capitalists of the entire world and of the Mensheviks, but that his speeches serve his political ends. In a speech he made later on 29 October (it was published in the Moscow *Pravda* on 3 November) he explained why he had spoken of faults and mistakes.[54] **It is a question, he explained, not only of giving a new orientation to the economic policy of the Soviet republic, which has been in operation since the month of March 1921, but it is also a question of realising the new policy. Now the party, which since autumn 1919 had carried out the most intractable policy of nationalisation, is not capable of changing at the blinking of an eye, and that is why it is necessary for it to become aware, under the most brutal form, of the intervening changes in the conditions of the development of the Soviet republic.** And this is what Lenin did by talking about past mistakes. In this speech Lenin sought to explain the nature of the mistakes made by making a comparison between the different tactics used by the Japanese General Nogi to capture Port Arthur.[55] To begin with, he attacked the stronghold by furious frontal offensives that cost him enormous losses. When he saw that Port Arthur could not be taken by these methods, Nogi then tried a slow and systematic siege, and took the city at the end of very hard struggles in which the work of the sappers and artillery played as great a rôle as the infantry offensives and assaults. Then Lenin asked: were the first assaults a mistake? The reply is: yes and no. It was a mistake because it later transpired that they were insufficient to capture the stronghold. But it was not a mistake because the enemy's capacity for resistance could not be determined without an attack, and a general must try to defeat the enemy as quickly as possible; finally, even the repelled assaults had weakened the enemy, and had therefore allowed him to be finally conquered by siege. Similarly, said Lenin, it was necessary to smash capitalism in Russia by a frontal assault. But when frontal assaults did not produce the expected results, our duty was to prepare the retreat and to organise the siege of the enemy, and defeat him by other means. Any comparison is unsatisfactory, but **this comparison of Lenin limps on both feet so to speak**, and the analysis of this comparison greatly helps to explain the causes of the policy of the Soviet republic in the period between autumn 1918 and March 1921 and its present alteration.

To begin with, we would like to say that the story of planning for war is an old tale against which all authentic war historians and historiographers of strategy have contended. The general staffs of all armies seek to develop a concept of the future war; outsiders call this a war plan. But there has not been a single war in history which was any more than a coup or a surprise attack that has proceeded in accordance with the planning of a general staff. A great debate began in German military history after the collapse of 1918 to know if the war had been conducted or not according to the Schlieffen Plan.[56] Historical investigation has shown that there was no war plan at all. Schlieffen had the idea of a situation in which Germany had to conduct a war on two fronts, and he formed the basic plan of preparing a corps of the German army in the event of the war being conducted in the conditions which he envisaged. Schlieffen counted upon a slow Russian mobilisation, and he therefore developed the idea of taking up a defensive position on the Eastern front before Russia could mobilise the bulk of its forces, while first attempting to overthrow France with decisive forces. He did not prepare a plan for the conduct of the war, because he knew all too well that a concrete plan can only be elaborated after the first engagements with the enemy forces had provided indications of subsequent developments. Schlieffen's prognostications were not realised, nor was it possible to apply his basic idea correctly. If in the conduct of the war no elaborated and foreordained plan for a general war exists, there nevertheless does exist a plan for **each particular battle**. The commander-in-chief is in possession of information on the state of the enemy's forces in a concrete battle situation. His own forces also represent a given and clearly defined quantity. He seeks to sift through all the possibilities for defeating the forces of the enemy, and then chooses the idea that seems the most favourable to him. He generally has **the possibility of choice**. It was the same for General Nogi. Nogi could have seen straightaway that the taking of Port Arthur was impossible by a frontal assault. He could have avoided the mistake made by correctly evaluating the enemy forces, but Nogi overestimated the chances of the attack and underestimated the forces of the defence, and that is why his attack was a mistake. **Now our Nogi, Lenin, estimated that the forces of world capital were very powerful.** In his speech of April 1918, he elaborated a war plan which proceeded from a correct estimation of the enemy forces and of our weaknesses.[57] This is why he proposed concessions to the peasantry and to capital, and that is why he carried out a policy of compromise with world capital by signing peace with Germany at Brest Litovsk and doing all in his power to avoid a war with the Entente. **What Lenin is at present defending under the label of the New Economic Policy does not amount to any other than a further development of his war plan of 1918.** But what was it that led him to abandon his ingenious plan in the autumn of 1918? **Lenin and the Soviet republic had no freedom of action, no freedom of choice.** Since the Czech uprising during the summer of 1918,[58] since the occupation of Archangel by the British,[59] **the enemy had seized the initiative.** It had dictated to the Soviet republic the action it must take. The enemy was far stronger than us, he took the initiative, and passing over to the offensive, he ruled out the possibility of a compromise. It was necessary to fight, and this fight developed not in accordance with a foreordained plan, but **under compulsion of the necessities of the struggle.** We understood perfectly that we were forced to a compromise with the peasants, who are petty producers of goods, are petit-bourgeois, and who could only be won over to Communist politics over generations through the great advantages offered by modern technical methods of agriculture. But despite this we were obliged to resort to **a policy of requisitions** which made us enemies in the village, and which, carried on for several years, weakened the agricultural forces considerably. To begin with Siberia was in the hands of the Czechoslovaks, and then of Kolchak, the Ukraine was in the hands of the Germans, then of Skoropadsky, then of Petliura,[60] and finally of Denikin. We had to feed the towns and the armies, increasingly more numerous, starting off from the reserves of central Russia and the Volga region. The peasants had in fact seized the land. They had returned to the village after a war that had strengthened their consciousness; they had weapons and an idea of liberty and of their relations with the state that were very close to the conception according to which the peasant had absolutely no need of anything so diabolical as the state. If we had then tried to impose taxes in kind, we would not have been able to collect them because we did not possess the necessary apparatus and because the peasants would not have provided them voluntarily. It was necessary to make them understand, to start off with by very vigorous means, that the state not only had the right to claim for its needs a part of the produce of its citizens, but also that it had the power to impose this right. Furthermore, given that starting from the autumn, our territory for provisioning was very limited, taxes in kind would of necessity have taken from the peasants all that was not necessary for their own subsistence. A tax in kind which confiscates the whole surplus product and is collected by military force is precisely none other than requisition.

But if we sought to take from the peasants the whole of the surplus product, it was necessary to avoid by all means their refusal to sell us only a part of the cereals of which we had an absolute need. We had to forbid them from selling cereals, and we had to suppress the town trade which constituted an encouragement to the black market in cereals.

And could we leave the **industrial and productive resources** in the hands of the bourgeoisie? We knew all too well that we could not administer small and medium industry on our own, our forces were insufficient for that. We knew that the captains of industry would be necessary to us, and that state cartelisation of industry with state participation, but under the practical management of capitalists controlled by the state, would for the moment be the form of industrial organisation most favourable to us. But these gentlemen captains of industry passed over to the enemy in order to overthrow us, first of all with the help of the Germans, and then with the help of the Allies. They did not wish to be our leaseholders, nor to find themselves under state control. **In short, they did not want to ally with us, because they had the hope of being able to overthrow us.** The policy of compromising with the leaders of big capital was impossible because they did not recognise our power, and were on the contrary convinced that they would come to overthrow us. But only the present recognition of our power has created the basis for a compromise. As far as small and medium industry were concerned, it was necessary from the outset of the great Civil War to close them down. Fronts in a civil war differ from fronts in a war between states in that the Whites, like the Reds, always have enemy forces behind their backs. The front lines only divide the country geographically, but not socially. On one side of the front line, the Reds have supremacy, but counter-revolutionary forces have not therefore disappeared from their territory. On the other side, power is in the hands of the Whites, but the forces of the Reds, the forces of the revolution, still exist and represent a great threat to the White dictatorship. In order to triumph at the front, the White dictatorship, like the Red, must totally suppress the enemy forces in the rear. The strength of the working masses resides in their organisation. This is why White dictatorship suppresses any form of workers' organisation. The strength of the bourgeoisie resides in the fact that it disposes of the means of production and the goods. **We can utterly suppress any political organisation of the bourgeoisie, but if we allow bourgeois trade, bourgeois industry and even small and middle industry to exist, then the bourgeoisie will maintain its cohesion and its unity as a class on the basis of the reciprocal economic relations between its members, and, as enemies of the working class, use its material means against us.** This is why we were forced to nationalise small and medium industry, even when nationalisation was only a pretext for closing down factories. The fight was on, and it was necessary to crush the enemy. Them or us, that is how the question was posed, and there was no room for compromise.

But nationalisation was also necessary for economic reasons. We had to conduct a war against an enemy who disposed of the most modern military and technical means. But we had to equip the army and provide it with weapons by means of an industry disorganised by world war, an industry that already before the war was on a far lower level than that of Western Europe. Consequently, we could only win by pulling together all the industrial forces of the country, and by using them single-mindedly for victory. We allowed the distant railways to get into disrepair, because it was necessary to strengthen the railway network in the area of war operations. I again recall the words of Trotsky to the party congress in 1920: 'We have ravaged the country in order to defeat the Whites.' This was surely not an economic policy, even less Communist construction. It was a policy of war and victory, and since we could not win otherwise, and did win in this way, history has judged these methods. And this judgement is set forth thus: **this way was not a mistake. It was the road to victory.**

But we had to take this road not only because of the policy of the bourgeoisie, and on account of economic necessity, we also had to take it because the principle strength upon which we relied was the working class. Each social class has its own maximum programme which it only gives up, or curtails, when it is forced to do so under the pressure of other classes, and under the pressure of necessity. Ever since the 1840s, bourgeois social reformers have always told the bourgeoisie that it was in its own interests not to treat the workers as slaves. They explained to the bourgeoisie that a well-rewarded working class, culturally developed, would work better; but the bourgeoisie paid absolutely no attention to all this advice, until the working class opposed its own will to the desire of the bourgeoisie to exploit it ruthlessly. The Russian bourgeoisie already felt the heat of the fire of the revolution, and yet it did not think to choke off the revolution by nationalising, by struggling against speculation, and by making concessions to the working class. The Russian peasants did not want to supply bread to the towns or to the workers, who had given them the land, until they were forced to do so. The Russian workers, who had been enslaved and oppressed by the bourgeoisie, had taken power, and took it by assault. The bourgeoisie seemed to be impotent, and in these conditions we could not wait for the workers to understand effectively the real relationship of forces, or for them to understand effectively the difficulties of the new regime, and the difficulties of establishing their power. In 1917, as in 1918, Lenin and the party leaders had a correct understanding of the relationship of forces, but the masses certainly did not. Lenin, in his speech on the immediate tasks of the Soviet government,[61] and Trotsky, in his speech on 'work and discipline',[62] addressed entire sermons, on the one hand against the mentality that they described as petit-bourgeois, individualistic mass psychology, which consisted of saying: 'industry belongs to us, every worker is master in his own house, and he can take what he wants', and on the other hand against aspirations which envisaged bringing in Socialism at one blow. Today, after four years of revolution and after immense privations of the masses, Lenin, in order to ensure the energetic and strict carrying out of the policy of compromise, considers it necessary to tell the party that the economic policy followed up to the present was a mistake; it is, however, highly improbable that the present policy could have been carried out in 1918, even without the attack of the Entente. It is sufficient to recall that in 1918, an influential group of party publicists and organisers, such as Bukharin, Ossinsky, Smirnov, Yakovleva, Lomov and myself,[63] carried out an attack against this policy in the *Communist*, a factional journal, and that there was not only a left tendency in the party, but that this tendency even had a central organisation. And it was in this spirit of the first successful frontal assault that the working class engaged in a very hard struggle against the Whites and against the intervention. It endured terrible privations, and it made the greatest sacrifices; and who should be surprised that Russia, the battlefield that was Russia, a besieged stronghold, had to live as if under siege? When the revolutionary fighters were suffering misery and hunger, could they abandon the least scrap of power and any privileges whatsoever to the class which with the help of the Entente was pouring cannon fire over them?

The necessities of the war and the necessities of the struggle were transformed in the heads of the masses into the religion of Communism. And each of our measures, even when they served very limited and transitory aims, was integrated and incorporated into a general Communist system. One petty Philistine, the Menshevik Abramovich,[64] asked when and how did the Communist Party describe its measures as temporary? Why did it talk about Communism? The brave man had not only never taken part in a revolution, but he had never even read with any sympathy the history of a great war of liberation. Otherwise he would have understood that revolution not only gives rise to coolness of judgement, but also to illusions, which are not 'mistakes', but which give wings to the offensive, give it strength, and lead it to the ends that are historically put before it. **It would be ridiculous to deny that we committed many mistakes in the struggle, or that we had ever carried out a mistaken policy; but it would be equally ridiculous to deny that ideology, which had taken on its own dynamic, very often transformed provisional, transitional measures into a system which in its turn influenced the measures and prolonged them beyond what was necessary.** In its entirety, as an historical epoch, the policy that we have had to modify at present was not a mistake; moreover, it was thanks to this policy, carried out resolutely, that we were able to push back the country's enemy, overthrow him within, and were thus able to create the conditions for the present policy. General Nogi missed his objective because of his erroneous estimate of the relationship of forces, because of his frontal assault on Port Arthur. Soviet Russia has not launched itself into any offensive of its own accord. The war against the Entente, with all its consequences, was imposed upon it, but our offensive was not repulsed. We have defeated the enemy, brought his aims to ruin, and prevented our own defeat; we have therefore created the conditions that permit us to attempt to conclude a compromise with him, which is necessary for the economic reconstruction of the country.

IV

The New Economic Policy was inaugurated in March 1921. It coincided with two events: the signing of the **Anglo-Russian Commercial Agreement** and **the crushing of the Kronstadt uprising.**[65] These two events are not only linked chronologically with the New Economic Policy; they also have an internal and structural link with it. The first event, the signing of the Anglo-Russian Commercial Agreement,[66] shows very well why we did not resort to the New Economic Policy in 1920, after the victory over Kolchak and Denikin. After the victory over Kolchak and Denikin, the foremost European power, Britain, began to negotiate with us, but for over a year it dragged out the negotiations at length. During this time, Europe's second capitalist power, France, mobilised Poland and Wrangel against us.[67] At the end of summer 1920 Wrangel was now officially recognised by France as the representative of the Russian government. Britain negotiated with us without even lifting her little finger to hinder French policy. British capital made the signing of a provisional commercial agreement drag on at great length, waiting for us to be vanquished eventually by the Poles and Wrangel, in order to be able to wash their hands innocently of us. Given that the New Economic Policy in part rests upon a compromise with world capital, it is clear that it was entirely suspended in mid-air for as long as the Anglo-Russian agreement had not been signed. Even today, many months after the signing of this accord, not a single important concessionary agreement has been concluded. All the contracts are at the stage of preliminary discussions. The famine this year awoke new hopes amongst the world bourgeoisie, and even that part of world capital that no longer hoped for our defeat waits before signing the agreements until the pressure of necessity is sufficiently strong for a compromise between it and us to be concluded in conditions most advantageous to it.

And what is the relationship of the Kronstadt events to the New Economic Policy? The Kronstadt events were only the echo of a deep process of fermentation amongst the peasant masses. They were the echo of the peasant uprisings in the Ukraine and at Tambov.[68] But what did these peasant uprisings mean? They showed that the imperialist war and the civil war had considerably weakened the rural economy. They showed that the Russian economic crisis had its origin not only in the disorganisation of industry, but also in the disintegration of its agriculture. They showed the necessity for a rapid and fundamental change in our policy; it had to take all the more an energetic and radical turn because the perspectives of a compromise with foreign capital were uncertain, and the course of the negotiations with foreign capital was dragging on at length. The agricultural crisis and the slowness of the negotiations with foreign capital have forced the Soviet government to alter the reconstruction plan that it had in view in spring 1920 after the defeat of Yudenich, Kolchak and Denikin. What did this plan consist of?

It rested on the hope of reinforcing economic relations with the foreign capitalist which were to help us obtain a mass of the means of production. In order to exploit this and to shorten the period of necessary preparatory work for using them, it was necessary to use the brute strength of the peasant masses in organisations of **labour armies**. Reconstruction had to begin with a frontal assault. Obviously this was not Communism, since we were prepared to rent out large sectors of industry to foreign capital. The outcries of the capitalist press and its Menshevik lackeys who were denouncing this as forced labour showed only the extent to which the bourgeoisie feared the rapid rhythm of economic construction in Russia. Given that this economic construction took account of the interests of both the workers and the peasants, the labour armies had nothing Communist about them. They were necessary measures which will be necessary every time the worker-peasant government has to achieve reconstruction at the most rapid rate. The plan ran aground to begin with because the labour armies, even before being organised, had to be militarily organised and equipped to fight against the Poles and Wrangel. It also got stuck because the foreign deliveries of the means of production were very slow. A frontal economic assault turned out to be impossible at the time. At the beginning of 1921 **it became clear that economic reconstruction would only take place very slowly.** World capital, which was incapable of overthrowing us, also showed itself incapable of concluding a rapid compromise with us. All these factors involved the necessity for a **retreat,** to the extent to which the Soviet government in 1920 dreamed of the rapid reconstruction of great statified industry thanks to the means of production provided by the foreigner and with the help of the strength of concentrated peasant labour. The essence of the New Economic Policy therefore consists in the Soviet government first of all mobilising the economic forces that will allow it to undertake Communist economic construction in the future.

V

The New Economic Policy of the Soviet government began with the abandonment of the policy of requisitions in the village, and its replacement by a tax in kind. The difference between the two policies first of all consists in the peasants henceforth having to pay only one tax of a fixed amount, whereas before they had been hit by requisitions varying in accordance with the current needs of the armies and the cities. The tax in kind takes much less off the peasants than hitherto. It therefore encourages them to extend the area sown, and to cultivate it more efficiently. This is because they now retain a surplus above what is needed for their subsistence and the tax, which they can exchange for industrial products. **By this, concessions to the peasants involve concessions to the urban bourgeoisie and to commercial capital** which preserved itself in the illegal form of speculation. In and of itself, concessions to commercial capital need not necessarily flow from concessions to the peasants. If Soviet Russia had at its disposal important stocks of merchandise, the peasant could exchange his surplus of cereals with the state against industrial goods via the cooperatives. The concessions to commercial capital result from the industrial weakness of the state, and from the lack of credits. But other consequences result from it. Even the commercial bourgeoisie does not possess sufficient stocks of merchandise. It seeks to accumulate merchandise whether by smuggling — foreign trade is in fact a state monopoly — or by purchase on the internal market. The commercial bourgeoisie can only procure merchandise among the kustari, the petty artisans. The domestic labour of the kustari, however, only produces a very restricted amount of goods — as regards quality as well as quantity.[69] If Soviet Russia does not want to aggravate artificially the lack of goods — and it is clear that it has no sensible reason to do this — it must very naturally allow the reconstruction of small and middle industry. The state must consciously renounce the management of this industry. This would in fact involve the dispersal of its forces of organisation which are none too numerous already. It is for this reason that the Soviet government has authorised the leasing of small and middling businesses by working class cooperatives as well as by private persons. But the limit of the concessions that the Soviet government is obliged to make in its retreat has not yet been reached. The Soviet government has need of foreign technical help, but its financial means are too weak to buy enough machines from abroad. To obtain these the Soviet government must seek to attract foreign capital by other means. These are the concessions, that is to say, the authorisation given to foreign capital to take over, on the basis of agreed conditions, industries which already existed or which it is necessary to start up from scratch. But great foreign capital thus rushes into an area whose control is vital for Soviet Russia: heavy industry.

The policy of the Soviet government contains concessions of very long duration, for the foreseeable historical period, and concessions of a more temporary type. The concessions to the peasants doubtless form part of the first type. In a country where the population is essentially petit-bourgeois, in a country where the small and middle peasant represent the great majority of the population, the progress to superior collective economic forms in the village can only take place when the proletarian state is capable of showing the peasants a life of progress thanks to great technical superiority, and important technical aid. For as long as Soviet Russia is not covered by a network of electric power stations, as long as modern agricultural machines have not had the widest distribution and use in the village, the peasant will remain a small, free and independent owner. Things are different as regards the concessions made to the commercial bourgeoisie and the small industrial capitalist leaseholders. As soon as large-scale industry begins to function, as soon as it is able to satisfy in one way or another the need for goods, it will vanquish small industry by means of competition. The development of the cooperatives will gain ground over retail trade, and all the more rapidly if the state supports the cooperatives more energetically. The concessions to foreign capital are linked to the international situation. They arise from a double necessity: on the one hand to obtain the means of production from foreign capital, and on the other hand to hold back the interventionist tendencies of world capital. The duration of these concessions is linked to the duration of the present and relative world equilibrium.

What social reconstruction of classes results from the New Economic Policy of the Soviet government? The peasantry forms a petit-bourgeois class. With it is linked the small and middle urban bourgeoisie in the process of restoration. Foreign concessionary capital forms the big capitalist class. The proletariat is opposed to these classes, on the one hand in the big state industry, on the other hand in small and middle leasehold industry, and finally in big concessionary industry. It is unnecessary to emphasise that this does not represent a favourable relationship of forces for the working class. The situation contains great danger in itself. The small and middle urban bourgeoisie, concentrated in the country's cultural centres, will try, on the basis of its commercial relations with the peasantry, to organise it as a class against the proletariat. In the first place, it will attempt to ally itself with the most powerful elements in the peasantry. To begin with, foreign capital, supported by the capitalist governments, will try to modify in its favour the conditions on the basis of which it was allowed into Russia by the Soviet government. Doubtless it will attempt to break the most important obstacle to its expansion: the state monopoly of foreign trade. The type of aid offered to starving Russia such as Lloyd George proposed in his speech of 16 September makes this perfectly clear. The whole plan in fact envisaged the assigning of trade credits by the British government to British firms which would then exchange in Russia industrial goods for foodstuffs under the form of free trade. In this way foreign capital would naturally forge independent economic relations with the Russian peasants.

The Soviet government is certainly not closing its eyes to the dangers which result from this; but they are counter-balanced by the fact that the proletariat holds state power. The proletariat as the ruling class is the owner of the means of production. Even if the peasant is exploiting the land freely, it nonetheless remains nationalised, that is, it remains in the hands of the state. This juridical right has a social significance. It prevents the formation of big private land ownership, and it holds back the formation of a rich peasantry as an organised counter-revolutionary force. It provides the proletarian state power with an entire series of means as regards the Russian and foreign bourgeoisie, whose industrial activity is linked to the question of the land. To the extent to which the state only leases industrial enterprises to private persons — when it does not keep control of them itself — to the extent to which it does not denationalise industry, it keeps control of it. It not only regulates the relationship of the leaseholders with the working class, which assures it, as the representative of the interests of the proletariat, of its link with the working masses and allows it to keep them as its social base, but it also has the possibility of influencing the economic activity of the leaseholders. It has the means to make this activity conform if possible with that of the state industry. In this context the possession of the means of transport and of communications is of decisive importance for influencing the economic activity of the bourgeois elements.

The general picture of the social situation, which is the objective and result of the New Economic Policy, is this: the proletarian state rests upon the ownership of the principal branches of industry. Obliged to allow these partly into the hands of foreign capital, it seeks permanently not only to strengthen its social base, but also to enlarge it, by doing all in its power to obtain new means of production. It controls small and middle leased industries, as well as that sector of industry it has been forced to lease to foreign capital. It is not only the protector of the proletarian workforce, but also, supported by real economic power, the regulator of economic life. The concessions to the peasantry have on the one hand the aim of renewing and strengthening the alliance between the working class and the peasantry which led to the victory of October, and on the other hand of obtaining from the peasantry thanks to the development of the rural economy fresh resources for heavy industry; the concessions to commercial and industrial rented capital on the other hand allow the state to obtain the goods necessary to satisfy the needs of agriculture. The concessions to big foreign capital have as their objective the freeing of resources for the development of state industry. **The result attained obviously does not represent a Communist organisation of society**, but it contains an entire series of measures that assure the development of the Russian economy. **It is on this basis that the power of the working class will be strengthened, and that the working class has the possibility of more and more organising economic life and controlling petit-bourgeois anarchy.**

VI

When the working class took power on 25 October 1917, the Revolutionary Military Committee, which had taken the power in the name of the soviet of the workers and soldiers of Petrograd, announced the change achieved to the Russian working class and the entire world by declaring: 'The cause of peace is in the powerful hands of the proletariat. The peasantry will finally obtain the land, and the **working class will extend its control over industry.**'[70] What was announced as the immediate aim of the revolution was not the immediate introduction of Socialism, but the solution of the question of peace, and of the peasant question; it was the setting in motion of transitional measures, for example, control over production. But revolutions do not respect the limits and definitions sketched out by their leaders. **The October Revolution was the prelude to the world proletarian revolution.** It was the prelude to the Communist uprising in the capitalist world; and however limited were the aims that the leaders of the revolution had set themselves, the blast of the Russian October Revolution was the blast of the proletarian revolution, the blast of the world Communist revolution. At the moment, the Russian Revolution has come up against a social limit which will be its limit for the next historic period. No revolution can achieve Communism at one blow. The revolution has only broken the resistance that the political power of the old ruling classes opposed to the development of the new victorious class. When throughout the whole world the revolution begins the struggle for economic transformation, then the path of this transformation will be shorter in one country and longer in another, depending on the extent of economic development which will help or hinder this transformation. The world proletarian revolution represents a long period of struggle; the road to power will be more arduous in the west, and will be far longer than in Russia. The organisation of Socialism, insofar as it concerns the conditions of industry, will be far easier in the capitalist countries than in Russia. The preponderance of industrial concentration and the high level of the technical skills of the proletariat will then be of decisive importance. But it would be false to assume that the proletarian revolution in western Europe will not have to surmount great economic difficulties. The greatest difficulty resides in its too narrow agricultural base. The industrialisation of Western Europe has made all the industrial countries dependent on the import of foodstuffs. The development of the proletarian revolution in the West is therefore closely linked to the development of the proletarian revolution in the East. It is necessary to take account of this when we pass judgement upon the problems of the proletarian revolution in Russia, on its ways, its necessities and its character.

The Russian Revolution has travelled through an entire cycle of development, from the struggle for the democratic republic to the struggle for the Soviet republic. The victory of the Soviet republic seems to be identical with the victory of Communism. But it is not by chance that its leaders have not retained the term 'Communism' in the name of the republic; and they have several times even given the words 'Federal Socialist Republic' the meaning of a **'republic struggling for Socialism'**. After four years of development, the Soviet republic has come up against the limit that constitutes its historic significance. This significance is the following: Russia is a rural country in which the working class has conquered power to hasten the development of the country towards Socialism. In this development it must as much take into account the petit-bourgeois nature of the country as well as the world relationship of forces. Depending on the development of the world revolution, it will realise its aims, or it will perish with them. The dominant position of the working class in Russia as regards the bourgeois tendencies and forces very much recalls the situation of the feudal elements in Russia as regards the bourgeois elements. Starting from the middle of the nineteenth century capitalist necessities and tendencies grew ever stronger in Russia. The feudal class made them economic concessions after economic concessions solely to maintain its political power. On the other hand, it knew how to delay political concessions for more than half a century. It was finally beaten because, under the pressure of the working class, it was forced to make political concessions to the bourgeoisie. The position of the working class as regards the bourgeoisie is naturally not comparable at all points with the position of the feudal elements. There exists in fact an essential difference: it is a question of the direction of the development of the entire world at the present time. Tsarism was forced to capitulate because world development was going in the direction of capitalism, in other words the victory of the bourgeoisie. The capitalist world is now in a state of increasing disintegration. The Russian bourgeoisie does not constitute a new, powerful class, sure of itself and dynamic, but a class atomised and broken, which is again supporting itself on the crutches offered it by the temporary strengthening of the bourgeois world after the overcoming of the demobilisation crisis of 1918-19. The new bourgeois elements in Russia, the peasants liberated from feudal yoke, would naturally form the basis for the reconstruction of a new and powerful bourgeoisie in Russia in the event of the international victory of capital. But in the event of the victory of the European proletariat, the Russian peasantry would be too weak to form a counter-revolutionary force opposed to the tendency of world development. This fundamental difference is decisive for passing judgement on the positions of so-called Marxists who assert, like Paul Levi,[71] that since economic relations are the decisive relations according to Marxist theory, Soviet Russia will be forced, after having made economic concessions to the bourgeoisie, to follow the road of development that leads to bourgeois democracy. This concept only shows that its author perhaps knows the ABC of Socialism, but that he is still ignorant of its grammar. **No Marxism can foresee at what rate economic conditions are transposed into political conditions.** If in the short run the decomposition of capitalism were to give way to decisive tendencies towards the re-establishment of capitalist domination, then the bourgeois pressure upon proletarian power in Russia would undoubtedly be strengthened from day to day, and the Soviet government would have the choice of two possibilities: either to go down fighting, or to transform itself into an instrument of bourgeois development. Whoever has not concluded from the events of these last three years that the capitalist social order will succeed in overcoming its forces of disintegration has no need to be of the opinion of our Marxist novice who thinks that economic concessions will involve political concessions.

The history of all revolutions in the capitalist era is the history of the struggle between capitalist and Socialist tendencies. The proletarian Socialist tendencies of the Levellers, the Diggers and the Millenarians in the English Revolution,[72] and of the Enragés in the French Revolution[73] were defeated by the bourgeois tendencies because capitalism was in the ascending phase of its development. The Russian Revolution is a part of the world proletarian revolution that is in the course of developing. Even if it is politically victorious, it can hardly fulfil the tasks of the world revolution, the transformation of capitalism into Socialism, because conditions are most unfavourable for it in Russia. In comparison with the programme of the historic period opened up by the uprising of 25 October 1917, the events of the Russian Revolution that have taken place up until now have only a very limited value. Basically, the Russian Revolution has only cleared the ground of the feudal classes and of feudal survivals. It has not been able to annihilate the bourgeoisie and bourgeois tendencies, for whilst capitalism dominates Europe these tendencies will feed off the peasant economy, and will be strengthened by the capitalist encirclement of Soviet Russia. The state power of the Russian working class is a means that allows capitalism to be methodically overcome. Isolated, Russia cannot overcome it. Only the victory of the world revolution in the industrialised countries will accelerate the development of this process. This will be a victory acquired not so much by means of Red Terror as by economic means.

Until the victory of the proletarian revolution in the industrialised countries, the duty of the Soviet republic is to maintain the power of the working class over this enormous country, so that it will not become a reservoir of human and material forces for the counter-revolution. If the Soviet republic only fulfils this negative task, it will have rendered an immense service to the world revolution. It will not allow world capitalism to suppress the growing revolutionary movements of the European proletariat with the bayonets of Russian peasants. If the Soviet government succeeds, through its realistic policy — which consists of recognising facts and taking account of realities — in strengthening Soviet Russia until it could play an active rôle in the struggles of the coming years, whether militarily, or by exporting food to the industrial countries in which the proletarian revolution had triumphed, then the question of the nature of the Russian revolution would be definitively solved. Until now the Russian Revolution was the first and therefore the most feeble link in the world Socialist upsurge. Its fusion with the powerful current of the world proletarian revolution would make the strengthening and development of Soviet Russia — as a power controlling the greatest agricultural base going in the direction of Socialism — **one of the main strategic tasks of the international proletariat.**

The opponents of the Russian proletarian revolution who deck themselves out in the plumage of Marxism, are exploiting the halt in the development of the world revolution and the New Economic Policy of the Soviet government, which is partly the result of the slow development of the world revolution, to undermine the confidence of the world proletariat and of the Russian proletariat itself; in fact they deny to the Russian Revolution its proletarian character, because it was not capable of gaining a victory over capitalism at one blow. They are recalling that they had envisaged for a long time that the Russian Revolution could only lead to the domination of the bourgeoisie, and that it would only be capable of overthrowing feudalism. But these representatives of the bourgeoisie in the revolution betrayed the Russian Revolution to forces which did not wish to liquidate feudalism. The Mensheviks, who supported the government of Prince Lvov[74] and prevented the peasants from liquidating big feudal land ownership, have no reason to boast about having immediately recognised the bourgeois limits of the revolution. They did not even dare to push the Russian Revolution to its bourgeois limits. The revolution has broken these limits and gone beyond them under the leadership of the Bolsheviks. It has taken the power from the bourgeoisie and has attempted to modify social relations in Russia thanks to this power. Each of its steps forward is an abomination to the enemies of the proletarian revolution. Each halt in its advance is hailed by them as collapse and bankruptcy. This does not trouble the revolutionary fighters. They know from the experience of their military struggles that a halt, or even a retreat, is often the precondition for a new victorious offensive.

Notes

1. Pamphlet published under the title *Wege der Russischen Revolution*, Verlag der Kommunistischen Internationale Auslieferungsstelle für Deutschland: Carl Hoym Nachf Louis Cahnbley, Hamburg, 1922.
2. GV Plekhanov, 'Socialism and the Political Struggle', *Selected Philosophical Works*, Volume 1, London, 1961, p119. Radek was wrong about the date of this work, which was in reality published in 1883.
3. *Iskra (Spark)* was the name of the paper of the Russian Social Democrats founded in 1900. The Economists were those members of the party who wanted to restrict its activity to supporting the economic struggle, and refrain from raising political demands.
4. The Party of the Socialist Revolutionaries (SRs), the main party of the Russian peasants led by Victor Chernov, was founded in 1901.
5. VI Lenin, 'Two Tactics of Social Democracy in the Democratic Revolution', *Collected Works*, Volume 9, Moscow, 1962, pp28-9.
6. Alexander Israel Parvus (Helphand, 1867-1924) was the first Marxist to apply the theory of the Permanent Revolution to the concrete conditions of Russia at the beginning of the twentieth century.
7. Karl Kautsky (1854-1938) was the main theoretician of German Social Democracy and of the Second International in the years before the First World War.
8. Rosa Luxemburg (1871-1919) was a leading theorist of German Marxism and leader of the Spartakusbund, and was killed during the German revolution.
9. The Congress of the Second International meeting in Amsterdam in August 1904 passed a resolution stating that Social Democrats 'cannot wish to take part in a government within the boundaries of bourgeois society'.
10. K Kautsky, 'Treibkräfte und Aussichten der russischen Revolution', *Neue Zeit*, twenty-fifth year, 1906-07, Volume 1, no 10, pp331-3.
11. K Kautsky, *Von der Demokratie zur staatssklaverei. Eine Auseinandersetzung mit Trotzki*, Freiheit, Berlin, 1921, p128.
12. Which came out in Moscow in 1919 in his pamphlet *Results and Prospects: On the Motor Forces of the Russian Revolution*, Sovjetski Mir editions. Cf *The Permanent Revolution*, New York, 1969, pp29-122.
13. LD Trotsky, *The Permanent Revolution*, pp69-70.
14. Op cit, pp101-2.
15. Op cit, p105.
16. Fyodor Andreyevich Cherevanin (Lipkin, 1868-1938) was a prominent Menshevik, and a member of his party's Central Committee in 1917.
17. Rosa Luxemburg, *The Mass Strike, the Political Party and the Trade Unions*, 1906.
18. Cf Dan's article 'Die Bedingungen des erneuten Aufschwungs des russischen Revolution', *Die Neue Zeit*, twenty-sixth year, Volume 2, no 27, 1 April 1908, pp4-10, and no 28, 3 April 1908, pp49-58.
19. Pyotr Bernhardovich Struve (1870-1944) was a prominent Russian economist who began as a Marxist and then moved over to the Cadets.
20. Karl Leutner (1869-1944) was a leading Austrian Social Democrat, and the editor of *Arbeiterzeitung*.
21. On 2 March 1917 (old style) Milyukov tried to get the Duma Committee and the Petrograd Soviet to accept the idea of a regency instead of a republic for the future government of Russia. His suggestion was firmly repudiated.
22. The Paris Commune was when the working class of Paris took over the running of the city in 1871 during the Franco-Prussian War.
23. Grigory Alexeyevich Alexinsky (1879-?) was an ex-Bolshevik who became a chauvinist during the First World War, and attempted to have Lenin tried as a German agent in 1917.
24. VI Lenin, 'The April Theses', *Collected Works*, Volume 24, Moscow, 1964, p24.

25. Lev Borisovich Kamenev (Rosenfeld, 1883-1936) was the main Bolshevik leader who opposed the overthrow of the Provisional Government in 1917. He was murdered by Stalin after the first Moscow Trial.
26. VI Lenin, 'Two Tactics of Social Democracy in the Democratic Revolution', *Collected Works*, Volume 9, Moscow, 1964, pp84-5; 'Letters on Tactics', *Collected Works*, Volume 24, p52.
27. VI Lenin, 'Letters on Tactics', *Collected Works*, Volume 24, p52.
28. VI Lenin, 'The Tasks of the Proletariat in Our Revolution', *Collected Works*, Volume 24, pp73-4.
29. Theobald Von Bethmann-Hollweg (1856-1936) was Prime Minister of Prussia and Chancellor of Germany, 1909-17.
30. Georgia was proclaimed an independent republic on 26 May 1919, with the Menshevik Noah Zhordania as its president. It was troubled by peasant uprisings, and gave passage to armies operating against the Bolsheviks during the Russian Civil War. It was reconquered by the Red Army in 1921.
31. K Kautsky, *Von der Demokratie zur staatssklaverei. Eine Auseinandersetzung mit Trotzki*, p16.
32. The Tenth Congress of the Communist Party meeting in March 1921 put an end to War Communism, and instituted the New Economic Policy.
33. After prolonged negotiations a treaty was signed between the Soviet republic and imperial Germany at Brest-Litovsk in Poland on 15 March 1918, by which the former dropped out of the First World War.
34. A left wing split from the German Social Democracy set up the Independent Social Democratic Party (USPD) in 1917 led by Haase, Kautsky and Ledebour. It later split, with the majority joining the Communist Party and the minority returning to the SPD in 1922.
35. During the German Revolution of November 1918 the USPD played a confused rôle, supporting both the workers' councils and the democratic republic.
36. Woodrow Wilson (1856-1924) was the liberal Democrat President of the USA who proposed a programme of 14 points as a basis for ending the First World War.
37. Georges Clemenceau (1841-1929) was Prime Minister of France during the First World War, and the main advocate of a war to the finish; David Lloyd George (1863-1945) was coalition Prime Minister of Great Britain for the second half of the war, and a supporter of the same policies.
38. Raymond Robins (1873-) was a member of the American intelligence service and the Red Cross mission in Russia.
39. This document figures in Radek's speech on the economic consequences of the Brest Peace published in the *Minutes of the First Congress of the Councils of the National Economy*. [Author's note]
40. Mieczyslaw G Bronsky (Varshavsky, 1882-1941) was Commissar for Trade and Industry in the first Soviet government.
41. Robert Hamilton Bruce Lockhart (1887-1970) was a journalist and British intelligence agent in Russia.
42. Otto Bauer (Heinrich Weber, 1881-1938) was one of Austrian Social Democracy's major theorists.
43. The first Soviet government was a coalition of the Bolsheviks and the Left SRs, who had split off from the rest of their party and had seven members in the Council of People's Commissars. But they went into opposition over the signing of the Treaty of Brest-Litovsk, and began terrorist activities against the government.
44. Admiral Alexander Vasilyevich Kolchak (1873-1920) led the White Guard attack upon the Soviet state from the Far East in the Russian Civil War; General Anton Ivanovich Denikin (1872-1947), Commander of the South-Western Front during the First World War, did the same in southern Russia and the Ukraine.
45. The Bolsheviks dissolved the Constituent Assembly in January 1918, since it did not accept the legality of the revolutionary government.
46. Arnold Struthan, 'Die Aussere und die innere Lage Sowjetrusslands', *Die Kommunistische Internationale*, 1919, no 3, pp9-27.
47. When the franc was finally stabilised by Poincaré in 1926, it was worth only a fifth of its prewar value.
48. *Programme of the Communist Party*, adopted at the close of the Eighth Congress of the Russian Communist Party (18-23 March 1919).
49. Arnold Struthan, 'Die Aussere und die innere Lage Sowjetrusslands', *Die Kommunistische Internationale*, 1919, no 3, pp9-27.
50. White Guard General Nikolai Nikolayevich Yudenich (1862-1933) attacked Petrograd during the Russian Civil War, backed by Britain.
51. VI Lenin, 'The Immediate Tasks of the Soviet Government', *Collected Works*, Volume 27, Moscow, 1964, p246.
52. VI Lenin, 'Resolution on the Attitude to the Middle Peasants', and 'The Middle Peasants', *Collected Works*, Volume 29, Moscow, 1964, pp217-20, 246-7.

53. VI Lenin, 'The New Economic Policy and the Tasks of the Political Education Departments', *Collected Works*, Volume 33, Moscow, 1964, pp62-4.
54. VI Lenin, 'Report on the New Economic Policy', *Collected Works*, Volume 33, Moscow, 1964, pp83-101.
55. The Japanese General Count Maresuke Nogi (1849-1912) attacked Port Arthur in August 1905 during the Russo-Japanese War.
56. Alfred, Graf Von Schlieffen (1833-1913) completed the famous Schlieffen Plan in 1905, which envisaged the solution to a two-front war with Russia and France with a knock-out blow delivered against France at the start of such a war, followed by a shift of the entire German army against Russia immediately afterwards.
57. VI Lenin, 'The Immediate Tasks of the Soviet Government', *Collected Works*, Volume 27, Moscow, 1964, p246.
58. Around 40 000 Czech soldiers, most of whom had been taken prisoner by the Russians during the First World War, were left stranded on the Trans-Siberian railway by the October Revolution. The Soviet government permitted them to leave the country via Vladivostok, but after a brawl with Hungarian prisoners of war led to them taking over Chelyabinsk on 14 May, it demanded that they be disarmed. The Czechs then staged a revolt, which led to the rapid collapse of Soviet rule along the Trans-Siberian Railway from the Volga eastwards, and permitted the establishment of an SR government in Samara, and the White regime in Siberia under Kolchak.
59. Claiming that they were protecting their supply dumps, the British army landed at Archangel in 1918 to assist the Whites in the Russian Civil War.
60. Pavlo Skoropadsky (1873-1945) and Semyon Petliura (1877-1926) were Ukrainian nationalists who opposed the Soviet government, the former in alliance with the Germans, and the latter with the Poles.
61. VI Lenin, 'The Immediate Tasks of the Soviet Government', *Collected Works*, Volume 27, Moscow, 1964, p254.
62. LD Trotsky, 'Work, Discipline and Order', 28 March 1918, *How The Revolution Armed*, Volume 1, London, 1979, pp28-48.
63. The Left Communist group first arose in the Bolshevik Party in protest at the signing of the Treaty of Brest Litovsk in March 1918. In addition to Bukharin and Radek, its leaders were Ossinsky (Valerian Obolensky, 1887-1938), Vladimir M Smirnov (1887-1937), Varvara N Yakovleva (1884-1944) and A Lomov (George I Oppokov, 1888-1937). Its platform, the *Theses of the Left Communists*, first appeared in *Kommunist* on 20 April 1918. An English translation was published by *Critique* in 1977. Cf RI Kowalski, *The Bolshevik Party in Conflict*, Pittsburgh, 1991.
64. Raphael Abramovich (Rhein, 1880-1963) was one of the main leaders of the Mensheviks in exile.
65. The sailors in the Kronstadt fleet base rebelled against the Soviet government in March 1921, and were suppressed at the cost of some bloodshed.
66. A trade agreement was signed by the Soviet and British governments on 21 March 1921. It covered more than just economic relations between the two states, with clauses prohibiting both governments from carrying out hostile propaganda and activities in each other's territories, the British Empire and independent countries that had been part of the Russian Empire.
67. Taking advantage of the Russian Civil War, the Poles advanced into the Ukraine in the spring of 1920, but their supply lines were over-extended, and the Russian army counter-attacked and invaded Poland. After the Russian defeat at the Battle of the Vistula, a peace treaty was signed at Riga in 1921. Coinciding with the Polish capture of Kiev, the White Guard Army of Baron Pyotr Wrangel (1878-1928) advanced from the south.
68. Apart from the nationalists, the south of the Ukraine was controlled by the Anarchist armies of Nestor Makhno for much of 1919-20; and there was a major peasant revolt against the Soviet government in Tambov in June 1920.
69. Kustari were cottage and small handicraft workmen producing in an amateurish fashion.
70. For the text of this proclamation, cf Sergei Mstislavskii, *Five Days Which Transformed Russia*, London, 1988, pp119-20.
71. Paul Levi (1883-1930) was the successor of Rosa Luxemburg as leader of the German Communist Party. He condemned the party's adventurism during the 'March Action' of 1921.
72. The Levellers, Diggers and Millenarians were radical sects thrown up by the ferment of the English Civil War.
73. The Enragés were radical revolutionaries led by Jacques Roux and Jean Varlet during the French Revolution.
74. Prince Georgi E Lvov (1861-1925) was a Cadet deputy and first Prime Minister of the Provisional Government.

Karl Radek

Lenin[1]

LIKE EVERYTHING else in nature, Lenin was born, has developed, has grown. When Vladimir Ilyich once observed me glancing through a collection of his articles written in 1903, which had just been published, a sly smile crossed his face, and he remarked with a laugh: 'It is very interesting to read what stupid fellows we were!' But I do not here intend to compare the shape of Lenin's skull at the age of 10, 20 or 30 with the skull of the man who presided over the sessions of the Central Committee of the party or the Council of People's Commissars. Our objective is not simply Lenin as leader, but as living human being. PB Axelrod, one of the fathers of Menshevism, who hates Lenin from the bottom of his soul, related, in one of the philippics[2] with which he sought to convince me of the harmfulness of Bolshevism in general and of Lenin in particular, how Lenin went abroad for the first time, and how he went walking and bathing with him. 'I felt at that time', said Axelrod, 'that here was a man who would become the leader of the Russian Revolution. Not only was he an educated Marxist — there were many of these — but he knew what he wanted to do and how it was to be done. There was something of the smell of Russian earth about him.' Pavel Borisovich Axelrod does not smell of the earth. He is one who reasons at home in his own study, and the whole tragedy of his life lies in the fact that at a time when there was no labour movement in Russia he thought out the lines upon which such a labour movement would develop, and when it developed along different lines he was frightfully offended — and today he roars with rage at the disobedient child. But people often observe in others that which is lacking in themselves, and Axelrod's words with regard to Lenin point out precisely those characteristics which make Lenin a leader.

It is impossible to be a leader of the working class without knowing the whole history of that class. The leaders of the labour movement must know the history of the labour movement; without this knowledge there can be no leader, just as nowadays there can be no great general who could be victorious with the least expenditure of force unless he knew the history of strategy. The history of strategy is not a collection of recipes on how to win a war, for a situation once described never repeats itself. But the mind of the general becomes practised in strategy by its express study; this study renders him elastic in war, and permits him to observe the dangers and possibilities which the merely empirically trained general cannot see. The history of the labour movement does not tell us what to do, but it makes it possible to compare our position with situations which have already been experienced by our class, so that in various decisive moments we are enabled to see our path clearly, and to recognise approaching danger.

But we cannot get to know the history of the labour movement properly without being thoroughly acquainted with the history of capitalism, and with its economic and political mechanism. Lenin knows the history of capitalism as do but few of Marx's pupils. It is no mere knowledge of the written word — here

Comrade Riazanov[3] could give him five points start — but he has thought out Marx's theory as no one else has done. Let us for instance take the small pamphlet which he wrote at the time of our conflict with the trade union movement; in it he calls Bukharin a Syndicalist, an eclectic and a great sinner in numerous other respects. This polemical pamphlet contains a few lines devoted to the differences between dialectics and eclectics, lines not cited in any collection of articles on historical materialism, but which say more about it than whole chapters from much longer books.[4] Lenin has independently grasped and thought out the theory of historical materialism as no one else has been able to do, for the reason that he has studied it with the same object in view as Marx had when elaborating the theory.

Lenin entered the movement as the embodiment of the **will to revolution**, and he studied Marxism, the evolution of capitalism, and the evolution of Socialism, from the point of view of their revolutionary significance. Plekhanov was a revolutionist too, but he was not possessed by the will to revolution, and despite his great importance as a teacher of the Russian revolution, he could only teach its algebra and not its arithmetic. Herein lies the point of transition from Lenin the theorist to Lenin the politician.

Lenin combined Marxism with general working class strategy, but at the same time he applied it correctly to the strategic task involving the fate of the Russian working class. It may be said that at the army staff academy he studied not only Clausewitz, Moltke[5] and their like, but he studied at the same time, as no one else in Russia, the territory of the future Russian proletarian war. Herein lies his genius — in his intimate contact with his field of activity.

I must take some other opportunity of debating why so great a mind as that of Rosa Luxemburg[6] was not capable of understanding the rightness of Lenin's principles on the origin of Bolshevism. I can only state the fact. Rosa Luxemburg did not grasp concretely the economic and political difference between the fighting conditions of the Russian proletariat and those of the proletariat of Western Europe. Therefore she inclined to Menshevism in 1904. Menshevism, regarded historically, was the policy of the petit-bourgeois intelligentsia, and of those strata of the proletariat most closely related to the petit-bourgeoisie. Russian Menshevism was an attempt at transferring the tactics of the West European labour movement to Russia. If we read an article by Axelrod or Martov on the need for the working class 'to learn to stand on its own feet', it appears exceedingly plausible to anyone who has grown up in the Western European movement. I remember very well that when I became acquainted with Russian Social Democratic polemics during the first revolution, but was not yet familiar with concrete Russian actuality, I could not comprehend how anybody could deny such elementary truths. Today it is historically proved that all the speeches delivered by the Mensheviks on the 'independence of the labour movement' were in reality only speeches on the necessity of the Russian labour movement subordinating itself to the Russian bourgeoisie.

Today, it is most interesting to read the controversy on the famous first paragraph of the party statutes, the paragraph which led to the split of the Social Democratic Party into Bolsheviks and Mensheviks.[7] At that time Lenin's demand that only the members of illegal organisations were to be counted as party members appeared highly sectarian. But what was the real point in question? Lenin sought to prevent the confused ideas of certain intellectuals from determining the policy of the labour party. Before the first revolution any malcontent of a physician or lawyer who happened to have read Marx styled himself a Social Democrat, though at bottom he was only a liberal. Even when they entered an illegal organisation, even when they had broken with their petit-bourgeois way of living, history shows many intellectuals to have remained liberals at the bottom of their souls. But the limitation of membership in the party to such persons as were willing to face the dangers of belonging to an illegal organisation had undoubtedly the advantage of lessening the danger of bourgeois ascendancy in the labour party, and permitted the revolutionary working class spirit to dominate the party organisations, however much filled with intellectual elements. But in order to be able to grasp this, in order to be even prepared to split the party on this account, it was necessary to be as closely bound up with Russian realities as was Lenin, in his capacity as Russian Marxist and Russian revolutionist...

Lenin's **way** of knowing Russian actuality is another point in which he differs from all others who have aspired towards leadership over the Russian proletariat. Not only does he **know** Russian actuality, he sees and feels it as well. At every turning point in the history of the party, and especially at the moment when we seized power and the fate of 150 million people hung on the decisions of the party, I have been amazed at Lenin's store of what the English call 'common sense'. It may be remarked that when we are speaking of a man of whom we are convinced that his like will not recur for a century, it is but a poor compliment to praise his common sense. But it is just in this that his greatness as a politician lies. When Lenin has to decide on an important question he does not think of abstract historical categories, of ground rents, surplus values, absolutism or liberalism. He thinks of Sobokavich, of Gessen, of Sydor from Tver province, of the Putilov worker, of the policeman on the street, and of the effect of the measures on the muzhik Sydor and on the workman Onufria as bearers of the revolution.

I shall never forget my talk with Ilyich before the conclusion of the Brest-Litovsk peace. Every argument which we brought up against the conclusion of the Treaty rebounded from him like peas from a wall. He employed the simplest argument: A war cannot be conducted by a party of good revolutionists, who, having seized their own bourgeoisie by the throat, is as yet incapable of finishing affairs with the German bourgeoisie. 'The muzhik must carry on the war', was the reply. 'But don't you see that the muzhik voted against the war?', Lenin asked me. 'Excuse me, when and how did he vote against it?' 'He voted with his feet, he is running away from the front.' And for him that settled the matter... It was necessary that the muzhik should touch with his hands the earth which the revolution had given him; it was necessary that he be confronted with the danger of losing this earth, and then he would defend it...

Lenin never permits himself to be blinded to reality by any preconceived formula; and he has the courage to throw yesterday's formula overboard as soon as it disturbs his grasp of this reality. Before our seizure of power we issued, as revolutionary internationalists, the slogan of the people's peace against the governments' peace.[8] And suddenly we found ourselves in the position of a workers' government, surrounded by peoples who had not yet succeeded in overthrowing their capitalist governments. 'How can we conclude a peace with the Hohenzollern government?', was the question put by many comrades. Lenin answered mischievously:

'You are worse than hens. A hen cannot make up its mind to step over a circle drawn around it with chalk, but it can at least justify itself on the ground that the circle was drawn by a strange hand. But we have drawn up our formula with our own hands, and now you see formula only, and not the reality. Our formula of peace to be concluded by the peoples had for its object the awakening of the masses against the military and capitalist government. Now you want us to go to ruin, and to let the capitalist governments carry off the victory, in the name of our revolutionary formula.'

His genius contains another trait. After he has set himself a certain goal, he seeks for the means leading to this goal through reality. He is not content with having fixed his aim, he thinks out **concretely** and completely everything necessary for the attainment of that aim. He does not merely work out a plan of campaign, but the whole organisation of the campaign at the same time... In Lenin's personality the great politician and the great political organiser are combined.

How all this happened to be combined in one man, God only knows (Comrade Stepanov and the Commission for Combating Religion will kindly excuse).[9] History has her own apparatus for distilling brandy, and no Cheka can detect her.[10] The German bourgeoisie could not manage to unite Germany, and somewhere, on a small landed estate grange, history set one of her machines in action, and with the aid of God or the devil, that is, by molecular work, she created **Bismarck**, who then fulfilled the task. If we read his first reports, if we follow his policy step by step, we are obliged to ask ourselves how it was possible for a landowner to possess such an understanding of the whole of European actuality.

The same thought arises every time we think over the history of our party, the history of revolution, and Ilyich. For 15 years we looked on whilst this man was fighting over every comma in the resolutions, against every **ism** invented during the last 25 years, from **Khvostism** to **Empiriocriticism**.[11] For Lenin every such **ism** has been the embodiment of some real enemy, existing either in other classes or in the working class, but in any case in reality. These **isms** were the symbols of reality, and he absorbed the whole of this reality into himself, studied it, thought it out, until the 'underground man' proved himself the most earthly man of Russian reality. History offers no second example of such a transition from subterranean revolutionist to statesman. This combination of the characteristics of theorist, politician, and organiser has made Lenin the leader of the Russian Revolution. And that he should be the only one universally recognised as such the 'human touch' was required — the quality which has made Lenin the beloved hero of the Russian Revolution...

For many people the truth is deadly; it is deadly even for many classes. If the bourgeoisie were to grasp the truth about itself, and were permeated with this truth, it would be defeated already, for who can go on fighting when the truth of history tells him that he is not only condemned to death, but that his corpse will be thrown into the sewer? The bourgeoisie is blind and dumb to its fate. But a revolutionary class needs the truth, for truth is the knowledge of reality... Lenin tells the proletariat the truth and the truth only, however depressing it may be. When workers hear him speaking, they know there is not a single empty phrase in all his speech. He tells us to inform ourselves on reality. At one time I was living at Davos with a Bolshevik workman dying of consumption. At that time the right of self-determination of nationalities was being debated, and we Polish

Communists were opposed to Lenin's views.[12] The comrade of whom I speak, after having read my theses against Lenin, said: 'What you have written is perfectly convincing to me; but whenever I have been opposed to Ilyich it has always turned out afterwards that I was wrong.' This is how the leading party functionaries think, and this is the reason for Lenin's authority in the party.

But the workers do not think so. They do not feel bound to Lenin because he has been in the right, a thousand times, but because, whenever he has been in the wrong, whenever a mistake has been committed under his leadership, he has always admitted openly: 'We have made a mistake, and therefore we have been defeated here; this mistake must be made good in such and such a manner.' Many have asked him why he speaks so openly of mistakes made. I do not know why Lenin does it, but the results of this course of action may be plainly seen. The workman is much too enlightened to believe in redeeming saviours any longer. When Lenin speaks of his mistakes he hides nothing, he leads the worker into his own laboratory of thought, he makes it possible for the worker to take part in forming the final decision, and the workers see in him the leader who represents their laboratory, the embodiment of their class struggle. A great class, itself needing absolute truth, loves with its whole heart a leader who is himself a truth-loving human being, one who tells the truth about himself. From such a leader the worker can bear any truth, even the hardest. Human beings have faith in themselves only when they conceal nothing, when they know everything about themselves, even the most unfavourable possibilities, and yet feel that they can say: 'In spite of everything...' Lenin helps the working class to a full knowledge of every decaying and decomposing element of its own existence, and yet enables it to say in the end: 'I am His Majesty the Proletariat, the future ruler and creator of life.' This is another factor in Lenin's greatness.

On the twenty-fifth anniversary of the party which not only bears the responsibility for the destiny of one sixth of the globe but which is at the same time the main lever of proletarian victory, the Russian Communists and all revolutionists amongst the proletariats of every country are filled with the thought and the wish that this Moses, who has led the slaves from the land of bondage, may pass with us into the promised land.

Notes

1. This text is reproduced from *The Plebs*, Volume 16, no 2, February 1924, pp52-8. It first appeared in *New Russia* some months earlier. It differs in some particulars from the version that appeared in *Inprecorr* for 22 March 1923, which was reprinted in *International Socialist Review*, Volume 34, no 10, November 1973, pp29-33.
2. Philippics is the general term applied to the speeches of the Athenian orator Demosthenes, which failed to galvanise the resistance of the Greeks to their conquest by Philip II of Macedon (359-336BC).
3. David Riazanov (Goldendakh, 1870-1938) was by common consent Russia's leading authority on the work of Marx and Engels. Cf *Karl Marx and Friedrich Engels*, New York, 1973, and the symposium edited by him, *Karl Marx: Man, Thinker and Revolutionist*, London, 1927.
4. VI Lenin, 'Once Again on the Trade Unions, the Current Situation and the Mistakes of Trotsky and Bukharin', 25 January 1921, *Collected Works*, Volume 32, Moscow, 1965, pp70-107. The section on dialectics is on pp90-5.
5. Karl Von Clausewitz (1780-1831) was a Prussian general famous for his three-volume treatise on the theory of war; Field Marshal Helmuth Karl Bernhard, Count Von Moltke (1800-1891) was the Prussian general responsible for victory in the battles that defeated France and Austria and united Germany.

6. Rosa Luxemburg, *Leninism or Marxism?*, London, 1973, originally published as an article in *Die Neue Zeit*, Volume 22, pp484-92, 529-35, Stuttgart, 1904. Radek here considerably misrepresents her views, for Rosa Luxemburg had a low opinion of his honesty.
7. Cf *1903: Second Ordinary Congress of the RSDLP: Complete Text of the Minutes*, London, 1978, pp311ff.
8. VI Lenin, 'Appeal to the Soldiers of All the Belligerent Countries', 4 May (21 April) 1917, *Collected Works*, Volume 24, Moscow, 1964, pp186-8.
9. Ivan Ivanovich Skvortsov-Stepanov (1870-1928) was an Old Bolshevik who sided with the Left Communists in 1918, and then with Stalin and Bukharin in the 1920s. A key figure in Soviet publishing, he wrote books on the theory of scientific atheism.
10. The Cheka (Extraordinary Commission for Struggle Against Sabotage and Counter-Revolution) was the Soviet state security service set up in December 1917.
11. Khvostism means tail-ending, trailing behind the masses, from the Russian word for a tail. Empiriocriticism was the name given by the Swiss thinker Richard Avenarius to his philosophical theories, combated in Lenin's book of 1908 *Materialism and Empiriocriticism* (*Collected Works*, Volume 14, Moscow, 1962, pp17-361).
12. Radek supported the view put forward by Rosa Luxemburg in her article 'The National Question and Autonomy' (R Luxemburg, *The National Question*, New York, 1976, pp101-287), denying that it was necessary for the working class to support movements for national self-determination. Lenin answered these arguments in 'On the Right of Nations to Self-Determination', February-May 1914, *Collected Works*, Volume 20, Moscow, 1964, pp393-454.

Book Two

Nikolai Bukharin, Lev Kamenev and Leon Trotsky

The State and Revolution

The aim of this section is to focus more narrowly upon the events of 1917-18 in Russia itself, to examine how the revolutionaries understood the state they destroyed, the new state they erected, and the mechanism by which they replaced the one with the other.

Although the structure of the Tsarist state more closely resembled an Asiatic empire than European feudalism, capitalism enjoyed a hothouse growth there during the last quarter of the nineteenth century. Much of it was due to foreign investment, often in association with the state itself, and developed spectacularly in the extractive industries, inhibiting the growth of a virile native capitalist class. Huge factories coexisted with petty commodity production and a backward peasant agriculture, making the development of a healthy domestic market almost an impossibility. Great strains were placed on a society just awakening from the sickening effects of a centuries-long sleep. The interaction of the old and the new can be gauged from the fact that in 1905 it took a failed workers' revolution for the Tsar to grant a feudal estates system, the Duma, such as Western Europe had discarded at the end of the Middle Ages.

The Tsarist state, an autocracy under a weak-willed Emperor, Nicholas II, could ill afford the foreign policy adventures by which it hoped to canalise domestic discontent. A disastrous war in the Far East with Japan in 1904-06 cost it defeat on land and sea, along with its port on the Liaotung peninsula and the control of the South Manchurian extension of the Trans-Siberian Railway. Domestic discontent united all the politically active sections of society after troops fired upon a peaceful demonstration petitioning the Tsar outside the Winter Palace in January 1905. Soviets appeared to organise the general strike that followed, and Trotsky emerged as a major figure in them for the first time. Since the peasantry as a whole failed to move, the army remained loyal to the regime, and at a critical moment the bourgeoisie abandoned its opposition to the autocracy. With some difficulty, the situation was brought back under control.

The warning of 1905 was wasted on Tsarism. Relations worsened with

Austria in the Balkans after Aehrenthal annexed Bosnia and Herzegovina, and Russia increased its pan-Slav propaganda and aid to Serbian nationalism, finally involving itself in a world war with the superpowers in 1914-18. After three years she had lost Poland, much of the Baltic littoral and the Ukraine, and 10 million men. Increasing anarchy within ruling circles led to the murder of Rasputin, who had presided grotesquely over all this mess. A demonstration of the capital's women workers in February 1917 showed that the regime could no longer rely upon the army to suppress its opponents, and the Tsar fell from power with practically no one to support him, or even to regret his passing.

In this political vacuum two meetings took place in different wings of the Tauride Palace. A committee of the Duma set up a Provisional Government under Prince Georgi Lvov to run the country until an All-Russian Constituent Assembly could come together to decide upon Russia's future form of government. At the same time a group of Menshevik and Socialist Revolutionary leaders proclaimed themselves to be the Executive Committee of the Petrograd Soviet, and called the soviets into existence beneath them in order to keep a suspicious working class and soldiery obedient to the Provisional Government. Once awakened from above, the soviets took on fresh life, and a weary period of 'dual power' followed for several months, in which one government, the official one, only ruled on the sufferance of the other (potential) government, the soviets.

When the soviets first reappeared, the Bolsheviks were a tiny minority within them, and in any case Stalin and Kamenev had pressurised their reluctant St Petersburg Committee to support the Provisional Government, whilst negotiations had begun for a healing of the split between the Bolsheviks and Mensheviks. Lenin's return to Russia armed with the *April Theses* had the impact of a bombshell. The Bolsheviks finally gained a majority in the soviets by demanding that the Menshevik and SR leaders break their links with the Provisional Government and take the power into their own hands. In the summer the Bolsheviks had taken on new strength when they were joined by the Inter-District Organisation led by Trotsky, whom they re-elected President of the Petrograd Soviet when they had gained their majority in it following the failure of the Kornilov coup. The Revolutionary Military Committee under Trotsky's direction brought the experience of 'dual authority' to an end by the seizure of power in the capital in October/November 1917. For a brief period its shadow returned with the election of the Constituent Assembly, which was dissolved by the Bolshevik authorities after meeting for a day.

Trotsky will need no introduction to anyone with a nodding acquaintance with Russian history, but perhaps a few words are not out of place here about the writers of the other essays we include, his brother-in-law, Lev Kamenev, and his chief rival up to the final triumph of Stalin, Nikolai Bukharin.

Lev Kamenev (Rosenfeld, 1883-1936) joined the RSDLP in 1901, met Lenin in exile, and went over to the Bolsheviks. He returned to Russia and took over the editorship of *Pravda*, as well as the leadership of the Bolshevik fraction in the Duma, with whom he was arrested at the outbreak of war in 1914 and deported to Siberia. His contribution to the 1917 revolution was a disastrous one. On his return from exile in March along with Stalin, he was responsible for changing the policy of the St Petersburg Committee of the Bolsheviks from suspicion towards the Provisional Government into support for it, and along with Zinoviev he opposed the actual seizure of power in October/November. He was closely associated with Zinoviev throughout the revolution, and they formed something of a team. Zinoviev was a flamboyant speaker, but Kamenev was of a retiring character, and was often assigned administrative tasks of a humdrum and day-to-day nature, which he invariably performed conscientiously. In 1920 he was sent to negotiate a commercial treaty in Britain, but was expelled by Lloyd George, allegedly for using Russian money to finance and influence *The Daily Herald*. From 1923 on he formed part of the ruling Troika along with Zinoviev and Stalin, which was set up to oppose Trotsky, but broke with Stalin in 1925 to lead with Zinoviev the Left/Centre (Leningrad) Opposition. They formed a joint bloc with the Left (Trotskyist) Opposition until 1928, when the Leningraders capitulated to Stalin. Kamenev was shot along with Zinoviev after the Trial of the Sixteen in August 1936.

Nikolai Bukharin (1888-1938) was the foremost theoretician of the Bolsheviks after Lenin himself, being the writer of *The Economic Theory of the Leisure Class* (1914), *Imperialism and the World Economy* (1915), *Historical Materialism* (1920), *The Economics of the Transition Period* (1920) and (with Evgeni Preobrazhensky) *The ABC of Communism* (1918). Like Trotsky, he was in New York at the outbreak of the February/March revolution. Along with Radek, he was leader of the Left Communists who opposed the signing of the Treaty of Brest-Litovsk in 1918, but later drifted over to the right, where he became Stalin's chief theoretician and the most fervent supporter of the New Economic Policy. After Stalin deposed Zinoviev in 1926 he became President of the Communist International, in which capacity he wrote the famous *Draft Programme* (1928) which attracted Trotsky's devastating criticism. But when the crisis of 1927-28 obliged Stalin to bring the NEP to an end, Bukharin and the other supporters of the Right (Moscow) Opposition led by him were removed from their positions. His drafting of the Stalin Constitution of 1936, 'the most democratic in the world', failed to prevent him from being the main defendant in the last of the Moscow trials, the Trial of the Twenty-One, in March 1938.

The articles by Bukharin and Kamenev allow us to examine how the Bolsheviks analysed the experiences of 1917, both before and after the seizure of power, and drew general lessons from them for the struggle of the working class in the rest of the world. Bukharin shows how the Russian bourgeoisie in February/March carried off the spoils of a revolution in which they had played no part, but that the further economic progress of Russia could only take place at the cost of their overthrow. Kamenev insists that the emergency measures of the proletarian dictatorship in Russia came about as a direct result of the resistance of the old possessing classes, and were in no sense part of a conspiracy to set up a totalitarian state. A successful workers' revolution, he argues, will almost certainly meet with even more determined resistance in countries where the bourgeois order is more deeply rooted and has more staying power, and working class rule will have to deal very firmly with them.

The first of Trotsky's contributions deals with the peculiar phenomenon known as 'dual power', whose reappearance in the course of many upheavals since (Britain in 1926, France and Spain in 1936, Greece in 1945, etc) shows it to be a recognised symptom of a deep-going revolutionary crisis and opportunity. He shows how society can only endure such a tension of authority for a comparatively short time before one power triumphs over the other. His essay on the dissolution of the Constituent Assembly confirms the fact that bourgeois democracy was not an option at all in Russia in 1917-18, where a Constituent Assembly dominated by the Right SRs would only hand back the power to a regime of the Kerensky type, which would itself in turn be only an interlude before the advent of a military dictatorship.

Nikolai Bukharin

The Russian Revolution and Its Significance[1]

THE FIRST Russian revolution of 1905 was the expression of a gigantic conflict between the growing forces of production on the one hand, and reactionary industrial and political conditions in Russia on the other. A rapidly growing capitalism demanded the freedom of the inner market, the failure of the Russo-Japanese War having made the extension of foreign markets impossible. But the home market was equally unresponsive. The predominating element amongst the Russian people is its peasantry, whose demands and whose buying power represented the basis for all further capitalistic development. They were equal, it is true, but equal in misery. A pauperised, not a proletarian nation of farmers, peasants who remained on their farms, did not go into the cities, and paid enormous sums for their little rent farms to the semi-feudal gentry landlords. Nobility landlordism on the one hand, hungry pauper tenantry on the other — such were the conditions in the agrarian sections of Russia. Capitalistic farm production had taken root only on the extreme outskirts of the nation, in the Baltic provinces and in southern Russia. But its extent was comparatively unimportant.

So the objective 'purpose' of the revolution was the creation of a home market, and the abolition of unbearable political conditions. The downfall of the revolution meant only the postponement of the great social catastrophe, and the possibility of a higher ultimate stage of development.

Nevertheless, the proletarian blood that flowed in 1905 was by no means shed in vain.[2] The old autocracy gave place to a new pseudo-constitutional regime, presenting a certain (though very limited) opportunity to conduct the broader work of revolutionary education among the proletariat.

But even from a purely economic point of view, the first revolution had consequences that are not unimportant. It was followed by fundamental changes in the national industrial structure, and by a consequent readjustment of class relations.

The large landlords, terrorised by the revolting farmers, sold their possessions, either directly to their tenants or through the agency of so-called 'farmers' banks' (Krestyansky Bank), the government institution that, as a rule, functioned as the business agency of the nobility. In this way, a small part of the possessions of the great landed nobility passed into the hands of the wealthier farmers. By his so-called agrarian reform programme, Stolypin, the Tsarist minister, dissolved the old 'Mir' (peasant communities), and divided the community lands in such a way that the best portions everywhere fell into the hands of a thin stratum of agricultural bourgeoisie. The result was a visible strengthening of this new class, whose members organised everywhere on a cooperative basis.

But the status of the great landholders, too, had changed. The modern capitalist wing grew stronger, a phenomenon that may be attributed mainly to altered conditions in the world market. The prices of wheat and rye were advancing almost hourly. It became more profitable to produce by modern capitalistic methods; the old primitive system went into discard. So agrarian capitalism gained a firm foothold in Russia.

All these changes kept step with the changes that were taking place on the industrial field. 'Our' industries before the revolution had been rather peculiarly constituted. 'We' had, on the one side, a primitive system of fragmentary, disorganised, small-scale production, on the other, gigantic undertakings which frequently employed 15 000 to 20 000 labourers and employees. After the revolution the concentration of capital advanced in leaps and bounds. In the era of the counter-revolution, mighty manufacturers' associations, employers' associations, trusts, syndicates and combinations, banking houses and banking corporations came into existence. In Russia today, monopolisation in a few branches of industry is very large indeed; so, for instance, the sugar, the metal, the naphtha, the textile and the coal mining industries are in the hands of a few syndicates. Thus there grew up in Russia the mighty power of the united bourgeois organisations, the power of financial capital, interested mainly in export and trade.

The revolution did not create a home market, it is true. This but increased the profit hunger of 'our' financiers. Protected by outrageous protective tariffs that enabled them to sell comparatively cheaply in the world market, the Russian capitalist began to sell his wares in Persia, in the Balkans, in Asia Minor, etc, and even in the Far East. Bank operations were augmented, state loans to China, Persia, etc, arranged; transactions that were diametrically opposed to the interests of English, French and German capital were on the order of the day.

The first revolution itself, as we have seen, resulted in no radical upheaval. But the greatest economic phenomenon of the counter-revolutionary period is the growth of **financial** capitalism and its policy of expansion, or **imperialism**.

Two classes were emerging out of the social chaos; the liberal bourgeoisie, which gradually developed into an imperialistic bourgeoisie, and the proletariat. During the first Russian revolution, the specific characteristics of the revolution were already quite evident, although the objective content of the revolution was wholly in harmony with capitalism. The demands made by the masses were characteristically bourgeois, and purely democratic and republican in their nature; even the economic reforms were compatible with the interests of capitalism — as, for instance, the eight-hour day, the confiscation of land, and others. But though the revolution of 1905 was the **bourgeois-democratic** revolution of Russia, the motive power behind this upheaval was by no means the liberal bourgeoisie, but the proletariat, and the revolutionary peasantry who fought in the struggle under the control of the proletariat. This seeming contradiction may be explained by the fact that the Russian revolution came too late, and came in an epoch in which the proletariat had already become a mighty factor in social struggles. So our liberalism was condemned to a vacillating position, between the revolution and Tsarism, a policy that finally resulted in the betrayal of the whole revolution. In the most critical period of the revolution, the liberals were already completely counter-revolutionary.

The outbreak of the war[3] almost completely levelled the Russian movement. It was the signal for an outbreak in the ranks of the bourgeoisie (including its liberal as well as its radical elements) of an indescribable patriotic fervour. The policy of conquest carried on by the nobility and the landowners was in accord with the thieving plans of the group which controlled the high finance of the nation. Mr Milyukov had long been singing the praises of the bloody policy of the Tsar's government in Persia and in the Balkan states. Thus the Russian civil peace was born, though a large part of the proletariat was actively and unalterably opposed to it.

But the calculations of the new liberal class were, after all, at fault. The Tsarist administration, in spite of the most energetic support of the liberals, proved ineffectual on every hand. Corruption, systematic thievery, and complete disorganisation of the whole administrative apparatus became more and more apparent. The needs of warfare had practically ruined the rickety economic organism of the Russian national economy. Instead of increasing the production of foodstuffs, the territory under cultivation was reduced. The strength of the whole nation was drawn off from productive labour, and a shortage in a number of important articles of consumption followed.

Chaos reigned in the finances of the state. Securities for enormous war loans and the payment of interest, staggering sums necessary to pay for all kinds of war manufactures — all these the Tsarist government attempted to cover by a promiscuous printing of paper money. This course was followed, naturally, by a steady depreciation in the value of paper money, until it was worth hardly 50 per cent of its face value. This meant an unbearable increase in the cost of living. High prices, in Russia, during the war, were caused, therefore, not only by actual shortage of supplies, not only by monopoly speculations, but also, to no small degree, by the ruinous financial policy of the government.

At the same time the collapse of the whole transportation augmented the general calamity by bringing about a complete disorganisation of the home market. For lack of means of transportation, the sale of products was limited to countless small markets in the immediate locality in which they were produced.

Increased taxes were another consequence of the war; all attempts to tax the wealthier classes as well were pushed back upon the shoulders of the proletariat and the peasantry by means of increased prices, intensified labour and the overthrow of the miserable Russian 'labour laws'.

Upon this 'economic foundation' was built up a corresponding 'political superstructure'.

The central administration, civil as well as military, was in the hands of Rasputin,[4] the Tsar and their followers, the clique of slovenly, religious, superstitious degenerate idiots and court thieves, who had always looked upon the Russian nation as their family property. The local administration was everywhere in the hands of autocratic governors, who ruled their territories like the satraps of the Ancient Orient.[5]

The story of a session of the magistracy of Moscow, in which a serious discussion as to the size of the bribe necessary to persuade the railroad officials to secure the transportation of Siberian meat to Moscow was the order of business, shows to what lengths corruption had gone.

'Civil peace' in Russia, as in all other countries, was rather peculiar. It meant, in effect, a system of gagging and oppression such as Russia had not known since the failure of the first revolution. The labour press was suspended, labour unions dissolved, and striking workers were sent to the front, thrown into prison, or summarily shot. In Ivanovo-Voznesensk alone more than 100 workers were killed.[6]

The proletariat and the peasantry were segregated on the battlefields, and were mechanically slaughtered. That Russia has been able to hold out against the Central Powers so long is due alone to its almost inexhaustible reservoir of cannon fodder.

These circumstances, which proved that the Tsarist regime was unable to realise even its own plans of usurpation, not to mention those of its liberal supporters, called forth the opposition of the liberal imperialists. The downtrodden and suffering proletariat cast its lot under the banner of civil war, assisted by large groups amongst the peasantry.

The liberal bourgeoisie (the Cadets and Octobrists) and with them the social-patriots, who are but their subservient vassals, were organised mainly in the Zemstva and in municipal units. They flirted with the Grand Duke Nicholas, with their democratic allies, and with the ruling circles within the army. In the Duma the so-called 'Progressive Bloc'[7] was formed as the parliamentary expression of the imperialistic bourgeoisie.

Their opposition was, as a matter of fact, rather innocent. They stood by the maxim: 'No infraction of the law.' In the words of Mr Milyukov: 'If victory means revolution, I want no victory.'

Not so the proletarian masses. In spite of the 'pacifying' manifesto of a few social-patriotic traitors, the proletarian vanguard developed an intense revolutionary activity. Street demonstrations, strikes, the general strike and revolts of workers and military groups that fraternised with them were the methods used in the struggle. These mass actions paved the way for the final overthrow of the Tsarist regime. The first wave of the second revolution shattered the Russian throne.

The first step in the revolution has been taken; the social structure of the state machine has been changed, a new class has come into power. The old, semi-feudal, noble, landowning class is overthrown. In its place stand the new rulers, the modern, capitalist bourgeoisie.

But the second step will inevitably follow: the transformation of the fatherland of the Guchkovs-Milyukovs into the fatherland of the proletariat.

How did it happen that the **imperialists** won the victory, although they were anything but revolutionary? The answer is plain. Everything points to a compromise between the ruling classes. The revolution was not yet strong enough to overthrow the capitalist system; it has only effected a shifting of the elements within the bourgeoisie as a whole, and has placed the more progressive wing at the helm, by pushing aside the reactionary nobility.

But the revolution is steadily growing. Even now, whilst these lines are being written, there exist in Petrograd two governments; one, that of the imperialist bourgeoisie, which was jubilantly greeted by the bourgeois classes of the other allied nations; the other, the governmental machine of the proletariat, the workingmen's and soldiers' council.

The struggle between the working class and the imperialists is inevitable. Even the reforms that have been proclaimed by the Provisional Government were concessions made out of fear of the threats of the proletariat. But the liberal government will not be in a position to fulfil the programme that has been forced upon it. The high cost of all necessaries of life and the growing burden of taxation can be decreased to a measurable degree only by liquidation of the war, by confiscation, by the annulment of state debts, by taxation of the possessing classes, by fixing hours of labour and wages, by organising public works, etc.

But Milyukov and his class must pay the debts they have incurred to the English, the French and the American bankers. They must defend the principle of private property, and must continue the policy of usurpation, a policy that is suicidal at the present stage of complete disorganisation. So the new government is staggering toward bankruptcy, to clear the way for the proletariat.

But the conquest of political power by the proletariat will, under the existing circumstances, no longer mean a bourgeois revolution, in which the proletariat plays the rôle of the broom of history. The proletariat must henceforth lay a dictatorial hand upon production, and that is the beginning of the end of the capitalist system.

A lasting victory of the Russian proletariat is, however, inconceivable without the support of the West European proletariat. And this support is fully guaranteed by the present international situation. To be sure, the Russian revolution has its specific abnormalities. But it is, as a product of the World War, only a part of the coming world revolution of the proletariat, whose first step it represents.

Wars and revolutions are the locomotives of history, one of our Socialist teachers once said. And the present war was destined to produce the revolution. The ruin of all national economy and with it the greatest conceivable concentration of capital; the formation of gigantic units of production; the adoption of state capitalism; the advance of great masses upon the scene of history — and the unbearable sufferings of these masses; the oppression of the people — and its armament — all of these conflicts must find their solution in a gigantic catastrophe.

More than 100 years ago, when the French bourgeoisie had cut off the head of its king, it lighted the torch of revolution in Europe. This was the signal for a whole series of capitalist revolutions. Today the bourgeoisie stands at its grave. It has become the citadel of reaction. And the proletariat has come to destroy its social order.

The call to arms of this great upheaval is the Russian revolution. Well may the ruling classes tremble before a Communist revolution. The proletariat has nothing to lose but its chains; it has a world to win.

Notes

1. Article printed in *The Class Struggle*, Volume 1, no 1, May-June 1917, pp14-21. We are greatly indebted to Sebastian Budgen for providing us with a copy of this text.
2. The 1905 revolution began with the massacre of a peaceful workers' demonstration on Bloody Sunday, 9 January 1905, and ended in barricade fighting in Moscow at the end of the year.
3. Bukharin is referring to the outbreak of the First World War in 1914.
4. Gregory Efimovich Rasputin (Novykh, 1864-1916) was a dissolute monk whose personal ascendancy over the Tsarina Alexandra gave him an enormous influence in the government until his assassination during the First World War.
5. Satraps were governors with full military and civil powers in the provinces of the ancient Persian empire, which they ruled on behalf of the Great King.
6. In the summer of 1916 the starving workers of Ivanovo-Voznesensk demonstrated in the streets, and were fired on by the Tsarist authorities.
7. The Progressive Bloc was an alliance of the Cadet, Octobrist and Progressive parties in the Duma in August 1915 to oppose the conduct of the war by the Tsar's ministers.

Leon Trotsky

The State in Russia, Old and New: The Farce of Dual Authority[1]

THE WAR conditions are twisting and obscuring the action of the internal forces of the revolution. But, nonetheless, the course of the revolution will be determined by these same internal forces, namely, the classes.

The revolution, which had been gathering strength from 1912 on, was, at first, broken off by the war, and later, owing to the heroic intervention by an exasperated army, was quickened into an unprecedented aggressiveness. The power of resistance on the part of the old regime had been once and for all undermined by the progress of the war. The political parties who might have taken up the function of mediators between the monarchy and the people suddenly found themselves hanging in the air, owing to powerful blows from below, and were obliged at the last moment to accomplish the dangerous leap to the secure shores of the revolution. This imparted to the revolution the outward appearance for a time of complete national harmony. For the first time in its entire history, the bourgeois liberalism felt itself 'bound up' with the masses — and it is this that must have given them the idea of utilising the 'universal' revolutionary spirit in the service of the war.

The conditions, the aims, the participants of the war did not change. Guchkov and Milyukov, the most outspoken of the imperialists on the political staff of the old regime, were now the managers of the destinies of revolutionary Russia. Naturally, the war, the fundamental character of which remained the same as it had been under Tsarism — against the same enemies, with the same allies, and the same international obligations — now had to be transformed into a 'war for the revolution'. For the capitalist classes, this task was equivalent to a mobilisation of the revolution, and of the powers and passions it had stimulated, in the interests of imperialism. The Milyukovs magnanimously consented to call the 'red rag' a sacred emblem — if only the working masses would show their readiness to die with ecstasy under this red rag for Constantinople and the Straits.

But the imperialistic cloven hoof of Milyukov was sticking out too plainly. In order to win over the awakened masses and guide their revolutionary energy into the channel of an offensive on the external front, more intricate methods were required — but chiefly, different political parties were needed, with platforms that had not yet been compromised, and reputations that had not yet been sullied.

They were found. In the years of counter-revolution, and particularly in the period of the latest industrial boom, capital had subjected to itself, and had mentally tamed, many thousands of revolutionists of 1905, being in no wise concerned about their labourite or Marxist 'notions'. And amongst the 'Socialistic' intelligentsia there were therefore rather numerous groups whose palms were itching to take part in the checking of the class struggle, and the training of the masses for 'patriotic' ends. Hand in hand with this intelligentsia, which had been brought into prominence in the counter-revolutionary epoch, went the compromise-workers, who had been frightened definitely and finally by the failure of the 1905 revolution, and had since then developed in themselves the sole talent of being agreeable to all sides.

The opposition of the bourgeois classes to Tsarism — upon an imperialistic foundation, however — had, even before the revolution, provided the necessary basis for a **rapprochement** between the opportunist Socialists and the propertied classes. In the Duma, Kerensky and Chkeidze built up their policy as an annexe to the 'Progressive Bloc', and the Gvozdyevs[2] and Bogdanovs[3] merged with the Guchkovs on the War Industry Committees. But the existence of Tsarism made an open advocacy of the 'government-patriotism' standpoint very difficult. The revolution cleared away all the obstacles of this nature. Capitulating to the capitalist parties was now called 'a democratic unity', and the discipline of the bourgeois state suddenly became 'revolutionary discipline', and, finally, participation in a capitalist war was looked upon as a defence of the revolution from external defeat.

This nationalistic intelligentsia, which Struve had prognosticated, invoked and trained in his paper *Vekhi*,[4] suddenly met with an unexpectedly generous support in the helplessness of the most backward masses of the people, who had been forcibly organised as an army.

It was only because the revolution broke out in the course of a war that the petit-bourgeois elements of city and country at once automatically took on the appearance of an organised force, and began to exert themselves upon the personnel of the Soviets of Workers' and Soldiers' Delegates, which won an influence which would have been far beyond the powers of these scattered and backward classes in any but war times. The Menshevist-Populist intelligentsia found in this great number of backwoods, provincial, for the most as yet hardly awakened persons, a support that was at first entirely natural. By leading the petit-bourgeois classes onto the path of an agreement with capitalist liberalism, which had again beautifully demonstrated its inability independently to guide the masses of the people, the Menshevist-Populist intelligentsia, through the pressure of these masses, acquired a certain position even amongst the proletarian sections, which had been momentarily relegated to a secondary position by the numerical impressiveness of the army.

It might have first seemed that all class contradictions had been destroyed, that all social fixtures had been patched up with fragments of a Populist-Menshevist ideology, and that, thanks to the constructive labours of Kerensky, Chkeidze and Dan, a national **burgfrieden** had been realised. Therefore, the unparalleled wonderment when an independent proletarian policy again asserted itself, and therefore the savage — in truth disgusting — wail against the revolutionary Socialists, the destroyers of the universal harmony.

The petit-bourgeois intelligentsia, after it had been raised by the formation of the Soviet of Workers' and Soldiers' Delegates to heights for which it was itself entirely unprepared, was frightened more by the idea of responsibility than by anything else, and therefore respectfully handed over their power to the capitalist-feudal government which had issued forth from the womb of the Duma on 3

June.[5] The organic terror of the petit-bourgeois in the presence of the sanctity of state power, which was perfectly transparent in the case of the Populists (labourites), was veiled in the case of the Menshevik-patriots by doctrinaire notions of the inadmissibility of having Socialists assume the burden of power in a bourgeois revolution.

Thus there came about the 'dual authority', which might with much more truth be termed a **Dual Impotence**. The capitalist bourgeoisie assumed authority in the name of order and of a war for victory; yet, without the Soviet of Deputies, it could not rule; the latter's relation to the government was that of an awed half-confidence, combined with a fear lest the revolutionary proletariat, in some unguarded gesture, might upset the whole business.

The cynically provocative foreign policy of Milyukov brought forth a crisis. Being aware of the full extent of the panic in the ranks of the petit-bourgeois leaders when confronted with problems of power, the bourgeois party began availing itself, in this domain, of downright blackmail; by threatening a government strike, that is, to resign any participation in authority, they demanded that the Soviet furnish them with a number of decoy Socialists, whose function in the coalition ministry was to be the general strengthening of the confidence in the government on the part of the masses, and, in this way, the cessation of 'dual authority'.

Before the pistol-point of ultimatum, the Menshevist patriots hastened to slough off their last vestiges of Marxist prejudice against participation in a bourgeois government, and brought on to the same path the 'labourite' leaders of the Soviet, who were not embarrassed by any supercargo of principle or prejudice. This was most manifest in the person of Chernov, who came back from Zimmerwald and Kienthal,[6] where he had excommunicated Vandervelde, Guesde, and Sembat[7] out of Socialism — only to enter the ministry of Prince Lvov and Shingarev.[8] To be sure, the Russian Menshevik patriots did point out that Russian ministerialism had nothing in common with French and Belgian ministerialism, being an outgrowth of very exceptional circumstances, as had been foreseen in the Amsterdam resolution. Yet they were merely repeating, in parrot fashion, the argumentation of French and Belgian ministerialism, whilst they continued constantly to invoke the 'exceptional nature of the circumstances'. Kerensky, under whose long-winded theatricality there is, nevertheless, some trace of reality, very appropriately classed the Russian ministerialism under the same category as that of Western Europe, and stated, in his Helsingfors speech,[9] that thanks chiefly to him, Kerensky, the Russian Socialists had in two months travelled a distance that it had taken the Western Socialists 10 years to accomplish. Truly Marx was not wrong when he called revolution the locomotive of history!

The coalition government had been sentenced by history before it was established. If it had been formed immediately after the downfall of Tsarism, as an expression of the 'revolutionary unity of the nation', it might possibly have held in check, for a time, the external struggle of the forces of the revolution. But the first government was the Guchkov-Milyukov government. It was permitted to exist only long enough to expose the full falsity of 'national unity', and to awaken the revolutionary resistance of the proletariat against the bourgeois propaganda to prostitute the revolution in the interests of imperialism. The obviously makeshift coalition ministry could not, under these circumstances, stave off a calamity, it was itself destined to become the chief bone of contention, the chief source of schism and divergence in the ranks of 'revolutionary democracy'. Its political existence — for of its 'activities' we shall not speak — is simply one long dissolution, decently enveloped in vast quantities of words.

To contend against a complete breakdown on the economic and particularly on the food-question side, the Economic Department of the Executive Committee of the Soviet of Workers' and Soldiers' Delegates worked out a plan for an extensive system of state management in the most important branches of industry. The members of the Economic Department differ from the political managers of the Soviet not so much in their political tendencies as in a serious acquaintance with the economic situation of the country. For this very reason they were led to conclusions of a profoundly revolutionary character. The only thing their structure lacks is the driving force of a revolutionary policy. The government, for the most part capitalistic, could not possibly give birth to a system that was diametrically opposed to the selfish interests of the propertied classes. If Skobelev,[10] the Minister of Labour, did not understand this, with his now proverbial '100 per cent' talk, it was fully understood by the serious and efficient Konovalov,[11] the representative of trade and industry.

His resignation was an irreparable blow to the coalition ministry. The whole bourgeois press gave unmistakable expression to this fact. And again began the exploitation of the panic terror of the present leaders of the Soviet: the bourgeoisie threatened to lay the babe of authority at their door. The 'leaders' answered by making believe that nothing special had happened. If the responsible representative of capital has left us, let us invite Mr Buryshkin. But Buryshkin ostentatiously refused to have anything to do with surgical operations on private property. And then began the search for an 'independent' Minister of Commerce and Industry, a man behind whom there stood nothing and nobody, and who might serve as an inoffensive letter-box, in which the opposing demands of labour and capital might meet. Meanwhile, the economic expenses continued on their course, and the government activity assumed the form, chiefly, of the printing of **assignats**.[12]

Having as his senior colleagues Messrs Lvov and Shingarev, it turned out that Chernov was prevented from revealing, in the domain of agrarian matters, even the radicalism in words only, which is so characteristic of this typical representative of the petit-bourgeoisie. Fully aware of the rôle that was assigned to him, Chernov introduced himself to society as the representative, not of the agrarian revolution, but of agrarian statistics! According to the liberal bourgeois interpretation, which the Socialist ministers also made their own, revolution must be suspended amongst the masses in a passive waiting upon the convocation of the Constituent Assembly, and as soon as the Socialist Revolutionaries enter the ministry of the landholders and manufacturers, the attacks of the peasants against the feudal agricultural system are designated by the term anarchy.

In the field of international policy, the collapse of the 'peace programmes' proclaimed by the coalition government came about more swiftly and more catastrophically than could possibly be expected. M Ribot,[13] the premier of France, not only categorically and unceremoniously rejected the Russian peace formula and pompously reiterated the absolute necessity of continuing the war until a 'complete victory' should be gained, but also denied the patriotic French Socialists their passports to the Stockholm conference,[14] which had been arranged with the cooperation of M Ribot's colleagues and allies, the Russian Socialist ministers. The Italian government, whose policy of colonial conquest has always been distinguished by exceptional shamelessness, by a 'Holy Egotism', replied to the formula of 'a peace without annexations' with the separate annexation of Albania.[15] Our government, and that includes the Socialist ministers, held up for two weeks the publication of the answers of its allies, evidently trusting in the efficacy of such petty devices to stave off the bankruptcy of their policy. In short, the question as to the international situation of Russia, that is, **the question of what it is that the Russian soldier should be ready to fight and die for**, is still just as acute as on the day when the portfolio of Minister for Foreign Affairs was dashed from the hands of Milyukov.

In the Army and Navy Department, which is still eating up the lion's share of the national powers and of the national resources, the policy of prose and rhetoric holds undisputed sway. The material and psychological causes for the patent condition of the army are too deep to be disposed of by ministerial poetry and prose. The substitution of General Brusilov for General Alexeyev[16] meant a change of these two officers, no doubt, but not a change in the army. The working up of the popular mind, and of the army, into an 'offensive', and then the sudden dropping of this catchword in favour of the less definite catchword of 'preparation for an offensive', show that the Army and Navy Ministry is as little capable of leading the nation to victory as Mr Tereshchenko's department was of leading the nation to peace.

This picture of the impotence of the Provisional Government reaches its climax in the labours of the Ministry for Home Affairs, which, to use the words of the most loyal Society of Peasants' Delegates, 'with partiality' filled the offices of the local administrations with the feudal landowners. The efforts of the active portion of the population to gain for them the communal self-governments, by right of conquest, and without waiting for the Constituent Assembly, are immediately designated in the state-police jargon of the Dans, by the term **anarchy**, and are greeted with the energetic opposition of the government which, by its very composition, is fully protected against all energetic action when it is really of a creative character.

In the course of the last few days, this policy of general bankruptcy has found its most repulsive expression in the Kronstadt incident.[17] The vile and out-and-out corrupt campaign of the bourgeois press against Kronstadt, which is for them the symbol of revolutionary internationalism and of distrust in the government coalition, both of which are emblems of the independent policy of the great masses of the people, not only took possession of the government and of the Socialist leaders, but turned Tsereteli and Skobelev into ringleaders in the disgusting persecutions of the Kronstadt sailors, soldiers and workers.

At a moment when revolutionary internationalism was systematically displacing patriotic Socialism in the factories and workshops and amongst the soldiers at the front, the Socialists in the ministry, obedient to their masters, were risking the hazardous game of overthrowing the revolutionary proletarian vanguard with one single blow, and thus preparing the 'psychological moment' for the session of the Pan-Russian Congress of Soviets. **To rally the peasant-petit-bourgeois democracy around the banner of bourgeois liberalism**, that ally and captive of Anglo-French and American capital, **politically to isolate and 'discipline' the proletariat**, that is now the principal task, in the realisation of which the government bloc of Mensheviks and Socialist Revolutionaries is expending all its energies. An essential part of this policy is found in the shameless threats of bloody repressions and the provocations of open violence.

The death-struggle of the coalition ministry began on the day of its birth. Revolutionary Socialism must do everything in its power to prevent this death-struggle from terminating in the convulsion of civil war. The only way to do this is not by a policy of yielding and dodging, which merely whets the appetite of the fresh-baked statesmen, but rather a policy of aggressive action all along the line. We must not permit them to isolate themselves: we must isolate them. We must answer the wretched and contemptible actions of the coalition government by making clear even to the most backward amongst the labouring masses the full meaning of this hostile alliance which masquerades publicly in the name of the revolution. To the methods of the propertied classes and of their Menshevik-Socialist-Revolutionary appendage in dealing with the questions of food, of industry, of agriculture, of war, we must oppose the methods of the proletariat. Only in this way can liberalism be isolated, and a leading influence on the urban and rural masses be assured to the revolutionary proletariat. Together with the inevitable downfall of the present government will come the downfall of the present leaders of the Soviet of Workers' and Soldiers' Delegates. To preserve the authority of the Soviet as a representative of the revolution, and to secure for it a continuance of its functions as a directive power, is now within the power only of the present minority of the Soviet. This will become clearer every day. The epoch of Dual Impotence, with the government not able and the Soviet not daring, is ineluctably culminating in a crisis of unheard-of severity. It is our part to husband our energies for this moment, so that the question of authority may be met with in all its size.

Notes

1. Reprinted from 'The State in Russia, Old and New: The Farce of Dual Authority', in *The Class Struggle*, Volume 2, no 2, March-April 1918, pp213-21. We are greatly indebted to Sebastian Budgen for a copy of this unusual text.
2. Kuzma Antonovich Gvozdev (1883-) was Minister of Labour in the Provisional Government.
3. BO Bogdanov (Oleynich, 1884-) began his political career as a Bolshevik, but later moved to the Mensheviks, and was a prominent member of the Executive Committee of the First All-Russian Congress of Soviets.
4. *Vekhi* was a journal published in 1909 by Pyotr Struve, Nikolai Berdyaev, Sergei Bulgakov and other former 'legal Marxists' who had moved to an idealist and elitist standpoint in the aftermath of the 1905 revolution. Considering that resistance to the Tsarist authorities was impossible, and that the masses were not capable of sensible political activity, its contributors called upon all oppositionists to come to a rapprochement with the Tsar, in order to encourage him to adopt democratising reforms.
5. The All-Russian Congress of Soviets meeting on 3 June 1917 was dominated by the Mensheviks and Socialist Revolutionaries, who continued to support the Provisional Government.
6. Chernov had signed the Zimmerwald anti-war declaration on 5 September 1915 and supported the follow-up conference at Kienthal on 24 April 1916, but later became a defencist.
7. Emile Vandervelde (1866-1838) was a leader of the Belgian Socialist Party and a member of the cabinet during the First World War. Jules Basile Guesde (1845-1922) had been a left wing Socialist before the war, but during it he supported the 'Sacred Union' and joined the French cabinet. Marcel Sembat (1862-1922), a well-known spokesman for the Socialist Party in the French chamber, was a social-chauvinist, and joined the cabinet as Minister for Public Works during the war.
8. Andrei Ivanovich Shingarev (1869-1918), a Cadet member of the Duma, was Minister of Agriculture in Prince Lvov's government, and Finance Minister under Kerensky.
9. Helsingfors was the old name for Helsinki, the capital of Finland. Kerensky spoke there shortly after becoming Minister of War in May 1917.

10. Matvei Ivanovich Skobelev (1885-1935), a leading Menshevik, was Minister of Labour in the Provisional Government. Because of the extent of the crisis he came up with the proposal to tax the possessing classes 'up to 100 per cent of their profits', apparently oblivious of the fact that this would mean expropriating them, something that could only be accomplished by a workers' revolution. Cf VI Lenin, 'Inevitable Catastrophe and Extravagant Promises', *Pravda*, 16 and 17 May (29 and 30 May) 1917, *Collected Works*, Volume 24, Moscow, 1964, pp424-30.
11. Aleksandr Ivanovich Konovalov (1875-1948), a member of the Cadet party, was Minister for Trade and Industry in the Provisional Government, and later Vice-Premier under Kerensky.
12. Assignats were government bonds first issued during the French revolution. They were intended to raise money to pay for war expenditure.
13. Alexandre-Félix Ribot (1842-1923) was Prime Minister of France in 1917.
14. A conference planned to be held in Stockholm on 18 May 1917 was intended to follow up the anti-war conferences of Zimmerwald and Kienthal. In the event it never took place.
15. The Secret Treaty of London of 26 April 1915 gave Italy 'special rights' in Albania.
16. General Mikhail Vasilievich Alexeyev (1857-1918) was Commander-in-Chief of the Russian army from February to May 1917.
17. On 27 May 1917 the Petrograd Soviet on the insistence of Tsereteli passed a resolution condemning the Kronstadt Soviet for 'anarchy' for refusing to accept the authority of the Provisional Government.

Leon Trotsky

The Principles of Democracy and Proletarian Dictatorship[1]

As MARXISTS, we have never been idol-worshippers of formal democracy. In a society of classes, democratic institutions not only do not eliminate class struggle, but also give to class interests an utterly imperfect expression. The propertied classes always have at their disposal tens and hundreds of means for falsifying, subverting and violating the will of the toilers. And democratic institutions become a still less perfect medium for the expression of the class struggle under revolutionary circumstances. Marx called revolutions 'the locomotives of history'. Owing to the open and direct struggle for power, the working people acquire much political experience in a short time, and pass rapidly from one stage to the next in their development. The ponderous machinery of democratic institutions lags behind this evolution all the more, the bigger the country and the less perfect its technical apparatus.

The majority in the Constituent Assembly proved to be Socialist Revolutionaries, and, according to parliamentary rules of procedure, the control of the government belonged to them. But the party of the Right Socialist Revolutionaries had a chance to acquire control during the entire pre-October period of the revolution. Yet, they avoided the responsibilities of government, leaving the lion's share of it to the liberal bourgeoisie. By this very course, the Right Socialist Revolutionaries lost the last vestiges of their influence with the revolutionary elements by the time the numerical composition of the Constituent Assembly formally obliged them to form a government. The working class, as well as the Red Guards, were very hostile to the party of the Right Socialist Revolutionaries. The vast majority of soldiers supported the Bolsheviks. The revolutionary element in the provinces divided their sympathies between the Left Socialist Revolutionaries and the Bolsheviks. The sailors, who had played such an important rôle in revolutionary events, were almost unanimously on our side. The Right Socialist Revolutionaries, moreover, had to leave the soviets, which in October — that is, before the convocation of the Constituent Assembly — had taken the government into their own hands. On whom, then, could a ministry formed by the Constituent Assembly's majority depend for support? It would be backed by the upper classes in the provinces, the intellectuals, the government officials, and temporarily by the bourgeoisie on the right. But such a government would lack all the material means of administration. At such a political centre as Petrograd, it would encounter irresistible opposition from the very start. If under these circumstances the soviets, submitting to the formal logic of democratic conventions, had turned the government over to the party of Kerensky and Chernov, such a government, compromised and debilitated as it was, would only introduce temporary confusion into the political life of the country, and would be overthrown by a new uprising in a few weeks. The soviets decided to reduce this belated historical experiment to its lowest terms, and dissolved the Constituent Assembly the very first day it met.

For this, our party has been most severely censured. The dispersal of the Constituent Assembly has also created a decidedly unfavourable impression among the leading circles of the European Socialist parties. Kautsky has explained, in a series of articles written with his characteristic pedantry, the interrelation existing between the social-revolutionary problems of the proletariat and the regime of political democracy.[2] He tries to prove that for the working class it is always expedient, in the long run, to preserve the essential elements of the democratic order. This is, of course, true as a general rule. But Kautsky has reduced this historical truth to professorial banality. If, in the final analysis, it is to the advantage of the proletariat to introduce its class struggle, and even its dictatorship, through the channels of democratic institutions, it does not at all follow that history always affords it the opportunity for attaining this happy consummation. There is nothing in the Marxist theory to warrant the deduction that history always creates such conditions as are most 'favourable' to the proletariat.

It is difficult to tell now how the course of the revolution would have run if the Constituent Assembly had been convoked in its second or third month. It is quite probable that the then dominant Socialist Revolutionary and Menshevik parties would have compromised themselves, together with the Constituent Assembly, in the eyes of not only the more active elements supporting the soviets, but also of the more backward democratic masses, who might have been attached, through their expectations, not to the side of the soviets, but to that of the Constituent Assembly. Under such circumstances the dissolution of the Constituent Assembly might have led to new elections, in which the party of the left could have secured a majority. But the course of events has been different. The elections for the Constituent Assembly occurred in the ninth month of the revolution. By that time the class struggle had assumed such intensity that it broke the formal frames of democracy by sheer internal force.

The proletariat drew the army and the peasantry after it. These classes were in a state of direct and bitter war with the Right Socialist Revolutionaries. This party, owing to the clumsy electoral democratic machinery, received a majority in the Constituent Assembly, reflecting the pre-October epoch of the revolution. The result was a contradiction which was absolutely irreducible within the limits of formal democracy. And only political pedants who do not take into account the revolutionary logic of class relations, can, in the face of the post-October situation, deliver futile lectures to the proletariat on the benefits and advantages of democracy for the cause of the class struggle.

The question was put by history far more concretely and sharply. The Constituent Assembly, owing to the character of its majority, was bound to turn over the government to the Chernov-Kerensky-Tsereteli group. Could this group have guided the destinies of the revolution? Could it have found support in that class which constitutes the backbone of the revolution? No. The real kernel of the class revolution has come into irreconcilable conflict with its democratic shell. By this situation the fate of the Constituent Assembly has been sealed. Its dissolution became the only possible surgical remedy for the contradiction, which had been created, not by us, but by all the preceding course of events.

Notes

1. Reprinted from *The Class Struggle*, Volume 3, no 1, February 1919, pp88-91. We offer our thanks to Sebastian Budgen for providing us with a copy of this piece.
2. Cf Karl Kautsky, *The Dictatorship of the Proletariat*, Ann Arbor, 1971.

Lev Kamenev

The Dictatorship of the Proletariat[1]

CONSERVATISM IN ideology, theories based on principles, slowness in their adaptation to rapidly-changing life, their constant lagging behind the constantly changing forms of the struggle, have frequently been noted by Marxists. In our struggle for Communism, we constantly meet with these facts, we constantly have to remark how great is the power of the old ideology even over the best men of the present labour movement — insofar as these men have grown up in the atmosphere of prewar Europe.

This mental conservatism is most strikingly observed in their approach to the question of dictatorship. Six years of war and revolution (1914-20), it would seem, should have elucidated this finally, from all points of view, by practice, by facts out of the everyday life of the masses; and yet, even among the comrades adhering to the Third International, we are often confronted with the question: 'What is the dictatorship of the proletariat?... Cannot the labour movement obtain its object without a dictatorship?... Why is dictatorship inevitable?' I have heard these questions not only from the members of the British trade union delegation,[2] but even from some of the members of the delegation of Italian Socialists.[3] When one hears such questions one thinks involuntarily that the persons uttering them must have slept through a whole historical period, and, first of all, through the World War of 1914-18. For these years constituted a model epoch of dictatorship; and the methods of carrying on the war were models of the application of dictatorial methods of ruling a country.

From the point of view of the government of a country, the imperialist war consisted in the assembling and placing under a single command of millions of men, in providing their equipment and transport, and compelling these many millions of men to carry out certain tasks. These tasks were foreign to these millions, and were accompanied for each of them separately, and for all together, with incredible sufferings, privations, and the risk of death. How did the governments of Europe, America and Asia accomplish the task? By what methods did they guarantee the assembling, equipment, transportation and command of these millions? By what methods did they secure the adaptation of the whole administrative, economic and social life of the state to carry out the tasks set by the government? Was this achieved by means of democracy? By means of parliamentarism? By means of the realisation of the sovereignty of the 'people'?

The sovereignty of the people, democracy, the state, parliamentarism, even from the point of view of their hypocritical bourgeois defenders, cannot but mean the discussion and decision, if only of the most important questions, of the state and social life by the citizens themselves, 'free' and 'equal' in the eyes of the law.

However, at present, even the most unenlightened peasant, in the most backward of all countries drawn into the war, knows that the government of his country in 1914-18 was, as a whole and in every detail, a clear, simple, elementary refutation of all these regulations of bourgeois democracy. Democracy, parliaments, elections, freedom of the press, remained — insofar as they did remain — a mere screen; in reality all the countries drawn into the war — the whole world — were governed by the methods of a dictatorship, which utilised, when it happened to be convenient and profitable, elections, parliaments and the press.

One must be a blind fool or a conscious deceiver of the masses not to see, or to conceal, this fundamental fact: at the most critical period of their history, at the moment of their struggle for existence, the bourgeois states of Europe, Asia and America defended themselves not by means of democracy and parliamentarism, but by openly passing over to the methods of dictatorship.

It was the dictatorship of the general staffs, of the officers' corps, and of large industry, to whom belonged, not only actually, but also formally, all power both in the army and in the country; who commanded, not only lives, but also the property of the whole country and of every citizen, not only living at the time but yet to be born (the military debts of Messrs Romanov, Hohenzollern, Clemenceau and Lloyd George will cover the lives and work of future generations).

During several years, before the eyes of the whole human race, a picture of the practice of dictatorship is unrolled — a dictatorship ruling over the whole world, determining everything, regulating everything, penetrating everything, and confirming its existence by 20 million corpses on the fields of Europe and Asia. It is natural, therefore, that to the question, 'What is dictatorship?', the Communists should answer:

'Open your eyes, and you will see before you a splendidly elaborated system of bourgeois dictatorship, which has achieved its object: for it has given that concentration of power into the hands of a small group of world imperialists which allowed them to **conduct their war and attain their peace** (of Versailles).[4] Do not pretend that dictatorship — as a system of government, as a form of power — can frighten anyone except the old women of bourgeois pacifism. The dictatorship of the proletariat suppresses, not 'equality', 'liberty' and 'democracy', but only the bourgeois dictatorship, which in 1914-18 showed itself to be the most bloody, most tyrannical, most pitiless, cynical and hypocritical of all forms of power that ever existed.'

The theorists of Communism, beginning with Karl Marx, proved, however, a long while ago that the dictatorship of the proletariat does not consist in replacing the bourgeoisie by the proletariat at the same governmental machine. The task of the dictatorship of the proletariat is to **break up** the machinery of government created by the bourgeoisie, and to replace it by a new one, created on a different basis and reposing on a new correlation of the classes.[5]

The dictatorship of the proletariat appears in the programmes of the Socialist parties not later than the seventies of the nineteenth century. However, during the whole period of the Second International,[6] it did not once, on any occasion, become the practical duty of the day, and attracted the attention neither of the practical workers nor of the theoreticians of the labour movement; and only when in 1914-18, through the veil of democracy, parliamentarism and political liberty, the unmistakable features of the bourgeois dictatorship became clearly discernible, did the idea of the dictatorship of the proletariat become a real force. It became a force because, as Marx says, it took possession of the proletarian masses.[7]

In the 1903 programme of the Russian Social Democratic Labour Party — a programme which aspired to be only a precise and improved statement of the programmes of the Social Democratic parties already in existence, and which at the time, in 1903, united both the Bolsheviks and the Mensheviks — the idea of the dictatorship of the proletariat was expressed as follows: 'A necessary condition for this social revolution is the dictatorship of the proletariat, that is, conquest by the proletariat of such political power as will enable it to suppress any resistance by the exploiters.'[8] This definition is embodied without alteration in the programme of the Russian Communist Party.

The authors of the 1903 programme could not foresee the actual circumstances in which the proletariat of any country would have to take the power into its hands. They certainly did not attempt at the time to define in what measure the dictatorship of the proletariat would be connected with the formation of a proletarian (Red) army, with the practice of terror, with the limitation of political liberties. They had to underline, and they did underline, not these changeable elements — varying in the various countries — of the proletarian dictatorship, but its fundamental and unchanging feature, inevitable for any country and any historical conditions under which the proletariat seizes power.

The proletariat not only seizes power; in grasping it, the proletariat gives to it such a character, such a degree of concentration, energy, determination, absoluteness, infinitude, as according to the words of the programme, 'will allow it to crush all resistance on the part of the exploiters'. That is the fundamental feature of the dictatorship of the proletariat.

The dictatorship of the proletariat is therefore an organisation of the state and a form of the administration of state affairs which, in the transitional stage from capitalism to Communism, will allow the proletariat, as the ruling class, to crush all resistance on the part of the exploiters to the work of Socialist reconstruction.

It is thus clear that the question itself of the necessity, the inevitability of a proletarian dictatorship for every capitalist country is connected with the question as to whether the resistance of the exploiters to their expropriation by Socialist society — or, more precisely, by society marching towards Socialism — is inevitable.

In the same way, the question regarding the degree of severity of the dictatorship, the extent and conditions of the limitation of the political rights of the bourgeoisie and limitation of political liberty in general, the application of terrorist methods, etc, is indissolubly linked with the question of the degree, forms, stubbornness and organisation of resistance by the exploiters.

Anyone who expresses a doubt as to the inevitability of the dictatorship of the proletariat as a necessary stage towards Socialist society, thereby expresses a doubt of the bourgeoisie showing any resistance to the proletariat at the decisive hour of the expropriation of the exploiters.

Propaganda based on this may be dictated by individual stupidity, or the interest of a group of persons in concealing from the proletariat the circumstances of the forthcoming struggle, and in preventing it from preparing for the same.

When persons calling themselves Socialists declare that the course of dictatorship, admissible and explicable for Russia, is in no wise obligatory or inevitable for any other capitalist country, they proclaim a thing directly contrary to truth. The actual Russian bourgeoisie always was — and up to the October Revolution remained — the least organised, the least conscious in the sense of class, the least united of all bourgeois classes in the countries of the old capitalist order. The Russian peasantry had not time enough to develop that class of strong and politically united peasants, which is the basis of a series of bourgeois parties in the West. The Russian middle class of the towns, crushed and politically unenlightened, never represented anything like such groups of the population which in the West create and support the parties of 'Christian Socialism' and anti-Semitism.

The first thunder claps of the proletarian revolution broke over this politically backward, inactive and unorganised class. 'The resistance of the exploiters' to the blows of the Russian proletariat must therefore be considered as comparatively weak — weak, naturally only in comparison with the activity which the bourgeoisie of any other European country will be able to develop. The actively resisting elements, which dragged on the struggle for three years, were not the unorganised forces of the Russian bourgeoisie, but, first of all, foreign interventionists, and then the bourgeoisies of the border countries (Finland, Lithuania, Poland, the Ukraine),[9] which, playing upon the centuries-old hatred against Tsarist Russia, managed to unite under the flag of nationalism certain organised groups for resistance against the Russian proletariat. If it were not for these external circumstances, the resistance of the Russian bourgeoisie would have been broken, not in three years, but in three months, and the proletarian apparatus of state power would naturally have directed all its energy towards other ends.

In conformity with the nature of the resistance which was to be expected from the Russian propertied classes and their organisations, the dictatorship of the proletariat in Russia had its period of 'rosy illusions' and 'sentimental youth'.

There can be nothing more mistaken than to assume that the Russian proletariat, or even its leader, the Communist Party, came into power with recipes, prepared in advance, of practical measures for the realisation of the dictatorship. Only 'Socialist' ignoramuses, or charlatans, could suggest that the Russian Communists came into power with a prepared plan for a standing army, Extraordinary Commissions,[10] and limitations of political liberty, to which the Russian proletariat was obliged to resort for self-defence after bitter experience. The cause of the proletariat was saved because it soon profited by its acquired experience, and, with unfailing energy, applied these methods of struggle when it became convinced of their inevitability.

The transference of power to the soviets, and the formation of the new Workers' and Peasants' Government, took place on 7 November 1917. The discomfiture and disorganisation of the bourgeoisie was so great that it was unable to muster any serious forces against the workmen. The resistance of the government of Kerensky was broken after a few days. The elections to the Constituent Assembly still continued. All the political parties — up to Milyukov's party — continued to exist openly. All the bourgeois newspapers continued to circulate. Capital punishment was abolished. The army was being demobilised. In the hands of the government there were no other forces than the volunteer detachments of armed workmen. The ministers of Kerensky's government, arrested during the first days (the leaders of the Socialist Revolutionary Party, Avksentiev, Gotz, Zenzinov, the Generals Boldyrev, Krasnov and others[11] — later on, all of them, leaders of the armed struggle against the Soviet power and members of the rebel governments of Siberia, the Don and the South),[12] were set free. Generals Denikin, Markov,[13] Erdeli and others remained in the hands of the Soviet power up to 20 November, and left its limits alive.

Yes, that was the period of 'rosy illusions'. It continued for a few months.

The conditions began to change by April-May 1918. In April 1918 the decree regarding the formation of a standing Red Army was published. Only in April the Extraordinary Commissions acquired the right to execute robbers caught in the act and officers going off to Kornilov,[14] according to his secret mobilisation. Only on 18 June did the Revolutionary Court pass its first sentence of death on the admiral commanding the Baltic Fleet.[15] Only in May were measures taken to stop the publication of the bourgeois papers (at the moment of this suppression there were 30 papers against three of the soviets in Moscow alone). Only in June 1918 were the Mensheviks driven out of the soviets.

Thus over six months (November 1917 to April-May 1918) passed from the moment of the formation of the Soviet power to the practical application by the proletariat of any harsh dictatorial measures. The increased severity in the dictatorship was called forth by a series of very elementary facts. In April the government of Skoropadsky was organised in Kiev; in May took place the rising of the Czechoslovaks, their seizure of the railway system, and the formation of the Socialist Revolutionary government in the East; in May, too, the Cossack counter-revolution on the Don — the Russian Vendée[16] — acquired increasing importance under the command of General Krasnov.

Parallel with this, all the attention and energy of the working class was concentrated on the tasks of the war; and the Soviet state was transformed into a camp of armed proletarians.

Such was the experience of the Russian proletariat. We have now before us the experience of the class struggle for proletarian power in Finland, Hungary[17] and Germany.[18] The fundamental difference between the experience of Hungary, Finland and Germany and that of Russia consists in the fact that the bourgeoisie of those countries proved, as was to be expected, to be much more organised, united and capable of fighting than the Russian bourgeoisie. Its period of confusion was much shorter; it organised a counter-attack against the proletariat much more rapidly and energetically; and by that very fact shortened the period of illusions of the proletariat itself as to the nature of its dictatorship.

The experience of the workers of Russia, Finland, Hungary and Germany allows us to establish an empiric law of the development of proletarian dictatorship, which may be expressed approximately in the following words. The fact of the conquest of the central political power by the proletariat in no wise completes the struggle for power, but only marks the beginning of a new and more determined period of warfare between the bourgeoisie and the proletariat.

After the first blow of the proletarian revolution and the seizure of the central apparatus of power by the proletariat, the bourgeoisie inevitably needs a certain time for the mobilisation of its forces, the bringing up of reserves, and their organisation. Its passing to a counter-attack opens up an epoch of undisguised warfare and armed clash of the forces of both sides.

It is just during this period that the rule of the proletariat acquires the harsh features of a dictatorship: a Red Army, a terrorist suppression of the exploiters and their allies, and the limitation of political liberty, become inevitable if the proletariat does not wish to give up without a fight the power it has won.

The dictatorship of the proletariat is consequently a form of government of the state which is most adapted to the carrying on of a war with the bourgeoisie, and to guarantee most rapidly the victory of the proletariat in such a war.

Are there any grounds for presuming that such a war in Europe will be carried on in less acute forms? That the European bourgeoisie will submit with a lighter heart to the expropriation of its riches by the proletariat? Can any reasonable person build his tactics on the supposition that the European bourgeoisie will not show all the resistance of which it is capable against the proletariat which has seized power? Can one presume that entering into the fight against the proletariat in power, the European bourgeoisie will prove to be less armed, less capable of fighting, less united and less prudent than the bourgeoisie of Russia, Finland or Hungary? Can one imagine that it will stop at any means, beginning with a far-reaching union with the betrayers of Socialism from the camp of the Second International, and ending with the bombardment of the workmen's quarters and the application of the latest technical methods for the suffocation of the enemy in war?

What under these conditions can be the meaning of a doubt in the inevitability of the methods of proletarian dictatorship, or a refusal to work, day in and day out, for the preparation of the proletariat to utilise all the methods of dictatorship in the coming struggle?

To move towards a seizure of power, not hoping to hold it, and not preparing the conditions for holding it, is simply foolhardiness; to recognise the necessity for the proletariat conquering power, and to doubt the necessity of a dictatorship of the proletariat, to refuse to instruct the workers in this direction — means consciously to prepare the betrayal of the cause of Socialism. Whoever does not recognise the necessity for the severest proletarian dictatorship during the transitional period from capitalism to Socialism, does not prepare the necessary conditions for the proletariat, on acquiring the central apparatus of power, at once directing it to the suppression of the resistance of the exploiters; whoever does not explain to the proletariat, as a necessary condition here and now of its victory, the inevitability of an armed struggle and harsh measures against treason and hesitation, and does not arm the proletariat with the suitable weapons — that person is preparing the ruin of the proletariat and the victory of the bourgeoisie.

But if the dictatorship of the proletariat is an organisation of power, which is best adapted to the carrying on of the war against the bourgeoisie and the suppression of its resistance, then we have an answer also to the question which is generally put to the Communists by the Syndicalists of various schools of thought. The latter, while admitting the dictatorship of the proletariat, cannot divest themselves of their old prejudices against a political party of the proletariat. The question, consequently, is: What organisation is capable of achieving a solution to the problems of dictatorship?

There can be no doubt that, at the moment of a decisive class war, the power of command and compulsion must lie in the hands of a definite organisation, capable of bearing the responsibility for each step it takes and of guaranteeing the logical sequence of these steps.

The army of the proletariat, moving in battle order, must have its general staff. When leading its regiments to the attack, that general staff must be capable of surveying the sum total of the international, political and economic conditions of the struggle. It must possess equal authority over all kinds of arms at the disposal of the working class. It must be in a position to carry out its decisions through the trade unions and the workmen's cooperatives, through the factory committees, and through the leagues of young workers, by means of written propaganda, and through the fighting militia of armed workers.

At the moment when the old power is overthrown and the apparatus of government is seized by the revolting proletariat, that general staff has new tasks to perform. The victory of the proletariat signifies the disorganisation of the old social system. The formation of a new army, the feeding of the country, the building up of industry on new principles, the organisation of law courts, the establishment of relations with the peasants, the diplomatic relations with other countries — all these matters become at once the immediate tasks of the general staff of the victorious proletarian army. Any delay in the accomplishment of one of these tasks, or any hesitation in the decision, is capable of bringing the greatest harm to the further victorious development of the proletarian revolution.

Consequently, this general staff must be an organised, responsible and centralised institution, prepared to deal with and decide all political, economic, social and diplomatic problems. An organisation which would satisfy all these conditions and solve all the problems incumbent upon it may be called, of course, by any name whatsoever; but in reality — and if we do not play with words — such an organisation can only be the political party of the proletariat, that is, an organisation of the most advanced, revolutionary elements of the proletariat, united by their common political programme and an iron discipline.

Such an organisation cannot be formed in a day, or even a week; it is the result of a prolonged process of assembling and selecting experienced leaders, who have proved by their daily work to be capable of estimating rightly each phase of the labour struggle and the interests of each separate group of the working class, from the higher point of view of the general interests of the entire working class as a whole.

The greatest misfortune which could befall the proletarian army after seizing the strongholds of capitalism, would be if the apparatus of leadership proved to be in the hands of men, groups or organisations whose previous work had been carried out only in the sphere of the labour movement.

The suppression of the resistance of the exploiters — which is the fundamental task of the dictatorship — is not only a military, or only a political, or only an economic task; it is all of them — military, political, economic. The resistance of the exploiters acquires only its most acute form during an armed conflict; but the rich peasantry, who will not give the bread for the famishing population, the engineers who sabotage industry, and the bankers who bring confusion into the mutual accounts of the industrial enterprises by concealing their books — are not less important factors in the resistance of the bourgeoisie. The suppression of all these various forms of resistance can be as little the work of an organisation created in the narrow sphere of the trade union movement, as, say, of a workers' cooperative organisation. It can be successfully achieved only by a general organisation of all the workers, in the shape of their soviets, in which are represented all the forms of the labour movement, and which are under the guidance of a political party, concentrating in itself the whole experience of the previous struggle of the working class.

In the epoch of the dictatorship of the proletariat, the Communist Party is still more necessary for the working class than in any other. It constitutes an essential condition for victory. A refusal to work for its creation and strengthening means a renunciation of the efficient carrying on of the class war — that is, a renunciation of dictatorship, of a condition of the victory of Socialism — and may engender, although unconsciously, the most cruel betrayal of the working class cause, by depriving the proletariat, at the most critical moment, of its most important weapon. Anyone who doubts the inevitability of the dictatorship of the proletariat, as a necessary stage of its victory over the bourgeoisie, facilitates the conditions for the victory of the latter; anyone who doubts or renounces the political party of the proletariat, is helping to weaken and disorganise the working class.
June 1920

Notes

1. This text is reproduced from an undated pamphlet of this title published by the Communist Party of Great Britain (probably 1920).
2. George Lansbury headed a British delegation visiting the USSR in February 1920.
3. The technical delegation visiting the USSR from Italy early in 1920 included Serrati and others from the Italian Socialist Party. The Comintern used the occasion to work on them to split their party in time for the Second Congress in July 1920.
4. The Treaty of Versailles was signed between the Entente powers and Germany in June 1919.
5. Karl Marx, 'Letter to Kugelmann', 12 April 1871, K Marx and F Engels, *Correspondence*, London, 1934, p309: 'The next attempt of the French revolution will be no longer, as before, to transfer the bureaucratic-military machine from one hand to another, but to smash it, and that is essential for every real people's revolution on the Continent.'
6. The Second (Labour and Socialist) International was founded in Paris in 1889. It still exists.
7. 'But theory also becomes a material force once it has gripped the masses', K Marx, 'A Contribution to the Critique of Hegel's Philosophy of Right: Introduction', *Early Writings of Marx*, Harmondsworth, 1974, p251.
8. *1903: Second Ordinary Congress of the Russian Social Democratic Labour Party*, London, 1978, p5.
9. A general strike in Finland was followed by a premature uprising on 27 January 1918, which was suppressed by General Mannerheim with the help of German troops, and thousands were massacred. The new state of Lithuania had been set up by the Entente powers at the Treaty of Versailles, and had been involved in the fighting on the side of Poland, which had attacked the Soviet Union in 1920. The Ukraine declared independence from Russia soon after the Bolsheviks seized power, remained separate under a variety of nationalist, pro-German and White Guardist regimes, and a stable Soviet regime was not established there until 1920.
10. The Cheka.
11. Nikolai Dmitriyevich Avksentiev (1878-1943) was Socialist Revolutionary Minister of the Interior in Kerensky's government; Abram Raphailovich Gotz (1882-1937), also an SR, was Governor-General of Petrograd; Vladimir Mikhailovich Zenzinov (1881-1953) was an SR member of the Constituent Assembly who took up arms against the Bolsheviks; General Boldyrev was placed in command of the army of the Constituent Assembly at Samara; Pyotr Nikolayevich Krasnov (1869-1947) led a revolt of the Don Cossacks against Soviet power during the Russian Civil War.
12. Admiral Kolchak set up a White government in Siberia in the spring of 1919, a Cossack Rada was set up at Ekaterinodar, and the SRs set up a government of the Constituent Assembly at Samara on 8 June 1918.
13. General Markov later fought against the Bolsheviks in the south in alliance with Wrangel.
14. General Lavr Georgevich Kornilov (1870-1918) was the Commander-in-Chief of the armed forces who tried to overthrow Kerensky in 1917; he later led a campaign against the Bolsheviks in the region of the Don and Kuban in the Russian Civil War, and was killed in front of Ekaterinodar.
15. Admiral Shchastny attempted to incite mutiny within the Baltic Fleet against the Soviet government. He was condemned to be shot by the Supreme Revolutionary Tribunal on 20 June 1918.

16. The Vendée was the scene of a royalist uprising against the French Revolution on 21 August 1792
17. The Hungarian Soviet republic was founded in March 1919 and crushed by a Romanian invasion in the following August.
18. The period 1918-20 saw a number of violent clashes between the revolution and the counter-revolution in Germany, including the mutinies in the High Seas Fleet, the Bavarian Commune, the Spartacist Uprising, and the Kapp Putsch. Cf *Revolutionary History*, Volume 5, no 2, Spring 1994.

Book Three

Leon Trotsky

Dreams and Reality

By 1922 Russia lay exhausted after four years of civil war and invasion from 21 foreign interventionist armies. Uprisings in Tambov and Siberia and the mutiny of the Kronstadt fleet base showed that the regime was isolated from its peasant population. A terrible famine spread along the Volga, accompanied by typhus and cholera. Despite this, these two articles show how the Bolsheviks attempted to counteract the avalanche of the misrepresentation of their revolution abroad, an accumulation of debris that is still being added to today. In sharp contrast with the shameless apologetics pumped out by Stalinist regimes since, Trotsky makes no attempt to disguise the reality of the situation by putting a utopian gloss upon it. Potemkin village scenarios of the Chinese, Korean or Cuban varieties had no place in a state where the workers wielded power, even a state convalescing in the New Economic Policy from the rigours of civil war. Trotsky's brief remarks here retain all their validity, all the more so because of the subsequent careers of his collaborators. Morizet returned to the Social Democracy, and Strong became a mouthpiece for Chinese Stalinism at the summit of the barbarities of the 'Great Proletarian Cultural Revolution', which was great, but only in the sense of being monstrous, whilst being neither proletarian, nor about culture, nor a revolution, but a noxious Stalinist purge. Trotsky's introductions remind us that the defence of a true workers' revolution does not mean lying about a happy land far, far away.

Book Three

Leon Trotsky

Dreams and Reality

Leon Trotsky
Defending the Revolution Abroad[1]

$\mathbf{D}$ear Comrade Morizet

The news that you have a book on Soviet Russia in the press has really cheered me up. You came to Russia as a friend. You were enabled to see everything deserving of your attention. You are assisting the cause of the French proletariat and the proletariat worldwide; you cannot therefore be influenced by any other than a desire to tell the truth to the working masses about the first workers' republic. This is a most important and precious thing.

You know better than I how many lies have been spread about us. Capitalist or Social Democratic international lying against Soviet Russia can be divided into two categories. To the first belong the fabrications of a hateful and hardly disinterested fantasy: reports about the feasting of Soviet dignitaries, their imprisonment of each other, the 'nationalisation' of bourgeois women by artillerymen, etc, etc. These lies are completely self-contradictory, and are stupid and monotonous. They only deceive the most ignorant of gossips and a few ministers. To the second group belong lies that contain bits of the truth. This is a superior sort of lying. Its scope of operation is wider, and its sources are richer.

Revolution is a harsh affair, above all in a country comprising of millions of backward peasants. Equipped with a camera and bad intentions, it is not difficult to take pictures of Soviet Russia today, which, taken in their entirety, would provide great pleasure to any reactionary bourgeois of whatever sort. Revolution consists of destroying in order to build up again. To be able to understand the revolution at its highest level as well as its darker sides, its inner necessities must be grasped, in the struggle of its living forces and the logical progression of its stages. I do not mean to say by this that the revolution must be infallible. But you must have a broad historical horizon to be able to understand its faults as well as its fruitful successes.

When we were attempting to create an army, there was still an important group of French officers in Russia; they witnessed the first of Soviet Russia's military undertakings. They regarded these undertakings with extreme scepticism. I do not doubt that their reports back to Paris could only arrive at one conclusion: nothing will come of it. These uniformed petit-bourgeois saw only destruction, cruelty, disorder and chaos in the revolution. And all this does form part of the revolution. But there is something greater than this in the revolution: it awakens to life millions amongst the backward masses of the people, provides them with great political aims, opens up new avenues for them, and rouses their dormant energy. That is why the revolution accomplishes miracles. This hardly needs proving to a people which has the Great Revolution in its own past.

In the course of these late years, I have often wanted to study the British press at the time of the Great French Revolution, the speeches and base politicking of the ministers of those days, the Clemenceaus and the Hervés[2] of the time, in order to compare the reactionary lying of the British ruling classes at the end of the eighteenth century with the falsehoods spread by *Le Temps* and its hangers on about Soviet Russia during these last years. Unfortunately, I have not yet found the time to do this work. But I am sure even beforehand that the parallelism would be striking. No doubt the British radicals who were Robespierre's[3] contemporaries looked for perfectly justifiable parallels at the time with the English Revolution of the seventeenth century, which would inevitably provoke the indignant protests of pious reactionary historians. In spite of its 'excesses', the English Revolution — they would go on to say — was a great event nonetheless, whereas the French terror is only the revolt of an ignorant and bloodthirsty populace. To sum up, even when reaction is armed with the worst intentions in the world, it is not inventive. The widespread French lying against the Soviet Revolution, amongst others, is but a literary pilfering, a miserable plagiarism from Pitt's scribbling journalists.[4]

You should see the evil rejoicing with which the Merrheims[5] and their employers talk about our economic difficulties. Now they are celebrating by proclaiming to all the world that we have returned to capitalism! Premature rejoicing! The Soviet Republic has nationalised the banks, the industrial concerns and the land. To give its owners back this property the revolution would have to be overthrown and crushed. We are further than ever from this. You can say this in all certainty to the French proletariat.

What is correct is that we have changed our mode of construction. Whilst keeping the factories completely in the hands of the workers' state, in order to estimate whether they are profitable or not, we are employing capitalist methods of accounting and market regulation. When we have attained an infinitely higher level of Socialist development, only then will we be able to direct all the factories from a single centre by distributing rationally between them the necessary input and resources according to a foreordained national plan. The present stage of development bears a provisional character. The market remains. Within certain limits, the industrial enterprises of the state have freedom of action, can buy and sell, and can thus create the vital foundations for the one future economic plan of Socialism.

It is true that at the same time we have agreed to give such and such an enterprise as a concession to capitalists. The backward economic system and Russia's inexhaustible natural resources afford a wide field of operation for concessionary capital. The state keeps control of the most important and essential enterprises of industry and transport. Thus we allow competition between the purely capitalist concessions and the coordinated enterprises belonging to the Socialist state, with the latter being indubitably dominant. The whole point lies in the relationship of forces.

Reformists have long cherished the hope that cooperation would swallow up capitalism little by little. While ever the power belonged to the bourgeoisie defending the right of private ownership of the means of production, this was a purely utopian hope. As far as Russia is concerned, while ever power belongs to the working class and the essential branches of industry remain in state hands, a slow and 'painless' restoration of capitalism by means of concessions is no more possible than Socialist regeneration of capitalism via cooperation.

Nothing allows us to talk of a return to capitalism. It is a matter of a change in the method used to build Socialism. Our experience and the results obtained along the new path will be to the great advantage of the working class in every land.

We have learned much during these five years of revolution. But we have given up nothing. I doubt if the capitalist world, such as it has emerged from the inferno of war, and as we see it today, gives us cause to proceed to revise our fundamental concepts. Capitalism has been condemned by history. The future belongs to Communism.

Fraternal Communist greetings

Leon Trotsky
Moscow
3 March 1922

Notes

1. LD Trotsky, Preface to André Morizet, *Chez Lénine et Trotski: Moscou 1921*, Paris, 1922, pp vii-xi, translated by the editor with the assistance of Harry Ratner. André Morizet was Mayor of Boulogne, and an early sympathiser with the Russian Revolution; he later rejoined the French Socialist Party. Socialist Platform is especially grateful to Malcolm Pratt for the gift of this splendid book.
2. Gustave Hervé (1871-1944) had previously stood on the left of French Socialism, but had become a chauvinist during the First World War.
3. Maximilien Robespierre (1758-1794) was amongst the most intransigent leaders of the French Revolution.
4. William Pitt the Younger (1759-1806) was Prime Minister of Britain, a fierce opponent of the French Revolution who paid professional writers to slander it.
5. Alphonse Merrheim (1871-1925) had been a French supporter of the Zimmerwald Manifesto, but in 1918 went over to the right and became a fervent anti-Communist.

Leon Trotsky
The First Time in History[1]

OF THE October Revolution and of Soviet Russia there is already a large literature. On account of the very character of the revolutionary epoch, each new book has characterised, with good will or with malice, a new step in the rapid course of revolutionary development.

There exist not a few books devoted to our civil war. Some of them paint our cruelty and blood-thirstiness; others tell of the heroism of the workers' vanguard, of the unexampled self-sacrifice of the toilers in the struggle for great new aims. Undoubtedly the breadth of the revolutionary struggle, its great sacrifices, have attracted to the cause of the Russian Revolution the sympathies not only of the toiling masses, but also of the better elements in the intellectual classes.

It is, however, necessary to state that the sympathies of these latter have not always proved stable. More than once we have observed that the very persons and groups amongst the intellectuals who accepted the revolution but sighed on account of her cruelties and destructive influence on culture, yet felt themselves not only injured but somewhat insulted when the revolution went over to the insistent drudgery of daily effort — from the heights of tragic poetry they, don't you see, were thrown down to the prosaic depths of the New Economic Policy.

The trouble is that the ethical-aesthetic standard by which is guided a considerable, and not the worst, part of the intellectuals, is entirely unfit for the grasping of great historical events. History is not at all guided in its movements by the rules of morals and beauty; it follows the logic of its inherent forces, the classes and material factors underlying the bases of all society. Ethics and aesthetics are already phenomena of second or third place. The new class, in the severe struggle towards a new epoch of history, by that very struggle lays down paths to new ethics and aesthetics.

'Alas! alas!', exclaim some of the injured 'friends' in Russia, 'behold the unlimited reign of Tsar NEP. Where is the tragic and bleeding Russia of 1918, 1919 and 1920?'

The author of the present book, Anna Louise Strong, does not belong to the number of such 'friends'. She approached the revolution not from the aesthetic or contemplative point of view, but from the point of view of action. Under the prose of the NEP, as well as under the dramatic events of the Civil War, she was able to see, or perhaps at the very beginning, merely to feel — the intense, stubborn, uncompromising struggle against age-long slavery, darkness, barbarism for new higher forms of life. When the Volga was stricken by famine,[2] Miss Strong arrived in Russia for the difficult, dangerous struggle with hunger and epidemics. She herself went through typhus. In her numerous articles and correspondence, she tirelessly made breaches in that wall of reactionary lies that made the most important part of the imperialist blockade around the revolution. This does not mean, of course, that Miss Strong was hiding the black spots; but she tried to understand and explain to others how these facts grew out of the past in its conflict with the future.

Thanks to such an approach, the only correct one, the NEP for the author of this book is not vulgar prose, and not a liquidation of the revolution, but one of its necessary stages. The very people who fought on all the fronts of the Civil War — except, of course, for the tens of thousands who fell victims to French, English and American imperialism — are working for the economic restoration of the country, in the name of the same aims, with the same energy, the same readiness to give themselves completely. The difficulties here are really incredible, our economic and cultural backwardness is immeasurable, but a knowledge of our own backwardness, when it takes hold of the wide masses of the people, becomes in itself the greatest force towards culture. This force has been awakened by the revolution. We have it, and on it we are building. One of the stages of our building, not infrequently mistaken, often awkward, but historically unconquerable — Anna Louise Strong shows in her book. That is why we think it has a right to attention.

L Trotsky
Moscow, 1923

Notes

1. LD Trotsky, Preface to Anna Louise Strong, *The First Time in History*, London, 1924, pp5-7. Anna Louise Strong (1885-1970) first came to Russia as a member of the American relief mission and became a literary fellow traveller of the Soviet Union. Despite her treatment by Stalin, she afterwards wrote a series of 'Letters from China' in *Peking Review* supporting the enormities of Mao's regime.
2. The American Relief Association estimated that five million people died of famine along the Volga in 1921-22.

Book Four

Vladimir Lenin, Leon Trotsky, Mikhail Tukhachevsky and Grigory Zinoviev

Defending Socialist Internationalism

Collected under this heading are a number of essays intended to illustrate what can loosely be described as the 'foreign policy' of the new Soviet state (inasmuch as an international state can be regarded as having a foreign policy in the true sense at all). What we see here is the mechanism of a state system in the process of being built, how it worked out a relationship with the proletariat outside its borders and the national minorities within them, and how it built up an army for offence and defence.

For the appearance of the Soviet state set a new pattern in international relations. In November 1917 it proclaimed 'the right of the peoples of Russia to free self-determination', shortly to be followed by its invasion by 21 foreign armies. In March 1918 it concluded a treaty with Germany by which it dropped out of the war. Yet this did not mean a shrinking of its horizons within national limits, for in March 1919 it founded the Third International to spread the Communist revolution throughout the world. These pieces can only be understood if we regard the defence of the revolution, the construction of a new army from scratch, the promotion of the world revolution, and the relations of the new state with its national minorities as so many components of the same basic policy.

Only two of the writers of these articles need any introduction here. Grigory Yevseyevich Radomysslsky (Zinoviev, 1883-1936) joined the RSDLP in 1900 and the Bolshevik faction in 1903, and for many years functioned as Lenin's right-hand man. He was the joint author with him of *Socialism and War* (1915), and accompanied Lenin in the famous sealed train in 1917. Along with Kamenev he opposed the seizure of power by the Bolsheviks in October 1917, but was appointed President of the Communist International at its founding conference in 1919. As Trotsky observed on several occasions, the fact that Zinoviev had been wrong-footed in 1917 led him to over-compensate by seeing revolutionary opportunities all over the world, which accounts for the note of urgency in his article here. Between 1923 and 1925 he allied with Stalin against Trotsky, and even went so far as to demand that administrative measures be taken against him long before Stalin was willing to entertain the idea. His subsequent break with Stalin to set up the Left/Centre (Leningrad) Opposition led to his expulsion from the Soviet Communist Party in 1927, and he was executed after the Trial of the Sixteen in 1936.

Mikhail Tukhachevsky (1893-1937) was a young officer in the Tsarist army who was taken prisoner by the Germans in the First World War. Upon his release he joined the Bolsheviks during the Civil War, and helped to build up an effective army, commanding the First Army in the capture of Simbirsk and the main forces during the war with Poland (1920-21). He was a brilliant pioneer of mobile warfare by means of tank armies, and it was largely due to his efforts that when Hitler invaded the USSR in 1941 he was faced by nearly 10 000 Soviet tanks of superb design. Tukhachevsky received no thanks for this achievement from Stalin, for he had been accused of plotting with the Germans four years earlier, and had been shot after the secret trial of the generals in June 1937.

In spite of the variety of subjects covered, our collection here shows a consistency of approach; that the Bolsheviks regarded their revolution as only the first of a series of revolutions; that they looked upon their army as an instrument of the international working class; that at this stage they rejected great power bullying of the Stalinist type in their relations with their national minorities; and that they envisaged their foreign policy and their armed forces alike as subordinate to the needs of the world revolution of the working class.

Those who are accustomed to politicians being more cynical but a good deal less frank will feel a shock at the realpolitik of Lenin's speech of 1920. But it should be borne in mind that in none of this material is there a hint of Russian nationalism of the 'Socialism in One Country' variety, suffused as it is throughout with the spirit of Socialist internationalism. For, like the English and French revolutions before it, the Russian Revolution could not be confined within the borders of a national state. History may have confirmed the opinion of Trotsky, Radek and Marchlewski that the decision to invade Poland in 1920 was a mistaken one. But it also indicates that no question of principle was involved in the decision as a whole, for after all an intervention of the Red Army in the German revolution could have spared us the rise of Hitler. Yet the circumstances surrounding the conquest of Georgia touched on in our last piece show that promoting the revolution at bayonet point was at best a two-edged weapon.

Grigory Zinoviev

International Socialism and the Proletarian Revolution in Russia[1]

IN AUGUST 1914 an International Socialist Congress was to have been held in Vienna which was destined to have a universal historical significance in the annals of the international working class movement. The year 1914 had completed the half-century since the foundation of the First International Working Men's Association (the First International). It had been proposed to organise a triumphant celebration of the half-centenary of the First International, and at the same time to settle once and for all the tactics of the struggle of the international proletariat against the imperialist world war, which was closing in with the inevitability of fate.

Instead of this, in August 1914 the world-wide imperialist war broke out, and is continuing to this day.

The International Socialist Bureau, led by Huysmanns[2] and Vandervelde, had published in Vienna on the invitation of the official Austrian Social Democracy a jubilee symposium-almanac of the Second International. In this symposium were gathered all the resolutions of the International on the subject of war, and certain speeches, articles and sayings uttered by the leaders of international Socialism against war. When the imperialist war began, accompanied by the bankruptcy of all the official Socialists and their acceptance of the banner of the bourgeoisie, the friends of Victor Adler[3] and Emile Vandervelde hastened to 'withdraw from circulation', that is, to hide the precious jubilee-symposium of the International. And they acted, from their point of view, correctly. Every line of this symposium lashed the official high priests of the governmental Social Democracy in the face. Every resolution, every one of the speeches and articles quoted in this symposium cried out aloud at the unheard-of treachery of the Scheidemanns,[4] Renners, Renaudels,[5] Hendersons,[6] Huysmannses & Company. Well might the leaders of the bankrupted Second International fear their own shadows! There was nothing else for them to do but to hide from their own past.

Indeed, how did the question of war and revolution stand at the beginning of the present war?

In the shameful renegade pamphlet *The Dictatorship of the Proletariat* published by Kautsky in the autumn of 1918,[7] this once-upon-a-time Socialist dissociates himself from civil war, brings arguments from every side to convince the working class that it is wicked to rush to arms, and that even the very words 'Socialist revolution' are impossible here and now. But then, it was this very Kautsky who wrote as far back as **10 years ago**:

'Socialism has already become an economic necessity today, only power determines when it will come. Getting this power for the proletariat through organisation and spreading consciousness is the most important task of Social Democracy today. Nothing is stranger than those Socialists who believe it is necessary to prepare for a further development of the power of capitalism.'

This was written by Kautsky as far back as 1907 in his pamphlet *Socialism and Colonial Policy* (p37, German edition).[8]

Another of the stoutest theorists of the Second International, Rudolf Hilferding,[9] wrote in his *Finance Capital*:

'The response of the proletariat to the economic policy of finance capital — imperialism — cannot be free trade, but only Socialism... Socialism ceases to be a remote ideal, an "ultimate aim" which serves only as a guiding principle for "immediate demands", and becomes an essential component of the immediate practical policy of the proletariat... Socialism must be given the most prominent place in propaganda, as the only alternative to imperialism...

'The tendency of finance capital is to establish social control of production, but it is an antagonistic form of socialisation, since the control of social production remains vested in an oligarchy. The struggle to dispossess this oligarchy constitutes the ultimate phase of the class struggle between the bourgeoisie and the proletariat... Even today, taking possession of six large Berlin banks would mean taking possession of the most important spheres of large-scale industry, and would greatly facilitate the initial phases of Socialist policy during the transition period, when capitalist accounting might prove useful.'[10]

The third high priest of the defunct Second International, Otto Bauer, also 10 years ago, in 1908, declared in his famous book *The National Question and Social Democracy*,[11] literally as follows:

'Undoubtedly the coming imperialist world war will involve a revolutionary stage. The imperialist universal catastrophe will unquestionably be the beginning of a world-wide Socialist revolution.'

Bebel[12] made a pronouncement in the same sense at the time of the Moroccan conflict.[13] In his celebrated speech in the Reichstag, Bebel declared:

'Then will come the catastrophe. Then [that is, when the world war begins] we shall have the greatest of European wars, in which from 16 to 18 million men, equipped with the finest weapons of slaughter, will hurl themselves upon one another. But it is my firm conviction that the price of the great world war will be the great world revolution. You will reap what you have sown. The Twilight of the Gods[14] is creeping over the bourgeois order. Yes, gentlemen, you may be assured, this twilight is very near. You are now at a point when you yourselves will be cutting away the foundations of your legal and social order. You yourselves have brought things to such a pass that you can hear the knell of your own legal and social state.'

But not only did single leaders of the Second International speak in this tone, but also the most responsible among its organisations. In an official document of the party, published in 1912 by the Central Committee of the German Social Democracy, it is written:

'If but 300 magnates of capitalism could be changed into men worthy of the trust of the proletariat, the whole of production, without further difficulty, could be conducted in the interests of the working class instead of the interests of the capitalists, and the transition to a Socialist organisation of production would have begun. So far as the preliminary conditions are concerned, they are ripe, and that work has been performed by the capitalists themselves.' (*Imperialism and Socialism*, 1912, p3)

An imperialist war will beget a Socialist revolution — such was also the declaration of the Second International in the celebrated resolution of the International Congress at Stuttgart[15] — such was the opinion which the most responsible, the most distinguished representatives of the Second International went on declaring right up to 1912.

Yes, right up to 1912. On the very eve of the beginning of the war — one may almost say 24 hours before the first shot — official representatives of the Second International continued to affirm just that very same thing. The industrious and pacifist professor Karl Grünberg (Vienna),[16] had collected in two bulky volumes all the resolutions, articles and speeches of the official Socialist organisations and leaders which had seen the light of day up to within a day or so of the outbreak of the war in 1914, and the result was exceedingly illuminating. All responsible politicians saw that here was the onrush of that very war, the approach of which the Socialists had heralded in the course of the previous 10 or 15 years. All the leaders of the Socialist parties were convinced that the Basle Congress[17] had been justified in its declaration that the Balkan War of 1912[18] was only the overture, merely a preface to the great all-European and world-imperialist war. Nay, even the general lines of the grouping of the powers at the beginning of August 1914 had already been clearly defined in 1912. And right up to the thunder of the first shot, the official Socialists continued by momentum to speak the truth. Every one of them, with one voice, affirmed that this war was not a war of justice, but of dishonour, and that this was to be a war for the interests of small cliques of capitalists. And all with one voice demonstrated to the workers of their country that their interest, their honour, demanded the very sharpest protest, the most decisive struggle against this overwhelming crime.

Professor Grünberg's book, a dry compilation of official materials, stands out as the most eloquent indictment against the Socialist apologists of all countries. Every line in this book is like a whip across the face of these social-traitors.

Hervé, the present market-place shouter, Hervé, the up-to-date moving spirit of the campaign of the French imperialists against the great Russian working class revolution — even Hervé wrote as late as 28 July 1914:

'A war for the defence of the small nations oppressed by the great powers! How nice that would be! But not by a long way is there in Europe one single great power whose hands are not soaked in blood. No! Not a war for the defence of the little Serbian nation, but a war for the defence of the prestige of our ally, the Tsar.

The prestige and honour of our ally! The honour of the Russian government! The bare word is enough to make Rabelais,[19] Voltaire[20] and Victor Hugo[21] turn in their graves. The Russian government was not so sensitive about its honour when it strangled Finland and Poland, and when it let loose its Black Hundreds on the Jewish populations of Kiev and Odessa.[22] To fight in order to safeguard the prestige of the Tsar! What an excellent motive for a people whose ancestors had brought about the Great Revolution! What a joy to die in such a noble business!' (*La Guerre Sociale*, 28 July 1914)

And the late Jaurès, murdered a few hours before the commencement of the war, in a speech delivered in one of the suburbs of Lyons four hours before his death, said:

'The colonial policy of France, the aggressive world policy of Russia, the imperious will of Austria — these are what cooperated in the creation of this terrible situation in which we find ourselves. Citizens, if this threat of war is turned into reality, it must become our chief concern as Socialists to save ourselves as soon as possible from this crime which the governing classes are committing.'

And the central organ of the official German Social Democracy up to 48 hours before the outbreak of war inserted article after article demonstrating that this war would be the greatest of crimes against the workers.

But no sooner did the first thunder of the guns resound than the official leaders of the governmental Social Democratic Party announced that black was white and white black. The most criminal of all wars was transformed under their pen into a 'great' war of 'liberation'. Each of the official Socialist parties urged the defence of their respective 'fatherlands', that is, their bourgeoisie, their masters. The principles of Socialism were forgotten, the red flags trampled in the mud. Honour and conscience were declared prejudices.

There was no treachery which these official leaders of the governmental Social Democracy did not commit against the workers of all countries. Every honest Socialist was denounced by the mass as a crank, madman or criminal enemy of his own nation. Upon every honest internationalist who raised the voice of protest against the imperialist massacre, the official high priests of the Second International flung their handfuls of mud. The sacred blood of the workers began to flow, and whole rivers of it are flowing down to this very day.

Now, as we write these lines, we are at the end of the third year since the Zimmerwald International Conference. It is not an exhilarating memory, this, of the time when there assembled in a dead and wretched little Swiss village somewhere about a score of Socialists of all lands, having at their back, in the best of cases, only a hundred or so supporters in the whole of blood-stained and tortured Europe.

In Germany, the internationalists, with Liebknecht at their head,[23] were only taking their first steps. Over the whole of Germany there reigned the peace of a graveyard. With boundless insolence, and with stupid self-confidence, the Scheidemannites were hectoring the courageous individual internationalists, being convinced that the working masses would continue to follow them, the official representatives of governmental so-called Socialism.

Matters were worse in Austria. In 1915, at the moment when the Zimmerwald

Conference was meeting, the individual internationalists of Austria could be counted on the finger-ends, while the official Austrian Social Democracy, led by Victor Adler, had bag and baggage gone over to the service of the Austrian government.

In France, in England, social chauvinism celebrated its orgies unreproved.

In Italy, the official party would not vote for the war credits, but the vast majority of the leaders became captives of the ideas of pacifism, and were unwilling to hear anything about open revolutionary revolt.

About Russia, mum's the word! Here there flourished the armament-contractors' 'Socialism', at the head of which marched, arm in arm, Guchkov, Potresov, Plekhanov and Milyukov.

Great had to be the faith in the working class to raise at that moment the flag of the international struggle for Socialism.

Which of those who were present at the Zimmerwald Conference dreamt that less than three years would pass before the Socialist revolution in Russia would be a fact, that Germany and Austria would be standing on the brink of a proletarian revolution, that in Italy and France there would begin to seethe the fiercest of class struggles?

But all this came to pass; we lived to see it.

When the March Revolution in Russia broke out, all the bourgeois governments of Europe, and in their train all the governmental social-patriotic parties, immediately pricked up their ears. Considerable sections of the European bourgeoisie could not help sympathising with the March Revolution so long as it remained a purely bourgeois revolution, so long as the matter appeared to be a change from the autocratic regime of Nicholas Romanov to the bourgeois regime of Milyukov and Guchkov.

But the tricksters of European imperialism began to exchange glances. The sharpened senses of the great property owners, who saw a grave danger arising from the mood of the rebellious slaves, immediately suggested to the leaders of the European bourgeoisie that the March bourgeois revolution would bring with it the germ of a revolution of the workers, that is, of a Socialist revolution.

As is well known, the very first moment of the March Revolution among us in Russia saw also the birth of the soviets (councils) of workers' and soldiers' delegates. The quickened scent of the butchers of world imperialism at once told them that these soviets had very serious chances of becoming the cradle of a Socialist upheaval in Russia. 'The soviets — they are the enemy.' Thus murmured to itself the European money-market.

'The participation of mobilised soldiers in elections [it was then a question of elections to the Constituent Assembly] would be full of risk' — so wrote the organ of the French government, *Le Temps*, on 21 March 1917. And this same Paris *Temps* on 22 March poured out its indignation with matchless frankness:

'We do not understand by what right 1000 delegates of the workers and soldiers have assembled in the Tauride palace, and from there dictate decrees. May not this improvised meeting play the part of a government? The English press yesterday uttered the first warning; we repeat it with all insistence, for if the Russian Revolution degenerates into a travesty, it will compromise the whole future of Russia, and the whole of its freedom.'

At the same time the principle organ of the British imperialists, *The Times*, also baited with rabid fury in the very first days of the March revolution the so-called 'extremists'. (This is what they called the Bolsheviks at that time in the West.) Already on 20 March 1917 it demanded the disarming of the Petrograd workers, and urged that if the Petrograd proletariat did not allow itself to be 'pacified' otherwise, one must not hesitate to employ force.

It was with good reason that the 'improvised meeting' in the Tauride palace took away the sleep of the London and Paris bankers. Oh, these people had not forgotten the movements of '48,[24] and very well remembered the Paris Commune of 1871, and they guessed that the soviets of workers' and soldiers' delegates promised nothing good to the European bourgeoisie.

Now that British imperialism is making open war on Socialist Russia, there are certain people whom the fact astonishes. About the middle of March 1917, when bourgeois rule in Russia had already outlived its honeymoon, at that very moment when the Russian bourgeoisie was proclaiming our revolution to be a 'great' one, just when it was so small — already at that time the stalwart freebooters of British imperialism had excellently well taken stock of what was going on. In the course of the last fortnight in 1917, London and Paris journals repeatedly expressed their warm sympathy with Nicholas Romanov; while the leader of the French bourgeois republic, from the tribune of the Chamber of Deputies, glorified Nicholas the Bloody as a man who had faithfully fulfilled his duty to his 'ally', the French 'people', whose renunciation of the throne was the noblest of actions, and whom the Russian people and all subsequent history were to hold in the utmost veneration.

European finance knew that in the struggle against the 'improvised meeting' of the workers and soldiers it was not going to be the only occasion when they would bend their knee before the Tsarist gang. The fire-eating 'veterans' and cunning rogues of bourgeois republicanism made it quite clear to themselves from the first moment of the March Revolution that they would be obliged in their own class interests to make the attempt to restore Tsarism in Russia against the working class and poorest peasantry.

The all-European bourgeoisie thus showed its teeth to the working class of Russia immediately. But the international proletariat? How did it answer the call of the Russian Revolution?

The rejoicings at the fall of Tsarism among the labouring classes of Europe were, as will be readily understood, universal. But of any active support, however small, to our soviets there was not at this moment any question. Everywhere the working class continued to be absorbed in their struggle for existence amidst the bloody war, and everywhere they continued to groan under the dead weight of a state of siege. A fresh wind had sprung up over the battlefields, but not for long. Nor was it strong enough to blow at once out of its path all those obstacles which history had piled up all over it.

On their part, the official Socialists of all countries continued their Judas work. They strove to make use of a revolutionary movement of an amplitude unknown in history in order to justify and to continue their work of treachery. The governmental and compromising 'Socialists' were helping the bourgeoisie of 'their' respective countries to throw mud and slander on the proletarian soviets emerging into the light in Russia, and to bait the Russian Bolsheviks who were raising the banner of a Communist revolution.

Yet the Russian proletariat felt with the true instinct of their class that the final result of the great struggle begun by them against the Russian bourgeoisie would be decided in the last resort by the echoes that their struggle would call forth in other lands. And the Russian working class fixed their gaze intently on the West, awaiting a fraternal response.

Like the earth after a long drought receiving the first drops of blessed rain, the Russian working class, worn out in an honourable internationalist cause, received every, even the very faintest, hint of international support on the part of the West European workers with avidity. With outstretched arms, the Russian working class received every Socialist coming from England or from France, even though he belonged to the 'patriots'. The trust which the Russian proletariat showed the representatives even of the most soppy European Socialism was truly boundless. And of this the Russian compromise-mongering Socialists took full advantage. Of set purpose they replaced the genuine representatives of international Socialism by make-believe Socialists. Consciously and of set purpose, they fed the Russian worker on substitutes. It was with the utmost deliberation and callousness that they offered him stones instead of bread. Who does not remember the disgusting spectacles at the Petrograd Soviet in those ever-memorable days when the Petrograd proletariat was 'patriotically' inclined, and the leaders of the Petrograd Soviet were Chkeidze, Tsereteli and Kerensky? Who does not remember, for instance, the arrival in Russia of the renowned Albert Thomas,[25] this Scheidemann of France? Who does not remember how in the overcrowded meetings of the Petrograd Soviet, Chkeidze, the old fox, rushed into the arms of the sharper Albert Thomas, and warbled *The Marseillaise*, and *The Internationale*? But among the simple workpeople there lived a genuine international enthusiasm, which made them believe that they were witnessing the fraternal welcome of genuine Socialists, and they never for a moment suspected that they were watching but a disgusting comedy of sanctimoniousness and hypocrisy. Many long months had to elapse before the scales fell from the eyes of even the most advanced among the Petrograd workers. But when at last our workers' sight grew clear again, there were no bounds to their detestation and contempt for the Jesuitical social renegades of the French, not less than of the German, brand. Nor was there a limit to their ardent attachment and love for those sincere Socialist internationalists of whose representatives stood out Karl Liebknecht in Germany, John Maclean[26] in Britain, Friedrich Adler[27] in Austria, and Eugene Debs[28] in America. 'The darker the night, the brighter the stars', was the word of the Russian working class to themselves.

An international proletarian revolution — such was the sacred goal of the onward sweep of the advanced Russian proletarians; such was the holy bright star which shone upon the struggles of the Russian proletariat! At the most difficult hour, when our working class perhaps grew faint in the struggle against superior hostile forces, when it was hungry, when it was besieged by enemies on every side, when it lost heart and sometimes murmured against its own soviets — in those hours it wanted but the momentary glimmer of a hope that the West was catching fire from the light of the revolution, that in the West the international Socialist revolution was beginning to loom — and fatigue, ill-will and mistrust would vanish. Once again, among the Petrograd and Moscow proletarians, the intrepid fighter would rise from sleep, would once again grip the rifle firmly in his hands, and would once again, without complaints and without murmur, carry forward the heavy burden which history had hoisted on his shoulders.

We call to mind the heavy days of Brest,[29] heavy, bitter days, unexampled in their oppressiveness. We remember those passionate discussions which took place in our midst in those memorable days. Weighing every pro and con of the tactics of 'respite', we staked everything on the question of whether we should injure thereby the proletarian revolution which was beginning to catch fire in the West or not. What we feared most of all was lest this step of ours should smother even for a moment the flame of proletarian struggle which was beginning to blaze in Europe. The Petrograd and Moscow proletarians trembled at the base thought that our 'respite' should be purchased at the heavy price of retarding the proletarian struggle in other lands. But the greatest fear of all for the heroic Russian working class was the sudden thought that the German workers would not understand us, that they would look upon this step as a reconciliation with German imperialism, that our halt for breath would intensify the difficulties of their struggle against Wilhelm, and our Brest peace would lead to new flashes of chauvinism in France and England. The working class Communists were tortured by these thoughts in those ever-memorable days.

But by good fortune we are now able to say that the proletarians of other countries understood us perfectly. Their class instinct whispered to them that our step was not dictated by any kind of egotistic national interests, but on the contrary just by the interests of international Socialism.

They understood that from the moment when the proletarian revolution had taken place in Russia, our land had been consecrated to Socialism, and that our Workers' and Peasants' Government was obliged to accept that disastrous peace for the very purpose of preserving the very first Socialist republic in the world. The advanced workers of all lands understood well that in signing the Brest peace we only wished to gain time for ourselves, and thereby give **them** time to make good their delay and collect their strength in aid of the first proletarian revolution in the world.

And the Russian proletariat kept its word. It has been able to sustain itself until the time when the world revolution has begun.

The world revolution will be begotten by the world war. This, among others, is the reason why the revolution has begun in the countries economically most backward; why, too, the first proletarian revolution was able to receive a real chance for a respite. Had it not been for the struggle of the two imperialist trusts among themselves, had it not been for the rabid rivalry between the Anglo-French and Austro-German imperialists, had it not been, in a word, for the world imperialist war, out of which the world proletarian revolution was bound to be born — had it not been for all this, a proletarian revolution in one single country would never have been able to maintain itself for a whole year. The bandits of world capitalism would have strangled it if these bandits themselves had not been clutching at each others' throats.

After Russia came Bulgaria — a country not less, but more backward, industrially speaking, than Russia. In Bulgaria there was no more manufacture and industry than in Russia. In Bulgaria the working class, both numerically and politically, was weaker than with us. Its power and weight were less than the power and weight of the working class in Russia before the March Revolution. Bulgaria was an overwhelmingly peasant country. But nonetheless it is plain that if the revolution triumphs in Bulgaria, this revolution will be a Socialist revolution.[30]

So it will be throughout Europe, throughout the civilised world. It must be so, because history has placed the Socialist revolution on the order of the day. It will be so, and Kautsky was right in 1907 when he said that Socialism even then was only a question of might. And Kautsky is wrong and falsified the facts when in 1918, he, the hypocrite and renegade, brings forward arguments to make us believe that the Russian proletarian revolution is not being swept by the spirit of the Communist Lenin, but by that of the lower middle class opportunist Eduard David.

An international revolution is not made to order. An international proletarian revolution cannot take place simultaneously in all countries. An international proletarian revolution is not produced according to the special prescription of this or that group of leaders. Here and there, the proletarian revolution may temporarily land into difficulties, and find itself between the hammer and the anvil. The immediate fate of Bulgaria, for instance, may possibly be very distressing. It is perfectly possible that when the workers' and peasants' revolution in Bulgaria has conquered, when it has mastered the hordes of Wilhelm, it may tomorrow find itself face to face with the no less reactionary hordes of Anglo-French imperialism. Perhaps Bulgaria and the Balkans will fall for a time into the jaws of Anglo-French imperialism. Perhaps the Bulgarian and Balkan revolutions will live to see their Brest. Perhaps the German proletariat, which tomorrow will take power into its own hands, and will have to liquidate that heavy heritage which Wilhelm and Hindenburg[31] have amassed for it — perhaps it, too, will have to undergo that bitter experience which will bring to mind our days of Brest. And perhaps the Ukrainian proletariat, which has already seen so much hardship, is destined to have yet bitterer experiences when its destinies will be tossed about like a tennis ball among the imperialist lords of the two coalitions. But nonetheless the future — and it is now possible to say with full confidence — the immediate future belongs to the proletarian revolution.

Even our revolution of 1905 had profound international consequences. Our first revolution itself had awakened hundreds and hundreds of millions of human beings in the East. But what was the revolution of 1905 in comparison with the revolution of 1917-18? — a child's toy, a flap of the unfledged wing! We still live too near the event, and cannot with one glance survey those colossal international consequences which flow out of our present revolution. But this is certain: this first great **proletarian** revolution of ours will arouse hundreds and hundreds of millions of people all over the world.

However much we may be slandered by the whole international bourgeoisie, however much the hireling social chauvinists may rush to its aid, however much they may describe our great movement as anarchy, as bloody chaos, as the depths of hell, they will not succeed in deceiving the proletarians of Europe and America. In his heart, in his inner feelings, every honest worker in Europe and America knows that the struggle we are carrying on in Russia is his affair. He feels that in Russia is being decided the great contest between labour and capital, that in our territory the first battle is being fought out — the first great skirmish of the outposts between the bourgeoisie, already in its decline, and the proletariat, pressing inevitably to power.

And whatever the pessimists and faint hearts say, we are most deeply convinced that we are going forward to fight the great fight and win the great victory.

The forecast of a revolutionary war outlined by Marx in 1848,[32] of which Engels still spoke in the 1890s[33] — this forecast is being wholly realised. If the proletarian revolution conquers tomorrow in Berlin, we shall unite with proletarian Berlin against bourgeois Paris and imperialist London. If tomorrow in Paris or Rome the workers should rise and take power into their own hands, we shall unite with proletarian Rome against bourgeois Vienna, or with the workmen's Paris against Hindenburg's Berlin. The idea of a revolutionary proletarian war takes on a most concrete bodily form. We do not yet know in all its details what will be the setting of the great world drama. We do not know in what precise grouping the portions of our Red Socialist Army will advance to war against the hordes of European imperialism. But one thing we know: under our very eyes the imperialist war is turning into a civil war — at first, it is true, in Russia alone, but other countries are coming into line.

The world proletarian revolution is at hand. There approaches a new Communist International, an International of the Soviets of Workers', Soldiers' and Peasants' Delegates.

Notes

1. Taken from a pamphlet published by the Socialist Labour Press in Glasgow. Although undated, the text indicates that it was written towards the end of September 1918. We are greatly indebted to Ray Challinor for the loan of the original text.
2. Camille Huysmanns (1871-1968), a leader of the Belgian Workers Party, was Secretary of the International Socialist Bureau, but became a chauvinist during the First World War.
3. Victor Adler (1852-1918) was a leader of the Austrian Social Democratic Party who supported the war and became Foreign Secretary of the provisional government after the collapse of the Austrian Empire.
4. Philipp Scheidemann (1865-1939), a leader of the right wing of the German Social Democracy, was Chancellor of Germany during the suppression of the Spartacist revolt.
5. Pierre Renaudel (1871-1935) was the editor of L'Humanité, the paper of the French Socialist Party, and became a social patriot during the First World War.
6. Arthur Henderson (1863-1935) was General Secretary of the Labour Party and a member of Lloyd George's war cabinet in 1916-17.
7. Karl Kautsky, Die Diktatur des Proletariats, Vienna, 1918. English edition, The Dictatorship of the Proletariat, Ann Arbor, 1964.
8. Karl Kautsky, Sozialismus und Kolonialpolitik, Berlin, 1907. English edition, Socialism and Colonial Policy: An Analysis, British and Irish Communist Organisation, 1975. The passage quoted is to be found in the English version on p26.
9. Rudolf Hilferding (1877-1941) was one of German Social Democracy's foremost economists, and later one of the leaders of the Independent Socialist Party (USPD).
10. R Hilferding, Das Finanzkapital: Eine Studie über die jüngste Entwicklung des Kapitalismus, Vienna, 1910; English translation by Sam Gordon (who got precious little credit for it), Finance Capital, London, 1981, pp366-8. Zinoviev's quotation alters the order of these sentences, and does not properly indicate the gaps between them. We have restored the order of the original.
11. Otto Bauer, 'Die Nationalitätenfrage und die Sozialdemokratie', Marx-Studien, 2, Vienna 1907.
12. August Bebel (1840-1913) was a friend of Marx and Engels, and a founder of German Social Democracy.
13. It is unclear as to which of the Moroccan conflicts this refers — to that sparked off by the Kaiser's visit to Tangier in 1905, or to the arrival of the gunboat Panther in Agadir in 1911, but the context suggests the latter.
14. The Twilight of the Gods was the cataclysm of German paganism, immortalised by Wagner in his operas.
15. The Seventh International Socialist Congress held at Stuttgart on 18-24 August 1907 passed a resolution affirming that the working class should do its utmost to use the crisis brought about by war to involve the people in political action to bring closer the collapse of capitalism.
16. Professor Karl Grünberg (1861-1940) was the well-known editor of a Socialist historical journal.

17. The manifesto of the extraordinary Congress of the Second International meeting in Basle in November 1912 called upon the Socialists of all countries to mobilise all the strength and energy of the proletariat to struggle against the coming war.
18. In 1912-13 Serbia, Bulgaria, Greece and Montenegro joined in an attack upon the Turkish Empire in Europe in the First Balkan War.
19. François Rabelais (1494-1553), one of France's foremost renaissance figures and author of *Gargantua and Pantagruel*, was a resolute opponent of arbitrary rule and priestly obscurantism.
20. François Marie Arouet de Voltaire (1694-1778) was a French philosopher famous for his opposition to religious obscurantism and arbitrary despotism.
21. Victor-Marie Hugo (1802-1885), the famous historical novelist, was a noted defender of democracy, and sat in the Constituent and Legislative Assemblies in France after 1848.
22. The Black Hundreds was an organisation of extreme Russian chauvinists founded in 1905 with links with the Tsarist police, and which carried out massacres of Jews. The pogroms of October 1905 referred to cost the lives of between 3500 and 4000 innocent people.
23. Karl Liebknecht (1871-1919) was a leader of the Spartakusbund who was jailed for his resistance to the First World War. He was killed by right wing irregulars in January 1919.
24. 1848 was a year of profound revolutionary convulsions in France, Germany, the Austro-Hungarian Empire and indeed, all over Europe.
25. Albert Thomas (1878-1932) was a right wing French Socialist who was Minister for Munitions in the First World War. He visited Russia on several occasions with the aim of keeping Russia in the war on the side of France.
26. John Maclean (1879-1923) was a Scots Socialist jailed for his opposition to the First World War.
27. Friedrich Adler (1879-1960), the son of Victor Adler, was imprisoned during the First World War for the assassination of the Austrian Chancellor, Count Stürghk, in 1916. He later became Secretary of the Second International (1923-1939).
28. Eugene V Debs (1855-1926) was American Socialism's most prominent figure. He was imprisoned in 1918-21 for his opposition to the First World War.
29. The Treaty of Brest-Litovsk, signed between Russia, Austria-Hungary and Germany on 15 March 1918, marked the withdrawal of the USSR from the First World War. By it, it had to give up Latvia, Lithuania, Estonia, Poland, the Ukraine and Georgia, losing much of its industry and the best of its agricultural land.
30. On 15 September 1918, inspired by the Agrarian Party, the Bulgarian regiments on the Macedonian front mutinied, proclaimed a republic, and marched on Sofia. The government was obliged to release the agrarian leader Stambolisky from prison to persuade them to submit to discipline. A fortnight later Bulgaria requested an armistice from the Entente.
31. Field Marshal Paul Von Hindenburg und Beneckendorff (1847-1934) was titular head of the German army towards the end of the First World War.
32. The entire international programme of the *Neue Rheinische Zeitung* of 1848 edited by Marx was that 'only a war against Russia would be a revolutionary war for Germany. In such a war it could wash away the sins of the past, vindicate its own manliness, defeat its own despots, advance the cause of civilisation by sacrificing its own sons in a manner worthy of a people which has flung off the chains of long-suffered and dull slavery, and win freedom at home by freeing itself externally.' (Franz Mehring, *Karl Marx*, English edition, 1948, p161)
33. Friedrich Engels, 'Socialism in Germany', October 1891, K Marx and F Engels, *Collected works*, Volume 27, Moscow, 1990, p245: 'This war, in which 15 to 20 million armed men would slaughter one another and devastate Europe as it has never been devastated before — this war would either lead to the immediate triumph of Socialism, or it would lead to such an upheaval in the old order of things, that it would leave behind it everywhere such a heap of ruins, that the old capitalist society would become more impossible than ever, and the social revolution, set back by 10 or 15 years, would only be all the more radical and more rapidly implemented.'

RUSSIA AND POLAND

LABOUR DECLARES AGAINST WAR
COMMITTEES OF ACTION TO BE FORMED LOCALLY

To the Secretaries of Local Trades Councils and Labour Parties

ORGANISED Labour has repeatedly made definite declarations in favour of a policy of Peace towards Russia. We have demanded the removal of the Blockade ; we have several times called upon the Government to institute negotiations for Peace. Notwithstanding these efforts, the reactionary forces inside our own Government and behind the Governments of our Allies, have at last succeeded in bringing us to open and declared war. There is no justification offered for this policy except an alleged menace to the independence of Poland. We are convinced the real object is to destroy the power of the Government of Russia and to re-establish in that country a form of government more in harmony with the capitalist interest who dominate the foreign and domestic policy of European States.

The workers of this country have nothing to gain by the contemplated attack on Russia. If War is declared we should again be involved in unlimited sacrifice of blood and treasure, and should be used as the tools of capitalist oppression. The national leaders have acted promptly ; all sections are united in denouncing the present policy of the Government. On this question there is no division or hesitation. A national body has been elected responsible for effec-tive resistance if War is declared. The Council of Action, appointed at a Special Conference at the House of Commons on Monday, is already at work. Plans have been prepared for mobilising the full resources of our movement. United industrial action, even to the extent of a General Strike, may be necessary. We must, however, act in strict accordance with a well-thought-out policy and plan. The Council of Action will sit in constant session to watch developments and will issue advice to the affiliated organisations. In the meantime, the action taken

Leaflet issued by the TUC leadership on 10 August 1920. Lenin's com-ments on the Councils of Action are on pages 145-6.

nationally must be followed immediately by similar action in the various districts, and we make the following suggestions :

1. Secretaries of local Trades Councils and Labour Parties should immediately convene a Special Conference for the purpose of electing a local Council of Action.

2. The local Councils should form sub-committees to deal with the following questions : (1) Supply and Transport ; (2) Strike Arrangements ; (3) Publicity and Information.

3. The name and address of secretaries appointed to act as secretaries of the local Councils, should be forwarded to the Joint Secretaries of the National Council immediately after the Conference.

The local organisations are urged to act speedily in connection with this important crisis in the history of our Movement. Ordinary methods of procedure should be suspended and special efforts made to get the local Conferences working in a few days. Points of contact between every district in the country and the National Council are absolutely essential. In the meantime spasmodic and ill-considered action should be avoided everywhere. The time has arrived for effective organisation and responsible officials are again urged to act in accordance with our advice.

W. ADAMSON, *Chairman*

J. R. CLYNES	FRANK HODGES
JOSIAH WEDGWOOD	J. BROMLEY
A. B. SWALES	ERNEST BEVIN
A. G. CAMERON	JOHN ROBERTSON
ROBERT WILLIAMS	A. A. PURCELL
W. H. HUTCHINSON	MARGARET BONDFIELD
J. O'GRADY	C. T. CRAMP
H. GOSLING	ROBERT SMILLIE
R. B. WALKER	J. W. BOWEN

F. BRAMLEY,
J. S. MIDDLETON, } *Joint Secretaries*
H. S. LINDSAY,

32 Eccleston Square, S.W.1
August 10th, 1920

Printed at the PELICAN PRESS (T.U.), 2 Carmelite Street, E.C.

Vladimir Lenin

The International Significance of the War with Poland[1]

Preliminary Note by the Translator

It is a pity that we have these remarkable documents in so unsatisfactory a form, but that circumstance is due to their very nature. Lenin spoke so frankly in these speeches that they were not considered suitable for publication, except in abridged and expurgated paraphrases. Consequently, the 'verbatim' reports remained until 1992 in the closed archives, unedited, and even uncorrected.

The result is that we have texts in which all the slips of the tongue, unfinished sentences, etc, that there may have been in what Lenin actually said are supplemented by all the mis-hearings and misunderstandings of the shorthand writers who recorded him. The Russian editors have frequently put their equivalent of 'sic' after what struck them as obvious errors, and they sometimes suggest what the right word must have been. The English translator can only wish that they had done this more often! I have inserted '[sic — BP]' in a few cases myself.

The attentive reader will, however, in many cases be able to make the needed correction from the sense of the context. For example, in a place where Lenin is made to say 'uninterested', what is clearly meant is the opposite, 'interested'. In the newspaper report of his first speech the statement — pointless as it stands in the text — that the Council of Action was 'unlike' (ne pokhozh) the first All-Russian Central Executive Committee of the Soviets was duly corrected to 'like' (podobnoe) — see *Polnoe Sobranie Sochineniia*, Volume 41, p283; English translation in *Collected Works*, Volume 31, p277.

The effort of imagination required in reading these texts is rewarded by their content as a source for Lenin's thinking at the time the speeches were given. He makes it plain that it was a hard decision for the Bolshevik leadership to cross the border of 'ethnographic Poland'. (That Trotsky argued against this move and favoured acceptance of the 'Curzon Line' is shown by his letter to the Political Bureau dated 13 July 1920, reproduced from *The Trotsky Papers* in *Trotsky's Writings on Britain*, Volume 1, 1974, pp100-1.) Lenin speculates on whether it might have been wiser not to do that in the given circumstances — but leaves no doubt that Soviet Russia would resort once more to 'offensive warfare' if circumstances turned favourable.

Amongst the reasons that have been suggested for the failure of the Soviet invasion of Poland in 1920 is that, like Hitler in his invasion of Russia in 1941, they pursued three objectives at once, instead of concentrating their forces. The Red Army advanced towards Warsaw with a view to establishing in the Polish capital a Communist regime which could then claim to be the de facto government of Poland. It also pressed forward to the north-west of Warsaw with a view to reaching the 1914 frontier between the German and Russian Empires. And it moved into Eastern Galicia, in the far south, with a view to opening a line of advance into Hungary.

Lenin dwells significantly on the 'contrary-to-nature' bloc which objectively came about in Germany during the Soviet-Polish war, between Communists and revanchists. We know from other writings of his in this period that he looked forward to a clash between Germany and the Entente powers in which the German workers would certainly not be advised by him to promote the defeat of their country. (For example, in his reply to Paul Levi of 25 July 1920, in which he urges Levi to consider a situation in which Germany goes to war against Britain and France: 'What should the workers do? Boycott? That would be quite mistaken. Participate, but guard their independence, and so utilise the **common** struggle so as to overthrow the bourgeoisie.' (*Polnoe Sobranie Sochineniia*, Volume 41, p458; not included in the *Collected Works*.)

During the successful period of the Red Army's campaign in Poland, the Soviet emissary Kopp told the German diplomat Von Maltzan on 19 July 1920 that when the new regime was established in Warsaw, Moscow would urge it to yield the Polish Corridor and Upper Silesia to Germany, and allow Germany and Russia to have a common frontier in the vicinity of Bialystok (Richard K Deles, *Survival and Consolidation*, 1992, p302, giving a German Foreign Ministry archive reference). Here we observe the preliminary approach that led to the secret military collaboration between the Reichswehr and Red Army which went on between 1921 and 1933.

Lenin also devotes particular attention to the question of Eastern Galicia, which the Soviets could have obtained, either by accepting the 'Curzon Line', or if the campaign in Poland had gone better for them. What interests him in this province is its proximity to Sub-Carpathian Rus (in the Western usage, sometimes 'Ruthenia'), the Ukrainian-inhabited tip of Czechoslovakia which touched Romania, separating Poland from Hungary. He had cabled Stalin on 23 July 1920: 'Zinoviev, Bukharin and I, too, think that the revolution should be immediately exacerbated in Italy. My own view is that, to this end, one should sovietise Hungary...' (Richard Pipes, *Russia under the Bolshevik Regime*, 1994, p177, giving a Soviet archive reference). This, perhaps, puts in a different light the persistence of Yegorov and Stalin in pushing towards Lvov instead of moving the forces of the South-Western Front towards Warsaw, for which they were later criticised by writers, some of whom may not have been aware of Lenin's objectives in the direction of Hungary. Incidentally, it was perhaps over-sanguine of Lenin to expect that if the Red Army reached the border of Hungary, it would then be easy to restart revolution in that country. Admiral Horthy's 'White Terror' following the collapse of Béla Kun's regime had been very thorough.

Explanation of Russian measures used in the texts

A verst is 3500 English feet, or 1.06 kilometres, a pood is 16.38 kilograms, or about 36 pounds, and a desiatina is 2.7 acres. The word 'concessions' is used here in two senses: firstly, in connection with the diplomatic negotiations with Poland, to refer to pieces of territory that Soviet Russia might agree to surrender to Poland as part of a peace settlement; secondly, in connection with the internal economic

problems of Soviet Russia, to refer to the licenses granted to foreign capitalists to exploit some of Russia's natural resources.
Brian Pearce

Russian Publisher's Preface

'**I request that less be taken down, this must not get into the newspapers.**'

The last 70 years have seen no decline in the world's interest in Lenin and his legacy. Scholars and publicists have written tens of thousands of books and articles on the subject. Yet, so far, there has been no really scientific biography of Lenin, describing his political thought, the way his ideas evolved, his creative laboratory.

There are many reasons why this is so. One of the most important is the incompleteness of the resource base available to the researcher.

From the mid-1920s onward the life and activity of Lenin were canonised in order to satisfy ideological dogma and the current political situation. Everything that had even the slightest connection with him was weighed and evaluated, and then either adopted or rejected, at the highest party and state level. In the first place, Lenin-connected documents were subjected to strict censorship.

Five editions of Lenin's *Collected Works* were published, together with 40 issues of *Leninskii Sbornik*. However, even the latest 55-volume collection of his works, entitled 'complete', cannot claim to be either complete or to be academically respectable. The texts of many documents were printed without the rules for scientific publication being observed, and there were frequent cases of their being edited and amended. A fairly large number of Lenin documents have never been published.[2]

Amongst the documents which have been unavailable to researchers is Lenin's political report on behalf of the Central Committee of the RCP(B) and his concluding speech in the debate on this report at the Ninth All-Russian Conference of the RCP(B), which was held in Moscow on 22-25 September 1920.

Here we have a unique case of a report by the founder and leader of the ruling Communist Party, presented in the party's highest forum, which has for 70 years remained unknown to his followers. It is at the same time typical as a striking example of the protective attitude to Lenin's biography which prevailed for many years. A speech that did not fit into the strictly-defined framework of the traditional interpretation of Lenin's views and ideas had no right to be published.

The political report of the Central Committee of the RCP(B) presented to the plenary morning session of the Ninth Party Conference on 22 September 1920 is a document which has many levels. Expressed in it first and foremost are the notions then held by the leader of the young Soviet state concerning the character of the Civil War, the tempos and prospects of the world-wide revolutionary process, and the rôles of the Republic of the Soviets, of the proletariat, and of other countries in the development of that process. The document shows that Lenin and the other leaders of the RCP(B) in 1920 still nourished the hope of a swiftly-coming world social revolution. Events occurring in Russia are treated in the report as the first stage of the world revolution, as a clash between one of the national units of the proletariat and the world bourgeoisie, united in the Entente. It is from these premises that the principal subject of discussion at the conference is evaluated, namely, the results of the military campaign in Poland and its international significance. The war with Poland is defined by Lenin as a turning-point in the class confrontation of the proletariat with the imperialist forces, a first and unsuccessful attempt by the Russian Communists to urge forward, by force of arms, the development of the revolutionary process in other countries.

The content of Lenin's report and concluding speech predetermined their subsequent fate. Being confidential in character, they were at that time not intended for immediate publication. 'I request that less be taken down, this must not get into the newspapers', Lenin warned the delegates to the conference. Judging by the shorthand report, he spoke freely, and was extremely frank. He did not choose diplomatic expressions when he described the country's international situation, and when analysing the outcome of the Polish campaign and the Party leadership's responsibility for the military situation.

Consequently, when the newspapers *Pravda* and *Izvestia TSIK* reported the conference a week later, on 29 September 1920, they published only a much-abridged version of Lenin's speech. In the publication *The Ninth All-Russian Conference of the RCP(B)*, which came out in Baku in that year from the state publishing house Azertsentropechet, the materials of the first and second plenary sessions of the conference were completely omitted.

In subsequent decades the materials of the Ninth All-Russian Party Conference remained practically closed to everyone. They recalled too vividly events in which was directly involved one of those principally responsible for the military defeat in the war with Poland — the former member of the Revolutionary Military Council of the South-Western Front, Stalin.[3]

The question of publishing Lenin documents re-emerged in the 1960s and the early 1970s. However, the negative decision which was then taken reflected the practice that had become established of whitewashing the life and activity of Lenin. The compilers and editors and those who ultimately decided the question of publication were evidently frightened by the sharpness of Lenin's appraisals, and their obvious failure to correspond to the officially-depicted image of the leader.

As a result, in Volume 41 of the *Complete Collection* of Lenin's works, and also in the publication *Proceedings of the Ninth Conference of the RCP(B)* (Moscow, 1972), all that was included, without any explanation being given, was that same newspaper report from *Pravda* of 29 September 1920. The shorthand report of Lenin's concluding speech on his report was not published at all, as was explained to readers, owing to the lack of a corrected copy of the text, such as existed in the speeches of the other delegates to the conference.

The record of Lenin's speech giving his report at the morning session, and of his concluding speech at the evening session of the conference, on 22 September 1920, was made by the shorthand writers serving the conference: Vladimirova, Lasman, Rozhdestvenskaia and Ostroumova. The gaps in the text correspond, as a rule, to the movements when one of the shorthand writers handed over to another. The uncorrected typescript made from the shorthand report of Lenin's speech is to be found along with all the other stenograms of the conference sessions which are held at the Russian Centre for Storage and Study of Documents of Recent History (RTsKhlDNI).

In the present publication the current rules of spellings have been observed. The words in square brackets have been inserted at the discretion of the editors.

The publication was prepared by AA Artizov and RA Usikov, candidates of historical sciences.

Political Report of the Central Committee of the Russian Communist Party (Bolshevik) to the Ninth Conference of the RCP(B)[4]

COMRADES, IT is natural that in a report to be given at this moment the centre of attention should be the war with Poland, and all the reversals of fortune we have experienced in this period. Permit me to begin [with] some [observations] from the beginning of this period, when the Polish war had not yet become a fact.

You know that before the Polish war, we approached the problems with extraordinary caution, and offered to the Poles, to the Polish bourgeoisie, in most solemn form, even in a special manifesto issued in the name of the Central Executive Committee, peace[5] on conditions that were in the highest degree [un]favourable to us, to a whole number of nationalities, [and to] the workers and peasants who were under the yoke of the Polish landlords and bourgeoisie. We offered peace on the basis of Pilsudski's[6] line, that is, the line on which the Poles stood before the beginning of their offensive on 26 April of this year, that is, a line by which they would obtain all Byelorussia and a substantial slice of the Ukraine, because they then had the province of Volhynia, and a lot of bits around Rovno, which they have now retaken. We agreed to make peace on this line, because we rated the peaceful economic work to which we had transformed the life of the army and that of tens of thousands of workers and peasants very much more highly than the possibility of liberating, by military successes, Byelorussia and part of the Ukraine, or Eastern Galicia.

Here, in the international political and economic relations, it has been repeatedly confirmed, and will be confirmed, that our new diplomacy, unusual, unforeseen in the history of monarchical and bourgeois states, can in no way be as yet accepted in other countries; that, when the Bolsheviks come forward with frank declarations, absolutely nobody in any state is capable of understanding that we are really pursuing a diplomacy based on public statements and the methods of a special kind of diplomacy. That is, if the Bolsheviks say 'We are ready to recognise Pilsudski's line' [the international bourgeoisie reasons like this] — it means that the Bolsheviks are extremely weak, and the concession is excessively big. [By our proposals] we gave support to the most frenzied chauvinism of the Polish bourgeoisie and landlords, the most frenzied chauvinism in France and in other imperialist countries, [because there] everyone reasoned that, in ordinary diplomacy, such things cannot be: 'How can this happen? It's weakness.' Thus, the offensive was decided on, not by the Poles alone, but also by France, because we, in a quite unusual way, said outright: 'For the sake of avoiding war, we are willing to retreat.' And in the negotiations which Marchlewski[7] conducted earlier, formally as representative of the Red Cross of Poland [sic], in those negotiations this line was fundamental as preliminary conditions for peace.[8] Consequently, through these earlier negotiations, we made such huge concessions. This conceding was understood as weakness on our part, and led to war.

You remember the beginning of the war, which was successful for the Poles, up to their capture of Kiev.[9] According to provisional calculations, they conquered territory with a population of four million. You remember how, after this success [for the Poles], [re]grouping of our forces brought success for us, and our forces, going over to the offensive, advanced quickly to Poland's most important line.

Here begins the major turn in the history of the Polish war, which in fact was a turn from peace [to] war. With this it is necessary to begin, so as to clarify subsequent history, and to proceed to the most important matter, which now concerns every party member, the most topical question — that profound, catastrophic defeat which we suffered as a result of the entire development of the operation.

On 12 July, when our troops, in an uninterrupted offensive, covering an immense stretch of territory, had reached the ethnographic border of Poland, the British government, [in] the person of Curzon,[10] addressed a note to us[11] which demanded that we halt our forces on a line 50 versts from the ethnographic frontier of Poland, as a condition for concluding peace on this line. This line followed the line [of] Bialystok to Brest-Litovsk, and gave us Eastern Galicia. Thus, this line was very favourable to us. This line was called the Curzon Line.

And now a fundamental question arose before us. The Central Committee had to take a very important decision. And this [decision] is the starting point to which, in my report, I must return in order to give my appreciation of the most important and fundamental question.

We were faced with the question — to accept this proposal, which would have given us favourable frontiers, and thus to take up a position which, generally speaking, was purely defensive, or to use this élan in our army and the advantage that we enjoyed in order to help sovietise Poland. There arose here the fundamental question of defensive and offensive warfare, and we in the Central Committee knew that this was a new question of principle, that we were standing at a turning point in the entire policy of the Soviet power.

Up to now, when waging war against the Entente, because we knew perfectly well that behind every separate offensive by Kolchak and Yudenich stood the Entente, we understood that we were fighting a war of defence, and would beat the Entente, but that we were not capable of winning final victory over the Entente, that it was many times stronger than us. And we merely sought to exploit as fully as possible the cracks that opened up between the different states of the Entente, so as to defend ourselves in good time. With Yudenich and Denikin, history showed us something unprecedented and improbable, from the standpoint of the calculation of forces. We beat them one by one. And the cleverest politicians in the world, who were only deeply involved from the colonial standpoint, like Britain, and deeply-involved France, concerned about its milliards in the former Tsarist house (and there are still some strange folk over there who hope to get them back), not only these deeply-involved politicians who hope to grab something from Russia, not only these major politicians interested in Russia, but also those indirectly uninterested, they all proved to be in a state of disintegration. Though they were a hundred times stronger than us, they were unable to put this potential into effect, because they were at odds amongst themselves, because they could not take a single step, could not carry out the simple task of uniting three or four elements, of uniting and coordinating three or four mighty powers which possessed infinite superiority over us, not only as regards finances, but also as regards naval forces, and so on. We had nothing, but they could not unite amongst themselves even in the financial matter, and this enabled us to win. And this was at a time when the entire bourgeoisie was seething with rage and hatred against Bolshevism. And it turned out that we were stronger than them. They launched our enemies against us separately, and, whilst shouting that they did not want to restore the Tsar, they were incapable of preventing Yudenich and Denikin from pursuing a purely monarchist policy, and thereby alienating the element which should have been for them, the muzhik, kulak elements.

And now this meant, in sum, that the circumstance came about that confidence grew in us that the military offensive of the Entente against us was over, that the defensive war with imperialism had ended, and we had won. Poland was the issue. And Poland thought that, as a power with imperialist traditions, it was in a position to change the character of the war. This meant that the appreciation was that the period of defensive war had ended. (I request that less be taken down, this must not get into the newspapers.) On the other hand, the offensive showed us that given the Entente's impotence to crush us militarily, its inability to do this with its own soldiers, it could only incite against us individual small states, worthless in military terms and maintaining the landlord-bourgeois system only at the price of those measures of coercion and terror which the Entente allows them to use. There can be no doubt that the Menshevik-democratic capitalism which still prevails in all the states bordering on Russia, formed out of the former Russian Empire, beginning with Estonia, Georgia, etc, maintains itself by means of what the Entente supplies. The Entente gives guns, soldiers, equipment and money so as to keep the workers in submission.

A new task faced us. The defensive period of the war with world imperialism had ended, and we could and must make use of the military situation to begin an offensive war. We had beaten them when they attacked us. Now we would try to attack them, so as to help to sovietise Poland. We would help to sovietise Lithuania and Poland, that was what our resolution said.

When this resolution was tabled in the Central Committee, there was no lack of appreciation amongst us of the awkwardness of this resolution, in the sense that it would be impossible to vote against it. How could one vote against helping sovietisation?

If we compare our relations with Poland with our relations with Georgia and Latvia, the difference becomes quite clear. We did not adopt a resolution to help by military means the sovietisation of Georgia or Estonia. We adopted a resolution to the contrary — not to help.

On this matter we had a number of conflicts with the revolutionaries and Communists of these countries. They made speeches full of bitterness against us, saying: 'How can you make peace with the White Guard Latvian butchers who have hanged and tortured the best Latvian comrades, who shed their blood for Soviet Russia?' Such speeches we heard also from the Georgians, but we did not help to sovietise Georgia and Latvia. And we cannot do that now, because we are not up to it. Saving and consolidating the republic is the overwhelming task before us.

In relation to Poland, however, we changed this policy. We decided to use our armed forces to help in the sovietising of Poland. From that decision followed our subsequent general policy.

We did not formulate this in an official resolution, recorded in the minutes of the Central Committee, and constituting law for the party until the next congress. But amongst ourselves we said that we must probe with bayonets to discover whether the social revolution of the proletariat was ripe in Poland. And here we posed a practical question which, as it turned out, was not completely clear, from the theoretical standpoint, to the best Communist elements in the international fellowship, the Communist International.

When the congress of the Comintern was in progress in July in Moscow,[12] that was the time when we were deciding this question in the Central Committee. We could not raise this question at the Comintern congress, because that congress had to proceed in public. In that lay its immense revolutionary, general-political, world significance, which is manifesting itself many times more than hitherto. At this congress were elements connected with the German Independents, who are now pursuing a most vile policy against the Soviet power. They had to be thrown out at that time. It was necessary to show to the world-wide Communist Party that we did not want to let them into our ranks. So we had to speak openly at the congress of the Communist International. Consequently, this question was deliberately not touched upon at the congress. Going over to the offensive against the allies of the Entente could not be brought up there, because there they were not at the stage of development necessary for considering this question. We had to be patient [with them].

Rote Fahne[13] and many others could not accept the idea that we should help with our own hands to sovietise Poland. These people regard themselves as Communists, but some of them are still nationalists and pacifists. Of course, those Communists who have had more experience, [to] which category belong the Finnish comrades, have not retained even a particle of these prejudices. I say that they have not retained them because they have been through a long period of war. When the British workers' delegates came to see me[14] and I told them that every honest British worker ought to wish for the defeat of the British government, they completely failed to understand me. They made such faces as, I think, not even the best photographer could catch. Their heads were quite unable to accommodate this truth, that, in the interests of the international revolution, the British workers should wish for the defeat of their own government.

The fact is that [in] Poland there is a well-developed proletarian population and a well-educated agricultural proletariat which said to us: 'You must help them to become sovietised.'

And that was the stage at which events stood, and at which our own party stood. This was a most important turning-point, not only in the policy of Soviet Russia, but also in world politics. Hitherto we had acted as a solitary force against the whole world, dreaming only of how to find chinks between our enemies so as to prevent them from crushing us. But now we said: 'We have now become much stronger, and to each of your attempts at an offensive we shall reply with a counter-offensive, so that you may know that you risk not only losing a few millions, such as you lost on Yudenich, Kolchak and Denikin, but you risk every offensive of yours resulting in an enlargement of the domain of the Soviet Republic.' Up to now Russia has been merely an object about which they pondered and judged how best to divide it between Yudenich, Kolchak and Denikin. But now Russia said: 'We shall see who is the stronger when it comes to war.' That was how the question stood now. This was a change in all politics, in world politics. Here it would be for the historian to note that this began a new period.

What were the results of this policy? The principal result, of course, was that we have now suffered a huge defeat. So as to arrive at that I must describe what preceded it.

To what extent did we succeed in sounding out with our bayonets Poland's readiness for social revolution? It must be said that this readiness was slight. Sounding out with bayonets meant achieving direct access to the Polish farm labourers and the Polish industrial proletariat, insofar as it existed in Poland. The industrial proletariat was in Warsaw, in Lodz, and in the Dombrowa mines, which were very distant from the frontier. On the other hand, in order really to sound out the degree of readiness of Poland's proletariat, the industrial workers, in the first place, and in the second place, the farm labourers on a basis of preponderance [sic], we should have had to clean up the Polish bourgeois troops and ourselves occupy not only the Warsaw area, but also those areas where the industrial proletariat is located. But those areas begin even sooner [sic: from the sense, evidently 'further'] than Warsaw, which we did not manage to take. Consequently, we had extremely little success in sounding out Poland's readiness for Socialist revolution.

We encountered a great national upsurge of the petit-bourgeois elements, who entered into a panic fear for their national existence as we drew nearer to Warsaw. We did not succeed in sounding out the real mood of the proletarian masses and the farm labourers, and in the ranks of the industrial proletariat of Poland.

As against that, a picture emerges in international politics which represents something in the highest degree favourable to us, and which was the centre of this event. One aspect of this picture will be shown you more completely, in all details, by Comrade Kamenev, who observed in London some of the developments [in these events].[15]

We did not succeed in sounding out the development and preparedness for Socialist revolution of the proletariat in Warsaw. Our advance showed that Poland cannot conquer us, but we came very near to conquering Poland.

It has turned out that all this is changing international politics. In drawing near Warsaw we approached so close to the centre of world imperialist politics that we began to do that. This sounds incomprehensible, but the history of the 'Council of Action'[16] in Britain showed, with absolute precision, that somewhere near Warsaw lies not only the centre of the Polish bourgeois government and the republic of capital, but also the centre of the entire present system of international imperialism, and that we are now in conditions when we are starting to shake that system, and practising politics not [only] in Poland, but in Germany and Britain. Thus, in Germany and Britain we have created a completely new field of proletarian revolution against world imperialism, because Poland, as the buffer between Russia and Germany, Poland, as the last state, remains wholly in the hands of international imperialism against Russia. It is the fulcrum of the entire Versailles Treaty.

The contemporary imperialist world is based on the Versailles Treaty. After beating Germany and settling the question of which of the two powerful worldwide groups, the British or the German, would dispose of the world's fate in the immediate future, the imperialists concluded [the war] with the peace of Versailles. They have no other means for consolidating world relations, both political and economic, than the Versailles peace. Poland is such a powerful element in this Versailles peace that, by breaking this element away, we would fracture the entire Versailles peace. We set ourselves the task of taking Warsaw. The task changed. And it turned out that what was being decided was not the fate of Warsaw, but the fate of the Treaty of Versailles. That was how the question was presented in all the bourgeois Black Hundred papers in Germany, and in the French press.

When our forces approached the frontiers of East Prussia, which is separated by a corridor of Poland which extends to Danzig, we saw that all Germany seethed. News began to arrive that tens and hundreds of thousands of German Communists were crossing our frontiers. Telegrams flew in [about the formation] of German Communist regiments. We had to take a decision not to publish [this news] of help, and to go on saying that we were fighting [Poland].

When newspapers which now reach us, which do not share the Bolsheviks' views, and which depict the situation in East Prussia, we get an extremely interesting picture, which reminds me of some periods of the Russian revolution of 1905, when there appeared in Germany [sic — BP] a standard [sic — BP] type of Black Hundred revolutionary. At that time the 1905 revolution in Russia was taking the first big steps to dig up and raise the extensive, and at the same time very backward, elements of the peasantry, and in this work we were helped by the Black Hundred elements which tried by their agitation to stir up the peasantry against us. This agitation was carried on, then, by Black Hundred priests and officers, and it happened that this newly-arisen Black Hundred political organisation was the first to unite the peasants and familiarise them with organisation. And these risen peasants, advancing today with Black Hundred demands, were next day demanding all the land from the landlords.

And now a similar thing has happened in Germany. I have not brought with me the correspondence in a certain German anti-Bolshevik paper (which, of course, I could not have read out to you, for lack of time) in which it is said that all Eastern Germany is seething, and all the Kappists (meaning those who supported Kapp[17] — our [sic — BP] Kornilov), all these Kappists are for the Bolsheviks. And it happens that when one talks with an immature young German fellow, who knows nothing about politics, he hesitates and says that Wilhelm ought to come back, because there is no order, and that at the same time he says the opposite, that one ought to go along with the Bolsheviks.

And we see that Eastern Germany is seething. A sort of contrary-to-nature bloc is being formed, at the head of which are Kornilovist generals who, being men of military common sense, and whose slogan is simply 'War against France at any price, never mind with whom or in what conditions' — these German officers are politically illiterate men who do not realise that war brings certain consequences after it (where should they acquire such understanding? That sort of German officer would need 10 years of study in various revolutions in order to learn anything at all), and now they have the idea of war against France at any price.

And so it has come about that we had strength, and substantial strength, to put against the Entente. And at this time we replied to Curzon: 'You refer to the League of Nations.[18] But what is this "League of Nations"? It isn't worth a damn. The question still remains, who will decide Poland's fate. The question can be decided not by what the League of Nations says, but by what the Red Army man says.' That was how we answered Curzon, if you translate our note into plain language.[19] And then in Germany they understood it in that way, and there came about that contrary-to-nature bloc which was not put together by a pact, and was nowhere written down and proclaimed, but a bloc in which Kappists and Kornilovists, the entire mass of the patriotic-minded element, were with the Bolsheviks.

That was how the problem stood at that time, and this problem could not then be solved by the German Communists — they could not solve it because they were at that time sitting here; here in Moscow, sitting and deciding the most elementary question of relations with the right wing Independents, whose leaders were like our Martov, but the workers were Bolshevik-minded. They were busy deciding that world-wide question which arises in all countries. And at that time events in Germany leaped over all decisions of these questions, and a bloc took shape between consistent and extreme patriots, on the one hand, and Communists, on the other, consciously declaring for a bloc [with] Soviet Russia. A bloc has come about such that in world politics only two forces exist, one, the League of Nations, which produced the Treaty of Versailles, and the other, the Soviet Republic, which tore up that Treaty of Versailles. And the contrary-to-nature bloc [in] Germany was for us.

Here appeared a gigantic fact of international politics, which I have observed more than once in particular cases and on which I had to dwell when I drew the lessons of the campaign against Yudenich, Kolchak and Denikin, and spoke of the conditions in which we made peace with Estonia, Georgia and Latvia. On the international plane it turned out not only that we beat Kolchak and Denikin and won over Russia's well-to-do anti-Communist peasants, which, amongst other things, settled the fate of Kolchak and Denikin, but we also won over the petit-bourgeoisie and the big bourgeoisie of the small countries which, though formally independent, were crushed by the Entente. This decided the conclusion of peace with us by Estonia,[20] the first country to make peace with us. It is entirely bourgeois, it is entirely in the pockets of the British and American billionaires, it was entirely opposed to peace with us, and it made peace with us — so harshly did international imperialism present itself to Estonia.

In Germany, the Communists stuck to their slogans. When the German Lefts reached the point of saying such nonsense as that there was no need for civil war, but on the contrary, an all-national bloc against France was needed, that was unheard-of stupidity. To put the question like that bordered on betrayal. Without civil war you won't get soviet power in Germany. If you form a bloc with the German Kornilovists, they will dupe you. In Germany there is a weak, small Communist Party and a strong party of Scheidemannists, right-wing Mensheviks, an immense proletarian party, headed by our Martovs — a policy between two stools.

And the first result was that the little states which all associated with us, despite their hatred for the Bolsheviks, and alongside their suppression of their own Bolsheviks, Estonian, Finnish and Latvian, had to make peace with us, and said that in international relations we, the little states, are closer to Soviet, Bolshevik, Russia. We showed in fact that for Germany, where the mood of the masses, the most backward and Black-Hundred-minded, is such that they are capable of saying 'Wilhelm rather than this', that in international relations there is no force for Germany except Soviet Russia.

Germany's national desires consist of two quantities, which it would be a big mistake not to distinguish between politically. One of them is the desire to throw off the Versailles Treaty, which is stifling them. On the other hand, the German imperialists, who associated themselves with this desire, said: 'We want not only to throw off the Versailles treaty' — and in fact they wanted to restore imperialist Germany [sic].

Not only in the little states, but also with regard to Germany we sounded out the international situation.

In my speech at the opening of the Comintern congress, which I gave in Petrograd, I spoke about the international situation,[21] and I said that the world's population now amounts to three milliards, and three quarters of them, of those three milliards, are in the colonies, and three quarters of a milliard in the countries that were vanquished, which means that 70 percent are in the colonies. I said that even with such a rough definition, if we speak of world politics, this seven-tenths of the population will, given a correct policy, stand for Soviet Russia. Here people may ask, 'How can they stand for Soviet Russia, when they are not Communists?' And how was it that Estonia and Georgia stood with us, although they were shooting Communists? In our international policy we have now proved that we have an alliance with all the countries that live under the Versailles Treaty. And that means 70 percent of the world's entire population.

Whilst in Germany things remained at the stage of thrilling and expecting, in Britain the situation developed differently. In Britain, Curzon had put to us an ultimatum — 'Either retreat, or we'll fight you.' They had got used to thinking that having signed the Treaty of Versailles they could dispose of the whole world. When we replied that we do not recognise the League of Nations, the French newspapers wrote that this was 'a cheeky reply', using an expression from the language of the schoolroom, where a teacher tells children that we [sic —BP] are being cheeky. In world politics, however, one can't employ such terms. The fact was that the League of Nations as such did not put in an appearance.

It turned out that in order to go to war with us, it was necessary first of all to ask permission of the British worker. As a result of our declaration, the British proletariat rose to a completely new revolutionary level. Standing before Warsaw, and unable to take that city and sound out the readiness of the Polish worker for revolutionary action, we sounded out the British workers, and lifted them to a new level of revolutionary action. When we were presented with the ultimatum, the British workers, nine-tenths of whom are Mensheviks of the most hardened type, answered this by forming the 'Council of Action'. The British press started to get worried, screaming that this meant dual power. And that was true. Britain was at that stage, as regards political relations, [at] which Russia was after February 1917. Alongside the government were the soviets, which had a concili-ation commission and, in practice, every step taken by the government was checked on, and then the world's bourgeoisie said that things couldn't go on like that. And now, in Britain, a Council of Action has appeared, and this Council of Action has prevented Britain from going to war against us. None of the threats that Lord Curzon put to us has been realised, and the labour movement in Britain has been raised to an incredibly high level.

The Council of Action created an organ of the toiling masses, a political centre which took its stand alongside the bourgeoisie, and is not acting in agreement with them. This Council of Action is headed by out-and-out Mensheviks and Right SRs, people such as we, in our time, put down.

[In order to cut ourselves off from the opportunists] we needed to have the Second Congress of the Comintern in Moscow, at which representatives of all countries were present. Only now has the full text been published of the resolution in which this policy has been adopted on the international scale. And what was the response? It is said that we have put forward unheard-of conditions.[22] A split has now arisen, a split, at any rate, between Bolsheviks and Mensheviks in all countries, without exception.

At a time when we, with the Comintern's help, did what we had not been able to do in a decade, and in conditions of complete rupture with international imperialism, at that time the Mensheviks and Bolsheviks united in Britain in the Council of Action. [At the Comintern congress] we had agonisingly to carry out a task of extreme difficulty. [But] the progress of the working class movement requires that we split with the Mensheviks ideologically, and yet at the [same] time act together with them in the Council of Action.

At first sight this appears to be a contradiction and opportunism, but we say: 'You have to continue again the Russian Revolution in its main features.'

The Council of Action in Britain is quite unlike our All-Russian Central Executive Committee in the days when Gotz, Dan and others ruled the roost there. This is a union of all the workers' parties without exception — Mensheviks and Bolsheviks — a union which competes with the bourgeois government, and in which Mensheviks are obliged to behave like Bolsheviks.

We understand that the ministry of 1914 [?], which the Mensheviks and Socialist Revolutionaries of the first convocation released [sic], said that the war is imperialist, let's protect the minority. They became confused and brought the masses over to us, and so Plekhanov was right. They said: 'We are for constitutional democracy, but you are for partial democracy.'

The Council of Action is still there. But this is an extreme case. It is a thing which we must read [sic], because it relates [to] the most imperialist country [with] unusually firm traditions of Menshevism. Whereas here Menshevism has a history of 15 to 20 years, over there all the trade unions without exception have a democratic system which is headed by Mensheviks. This has all been ruined by the British Mensheviks, and they have to advance to the method of the dictatorship of the proletariat [sic].

We have obtained the possibility of saying to the British and French workers that you have got to learn to be Communists. The Comintern [Commune?] has taught that. British politics is beginning to teach politics to the French. Along with that you must learn, on the basis of the mass organisations, to form a bloc with the British Bolsheviks, when they are obliged to act constitutionally, so that the British masses may learn this in action [sic. After this there is a gap in the transcript].

We in Russia have ourselves painfully experienced how many times it had to happen that the Mensheviks and SRs duped the Russian workers, so that they ceased to believe them. They duped the Russian workers before the February Revolution, they duped them between May and the July offensive, they duped them again, and, finally, by October the Russian worker had matured to the point where he no longer let himself be duped.

How many times the British workers will have to be duped by the British Mensheviks is not written in any book, and cannot be written. That remains to be seen. But the British Bolsheviks must know how always to stand together with the masses, to enlighten them, to show and to say to them: 'Here they are, duping you again, see how they have duped you once more!' And in the process of current events in Britain you will see, and Comrade Kamenev will summarise his impressions,[23] that the British Mensheviks already feel that they are the government. They know that the bourgeois government cannot hold on in Britain, and that it will be overthrown. They see governmental positions before them. 'Welcome [the British Bolsheviks must explain], but you too will fall from these governmental positions, just as your bourgeois government fell, and fall in such a way that nothing more of it will be left.'

That is the result of our international policy, and the way relations have taken shape in Western Europe.

And now I must proceed to the chief and grievous conclusion which has now emerged from that result. We have been thrown back at the front to such an extent that we have retreated so far that the fighting is going on near Rovno,[24] and the Poles are approaching the line on which Pilsudski earlier boasted that he was on his way to Moscow, which remained mere boasting. It must be said that despite the fact that we have been thrown back, our troops have nevertheless done wonders. The enemy forced them back hundreds [of versts] in the east and in the west, but to the place at which we earlier offered to make peace with Pilsudski they have not forced them back. And now Pilsudski is going for peace in conditions worse for him and better for us than our original offer. All the same, though, we have suffered an enormous defeat, [and] a colossal army of 100 000 has either been taken prisoner, or is in Germany. In short, [it is] a gigantic, unprecedented defeat.

What does this mean? It means that, without doubt, a mistake was made. We had victory in our hands, and we let it slip. That means there was a mistake. This question arose before all of us, and we in the Central Committee sought the answer. What was the mistake? Where is it, and can it be found?

A mistake, clearly, there must have been, both in policy and in the strategy of the war. But you know that strategy and policy are inseparably connected. During the Civil War we [in] the Political Bureau had to decide purely strategic questions, such purely strategic questions that we looked at each other with a smile: How have we come to be transformed into strategists? Amongst us were people, even, who had never seen war, even from afar. But, in spite of that, we had to concern ourselves with strategy, because strategy is subordinate to policy, and they are unbreakably linked. Now, just as in the time of the offensives by Yudenich and Denikin, we had more than once to decide purely strategic questions. That did not even surprise us. But now it is necessary to remember that every strategy is none other than a policy.

Where now to seek the mistake that was made? A political mistake is possible, and also a strategic mistake. I do not claim in the least that I know military science, and for such I apologise beforehand to comrades who know that science theoretically and practically. I am going to investigate from the standpoint of where to seek the possible mistake, either political or strategic.

I say now that the Central Committee has looked into this question, and left it open. We consider that in order to subject this question to investigation, in order to decide it properly, we should have to assign more forces to the task, forces which we have not got, because the future has us wholly in its grip. And we decided — let [the riddles] of the past be solved by historians, let this question be investigated later. That was what we arrived at.

A mistake, either in politics or in strategy, or else in both. There was possibly a mistake in the way we replied to Curzon's note of 12 July, when we simply said: 'We spit on the League of Nations. We are going ahead.'

It goes without saying, we took an incorrect decision. From revolutionaries who have found themselves in conditions of difficult politics, who have become used to deciding questions victoriously, when there is unprecedented heroism and an upsurge of the masses, a correct decision is required. In deciding this question we predetermined a general offensive line. Basically — we are convinced of this — this line was correct. Basically it was sound, and really coincided with the new period of world history, when Russia, which had been until then an object of decisions as to whether Yudenich or Kolchak would eat it, and with what garnish, was determining the internal politics of Britain.

And here, perhaps, we ought to have replied differently. We said that, basically, we accept Curzon's proposal, but we shall haggle. And we haggled on the basis of our decision until Kamenev succeeded, in unforeseen circumstances, in so haggling that they expelled him.[25] He received the help of the Council of Action, so that in the end it was Kamenev who won, and not Lloyd George.

Perhaps we ought to have replied like this. 'We agree on the basis that we halt at a distance of 50 versts, on the frontier that you lay down.' This will be determined by the conditions at the war fronts. By acquiring Eastern Galicia we [should have] acquired a base against all contemporary states. Under these conditions we should have bordered on Sub-Carpathian Rus, which is seething even more than Germany, and had a direct corridor into Hungary, where a small push would be enough to light the fire of revolution. We [should] have retained, on the international plane, the aureole of a country unbeatable, and a great power. That is great praise.

But here a different policy emerged. We should not have obtained the seething that occurred. Probably we should not have obtained the Council of Action. We should not have obtained the transference of all British politics, proletarian and bourgeois, to a new stage. But we [should] have gained a sound, quiet, firm base for operations against Central Europe through the designated frontiers.

It may be, I repeat, that here a political mistake was made, for which the Central Committee as a whole will answer, and for which each one of us bears responsibility. This is the fundamental mistake — strategy is subordinate to policy.

Another explanation is possible, which runs thus: since the Central Committee decided the political line, since it decided the position to be taken by all Soviet organs, since it determined the limits beyond which our command could not act: 'You set the task of helping sovietisation, of crossing the ethnographic frontier, and establishing a frontier with Germany. From the place where we stood, from Bialystok, the strategy could have been changed, and our strategic conditions and tasks altered.' One could argue that strategists ought [not] to have been set to carry out the fulfilment of the task. But talk, motives, feelings are one thing, and decisions another. 'One can talk, but if you do not fulfil the decision, worthy People's Commissar, you will be sacked or sent to prison.' Without awareness of that we should have gone to pieces long ago.

Here strategy, perhaps, provides understanding, and says: 'We did not have the strength for that offensive, and if, after advancing 50 or 180 versts, and stopping at that, we had halted at ethnographic Poland, we should have had a real, secure victory, we should certainly, if we had halted then, have had peace by now, an absolutely victorious peace, retaining all that aureole and all that influence in international politics.' It may be that a strategic mistake was made.

These are the basic limits of the possible mistakes about which, naturally, the Central Committee's thinking revolved.

You see why the view prevailed in the Central Committee that no, we will not set up a commission to study the conditions of the offensive and of the retreat. We lack the forces for studying that question. We now have a number of other questions which demand immediate solutions. We cannot assign any forces, even second-class ones, to this task. And we have to solve other questions, very complicated questions of politics and strategy, for we remember how we beat Denikin, drove him to the Donets area, and because we were not able to beat him completely, he hustled back as far as Orel. We saw how we beat Kolchak. When we drove him to Ufa, and then when he drove us back to Samara, a time when the whole press of Europe gave a new date for the fall of Moscow and Petrograd.

It is interesting that yesterday I saw an American publication[26] in which some people in a small publishing house had assembled a complete collection of what the best American newspapers had written about Russia. One couldn't imagine better agitation in the Bolsheviks' favour. They study how many times the fall of Moscow and Petrograd was announced. This little pamphlet is made up of what American newspapers said from October 1917 until 1920 and, in two words, what came of that. There is nothing better, more successful, than this short history of an offensive. We shall try to publish [the pamphlet] in Russian.

You will recall that our Red Army, after 150 versts of defeat, did beat Kolchak. It accomplished the impossible, as I was told by a comrade from the Red Army, before that halt 50 versts before Chelyabinsk, when it had reached a state of uselessness. Comrade Smirnov[27] said: 'Look at the Russian soldier, if we had not advanced, we should [not] have mobilised new forces. In a desperate situation as regards boots, marching was impossible: heroes did it, heroes who can by their nature perform miracles.'

The Red Army man began to perform miracles. He marched 800 versts. Whether he was to march another 100 [versts] or had to halt after 100 versts because he was not to go any further, that was a strategical problem of unprecedented difficulty for the new strategy.

You see that we have outlived Kolchak. You see what the elements of the problem were, from which the Central Committee drew its conclusion. The Central Committee itself was extremely concerned that we had made a mistake and suffered defeat: it did not undertake to correct this mistake [and] appoint a commission.

We have to settle questions of current policy — the negotiations in Riga.[28] We are faced with an offensive against Grodno, and Wrangel has taken Aleksandrovsk [now Zaporozhé], and is advancing on Ekaterinoslav [now Dneipropetrovsk].[29] We need to strain all our strength to survive this question. And it would be good to redouble all our strength. We have applied ourselves to this question, and on it I must focus your attention.

It is clear that the Polish offensive and Wrangel's constitute a single offensive by the Entente. It is committing all it has.

Today a letter arrived from a comrade[30] who was working in Britain. He says the mood there is changing. Yesterday the German Kornilovists were for the Bolsheviks, now they are for the Entente. But we have seen even bigger turnabouts.

We must take account of what conditions are now. In all probability a winter campaign has been decided on.

A whole series of pointers indicate what Poland and the Entente imperialists count on. The French are wagering on Wrangel, and are saying to the Poles: 'Be sure that if you receive from the Bolsheviks a frontier that would run not far from Warsaw, your cause is lost. Wrangel stands for us, and we are your only friends.' Politics is not too important. And the French and the Poles [are three independent elements]. It is not so simple to draw these three elements into joint action. It is even almost impossible to unite the forces of three governments against the Bolsheviks.

It might seem that this could be done easily and sufficiently, since they all hate the Bolsheviks. One must observe how Pilsudski, Wrangel and the French imperialists are ready to commit all their forces to crushing the Bolsheviks. All three declaim against the Bolsheviks, and they can do nothing, even if they were 10 times cleverer and acted 10 times more cleverly than our Soviet people. Now, on the other hand, the French are applying all their efforts to the support of Wrangel, and he is having success. They are sending him reinforcements. On the other hand, the French have to sustain the Polish front, and are saying: 'Wait, don't make peace.' The Polish petit-bourgeoisie, petit-bourgeois, patriotic and chauvinist Poland, the representatives of the PPS party,[31] the party of the landlords and the Ludowa [party],[32] and the party of the well-to-do peasants, the kulaks, all say: 'We prefer peace, because the war is bringing ruin.'

Already before the war the situation in Poland was full of crisis, and their representatives said that they would come out of the war in an utterly ruined financial situation. That is true, because they know very well that this war will have to be paid for, that France recognises 'the sanctity of private property'.

Again, there is news that 60 ships have once more reached Poland. I don't think that they have consolidated their position by means of these 60 ships.

Here a comrade who gave us a report[33] said that the social composition of the Polish army has changed. From him that remark passed unnoticed, and I mention it because here is the whole essence of the matter. If we beat Kolchak and Denikin, we beat them only because the social composition of their army changed. And Wrangel feels strong at present only because his is an army made up of officers. He himself knows that if he starts to rely on the masses he will fall as rapidly as, in their time, the Kolchaks and Denikins fell.

The Poles attacked us with an army which was originally [composed] exclusively of youngsters, who could be thoroughly 'processed'. Now, however, they have called up those age-groups who have experienced a much harsher war, now they have an army of grown-ups, an army made up of men who are not youths, men to whom one can't teach whatever one likes. The Poles have now crossed that line which Kolchak and Denikin crossed in their time, the line at which there was at first the greatest victory and the line at which the greatest defeat was ensured. That is the state of affairs in Poland today.

And in these circumstances we nevertheless say that we need to avoid a winter campaign, because [for] us tens of thousands of lives of Russian workers and peasants are far more precious than everything else. We realise perfectly well that much is now at stake, that we are strong, that by holding Galicia, where the Soviet order has been secured, by holding Galicia, which is connected with Czechoslovakia and Hungary, where everything is seething, we thereby develop a direct road for the revolution. It would be worth fighting for that, one cannot disregard such a fact. But at the same time we know that a winter campaign would demand many lives, and we say: 'We must avoid a winter campaign.'

Our chances of doing that are not great, because Wrangel and Poland, however much they may curse one another, constitute a single international front. But here we are going horizontally [sic — the sense requires 'contrariwise'] as we always have done, we are going horizontally to all previous international usages. We know well that the international predators don't trust us, but there is this one and that one who always does trust us [sic].

And we are going to make a clean cut. We propose to say, in the name of the session of the All-Russian Central Executive Committee, that we do not want a winter campaign. Please sign peace within 10 days, and we shall renounce Galicia and offer a frontier considerably further to the east than the Curzon line. Because for us these concessions are not burdensome, but it is more important for us to avoid a winter campaign, [because] we are firmly engaged in peaceful constructive work. But we propose that this be done within 10 days. But we say that, for it to be done, it will be necessary for your patriotically-inclined petit-bourgeoisie [and] your workers to overcome your bourgeoisie and landlords. And that is hardly possible, since they are strong, because the peasantry have always been patriotic lackeys — that is inevitable for economic reasons, by force of inevitable private property, and it is inevitable also in political relations. But in any case there is a chance, and in any case [at] private meetings of these parties a coincidence of opinion with us has already come about. Representatives of these parties said: 'We know that Warsaw and Poland were not saved by the Entente, they were unable to save us. We were saved by the patriotic upsurge.' And these lessons will not be forgotten. We want to make use of this opportunity.

We are offering immense concessions in a short period of time so as to settle the question of a winter campaign. Therefore we are proposing to the Poles that we make peace at once. We offer a line to the east of Brest-Litovsk. We gain from the military standpoint by ensuring a rapid victory over Wrangel. That will be a sufficient gain for us.

In relation to West European politics, we must turn to consider the consequences of our first attempt at an active policy. These consequences are not so terrible. The military consequences do not signify consequences [for] the Communist International. Under cover of the war, the Comintern forged its weapon and sharpened it so that Messrs imperialists won't break it. All the parties will henceforth develop in our way, as prescribed by the Comintern. Without any exaggeration, we can say that we can be at ease in that matter. It comes down to the tempo of development, to the conditions of development. We were not in a position to bring off a decisive military victory, which would have smashed the Versailles peace. We would have had before us, torn up, the Versailles Treaty of world-triumphant imperialism, but we were not strong enough for that. Our fundamental policy has remained the same. We shall make use of every possibility to go over from defence to attack. We have already slashed at the Treaty of Versailles, and we shall finish the job at the first opportunity. But today, in order to avoid a winter campaign, we must make concessions.

I haven't at hand at this moment the text of the declaration which will be presented to the party conference for confirmation and despatch to the session [of the All-Russian Central Executive Committee]. I have set out its political content.

In order to avoid a winter campaign we are offering the Poles a short, 10-day truce. Our chances are not great, but we shall gain in either eventuality. We have shown our forces that we have done everything to avoid the hardships of a winter campaign. For us the question of territorial frontiers is a twentieth-rate question compared with the question of ending the war as quickly as possible. We have offered our terms, and however difficult a winter campaign may be, such as they may force on us in spite of our peace proposal, we shall nevertheless bring it to a victorious end.

I have gone over the time allotted to me, and I want now to proceed briefly to the internal situation. We shall end a winter campaign victoriously, despite our immense weariness. We have achieved great successes, and we stand on ground such that from the economic point of view it is clear that we have acquired a basis, a foundation. If we take the case of grain, in 1917-18 30 million [poods] were procured. In the following year, 110. We are now secure, [because] we have more than 300 million poods of grain, possibly even up to 360. That means between 25 and 30 million poods per month. These figures exceed the meagre figures in which we writhed in the years of hunger. Having **this** basis, we shall not look with such horror at the pieces of coloured paper, those millions, hundreds of millions and milliards which have to be signed every day and which show that basis is a plaything, [it] has been broken, that these are remnants, tatters of utterly aged bourgeois clothing. But when 250 million poods [sic] of grain per year are in the hands of the state, which has taken them by requisition from the peasantry as a defined condition for the needs of industry, so that we have a basis for construction, then we shall cope quite freely with the task of correct distribution.

Our economic situation has considerably improved. We know that we have more than 100 million poods of oil. We know, too, that we have between 20 and 30 million poods of coal in the Donets basin. And we know that our position has improved with respect to firewood, which we had to manage with last year owing to the lack of coal and oil. This shows that our economic basis, despite the unprecedented losses we have suffered, the incredible weariness, the nervous exhaustion, the bureaucratisation, despite the deterioration of the entire party apparatus, despite all this, despite the hardships of the impending winter campaign, we are continuing to ensure our fundamental economic base, and will ensure it. We have the basic supply of grain for the population, and industry's grain, meaning fuel, is in much greater quantity than last year. And that is why, taking account of the difficult situation that we have experienced, we say that if we rally and strain our forces once more for a winter campaign, victory will be ours.

I must now speak about concessions. We have talked a lot about concessions. We have disputed about whether they are permissible from the standpoint of principle. Of course, we shall give to the imperialists only what we cannot develop by ourselves. In Britain our comrades have concluded a concession for 10 000 desiatinas of timber. In the northern Archangel district we are beginning this work ourselves, and this is absolutely to our advantage. We are offered a 15-year redemption period. This period is perfectly acceptable. There is no reason to fear concessions, they are a gigantic plus for us.

I read recently a small book by the American social chauvinist Spargo,[34] a real Alexinsky, who writes that we are obviously heading for collapse if we conclude concessions with the bourgeoisie. Attacks of this sort from an American Alexinsky are quite groundless, and we must meet them quite calmly, for every sensible worker knows that we are right.

We are striving to help Russia achieve the Communist order, but we cannot do this with Russia's forces alone. We say that the revolution can be brought about only through the efforts of the advanced workers of the advanced countries. On that point no conscious Communist has ever had a shadow of doubt.

This transitional period, when one weak side is holding out against all the other sides, will be a period of complex and confused relations. We can be sure that we shall not get confused, but the others will, for we have already demonstrated our international policy in relation to the small states. Then, of course, we shall exist as a Socialist republic ruined by the imperialist war and possessing incredible riches that we won't be able to work up in 10-15 years. Drawing foreign capital into this task, paying with our riches only because we cannot [with our own forces] catch up with them — this now means securing a basis for world relations.

Britain drove away our trade union organisation, quarrelled with Kamenev, and expelled him. That is not so terrible. Communists have learned not to fear actions for show. And at the same time, a treaty has been signed by which they have supplied us with a million sleepers. 'We are not able to fight over these conditions. We have sleepers which we are not in a position to make for ourselves, there is timber which we are not in a position to use, and which you can. Take timber from our outlying areas which we are not in a position to use, and, by receiving concessions from us, you will create the basis for peace, political and economic. You can't attack us, for any attempt at an attack will mean a Council of Action in any country. The Comintern has dozens of connections and agents in every country. To Moscow come representatives of various countries. We shall stand, independently of all the other conditions of development...' [after this there is evidently a gap in the transcript].

This weapon is permissible from the standpoint of principle, although it is double-edged. And moreover, though we are convinced that it is permissible from the standpoint of principle, in practice we have to learn to control it. American politicians write long notes in which they accuse us of being bad democrats. A well-known American millionaire arrives and says: 'Let's make a deal...'[after this there is a gap in the typescript]. From all this we shall certainly gain.

In the present international situation we are having to confine ourselves to a defensive position with regard to the Entente, but despite the complete failure of the first case, our first defeat, we shall again and again go over from a defensive to an offensive policy, until we have finally smashed them.

Concluding Speech in the Debate on the Political report of the Central Committee of the RCP(B) to the Ninth Conference of the RCP(B)[35]

COMRADES! IT remains for me to make a few remarks. Comrade Trotsky tried in his concluding speech to interpret his expression 'half sleepwalking' in a more acceptable form. In the debate it was pointed out to Comrade Trotsky that if the army was in a half-sleepwalking or, as he expressed it later, half-tired-out condition, the central strategic command was not, or at least ought not to have been, half-tired-out. And the mistake undoubtedly remains. I showed that this is a mistake, which has been confirmed by the whole course of development of our military operations. The conclusion from this is that if we did not learn, after Denikin and Kolchak, to set up [sic — BP] this wall of inward fatigue, if the state of morale is one-third semi-sleepwalking, then we must say to every political leader: be so kind as to confirm our directives and change [sic — BP]. We have still not learned to do this, although we have twice had experience, with Denikin and Kolchak and with Poland.

Regarding Bukharin's speech, it must be said that he went too far on the second question of principle, just as, for example, Comrade Stalin did. Western Europe was in a state of great agitation. To say now, about that, that they let us down, calls for a fully legitimate defence of the Red Army. I began my report by saying that a commission to study the conditions of the retreat was functioning — the Central Committee rejected the retreat [sic — BP]. Here there is nothing to justify the appointment of a special commission. What matters is not that, but the fundamental political blueprint. We shall not examine that, and we shall draw the lesson from it [sic — BP]. Bukharin said that one can't count on revolution and on war as well. Revolution is distinguished by the fact that the tempo of the struggle and the number of fighters increases 10 and 100 times, like the strikes in Russia in 1905. We continue to retain the confidence which the West European front deserves, and in the central command, for it has withstood the test in a whole series of very difficult campaigns, and this more than makes up for all partial mistakes.

The comrade who said 'you are not analysing the mistakes' was wrong. [He means SK Minin, a member of the Revolutionary Council of the First Cavalry Army.][36] We have begun to do that. I constructed my report on that. There has been a mistake, let's investigate it. This means that all party members spoke about it, that all appraisals were presented here. Perhaps we might have made a mistake with Denikin, but it is not at all inevitable that we made this mistake four times over.

When Comrade Bukharin spoke against Dzerzhinsky [a mistake in the transcript: DV Poluian is meant], saying that he is only introducing green sickness, I understand the factual situation that Dzerzhinsky [Poluian] spoke about. But how can one call it green sickness when a man is evaluating facts? Where's the green sickness here? Only in that these facts are very sad, that they show that the task was too difficult, it is for that that Poluian is being abused for introducing green sickness.

Bukharin (from his seat): I was referring to Kon.[37]

Lenin: Both Kon and Dzerzhinsky adduced facts and showed the incorrectness of Poluian's[38] tactical appraisal that the situation is complicated, that it is impossible to take stock of the position in a country in which one has to act so severely, where we have a purely proletarian population [sic — BP]. But it was proved that Poluian was mistaken. But to say that he introduced green sickness means saying nothing. It gives a definitely negative line in the sense that you don't select the negative facts, and then they call you green sickness. No, we, on the contrary, will learn to select them.

I can now bring forward some conclusions which coincide with the line of the resolution drawn up here. Comrade Trotsky was right when he compared what happened in Poland with the July demonstration in 1917, but on the scale of the international revolutionary calendar. That was correct. We ourselves, through the February, March, June demonstrations, and the demonstration on 20 April, which we called semi-demonstrations and semi-uprisings — we said: 'A little more than a demonstration and a little less than an uprising.' — we passed through these 'a little more than a demonstration', through successful uprisings to our own goal... [After this there is a gap in the transcript].

And that we shall really proceed, on the international scale, from semi-revolution, from successful sallies, to that, so that there may be no error, and we shall learn this in offensive warfare.

We shall not speak of that in the resolution. We shall bring forward what the Polish Communists put to us, and say that this is the only true decision which can be adopted. We shall proceed through a series of steps in which the oppressed proletarian masses will develop, enabling them to grow, to develop and grow stronger, and to avoid those mistakes which inevitably occur on the way.

This is not at all a conclusion drawn by the members of the Central Committee, but the conclusion drawn by comrades who were at the front and are delegates, and so here there was no talk of distrust. The legitimacy from the standpoint of principle of offensive action in the sense of revolutionary decisions is recognised, clarity in calculation of forces, carefulness in checking negative and positive facts, is needed.

A note has been handed to me: Why so little said about Italy? Because, apart from newspaper reports about Italy, we have no information. Perhaps this is for the best, since the bourgeoisie, had their side won, might have announced it. But perhaps it is for the worst. And, in general, it can be said that the international situation, quite independently of the steps we take in Poland, is generating a new international revolution, and that the Italian revolution has acquired fresh sweep.[39] If there were already a Soviet Poland or a Soviet Hungary, it would be still better. It is not at all out of the question that tomorrow we may take a risk for Hungary, too. I am sure that the conference will agree with us on that. But we say that we shall take a risk in such a way that with each double step we shall remember where we have got to. We shall take a risk, reckoning to bring help to Italy, although, unfortunately, at present this is impossible in practice.

But it is important, in the last analysis, that now, by way of consolation, Comrade Trotsky emphasised that it is absolutely necessary to smash Wrangel, to smash him completely by the winter, because, of the two fronts, we are giving great territorial concessions to Poland, but, as against that, we shall not be threatened from that quarter with the development of civil war, cutting off of supplies of grain, oil, etc. Consequently, Wrangel occupies first place for us, and the territorial concessions to Poland are not so important. No objection was raised here to our declaration of principle regarding Poland, and this guarantees that we shall unite our forces.

It may be that we shall hold a supplementary meeting devoted exclusively to military supplies, so comrades may share their impressions, like, for example, the comrade from Kharkov,[40] [who] could relate what he told us about their initiative taken in the matter of military supplies, when they did what was not done in other places, and then such examples might easily be transferred to these other places.

And I will finish by reading the text of the declaration which has now been finally drafted and is presented for confirmation by the conference so that the

Communist fraction can introduce it at tomorrow's session of the All-Russian Central Executive Committee and be approved there, and so that tomorrow night this declaration can be in our delegates' hands [VI Lenin then reads the declaration.][41]

Notes

1. The following speeches were delivered by Lenin on 22 September 1920, and were kindly translated for us by Brian Pearce from the section 'The Leader's Archive' in *Istoricheskii Arkhiv* (new series), no 1 (1992), pp12-30.
2. Information about the quantity and composition of Lenin documents which have remained unpublished is contained in the memorandum of the Director of the Institute of Marxism-Leninism attached to the Central Committee of the CPSU, GL Smirnov, dated 14 December 1990, which is published in this issue. Cf the material 'Publication seems inexpedient', in the section 'Archival Miscellanea'. [Russian editors' note]
3. It was the capture of Lvov by the Southern Front armies led by Yegorov and Budienny, to which Stalin was attached as Commissar, that opened up the gap with Tukhachevsky's armies to their north, into which Pilsudski threw his troops, so turning Tukhachevsky's flank and leading to the Russian defeat at the Battle of the Vistula in August 1920. It has generally been mistakenly ascribed in the past to insubordination to Trotsky on Stalin's part, due to his ambition to prove himself.
4. Shorthand report of the speech at the Ninth Conference of the RCP(B), 22 September 1920.
5. What is indicated here is the 'Appeal of the All-Russian Central Executive Committee to the Polish People' which was broadcast by radio on 2 February 1920, in which were repeated the proposals made in the statement by the Council of People's Commissars of the USSR, 'On the Bases of Soviet Policy towards Poland', 28 January 1920 (*Dokumenty vneshnei politiki SSSR*, Moscow, 1958, Volume 2, pp331-333, 355-357). [Russian editors' note]
6. Field Marshal Jozef Pilsudski (1867-1935) was a prominent Polish nationalist, and commanded the Polish forces during the war with the Soviet Union. He later set up a military dictatorship in Poland.
7. Julian J Marchlewski (Karski, 1866-1925) was a prominent figure in the Polish and international revolutionary movement. In October-November 1919 he was the representative of the Russian Red Cross Society in its negotiations with the Polish Red Cross Society. In 1920 he was a member of the Polish Bureau of the Central Committee of the Russian Communist Party and Chairman of the Provisional Revolutionary Committee for Poland. [Russian editors' note]
8. This refers to the negotiations which took place in October-November 1919 at Mikaszewicze station in Byelorussia between delegates of the Russian and Polish Red Cross Societies, as a result of which were signed an 'Agreement on Final Solution of the Question of Polish Hostages in the USSR', and an 'Agreement on Reciprocal Exchange of Civilian Prisoners'. [Russian editors' note]
9. The Polish army captured Kiev on 6 May 1920.
10. George Nathaniel, Viscount Curzon (1859-1925) was British Foreign Secretary from 1919 to 1923.
11. VI Lenin gives the date of receipt of the note from Curzon as 11 July 1920. The note contained a detailed statement of a frontier-line between the Soviet and the Polish forces (*Dokumenty Vneschei politiki SSSR*, Moscow, 1959, Volume 3, pp53-5. [Russian editors' note]
12. The reference is to the Second Congress of the Communist International, which was held on 19 July in Petrograd and then from 23 July to 7 August 1920 in Moscow. [Russian editors' note] Cf *Workers of the World and Oppressed Peoples, Unite!: Proceedings and Documents of the Second Congress*, two volumes, New York, 1991.
13. *Rote Fahne* was the main daily paper of the German Communist Party.
14. VI Lenin met a British workers' delegation on 21 May 1920 in Moscow (*Vladimir Ilyich Lenin: Biograficheskaia khronika*, Moscow, 1977, Volume 8, p592). [Russian editors' note]
15. In July 1920, at the moment of the greatest successes of the Red Army on the Polish front, LB Kamenev arrived in London to conduct negotiations. On 4 August 1920 he had a meeting with the British Prime Minister, Mr David Lloyd George, at which the head of the British government demanded that the offensive by the Soviet forces be halted. After the defeat of the Red Army before Warsaw negotiations were broken off, and on 1 September 1920 LB Kamenev was expelled from Britain. The formal reason given for his expulsion was LB Kamenev's subsidising

the activity of the workers' newspaper *The Daily Herald*. LB Kamenev's speech mentioned by VI Lenin was given after the political report of the Central Committee of the Russian Communist Party (Bolshevik) at the first session of the conference on 22 September 1920 (*Deviataia Konferentsiia RKP(B). Protokoly*, Moscow, 1972, pp12-23). [Russian editors' note]

16. The Council of Action was the organ created by the British workers for the purpose of preventing their country from going to war against Soviet Russia. It was formed in London at a joint conference of the Parliamentary Committee of the Trades Unions and the Executive Committee and the parliamentary group of the Labour Party on 9 August 1920. Besides the central 'Council of Action' local 'Committees of Action' were set up. [Russian editors' note]

17. Dr Wolfgang Kapp (1858-1922) attempted to overthrow the Weimar government in Germany in March 1920 and restore the imperial system with the help of a section of the army and Freikorps irregulars. He was defeated by a general strike of the German workers.

18. The League of Nations was the brainchild of the American President Woodrow Wilson, and was incorporated into the Treaty of Versailles in 1919. It aimed to preserve peace and encourage disarmament. It held its inaugural meeting in 1920.

19. The text of the note of the government of the USSR to the government of Great Britain, 17 July 1920 (*Dokumenty Vneschei politiki SSSR*, Volume 3, pp47-53. [Russian editor's note]

20. The peace treaty between the USSR and Estonia was signed on 2 February 1920 in Tartu. [Russian editors' note]

21. VI Lenin has in mind the 'Report on the International Situation and the Fundamental Tasks of the Communist International' which he gave at the opening of the Second Congress of the Comintern on 19 July 1920 (VI Lenin, *Collected Works*, Volume 31, Moscow, 1966, pp215-34). [Russian editors' note]

22. This is a reference to the 'Theses on the Conditions of Admission to the Communist International', the famous '21 Conditions' proposed by Trotsky to the Second Congress. Cf *Theses, Resolutions and Manifestos of the First Four Congresses of the Communist International*, London, 1980, pp92-7.

23. Cf note 15 above.

24. Rovno was captured by the Polish army on 18 September 1920.

25. Cf note 15 above.

26. This evidently refers to the collection of documents *Russian-American Relations, March 1917-March 1920: Documents and Papers*, New York, 1920, published on the initiative of the American organisation called the League of Free Nations Association. [Russian editors' note]

27. Ivan Nikitich Smirnov (1881-1936) had been a member of the RSDLP since 1899. From August 1918 to April 1919 he was a member of the Revolutionary War Council of the Eastern Front, and from April 1919 to May 1920 of the Revolutionary Council of the Fifth Army, whose troops liberated Chelyabinsk from Kolchak's troops in July 1919. [Russian editors' note] He perished during the first of the Moscow Trials.

28. This is a reference to the regular session of the Soviet and Polish delegations held in Riga on 21 September 1920 to negotiate for the conclusion of a treaty of peace. [Russian editors' note] The Treaty of Riga was finally signed in March 1921.

29. Wrangel captured Alexandrovsk on 19 September 1920. On 23 September he took Sinelniko, 30 kilometres south-east of Ekaterinoslav.

30. It has not been possible to establish what letter from Britain is meant here. [Russian editors' note]

31. The Polish Socialist Party (PPS) was the more right wing of the two prewar Socialist parties in Poland, to which at that time Pilsudski himself belonged. The more left wing organisation was Rosa Luxemburg's Social Democratic Party of the Kingdom of Poland and Lithuania (SDKPil). The PPS split, and its left wing fused with the SDKPil to form the Polish Communist Party. Members of the PPS frequently took part in government in Poland in 1918-19.

32. This is a reference to the Polskie Strannictwo Ludowe party (PSL) 'Wyzwolenie', which represented the interests of the peasantry. [Russian editors' note]

33. This is a reference to W Uljanowski (1893-1937), who represented the Communist Workers Party of Poland at the Ninth All-Russian Conference of the RCP(B). [Russian editor's note]

34. This is obviously a reference to John Spargo (1876-1946), an American Socialist and author of a number of works on social and economic subjects. Speaking on 21 and 26 November 1920 and 11 April 1921, Lenin described Spargo as a social-chauvinist, 'something like an American Alexinsky' (VI Lenin, *Polnoe Sobranie Sochineniia*, Volume 42, pp24, 43, and Volume 43, p189). [Russian editor's note]

35. Speech delivered at the Second Session of the Ninth Conference of the RCP(B), 22 September 1920.

36. SK Minin (1882-1962) was a member of the Revolutionary Military Committee of the First Cavalry Army in 1920-21.

37. Felix J Kon (1864-1941) was a figure in the Polish and international revolutionary movement. He was from 1919 Secretary to the Central Committee of the Communist Party (Bolshevik) of the Ukraine, and at the same time in 1920 a member of the Provisional Revolutionary Committee for Poland and a member of the Polish Bureau of the Central Committee of the CPSU(B). [Russian editors' note]

38. DV Poluian (1886-1937) was Chairman of the Cossack section of the All-Russian Central Executive Committee and a member of the Praesidium of the latter from December 1919; in July-September 1920 he was at the same time head of the political section and acting member of the Revolutionary War Council of the Fifteenth Army. [Russian editors' note]

39. The engineering workers occupied factories all over Italy on 1-4 September 1920.

40. The person indicated here is EG Yevdokimov (1891-1941), Deputy Head of the Special Section of the South-Western Front. In the publication *Deviataia Konferentsia RKP(B). Protokoly* (pp62-63, 386) it is unmistakably stated that he spoke at the second evening session. [Russian editors' note]

41. For which see *IX Konferentsiia RKP (B). Protokoly*, Moscow, 1972, pp79-81. [Russian editors' note]

How We Built the Red Army: An Interview with Trotsky[1]

LAST YEAR, at the time of the war with Poland, we had 5.3 million soldiers under arms...

The army was officially set up by a decree of 18 January 1918 signed by Lenin and Dybenko and Podvoisky,[2] the Commissars of the army and navy. I was then negotiating the peace of Brest-Litovsk as Commissar for Foreign Affairs, and I assumed my new responsibilities in March.

There was nothing left. The old army had dissolved, vanished into thin air. The men had gone home, the equipment was stranded almost everywhere, abandoned haphazardly by the trains breaking down. The local soviets, as yet still new and very primitive, were telegraphing me: 'I have 10 artillery pieces... I have an airfield of planes... Ten soldiers... Five seamen...' You see what a mess it was!

My office in Smolny was a funfair. Men were coming there from all corners of the country: 'Give us boots! Don't you have a colonel?' Remind yourself of the description Lissagaray gives of the Ministry of War under the Commune.[3] It was like that.

It wasn't easy bringing order into that. I had no experience, and to begin with I had hoped that I could get help from the foreign missions who cherished the hope that we would resume the war. But when I saw General Niessel,[4] the head of the French mission, making sport of me and playing at being a German general by putting his boots on my table, and especially when I ascertained the scepticism of all these professionals, I showed them the door. They went back to their own country shortly afterwards.

A party comrade, Bonch-Bruevich,[5] introduced me to his brother, a Tsarist general. I took him on and invited him to form a general staff, and attached two Communists to him to supervise him. He always performed his functions perfectly. He now teaches surveying in the university.

We began to unravel the situation along with him. But you see that? A Tsarist general? They began by crying betrayal and refusing to obey me. But happily the Central Committee understood and helped me. We had to deal ruthlessly in order to re-establish discipline. It had to be done.

There were all sorts amongst those who offered me their services: brigands and semi-brigands. One man, who came with a small detachment, had his pockets full of gold and watches; he was shot. There were informers and spies. It was necessary to carry out operations of revolutionary hygiene.

Interesting initiatives saw the light of day everywhere, and in what manner! Whenever a nucleus formed, a federal spirit got mixed up with it. We had a Tver army, or a Vladimir one. General disgust of militarism prevented any cohesion. It was madness!

Class peace or civil war? From *The Communist*, 24 June 1922.

Finally, the essential apparatus was put into operation in May: seven regions were formed with gubernia, cantonal and volost subdivisions.

I did not dare begin by reinstating compulsory military service; only volunteering was in operation. That then gave us about 200 000 men, mainly old soldiers and members of the Communist youth. The Czechoslovak affair arose and the necessary drive came into being.

Do you remember this incident? Entire Czechoslovak divisions had passed over into our ranks from the Austrian army during the war. We had them billeted on the Volga. Worked on by Savinkov[6] and the Socialist Revolutionaries, they arose and occupied Kazan, Simbirsk and Samara.

Tukhachevsky,[7] an old Tsarist officer who had been won over to Bolshevism during his captivity in Germany, who was Commander-in-Chief in the war against Poland last year, was leading our First Army in front of Simbirsk; Vatsetis,[8] a Lett, who had been our first generalissimo, led the Fifth Army in front of Kazan. These were poor armies, with only between 6000 and 8000 bayonets each. I established myself near him, at Svyazhsk.[9]

To begin with we mobilised the Communists at the front, and then six classes from the Volga gubernias. The order was: 'Victory or death!' The peasants came in masses against the Whites, but they lacked confidence in their own strength. This is what gave it to them.

I was living in a much talked-about train made out of wagons reinforced by sacks of earth, defended by a piece of artillery and machine guns, followed by another train. This had 300 cavalry on board, with an aeroplane, a garage wagon for five cars, a radio telegraph, a printshop and a courtroom; a small military town, in other words.

To start with, it was nearly captured. Savinkov, Kappel and Fortunatov[10] were so sure of their success that they announced it beforehand. They surrounded us with a thousand men. We dug trenches and endured a siege, and finally they were pushed back.

The same night as our rescue, in order to profit from our advantage, along with Raskolnikov,[11] a young naval officer who is today our representative in Afghanistan, I risked a decisive blow.

Raskolnikov had four old torpedo boats brought up by canal from Kronstadt. Together we planned to annihilate the enemy fleet with them, which was composed of flat bottomed barges armed with artillery moored in front of Kazan. We were separated by a bend in the river on which arose a steep hill. At one o'clock in the morning we cleared the narrows with the first torpedo boat, and with the first shot we were fortunate enough to set fire to the petrol tanks of one of the ships. Everything caught fire.

Our other torpedo boats could not join us, and I still ask myself how we escaped. No doubt the fire had prevented the distracted enemy from seeing us. We finished by getting back unhindered, and with a broken rudder.

The impact was enormous. As soon as dawn came, after a short struggle, the Whites evacuated Kazan. Tukhachevsky took Simbirsk the next day.[12] Our army finally gained confidence. Since then it has only known success.

Then began the real work of organisation. Our partial, makeshift mobilisations had not produced much. We mobilised regularly, by age group. The numbers of those disobeying orders went down. Posters, meetings, the performance of satirical plays in the countryside, the courts — all methods were used.

We called up the old officers. Out of 15 000 royalist officers the French Revolution picked up between 5000 and 6000. Out of a million we gained hundreds of thousands. Some have betrayed, that is true. For example, our Eleventh Division, the division of Nizhni-Novgorod, which was our pride and joy, was massacred in the spring of 1919 during Krasnov's cossack rebellion by the premeditated fault of its officers.[13] We arrested the families of the suspect officers and took them hostage. Moreover, the threat alone was enough.

We created military commissars. The Convention[14] only put them amongst the top generals. We have placed them in every division, in every brigade and in every regiment, and we have attached 'political guides' to them in every company to back up their activity. Untouchable, but responsible for any betrayal, they possess the right of life and death over everyone, but without being able to interfere with the conduct of operations.

This is how the military organisation has grown and functioned that has won all our victories, and whose numerical strength has so surprised you.

Notes

1. Interview with LD Trotsky as reported by André Morizet in *Chez Lénine et Trotski: Moscou 1921*, Paris, 1922, pp102-7, translated by the Editor with the assistance of Harry Ratner.
2. Pavel Yefimovich Dybenko (1889-1938) was a Bolshevik sailor at the Kronstadt fleet base, and afterwards army commander in the Ukraine; Nikolai Ilyich Podvoisky (1880-1948) had been an organiser of the Red Guards, and was afterwards Commissar for the Defence of the Ukraine in 1919.
3. Cf POH Lissagaray, *History of the Commune of 1871*, London, 1902, pp220-3.
4. General Henri Albert Niessel (1866-1955) was sent in 1917 to head the French Military Mission in order to try to keep Russia in the war.
5. Vladimir Dimitriyevich Bonch-Bruevich (1873-1955) was the first organiser in Petrograd of the Cheka, the Soviet intelligence service, before its offices were transferred to Moscow.
6. Boris Viktorovich Savinkov (1879-1925) was head of the military organisation of the Socialist Revolutionaries, who opposed the Russian Revolution and fought on the side of the Whites in the Civil War.
7. Mikhail Nikolayevich Tukhachevsky (1893-1937) was a Tsarist officer who had been a prisoner of war in Germany. On his return in 1918 he joined the Bolsheviks and commanded the Fifth Army against Kolchak and Denikin. A brilliant pioneer of tank warfare, he was murdered in the purge of the generals.
8. Ioakim Ioakimovich Vatsetis (1873-1938) was a colonel in the Tsarist army who joined the Bolsheviks after the Russian Revolution, and was Commander-in-Chief of the armed forces from September 1918 onwards.
9. Cf Larissa Reissner, 'Svyazksk', in *Leon Trotsky: The Man and His Work*, New York, 1969, pp112-8.
10. Fortunatov was a prominent member of the anti-Soviet Samara government that was set up in 1918 by Socialist Revolutionaries under the protection of the Czechoslovak legions. Vladimir Oskarovich Kappel (1883-1920) was first of all commander of the troops of this government on the Volga, and then in charge of Kolchak's troops in the same area.
11. Fyodor Fyodorovich Raskolnikov (1892-1939) was a naval officer and leader of the Kronstadt sailors during the Russian Revolution. He was Commissar for Naval Affairs in the Soviet government, and was in charge of the Volga-Caspian flotilla during the Civil War.
12. Simbirsk was captured on 12 September 1918.
13. On the treachery at Nizhni-Novgorod, cf LD Trotsky, *How the Revolution Armed*, London, 1979, Volume 1, p444.
14. The Convention was the revolutionary assembly which directed the government and the defence of France during the revolutionary war.

Mikhail Tukhachevsky
The Red Army and the Militia[1]

FORMERLY IT seemed thoroughly self-evident and appropriate for the Socialist state to provide for its necessary capacity for defence by means of a militia army. Now this point of view is undergoing an ever more critical examination and even a rejection by judgement.

The past plays no small rôle in this question; belief in the infallibility of knowledge once acquired is very slowly lost. This belief has led many not to examine this problem on its own basis, but to consider it in the sense of this or that generalisation of a meaningless system within the postulates of a Socialist state.

But there are also those who not only consider it superfluous to examine this question afresh, but who — persisting in a once fundamentally understood idea — even demand the immediate establishment of the militia system in Soviet Russia.

This essay proposes to enquire into the question. For this it is necessary not only to examine the utility of the militia system for the dictatorship of the proletariat, but also the nature of the militia system and finally likewise of that system of the Socialist army that responds to the requirements of a truly Socialist armed force and its tasks.

Defence and Attack

In the epoch of the Second International the dominant idea in the heads of the Socialists was that of the 'defence of the fatherland'. Armed attacks were — without seeking their motives, aims and causes — indiscriminately rejected. Therein is shown the specific form of the Second International's struggle against imperialism. That is precisely why this problem has been illustrated in a somewhat one-sided way. This struggle — or, better said, this passive half-struggle — with imperialism has driven out of the working class the idea of activity — the idea of an attack of the proletariat on the bourgeoisie — and has rendered it more difficult for it to have a clear vision of the possible consequences of such an attack.

The present military situation of Soviet Russia as the propagator of the Socialist revolution throughout the world is above all not taken into consideration. But this situation can never occur among imperialist states in a military respect.

But not only the details of this question betray the erroneousness of such a passive conception. The whole foundation of the idea of a military attack by the proletarian class on the bourgeoisie is unsuitably limited from a military point of view. The Second International inoculated everyone with the notion that such a war of attack was permissible only within the narrow limits of a state territory.

Naturally, life and the Socialist revolution, in their rich multiplicity, do not allow themselves to be squeezed into limits. Uncheckably they spread over the entire world, and their extension will continue as long as there is a bourgeoisie in the world.

By what means shall it seek its goal? By means of an armed uprising in each state, or by means of the armed uprising of the Socialist states against the bourgeois states, or by means of both together? That cannot be said in advance; the course of the revolution will show us. One thing is sure; if anywhere a Socialist revolution reaches power, then it has the self-evident right to expand, it will strive with elemental force to spread by direct action to all neighbouring countries to involve the whole world. Its most important instrument will naturally be its military power.

We see therefore that the Socialist revolution requires of its army a readiness for active offensive operations within its own frontiers and, if the turn of events compels it, outside them.

The Recruiting System

The structure of an army is determined on the one hand by the political goals that it has to attain, and on the other hand by the recruiting system in practice. These are the two decisive components of the system of building an army.

In the period before the French Revolution, when the political and sometimes active goals of the monarchs and their courts were determined without any participation by the people, and when the army was recruited from mercenary soldiery, the entire structure of the relatively small army had a rare regular character. The size of the army depended on the means available to the court, but it had to be regular, because a mercenary army requires long hard training and is not quickly recruited.

The great French Revolution brought about a decisive turn in the nature of the army. Political aims, still active because of their nature, lay close to the hearts of the popular masses. The most fundamental change concerned the system of recruiting. It was changed into a national and obligatory system. It provided the French Revolution with enormous, hitherto unseen, masses of troops, and also changed the whole of strategy by introducing methods that arose from the new form of army.

This system formed the basis for all European armies of the nineteenth and twentieth centuries. The Germans were the first to grasp this new form theoretically, and made this principle the basis of their 'people in arms'. This system developed uninterruptedly. The size of the peacetime standing army did not vary much, but the length of military service grew ever shorter, which had as a result that ever broader layers of the population were made liable to serve militarism. In case of war this trained mass of reserves was called to the colours, and in this way an enormous, many-millioned section of the people could be immediately moved into the field.

The development of this system of the people's army progressed in parallel with the development of industry, technique, transport, etc. The manipulation of this colossal army presupposed a big complete railway network and plans worked out to the smallest detail.

The real cadre-troops, however, were no longer so fit for war and so capable of resistance as formerly. With the shortening of military service, the quality of the training of the army and its efficiency had also diminished. All that led to a quicker perfection of military-technical means whereby to strengthen — or, better said, to replace — the morale of the troops. In recent times war techniques have obtained unexpected successes.

This circumstance also forced — in order to use the technical means more and more for the purposes of mobilisation — assigning only insignificant means to the cadre-troops. Indeed, if we think of the importance that automobiles, aeroplanes, etc, now have, then it becomes clear that these technical means, which are of the very greatest importance for the state, cannot be constantly withdrawn from the life of the nation, and can be turned over to the military apparatus only at the beginning of mobilisation.

In the same way it has become impossible, as time goes by, to occupy the necessary number of factories with the production of military equipment. Half of all industry would be needed for this. Hence, for example, it is only at the beginning of mobilisation that industry is used to the proper degree for the production of individual firearms. And it is the same case with all the other fields of military equipment.

The nation invested its strength ever more in the economic life of the country. But at the moment of the mobilisation call it engaged with its whole weight in the state of war. This system has very appropriately been termed the system of 'the people in arms'.

In general, the military apparatus developed with the growth in population figures, and the increase in technique and industry. The army, insignificant in peacetime, swelled up in the few mobilisation days to a gigantic size. And so strategy also had to adapt itself to this system. It became, through its strong dependence on the railways, much less free, and was bound up with the size of the army and technique. The training of the army steadily fell behind, while that of the staff moved into the foreground; tactics depended almost entirely on the adequacy of numerical calculations, and on the degree of precision with which the troops could be moved by means of the railways. The enormous and cumbersome mass armies rendered the active conduct of war ever more difficult, unless an excellent technique and an efficient and widely ramified railway network could be counted on.

These conditions set the limits for the increase in the size of the army, which in addition had to keep pace with the country's industrial development. With the increase of industry, the numerical strength of the armed forces could also increase. By the utmost development of technique and industry, the army also could be brought up to its maximum size; if the most perfect technique of war was taken for granted, the quality of an army could be almost entirely replaced by its quantity. Through an ideal and efficient railway network, such an enormous army, even if it did not know how to manoeuvre, could, with the help of a well-trained army leadership, carry out the most complicated movements. Such an army, which in case of war approximates to almost the whole male population of the country, would not in peacetime divert these masses from productive labour. If such an organisation must also lead to an inferior training of the troops, it could nevertheless by means of technical perfection successfully solve its active tasks, and overwhelm its adversary by its numbers and technique.

What limit is therefore set to the development of the idea of a bourgeois army based on general national military service? This limit was unconsciously known; it was called 'the militia system'.

But a misunderstanding appeared. The idea of a militia army did not proceed as a logical result of previous military thinking, but emerged quite accidentally and unexpectedly in the Socialist camp, and here made itself at home — in the same camp that was fighting against the proponents of 'the people in arms'.

The demand for the militia was already set forth in the **democratic** programmes of 1848. Democratic ideology knows no classes; for it there is only a single indivisible 'people' whose rights have been usurped by 'tyrants', 'the state', or whatever else. The defence of 'the people's freedoms' requires a 'people's army'.

The idea of 'the people in arms' and the idea of the militia — the latter being only the logical development of the former, but not recognised as such by the two enemy adversaries — these ideas were long considered to be opposed extremes.

Why was the militia system fought against with such determination and obstinacy by the leaderships of the regular armies? This was not at all for the reason that such a gigantic army with its inferior discipline caused anxiety to military experts. Such a conception can only be attributed to frivolity. Their fear was much more that the militia army cannot carry out large-scale movements on foot; but the technical levels did not up till then allow in a single country the use of such a giant army as a movable force, ready for action, for railway, automotive and other means of transport were not yet sufficiently developed. The officers' corps, however, which had everywhere grown up with imperialist conceptions, could not accept the militia army, which in its nature is passive and serves only the purposes of defence. The commanders could not use such an army. They dreamed of conquests and victorious campaigns.

The Second International, therefore, in its struggle with imperialism, understandably defended the militia system. This system became the tradition of the Socialists. Gradually, the real purpose of an army was forgotten; an active Socialist war was not thought of, and the fundamental task of an army was considered to be what would disturb as little as possible the economic life of the country.

In this way, there was established a lasting misunderstanding about these important questions. One side did not understand that the militia system is the most consistent and powerful military system of the bourgeois state at the highest point of its capitalist development, whereas the other side, in its struggle against capitalist designs, strove to validate the militia system, which had to be used, on account of the relatively inferior development levels of industry, only for defence. In this struggle, the understanding of the real purpose of any army was forgotten, and thinking descended to the fanatical belief in the absolute suitability of the militia army to the Socialist order of society.

Now, in the period of the building of Socialism, there are still many advocates of this old idea, or, better said, of this old superstition. These admirers of the militia never once make the effort to analyse the significance of this problem for the country and the class. Obstinately and unreflectingly, they require the immediate introduction of the militia system in Soviet Russia. They cannot grasp that any new social order — especially when it follows after powerful revolutionary convulsions — makes a new army system necessary.

Let us try to examine more closely the problem of the armed forces of a state founded on the dictatorship of the proletariat.

It is self-evident that the proletariat, emerging victorious from the class struggle, cannot undertake the recruiting of its army by means of general national conscription. Recruitment can be based only on the obligatory conscription of the working class. Such a system would be distinguished from the bourgeois national one in another way as well. From the fact that the recruiting system of an army is based essentially on the working class, this system itself becomes international. The admission of poor peasantry into the Red Army does not alter this principle.

We see now that the Socialist revolution has set up a new recruiting system — the international class army — in opposition to the bourgeois system, which has hitherto produced the national and democratic army.

We know that the system of recruiting influences the composition of the armed forces of a state, and also its military science. And our revolution has in fact also overturned the whole of the military art.

We see that the two classes do not fight under the same conditions. The sources of recruitment of the proletariat and the classes close to it are almost inexhaustible, whilst the sources of the bourgeoisie are extremely limited. Both one side and the other can during an offensive advance count only on those classes close to themselves in the occupied territories. That is why the chances of the Red Army for an accession of new forces are very favourable, whilst those of the bourgeois army are generally not. True, the bourgeoisie also mobilises the labouring strata of the population, but this increase only diminishes the quality of its army.

This extremely characteristic component of our Socialist wars alters the whole nature of the conduct of war; and it is above all this component that gives a Socialist army and its recruiting system its international character. It gives the Red Army the possibility of almost unlimited recruitment, and allows proletarian strategy to accomplish tasks and aims which are out of the reach of any other strategy.

The Organisation of the Armed Forces

Before we can solve the problem of the structure of a Socialist army, we must cast a closer light on some constituents of the armed forces in general, and the conditions of war in different circumstances.

Let us consider the conditions for the use of the militia system. The militia system, like the system of the regular standing army, requires complicated and extremely precise preparatory work if it is to be able in case of war immediately to put the required military forces on a war footing. That presupposes an ideally constituted military administrative apparatus. A mobilisation plan, worked out down to its last details, is unconditionally necessary, training must be perfect, and many other things. The militia army, just like the modern standing army, must be organised according to territorial principles. The different districts must form firm and autonomous units. The technical administrative apparatus must work with absolute precision. This whole preparatory work requires a long time, that lasts not months, but years. And finally it must be said that a militia army, just like the standing army, presupposes a homogeneous population — in any case the population must not be split up by the class struggle.

All these conditions having been assumed, the apparatus of a militia army, after systematic preparatory work over many years, can, upon the call to mobilisation, immediately set on foot an enormous mass army ready to march.

Now let us see how a revolutionary Socialist army is constituted.

Above all it is to be noted that the whole way in which it is set up is diametrically opposed to that of the militia army. The latter is formed at the end of long preparatory work of the military administrative apparatus, whereas the Socialist army begins to be formed immediately after the revolution in a wholly elemental way; administrative authorities neither are on hand nor are organised. Little by little, the organisation automatically develops itself. The army grows and becomes strong. Suffused by a strong class consciousness and by a revolutionary will to victory, it rapidly becomes a regular army ready for war. The military administrative organs are far from developing with the same success. Since they are predominantly composed of specialists, who belong to the class that has been overthrown, they remain for a long time unviable and attached by an umbilical cord to the active army.

It has already been said that the organisation of the Red Army is built on the principle of the class struggle. The application of this system produces great difficulties.

At the first stages the Red Army recruits volunteers who come from the labouring classes. These become the Red Army's iron nucleus of troops, consciously defending their class interests, who later can also admit unenlightened elements, educate them, and raise them to the necessary political consciousness.

But even on the supposition that strong class-conscious proletarian cadre troops are available, recruiting runs into many difficulties in many regions with a predominantly bourgeois rural population, and is not without its dangers. Everyone knows what enormous significance the work of political clarification has amongst our troops, and how hard the newly arrived, indifferent peasant masses are to assimilate. It is only when strong and politically well-educated cadre troops are available, with many Communists well distributed amongst them, that the unenlightened peasant masses can be easily and rapidly worked upon.

It is completely incomprehensible how a militia army, which would be composed in its overwhelming majority of peasants, might become, immediately after its mobilisation, highly qualified politically, and prepared to take the field with Communist banners, ready for victory. It is quite clear that such a supposition is completely senseless.

It suffices to observe the Ukrainian partisan leader Makhno — who lived only at the cost of the rich Ukrainian peasantry, which provided him with the requisite human material, and furnished him with horses, food supplies, etc — to understand fully that the introduction of the militia system in this area would be only cutting into one's own flesh.

In the same way, the peasant revolts occurring in many districts provide a good example. It would be not uninteresting to learn how the proponents of the militia system conceive of the struggle with the elements in revolt in these districts by means of a militia army, and how they imagine carrying out mobilisation in these regions.

Tasks and Duration of a War

The tasks of a Socialist army can be very varied. The Red Army can fight against domestic counter-revolutionary troop formations with the purpose of completely destroying them; it can fight against the bourgeoisie of neighbouring countries if their governments want to strangle the Socialist state — in this case also the struggle can hardly end until one or the other adversary is crushed. In general, war, even with interruptions, will last until either the Socialist state is completely destroyed and ceases to exist as such, or the revolution has taken over the entire globe.

What is impossible and untenable is the supposition that this world, shaken to its foundations by the Great War, might quite peacefully divide itself into two halves, one Socialist and the other capitalist, which could now live together in peace and good neighbourliness. It is as clear as day that such a situation can never occur, and that the Socialist war will last until the final victory of one side or the other.

We see therefore that until the final decision in this struggle, the moment will never occur in which the proletarian state could dissolve the Red Army it has had to date, to undertake the years of work needed to organise a militia army.

It is true that after the final victory of the proletarian revolution — that is, if a single Communist social order is introduced in the entire world — the militia system could then be introduced. But who would then need it? In any event, the state organism, withering away, would render it quite impossible for this system to produce any army — despite all the imprecatory formulae from the advocates of the militia army.

We have therefore found that the militia system has nothing to do with the Socialist revolution, from the first moment of its birth up till its greatest extension, embracing the entire world.

Strategic Peculiarities of Armies and the Auxiliary Resources of the Nation

The characteristic traits of a militia army are its enormous size, its relatively limited readiness for combat, and outstanding equipment with the most modern matériel of military technique. All these detailed characteristics are in close relationship one to another.

The big mass armies which are called up by mobilisation, which have no cadre troops and therefore have not been able during peacetime to receive any fundamental training in regular troop formations, will obviously have only limited discipline and combat-readiness. Their weakness will be shown with quite particular clarity in the areas of field manoeuvres and tactics. These lacks must be absolutely compensated for in one way or another by some means, and the technique of war is precisely the suitable means. It will be sought to deploy them in their full strength, to demoralise the adversary, and to protect one's own troops. Thanks to these circumstances, a militia army is better suited to defence than to attack.

Nevertheless, this characteristic of the militia — its enormous numerical strength — can render very good service in the theatre of operations. For this purpose, there is needed only an exceptionally well-built network for transportation by railways and trucks, as also by waterways. Under these conditions, even cumbersome troops of limited combat-readiness can by their well-concentrated mass crush the adversary. But this advantage of the militia operates only if there are excellent means of transport and ideal technical equipment. If we furthermore call to mind what inevitable quantities of defence equipment, food supplies, equine material, etc, this involves, then we shall recognise that such a militia army can fulfil its task only in a country with a most highly developed industry. It would be senseless to think that a militia army requires only limited economic expenditures in peacetime. It must not be forgotten that guns, cannons and in general all matériel must be on hand before the war, and kept in the best condition.

And so the militia system would be an enormous force, but only if the state is extremely cultivated, and has at its disposal a highly developed industry and great wealth. These great means are especially necessary during the war. It is necessary to think only of the millions of guns, the hundreds of thousands of machine guns, the tens of thousands of cannons, the hundreds of millions of shells, the many thousands of millions of bullets, and so on and so forth, quite apart from the losses in men's lives. Let us only remember the dimensions of the last war of 'the peoples in arms', which is to be considered merely a foretaste of the dimensions of a fight between militia armies. Can any Socialist state in its transitional period face up to such expenditures? Without these enormous human masses and without this military technique pushed to its peak, a militia army isn't worth a whistle.

If we now examine more closely whither the militia system would lead our republic, then we shall see the following: above all, we should not be able to organise the military apparatus in time before the beginning of the next war. Secondly, in a whole series of regions of our country, we should only be arming our own counter-revolutionary adversaries. Thirdly, we should be able neither to clothe nor equip the mobilised millions. Fourthly, we should not be able within the necessary time to bring this enormous military mass to the threatened frontier, and the Poles, for example, would have already occupied Moscow before our militia army would have time to concentrate itself in the Volga region. Fifthly, our means of transport would not suffice to move the militia army at will to the theatre of war, and an adversary who was considerably weaker, but on the other hand well equipped with technical means, could easily beat isolated troop formations. Lastly, we should ourselves be condemning our immense army to death, for we could not provide it with food supplies or with any other equipment.

I have on occasion heard from fanatical admirers of the militia system statements from which it follows that they consider themselves the consistent representatives of the idea of a militarily powerful Soviet Republic. Personally, I should have nothing to say against the militia system if it really led to that goal. But unfortunately, this system would only result in Communist defeats. With us the introduction of the militia system would mean a crucifixion of the Soviet Republic.

There are also many all-too-zealous generals who understandably see their last hope in the introduction of the militia system in Soviet Russia, and for that reason become enthusiastic about this system.

In recent times, when there are many party comrades who sharply reject the militia system, the supporters of it are heard to say that they are thinking about another kind of militia than that of the Second International, that the militia should be organised in a quite new way, and so on.

Such arguments mean only that these comrades have not reflected at all seriously about the problem. Without examining more closely the question of the armed forces of a proletarian state, they have grasped at this thing that has long been known — the militia system. But when they saw that such a system is not practicable, they imagined new forms which they obstinately call by the old name. The notion of 'the militia system' is something wholly defined — it cannot be transformed at will into another system.

Now let us get on to the question of what conditions the resources of our republic, as well as any other republic of councils, afford to the armies that are necessary in the transitional period.

There is not much to be said about this. Anyone will understand without more ado that an impoverished country needs above all a small army, whose insufficient quantity must necessarily be compensated for by its quality, for its first task is effectively to guarantee the existence of the Soviet republic.

The System of the Socialist Army

The quality of an army lies above all in its combat-readiness developed to the highest degree, and in its precise and easy mobility. It is not easy to fulfil these requirements, and that is why they involve a long hard period of preparation. Only a regular army can receive such training. We thus observe that a Red Army can be only a regular army.

We should now like to see how the Socialist system of recruiting affects the army and the whole military apparatus. We reached the conclusion above that this system is based on the class principle, and is an international system. That shows that for the mobilisation of the state, the registration of the population must be undertaken according to what class they belong. The whole military training of the youth before they are called up must also take this principle into account. It is self-evident that this principle extends to all areas of military reality, including the training of leaders.

The structure of the army itself fundamentally involves nothing essentially new. All troop units must constantly show their mobile strength, deviations from this rule being permissible only within the country.

But the deeper hinterland, which requires the most human material, in quiet times permits a reduction to a minimum in troop strength. The active troop units can generally be revictualled by the civil authorities.

Such an army can, without depending on the complex process of mobilisation, be immediately thrown on to the chosen front; meanwhile, the mobilisation is completed, the necessary staging areas are organised, and the reserves of the army filled out. In addition, in case of danger from abroad, reserve formations can be built up. That depends on the available stocks of weapons, equipment, etc.

The fact that the Red Army built upon this system is far from requiring the whole human material of the state shows that in the most important industrial areas military mobilisations can become entirely unnecessary. On the other hand, a militarising of labour will be very useful for increasing its results.

The advocates of the militia will furiously attack such a system; they will claim that it is economically untenable, that it renders impossible the construction of a Socialist economy, and so on and so forth.

But these objections are unfounded. Firstly, it has never been claimed that a military system, of whatever nature it may be — hence also of the militia system — can be useful to the economic life of a state. Whether it be agreeable or not, the state must for its own defence maintain an armed force, and such a one as corresponds to its military situation.

The guarantee of the existence of the Soviet state is the main task; everything else — even economic requirements — must give way to it. Secondly, though the militia army in peacetime requires less upkeep costs, it yet requires far greater quantities of clothing and equipment than the standing army — not to mention the enormous stocks of armaments that must be held ready for the militia. It would be necessary to make a colossal war industry specially for the militia. Thirdly, it must not be forgotten that it is not the peacetime but the wartime army that ruins the country. During war all the economic advantages are on the side of the standing army, for a few thousand guns that one could otherwise do without already cost enormous sums. These costs increase proportionally to the increase in the army's size.

We have a striking example of this in the great impoverishment that the war of 'the peoples in arms' brought to the entire world. We have examples in history for this, that even the poorer peoples with small but well-trained armies can carry on long wars with comparatively more powerful adversaries with numerically far greater armies. It is clear that Soviet Russia, in its arming for new wars that will undoubtedly be forced upon it, dare not introduce an army system that in case of war would wholly ruin the country.

Thus we have sought what type of army corresponds to a state, like Soviet Russia, based on the dictatorship of the proletariat. It remains only for us to study this system in its utilisation in connection with any international policy that the Socialist revolution must carry out.

We have demonstrated above that this revolution has produced a complete overturn in strategy. And indeed, our Red Army has never fought alone against its adversaries. It immediately finds the expected support from the working class of that land against whose bourgeoisie it is waging war. This support is not limited to revolutionary outbreaks in the bourgeoisie's rear; it consists above all in the fact that the Red Army can fill out its troops from the working class of the occupied territories. This influx is produced not only at the cost of the local population, but also at the cost of the capitalist armies, which the workers and peasants gladly desert so as to enter the Red Army.

This accession of international fighting forces is just the characteristic mark of the war leadership of the Red Army.

On all fronts of the different nationalities we observe this same phenomenon. It is particularly the case when the bourgeois army has suffered a defeat. At the time of our penetration into Polish areas, Polish soldiers began immediately to come over to us, despite the fact that the army of the capitalist Poles still had its full fighting capacity. This was particularly the case at Bialystok, where the workers greeted our army with enthusiasm, and wanted to enter its ranks.[2] Only our rapid retreat prevented the fulfilment of their intentions.

Thus our Red Armies may be considered outside the frontiers of the Soviet Republic to be an international cadre formation.

This system of a World Red Army must be clearly brought to our consciousness.

Can we then view our military tasks only within the frontiers of the republic? Naturally not, for in the republic itself serious military tasks do not lie before us, whereas foreign tasks depend not so much on us as on the outer world, that is, first of all on the development of the international revolution.

In view of this, every task of our republic must be most closely bound up with the tasks of the world revolution. This is, naturally, particularly valid for the question of the organisation of our Red Army, the first cadre-troops of the World Red Army.

If we are conscious of this task, then the question of the system for the Red Army seems even more serious. This army must be a valid model in every regard, including in the political sense. This army must have forgotten of what nationality it was in its majority composed. It must be aware that it is the army of the world proletariat, and nothing else. Wherever this army may arrive, the people must be able immediately to feel that it is a Red Army, and not a Russian army. Only such an army, composed of class-conscious revolutionaries, can be the instrument for the propagation of the world revolution and for the destruction of capitalism.

Conclusion

Now that we have cast light from all sides on the question of the use of the militia system for a state with the dictatorship of the proletariat, we must recognise that it is completely unusable.

We have seen that the militia system can be a dangerous weapon in the hands of an extremely highly developed capitalist state. We have seen that a Communist social order that extends over the entire world could introduce this system. We have, however, also learned that this system in the transitional period might be a deadly pit for the Socialist state, for it is not even usable for defensive purposes. We have seen that the Red Army is set up in a diametrically opposite way to the militia army. But since the Socialist state must reckon on an uninterrupted struggle against the capitalist world, the technical possibility of the organisation of a militia army is automatically forever ruled out. We have seen that the militia system, in a whole series of areas, cannot be introduced on grounds of their unsuitable class composition. Such are the grounds for which the introduction of the militia system in the Soviet state is on principle excluded.

On the other hand, we have also seen the basic characteristics that the Red Army of a Soviet state must have. We have learned that this army must be a standing army, and that it must be based on the principle of the class struggle and international recruiting.

We saw that this army is destined to take part in the world revolution, and that our Red Army has the rôle of being the cadre-troops of the World Red Army. What its actions must be does not fall within the limits of our considerations here.

It seems to me that the introduction of the militia among us would be very much in contradiction to the givens of the situation, and that as it is rejected by so many Communists it would not really be worth the trouble of discussing this problem, which could not have been solved in any other way. This is correct, but it was desirable once more to examine the question more closely, since it was again brought on to the agenda.

The sterility of the Second International was shown in its fetishism about the militia army, just as about the idea of the national assembly. And, like the latter, the militia army also will soon vanish from our horizon.

The Communist International — the leader of the Socialist world revolution — cannot base itself on this militia. The Red Army will, under the leadership of the Communist International, take on a new form — the form of the international armed forces of the world proletariat.

Notes

1. M Tukhachevsky, 'The Red Army and the Militia', from *Fourth International*, no 6, Spring 1959, pp61-7, translated from the pamphlet series *Kleine Bibliothek der Russischen Korrespondenz*. It is an extract from a discussion that took place on 11 January 1921 at the Military Scientific Committee attached to the Red Army Military Academy presided over by Leon Trotsky, who provided an introduction and a summing up.
2. Bialystok was the first large town captured by the Red Army in Poland in 1920. Encouraged by their reception, they set up a 'Revolutionary Committee of the Polish Republic' there on 31 July.

Leon Trotsky
On the National Question[1]

'A' IS a member of the Young Communist League. A capable and devoted young revolutionary, he fought as a volunteer in the Red Army. However, his Marxist education and political experience are to some extent inadequate. 'B' is a better grounded comrade.

'A' Of course, nobody can object to the resolution of the Twelfth Congress on the National Question.[2] All the same though, this question was brought up artificially. For us Communists the national question is not of acute importance.

'B' Why do you say that? After all, you've just declared that you agree with the resolution, haven't you? Yet the main idea of this resolution is that the national question does not exist for the benefit of the Communists, but the Communists exist to solve the national problem as a constituent part of the more general question of the organisation of man's life on earth. If, in your self-education study group, with the aid of the methods of Marxism, you have freed yourself from various national prejudices, that is, of course, a very good thing, and a very big step forward in your personal development. But the task confronting the ruling party in this sphere is a more far-reaching one: we have to make it possible for the many millions of our people, who belong to different nationalities, to find through the medium of the state and other institutions led by the party, practical living satisfaction for their national interests and requirements, and therefore enable them to get rid of national antagonisms and prejudices — all this not at the level of a Marxist study group, but at the level of the historical experience of entire peoples. Therefore there is an irreconcilable contradiction between your formal acknowledgement of the resolution and your statement that for us Communists the national question is not of great importance. Thereby you testify that you do not acknowledge the resolution, or, to put it bluntly — in a purely comradely spirit and without meaning any offence — you do not grasp the political meaning of the resolution.

'A' You misunderstand me.

'B' Hm... hm...

'A' All I meant to say is that the class question is for us Communists incomparably more important than the national question. Consequently, we must keep a sense of proportion. I am afraid, however, that the national question has recently been very much exaggerated by us, to the detriment of the class question.

'B'. Perhaps I have again misunderstood you, but in this statement you have just made it seems to me you have committed another and even bigger mistake in principle. The whole of our policy — in the economic sphere, in the building of the state, in the national question and in the diplomatic sphere — is a class policy. It is dictated by the historical interests of the proletariat, which is fighting for the complete liberation of mankind from all forms of oppression. Our attitude to the national problem, and the measures we have taken to solve it, form a constituent part of our class position, and not something accessory or in contrast to it. You say that the class criterion is supreme for us. That is perfectly true. But only insofar as it is really a class criterion; that is, insofar as it includes answers to all the basic questions of historical development, including the national question. A class criterion minus the national question is not a class criterion, but only the trunk of such a criterion, inevitably approximating to a narrow craft or trade union outlook.

'A' According to you, then, concern about solving the national question, that is, about forms of coexistence of national groups and national minorities, is just as important for us as the retention of power by the working class, or of the dictatorship of the Communist Party! From such a position it would be easy to slide into complete opportunism, that is, to subordinating revolutionary tasks to the interests of agreements between nationalities.

'B' I feel I have a presentiment that I'm going to find myself today amongst the 'deviators'... Nevertheless, I'll try, my young friend, to stick up for my point of view. The whole of the problem, as it faces us today, if we formulate it politically, has this significance for us — **how, that is, by what measures and methods of action, by what approach, can we maintain and consolidate the power of the working class in a territory where many nationalities live side by side**, with the central Great Russian nucleus, which formerly played the rôle of a great power amongst these nationalities, constituting less than half of the entire population of the Union? It is precisely in the process of developing the proletarian dictatorship, in the course of our entire state building activity and our daily struggle to retain and strengthen the workers' power, that we are at this moment being faced more urgently than ever before with the national question in all its living reality, its daily concrete manifestations in state, economic, cultural and everyday life.

And just now, when the party as a whole is beginning to present the question in this way — and it cannot be presented in any other way — you (and unfortunately not you alone) declare with naive doctrinairism that the question of the dictatorship of the proletariat is more important than the national question. Yet it is precisely for the sake of the dictatorship of the proletariat that we are now in practice going more deeply (and shall in the future go still more deeply) into the national question. What is the meaning of the contrast that you make? Only people who do not understand the significance of 'National Factors in the State and Party'[3] can present the question in this way. And, in any case, all those who adopt a nihilistic or contemptuous attitude to the national question will eagerly seize upon such a formulation as yours. To turn one's back on the demands and interests of the formerly oppressed small nationalities, especially those which are backward and consist mainly of peasants, is a very simple and perfectly easy thing to do, especially if this sort of lazy indifference can be covered up with general phrases about internationalism, about the dictatorship of the Communist Party being more important than any and every national question...

'A' As you please; but presenting the question in this way seems to me to be bending over backwards to an impermissible extent in the direction of the backward peasant borderlands, and thereby incurring the risk of doing very great harm to the proletarian centre, upon which our party and the Soviet power rely. Either I have understood nothing of what you have said, or you really are deviating towards the backward, predominantly peasant nationalities.

'B' Here it is, we've reached it at last — my peasant deviation; and I expected as much, for everything under the sun, including political mistakes, has its own logic... 'A deviation in favour of the backward, peasant masses' — but did you hear what the Twelfth Congress had to say about that?

'A' About what?

'B'. About the mutual relations between the proletariat and the peasantry — about the 'link'?[4]

'A' The 'link'? What's that got to do with it? I'm absolutely in agreement with the Twelfth Congress. The link between the proletariat and the peasantry is the basis of everything. The question of the link is the question of the fate of our revolution. Whoever is against the link is...

'B' Yes, yes. But don't you think that the dictatorship of the working class and of our party is more important for us than the peasant question and, consequently, than the question of the link?

'A' How so?

'B' It's very simple. We, the Communist Party, the vanguard of the proletariat, cannot subordinate our social-revolutionary aims to the prejudices, or even to the interests of the peasantry, which is a petit-bourgeois class in its entire tendency. Isn't that so, my left wing friend?

'A' But pardon me, that sophistry — that is a quite different matter, and has nothing to do with the question. The link is our basis, our foundation. Lenin wrote that without the link with the peasantry we should not attain Socialism; more than that, without the achievements due to the economic link, that Soviet power will inevitably be overthrown.

'B' That's it, precisely. Therefore — you'll agree, I think? — it is absurd, politically illiterate, to counterpose the link with the peasantry to the dictatorship of the proletariat. Of course the dictatorship of the proletariat is the basic idea of our programme, the basic criterion of our state and economic constructive work. But the whole point is that this very dictatorship is unthinkable without certain definite mutual relations with the peasantry. If you separate the link with the peasantry from the question of the dictatorship of the proletariat, you are left, so far as the given historical period is concerned, with an empty form, a meaningless abstraction.

'A' I don't disagree with you, but what has this got to do with our subject?

'B' It is very directly and closely connected. In our Soviet Union the link with the peasantry naturally presumes not merely a link with the Great Russian peasantry. We have a large non-Great Russian peasantry, and it is distributed amongst numerous national groups. For these national groups each national, political and economic question is refracted through the prism of their native language, their national-economic and folk peculiarities, and their national mistrust, which has its roots in the past. Language is the most basic, most broadly embracing and deeply penetrating instrument of the link between man and man, and so between class and class. Whilst in our conditions the question of the proletarian revolution is, as you acknowledge, above all a question of the relations between the proletariat and the peasantry, this latter question amounts, more than 50 per cent, to the question of relations between the more advanced and influential Great Russian proletariat and the peasant masses of the other nationalities, which were mercilessly oppressed in former times and still remember very well all that they suffered. What's wrong with you, friend, is that all your would-be-radical, but essentially half-baked, nihilistic arguments strike not only at the national question, but also at the fundamental question of the link between the workers and the peasants.

'A' But, look here, there was the time when our army went into Georgia to drive out the Menshevik agents of the imperialists without waiting to be asked first by the people concerned, which meant a plain breach of the principle of self-determination. And there was the time when our army advanced on Warsaw...

'B' Yes, of course, there were those times, and I remember them very clearly, and don't disavow them in the least. But there was also, not just times, but a whole period when we confiscated from the peasants all their surplus, and sometimes even what they needed themselves, by means of force, not shrinking from the most extreme methods.

'A' What do you mean by that?

'B' What I say. The revolution not only seized the peasants' surplus, arms in hand, but also introduced a military regime in the factories and mills. If we had not done this in a certain very acute and grave period we should have perished. But if we were to wish to apply these measures in conditions when they are not called for by iron, inexorable necessity, we should perish still more surely.

This applies also, of course, to our policy on the national question. Revolutionary self-defence required at certain moments a blow at Tiflis and a march on Warsaw. We should have been pitiful cowards and traitors to the revolution (which includes both the peasant question and the national question) if we had baulked at the empty fetish of the national 'principle', for it is perfectly obvious that there was no real national self-determination in Georgia under the Mensheviks: Anglo-French imperialism held unrestricted sway there, and was gradually subjecting the whole of Caucasia, and menacing us from the south. In the national question, as in all others, what matters to us is not juridical abstractions, but real interests and relations. Our military invasion of Transcaucasia can be justified, and has justified itself in the eyes of the working people, insofar as it dealt a blow at imperialism, and established the conditions for real, actual self-determination for the Caucasian nationalities.

If through our fault the masses of the people in Transcaucasia should come to look upon our military interference as an act of conquest, then this interference would thereby be transformed into a very great crime — not against the abstract 'principle' of nationality, but against the interests of the revolution. Here we have a complete analogy with our peasant policy. The confiscation of the peasants' surplus produce was a very harsh thing. But the peasantry accepted it as just, even though after the event, insofar as they were convinced that, as soon as conditions permitted, the Soviet power would go over to the fulfilment of its basic task — all-round easing of the lives of the working people, including the peasants.

'A' But still, you can't deny that the class principle ranks higher for us than the principle of national self-determination. After all, that's ABC.

'B' The realm of abstract 'principles' is always, my dear friend, the last refuge of those who have lost their way on this earth. I've already told you that the class principle, if you understand it not idealistically, but in a Marxist way, does not exclude but, on the contrary, embraces national self-determination. But this latter we also understand not as some supra-historical principle (on the model of Kant's categorical imperative)[5] but as the aggregate of real, material conditions of life that make it possible for the masses of the oppressed nationalities to straighten their backs, to advance, to learn and to develop, getting access to world culture. For us, for all Marxists, it must be beyond dispute that only a consistent, that is, a revolutionary application of the class 'principle' can ensure the maximum realisation of the 'principle' of national self-determination.

'A' But didn't you yourself say, in explaining our Transcaucasian intervention, that revolutionary defence takes priority with us over the national principle?

'B' Possibly I did, even probably. But in what conditions and in what sense? In the fight against the imperialists and Mensheviks, who transform national self-determination into a metaphysical absolute, insofar as it is directed against the revolution — whilst they themselves, of course, trample upon national self-determination. We answered the sorry heroes of the Second International that the interests of the defence of the revolution mattered more to us than juridical fetishes;[6] the real interests of the oppressed weak nationalities are dearer to us than anything else whatever.

'A' But what about the keeping of Red forces in Transcaucasia, in Turkestan and in the Ukraine? Isn't that a breach of national self-determination? Isn't there a contradiction there? And isn't this to be explained by the fact that the revolution is for us higher than the national question?

'B' When the working people of those countries understand (and when we do everything we can to help them understand) that these forces are on their territory only to ensure their security against imperialism, there is no contradiction here. When these forces indulge in no insult to the national feelings of the native masses, but, on the contrary, display purely fraternal care for them, there is no contradiction here. Finally, when the Great Russian proletariat does everything it can to help the more backward national elements of the Union to take a conscious and independent part in the building of the Red Army, so that they may defend themselves first and foremost with their own forces, then that must mean the disappearance of even the shadow of a contradiction between our national programme and what we do in practice.

All these questions will be solved, of course, not only as a function of our good will, but it is necessary that we display the maximum good will for their genuine solution in a proletarian way... I recall that I read two years ago some reports by a certain former Tsarist general in the service of the Soviet power about how the Georgians were frightful chauvinists, how little they understood Moscow's internationalism, and what a lot of Red regiments were needed to counteract Georgian, Azerbaijani and every other sort of Transcaucasian nationalism. It was quite obvious that in the case of this general, the old-time forceful great power attitude was barely disguised under the new terminology.

And there is no point in hiding sin: this general is not exceptional. In the Soviet administrative machine, including also the military machine, tendencies of this kind are powerful to an extreme degree — and not only amongst former generals. If they were to get the upper hand, the contradiction between our programme and our actual policy would inevitably lead to a catastrophe. This is why we have raised the national question sharply, so as by concentrating all the party's efforts to eliminate this danger.

'A' All right. But nevertheless, how do you explain the fact that those very comrades who fully grasp the significance of the link with the peasantry take up at the same time, as I do myself, a much more reserved position where the national question is concerned, regarding this question as exaggerated and pregnant with the danger of distortions in favour of the backward border-lands?

'B' How do I explain such a contradiction? Logically it is to be explained by the fact that not everybody thinks things out properly. But a logical explanation is not sufficient for our purpose. The political explanation is that the leading rôle in our party here is played — and in the immediate period cannot but be played — by its Great Russian kernel, which through the experience of these last five years has fully taken to heart and thoroughly thought out the question of the relations between the Great Russian proletariat and the Great Russian peasantry. By simple analogy we extend these relations to the whole of our Soviet Union, forgetting, or insufficiently taking into account, that on the periphery of Russia there live other national groups with a different history, a different level of development, and — what is most important — with a mass of injuries they have suffered.

The Great Russian kernel of the party is, in the main, as yet inadequately aware of the national side of the question of the link, and still more inadequately aware of the national question in its entire scope. From this there also derive the contradictions of which you speak — sometimes naive, sometimes stupid, sometimes of a flagrant character. And that is why there is no exaggeration in the decisions of the Twelfth Party Congress on the national question. On the contrary, they answer to the most profound needs of our life, and we must not only adopt them, but develop them further.

'A' Whilst the Communists of the Great Russian centre carry out a correct policy in Great Russia, surely there are in the other parts of our Union local Communists who are carrying on the same work in different national circumstances? This is merely a natural and inevitable division of labour. The Great Russian Communists must and will fight against great power chauvinism, whilst the Communists of the other nationalities fight against their own local nationalism, which is directed, in the main, against the Russians.

'B' What you say contains only part of the truth, and half-truths sometimes lead us to completely false conclusions. Our party is not at all a federation of national Communist groups with a division of labour according to their respective national features. If the party were so constructed, that would be extremely dangerous.

'A' I am not proposing any such thing...

'B' Of course you aren't. But your idea would be developed towards such a conclusion. You insist that the Great Russian Communists must fight against great power nationalism, and the Ukrainian Communists against Ukrainian nationalism.

This recalls the formula of the Spartacists at the beginning of the war: 'The main enemy is in your own country.' But there it was a matter of a struggle by the proletarian vanguard against its own imperialist bourgeoisie, its own militarist state. There this slogan had a profound revolutionary content. Of course, the task of the German revolutionaries was to fight against Hohenzollern imperialism, not to expose French militarism, etc.

It would, however, be a complete distortion of perspective to transfer this principle to the constituent parts of the Soviet Union state, for we have a single army, a unified diplomacy and, what is most important of all, one centralised party. It is perfectly correct that those best fitted to combat Georgian nationalism are the Georgian Communists. But this is a question of tact, not of principle. The root of the matter is the need clearly to grasp the historical origins of the great power aggressive nationalism of the Great Russians and of the defensive nationalism of the small peoples. It is necessary to appreciate the true proportions between these historical factors, and this appreciation must be the same in the mind of the Great Russian and of the Georgian and of the Ukrainian, for these very proportions do not depend upon the subjective approach — local or national — but correspond (and must correspond) to the real balance of historical forces. The Azerbaijani Communist working in Baku or in the Muslim countryside, and the Great Russian Communist working in Ivanovo-Voznesensk, must have one and the same conception where the national question is concerned.

And this uniform conception must consist in a non-uniform attitude to Great Russian and to Muslim nationalism: in relation to the former, ruthless struggle, stern rebuff, especially in those cases when it is displayed in the administrative and governmental sphere; in relation to the latter — patient, attentive, painstaking educational work.

If a Communist on the spot shuts his eyes to the national question in its full scope, and begins to fight against nationalism (or, often, against what seems to him to be nationalism) by summary and oversimplified methods, intolerant negation, persecution, denunciation, etc, then he will perhaps gather around him active, revolutionary, 'left' young people, subjectively devoted to internationalism, but he will never furnish us with a lasting and reliable link with the native peasant masses.

'A' But it is just the 'lefts' in the border republics who call for a more revolutionary, more vigorous solution to the agrarian question. And, after all, isn't this our main bridge to the peasantry?

'B' Undoubtedly the agrarian question, above all in the sense of the abolition of all remnants of feudal relations, must be settled everywhere. As we now have an already firmly established Union state, we can carry through this settlement of the land question with all the resoluteness that it calls for; of course the settlement of the land question is a most important task of the revolution... But the abolition of landlordism is an act that is carried out in one blow, once and for all, whereas what we call the national question is a very lengthy process. After the land revolution has been completed, the national question will not disappear. On the contrary, it will only then come into the foreground. And responsibility for all shortages and shortcomings, all injustices and cases of lack of attention or harshness in relation to the native masses, will be attributed in their minds — and not without reason — to Moscow. It is necessary therefore that Moscow, as the centre of our Union, should be the invariable initiator and promoter of an active policy permeated through and through with fraternal attention to all the nationalities that make up the Soviet Union. To speak of exaggeration in this connection is truly to show a complete lack of understanding.

'A' There is a good deal of truth in what you say, but...

'B' Do you know what? Just you read over again the resolution of the Twelfth Congress now that we've had this talk, and then perhaps, one of these days, we'll discuss these matters again.

Notes

1. This article first appeared in *Pravda*, 1 May 1923, and was reprinted in Trotsky's *Sochinenya*, Volume 21, Moscow, 1927. This English translation by 'Leonard Hussey' first appeared in *International Socialist Review*, Volume 19, no 3, Summer 1958, pp99-103. Leonard Hussey was a pseudonym being used at the time by Brian Pearce, and we are grateful for his permission to reprint his translation here.
2. The congress resolution on the national question was drafted by Stalin. Cf JV Stalin, *Marxism and the National and Colonial Question*, London, 1936, pp279-87.
3. That is, the resolution referred to above, n2.
4. The 'link' referred to is the worker-peasant alliance, on which the Soviet state rested.
5. The categorical imperative of Immanuel Kant (1724-1804) was the means whereby for him practical reason affirms its domination over natural impulses. He thus describes it as the 'ought of that which has never happened', the basis of his theory of free will.
6. Trotsky's answer is contained in *Social Democracy and the Wars of Intervention*, London, 1975 (formerly entitled *Between Red and White*).

Book Five

Nikolai Bukharin and Leon Trotsky

Capitalism and Communism

The items in this section deal with the changing economic policies adopted by the Bolsheviks over the period 1917-23. They show that contrary to legend they were not doctrinaires who came to power armed with patent prescriptions to impose upon a country a sixth of the earth's land surface, which stretched from Europe across Asia, and included almost every social formation from stone age hunter-gathering to some of the largest factories in the world. Within the time span included here the Russian economy experienced increasing nationalisation of industry under the Tsar, the decentralisation of workers' control in 1917, central regulation through one-man management, nationalisation and requisition during the Civil War, and decentralisation again under the New Economic Policy.

The interview with Trotsky makes clear that to begin with the Bolsheviks had no intention of nationalising the whole of industry, not even all of heavy industry; that the widespread nationalisations and the resort to requisitions in the countryside after 1918 were imposed upon the government by the necessities of the Civil War, and that, as Radek has already informed us in Chapter Three of Book One, the NEP was in many respects a return to the plans they had originally formulated for the economy when they came to power in 1917. Trotsky also shows that Socialist planning in the conditions of the early 1920s meant a conflict between state capitalism and the private sector, and that the failure to impose a proper system of accounting and of managerial responsibility was a source of future danger. The complete triumph of the market, so he says, would mean an end of the regime.

Leon Trotsky

Workers' Control and Nationalisation[1]

It WAS on a short Petrograd December day but a little over a month after the capture of power by the Bolsheviks that I ran the gauntlet of the soldiers that guard the long corridors of the Smolny institute, and was ushered into the presence of Leon Trotsky, née Bronstein, Minister of Foreign Affairs for the Bolsheviks and right-hand man of Lenin, née Ulyanov, the economist and strategist of Russian Socialism. I found a square-shouldered man of medium height whose advertisement of intellect in his broad wall-like forehead was balanced by a firm, square chin announcing will.

After telling him I was interested in his economic programme rather than his peace programme, I asked: 'Is it the intention of your party to dispossess the owners of industrial plants in Russia?'

'No', he replied, 'we are not ready yet to take over all industry. That will come in time, but no one can say how soon. For the present, we expect out of the earnings of a factory to pay the owner five or six per cent yearly on his actual investment. What we aim at now is **control** rather than **ownership**.'

'What do you mean by "control"?'

'I mean that we will see to it that the factory is run not from the point of view of private profit, but from the point of view of the social welfare democratically conceived. For example, we will not allow the capitalist to shut up his factory in order to starve his workmen into submissiveness or because it is not yielding him a profit. If it is turning out economically a needed product, it must be kept running. If the capitalist abandons it, he will lose it altogether, for a board of directors chosen by the workmen will be put in charge.

'Again, "control" implies that the books and correspondence of the concern will be open to the public, so that henceforth there will be no industrial secrets. If this concern hits upon a better process or device, it will be communicated to all other concerns in the same branch of industry, so that the public will promptly realise the utmost possible benefit from the find. At present, it is hidden away from other concerns at the dictate of the profit-seeking motive, and for years the article may be kept needlessly scarce and dear to the consuming public.

'"Control" also means that primary requisites limited in quantity, such as coal, oil, iron, steel, etc, will be allotted to the different plants calling for them with an eye to their social utility. On a limited stock of materials of production, concerns that produce luxuries should have a slighter claim than those which produce necessaries.

'Don't misunderstand me', he added, 'we are **not** ascetics. Luxuries shall be produced, too, when there is enough of fuel and materials for all the factories.'

'On what basis will you apportion a limited supply of the means of production among the claimant industries?'

'Not as now, according to the bidding of capitalists against one another, but on the basis of full and carefully gathered statistics.'

'Will the workmen's committee or the elected managers of a factory be free to run it according to their own lights?'

'No, they will be subject to policies laid down by the local council of workmen's deputies.'

'Will this council be at liberty to adopt such policies as it pleases?'

'No, their range of discretion will be limited in turn by regulations made for each class of industry by the boards or bureaux of the central government.'

'In a conversation last week with Prince Kropotkin',[2] I said, 'he urged that each centre be autonomous with respect to the industries carried on within it. Let the city of Moscow, for example, be owner and mistress of all the mills in and around that city. What do you think of it?'

'Kropotkin's communalism', replied Trotsky, leaning forward a little in his earnestness, 'would work in a simple society based on agriculture and household industries, but it isn't at all suited to the state of things in modern industrial society. The coal from the Donets basin goes all over Russia, and is indispensable in all sorts of industries. Now, don't you see that if the organised people of that district could do just as they pleased with the coal mines, they could hold up all the rest of Russia if they chose? Entire independence of each locality respecting its industries would result in endless friction and difficulties in a society that has reached the stage of local specialisation of industry. It might even bring on civil war. Kropotkin has in mind the Russia of 60 years ago, the Russia of his youth.'

'Then you are centralist rather than federalist?'

'Not at all', he answered quickly, 'on economic matters the degree of centralisation should correspond with the actual stage of development of industrial organisation. But unitary regulation of production is very different from the centralisation that characterised the old regime. There is no call for the steamroller to crush the different nationalities amongst us into conformity of speech, religion, education, etc.'

'What should be done to meet the wishes of the diverse nationalities in Russia, Finns, Letts, Lithuanians, Little Russians,[3] Georgians, Armenians and Tartars?'

'The only solution is a federal union such as you have in the United States. Let each of the states of future Russia be free to do as it will in respect to language, schools, religion, courts, laws, penal systems, etc.'

'Do you propose that the profits earned by a concern shall be divided among its workers?'

'No, profit-sharing is a bourgeois notion. The workers in a mill will be paid adequate wages. All the profits not paid to the owners will belong to society.'

'To the local community or to the central government?'

'They will be shared between the two according to their comparative needs.'

'What will be shared — everything above running expenses? Or will you set aside something for depreciation, so that when the plant is worn out there will be money enough to replace it?'

'Oh, of course, it is only **pure** profit that will be divided.'

'By sticking to this principle you can keep up the existing industrial outfit. But in some branches — say the making of motorcycles or tractors — new factories are called for to supply the expanding needs of the public. Where will the money come from that will build these new factories?'

'We can impose on the capitalist to whom we allow a dividend of five or six per cent on his capital the obligation to reinvest in some industry — a part, say, 25 per cent — of what he receives.'

'If in Russia you hold the capitalists down to five or six per cent whilst in other countries they can hope for twice or thrice as much return, won't Russia be stripped of capital?'

'They won't be allowed to remove their capital from Russia at will', said Trotsky significantly.

'Besides', he went on, 'do you imagine that capitalist control is going to survive everywhere save in Russia? In all the European belligerent countries I expect to see social revolution after the war. So long as they remain in the trenches, the soldiers think of little but their immediate problem — to kill your opponent before he kills you. But when they go home and find their family scattered, perhaps their home desolate, their industry ruined, and their taxes five times as high as before, they will begin to consider how this appalling calamity was brought upon them. They will be open to the demonstration that the scramble of capitalists and groups of capitalists for foreign markets and exploitable "colonial" areas, imperialism, secret diplomacy and armament rivalry promoted by munition makers brought on the war. Once they perceive that the capitalist class is responsible for this terrible disaster to humanity, they will arise and wrest the control from its hands. To be sure, a proletarian Russia cannot get very far in realising its aims if all the rest of the world remains under the capitalist regime. But that will not happen.'

'Everywhere in Russia I go I find a slump of 40 or 50 per cent in the productivity of the workmen in the factories. Is there not danger of an insufficiency of manufactured goods if the workmen of each factory follow pretty much their own gait?'

'The current low productivity is a natural reaction from the labour-driving characteristic of the old regime. In time that will be overcome by standards of efficiency being adopted by each craft union, and the denial of the advantages of membership to such workmen as will not or cannot come up to these standards. Besides, collectivist production will make great use of the Taylor system of scientific management.[4] It has not been popular amongst the proletariat because as now applied it chiefly swells the profits of the capitalist with little benefit to the working man or the consuming public. When all the economy of effort it achieves accrues to society as a whole, it will be cheerfully and generally adopted, and premature labour, prolonged labour and overwork will be abandoned because they are needless.'

Notes

1. This text is taken from EA Ross, 'A Talk with Trotsky', *The Independent* (USA), 9 March 1918, which was later reprinted in *Intercontinental Press*, 13 July 1981, pp743-4. Edward Alsworth Ross (1886-1951) was a liberal academic who later served on the Dewey Commission.
2. Prince Peter Kropotkin (1842-1921) was the foremost Anarchist advocate of the theory that society should consist of freely associated communal units, an argument he put forward in *Mutual Aid* (English edition, London, 1939).
3. A term in use during this period for Ukrainians.
4. The Taylor system was the name given to the most extreme methods of exploitation of labour advocated by the American Frederick Winslow Taylor (1856-1915) in his book *Shop Management* (1911).

Nikolai Bukharin

The New Economic Policy of Soviet Russia[1]

IN ORDER to understand the new policy and its practical importance, we should consider it in connection with the economic and social crises through which we had to go this spring. The experience of the Russian Revolution has proved that our former notions of the revolutionary process were rather naive. Even the orthodox Marxian section thought that all the proletariat had to do to take over the technical apparatus after ejecting the upper layers of the bourgeoisie was to capture the reins of power. Experience taught us something very different from that. It proved that during the proletarian dictatorship the complete dissolution of the old capitalist apparatus is a necessary stage in the revolutionary development.

Perhaps some will object that this experience does not give us a theoretical proof, and that the development in other countries may assume a different character from that of Russia. They say that Russia is backward, her proletariat is not numerous, and big industry constitutes a small proportion of the economy of Russia. In Western Europe and in America, however, the development will take quite a different direction. This idea can be refuted not only by Russian experience — we are convinced of the absolute inevitability of an economic disorganisation generally during the revolutionary process.

Every revolution is a process of reorganisation of social relations. In a bourgeois revolution this process is not so thorough nor as extensive as in a proletarian revolution, because capitalism has already been developed, and only a political transformation becomes necessary. Feudal property had already become private property, and the bourgeois revolution had only to secure this private property and allow it a wider scope of action. It was mainly a question of transferring the political machine from one set of owners to another. But even in this case it was necessary to undergo a certain process of reorganisation, which had to be paid for dearly. Even a bourgeois revolution is accompanied by a temporary decline in productivity. Such was the case in the great French Revolution.

The same was manifested in the American Civil War, where economic development was thrown back for a decade.[2] In a proletarian revolution the same thing takes place on a much larger scale. During a proletarian revolution we must not only destroy the state machine, but completely reorganise the industrial relations. That is the most important point.

What are the industrial relations in the capitalist system? First of all, there is a capitalist hierarchy, the subordination of one group to another; higher up there is the class of capitalists, then follow the directors, then the technical intelligentsia, the so-called new middle class, then the skilled workers, and finally the rank and file workers. If these industrial relations are to be reorganised, it means that we must first of all and immediately destroy the various ties that bind these groups. The workers achieve this not by street fights only, but by struggling industrially by means of strikes, etc. The working class cannot win the army in time of revolution if the soldiers obey their officers. It is equally necessary to bring about a breakdown in industrial discipline, if the proletariat is to gain a hold over the economic apparatus.

Once these ties between the classes and strata are severed, the whole process of production will be brought to a standstill. When the workers strike or fight on the barricades, no work can be done. When there is sabotage on the part of the technical intelligentsia, the whole process of production is interrupted. Only when the proletariat is fully in possession of the whole government machine can it put down such attempts. Until that time the process of production will be paralysed. Kautsky and Otto Bauer were talking utter rubbish when they spoke of the continuity of the process of production, and wish to connect it with the revolution. It would be the same if an army wishing to defeat its officers were to preserve a strict discipline under their command instead of killing them. Either the revolution will win, and then there is an inevitable disorganisation of the process of production, or discipline will be maintained, and then there will be no revolution at all. Every revolution is paid for by certain attending evils, and it is only at that price that we can bring about the transition to higher forms of economic life of the revolutionary proletariat. We need not be afraid of that temporary disorganisation. One cannot make omelettes without breaking eggs.

Proletarian Dictatorship and the Peasantry During the Civil War

Now it becomes clear that the price to be paid for the revolutionary process is greater where there is a more stubborn resistance on the part of all the other classes and groups to the proletariat, attaining its maximum in the country which is first in adopting the dictatorship. In Russia, the class struggle involved not only a civil but also a foreign war. Where civil war is transformed into foreign war against powerful states, the revolution has to be paid for at an outrageous rate. This is the chief cause of our impoverishment in the course of the last few years. Nearly 75 per cent of our small supplies and of our latest products had to be given to the Red Army. Every intelligent man will understand what this means to our economic life.

It is impossible to live without bread. The bread question is the most difficult problem of the revolution. The process of economic disintegration during the revolution is also expressed by the severance of ties which connect town and country. When the battle of classes is raging, and the process of production in towns is paralysed, communications with the rural districts cease. The ties of finance and capital which bind the large landowners and the rich farmers to the banks are immediately severed. The same happened to the connecting links between the various peasant cooperative organisations. All exchange between town and country ceases. The credit system in particular is ruined. When towns cease to supply anything to the country, there is no stimulus to give anything to the towns. The economic equilibrium is destroyed.

As the town population must exist also in time of revolution, special means must be found to feed it. First the supplies stored in towns are consumed. Then compulsory means may be adopted against the peasants. The third expedient is the consciousness of the peasants that only the proletarian state defends them against the landowners, the usurers and others.

The peasants were greatly influenced by that consideration during the Civil War against foreign counter-revolution. Our compulsory methods found their economic justification in this circumstance. As regards the arguments of the opportunists that the peasantry was opposed to the Bolsheviks, and that the latter rule by sheer force, every Marxist will say that this is nonsense. Not even the Tsar's government was capable of performing such a feat. Our compulsory actions found their economic justification in the fact that the peasants, as a class, fully understand that there is no other force that can defend them from the landowners, of whose estates the peasants have taken possession. In Russia, 82 per cent of land formerly owned by large landowners was given to the peasants. The close-fisted peasant will not allow this land to be taken from him. He was wise enough to perceive that the main economic problem is to keep fast to the land, as land alone gives him the certainty of growing food. That is why he put up with our methods of requisitions, and that is why we were on the whole able to maintain an equilibrium in our social structure. We felt the ground under our feet.

Of course, every war has its laws. The experience of capitalist countries has shown that the economic changes can more easily be effected in war than in peacetime. The same can be observed in our country. Certain classes, especially the petit-bourgeoisie, were honestly convinced that everything must be sacrificed for war. Due to this, we were able to estimate our resources and regulate our economy by strongly applying the dictatorship of the proletariat.

But after the war was over, the contradictions of this economic system came to the surface at once, first and foremost the contradictions between the regulating tendencies and the anarchical tendencies of the peasantry.

The Inflexibility of the Peasant and the Declassing of the Proletariat

It was proved economically that if we take away all the surplus of the peasants' produce, we take away almost all the incentive to further production. If the peasant knows that he will be deprived of all surplus produce, he will only produce for himself and nothing for others. The only incentive that remains is of an intellectual kind, the knowledge that he must support the workers who defend him from the landlord. After the victory at the civil war fronts, the effect of this incentive was destroyed. It was observed that the cultivated area diminished. This was also due to the drafting of the labour forces to the army, to the decrease of the stocks of cattle, peasant stock generally, etc. Agriculture was in a critical condition, and we were in danger of being left without sufficient bread.

Naturally, this state of agriculture reacted on industry. It is not true that our technical apparatus is totally disorganised. In many important branches of the textile and metal industries, as well as others, we possess a good technical apparatus. But the great problem facing us is how to provide the towns with the necessaries of life. In our country the workers are hungry because the exchange of goods between town and country is paralysed.

These economic conditions have their social consequences. When large industry is in such a miserable condition, the workers seek to find a way, for example, by manufacturing small articles of everyday use at the places where they work, which they subsequently sell. By such methods the proletariat becomes declassed. When in this way the worker becomes interested in free trade, he begins to regard himself as a small producer, a petit-bourgeois. This means the transformation of the workers into petit-bourgeois with all their characteristics. The proletariat goes back to the village, where it works as small craftsmen. The greater the disorganisation, the stronger the process of degeneration of the proletariat, now demanding free trade.

The proletariat as such is weakened. Moreover, the flower of the proletariat was destroyed at the front. Our army consisted of an amorphous peasant mass which was like wax in the hands of the Communist and non-party men. We have lost an immense number of these proletarians, and it was precisely these who enjoyed the greatest esteem and confidence in the factories. Moreover, we were compelled to utilise the best strata of the proletariat for the state machine, the administration of all the villages, etc. To organise a proletarian dictatorship in a peasant country meant to distribute the proletarians amongst certain localities like so many pieces on a chess board, in order to guide the peasants. One can imagine how the factories suffered in consequence through lack of proletarian forces. Only the worst elements remained in the factories. And on top of it all came the declassing of the workers. Such is the social crisis within the working class.

The peasantry also had to suffer, but not to the same extent. If we take an economic view of the subject, that is, not in the sense of power and political rights, the peasantry has derived more benefit from the revolution than all the other classes. Economically, the peasantry is better off than the proletariat, though the latter is the privileged class. The peasant feels himself stronger than ever. There are other, secondary causes. The peasant obtained a good training in the army. He returned from the war a different man. He is now on a higher intellectual and moral level than he was before. Now he understands politics very well. He says: 'We are the predominating force, and we shall not allow others to treat us as silly children. We want to feed the workers, but we are the senior partners, and demand our rights.'

As soon as the war was over, the peasants immediately presented their demands. They are interested in small trade. They are supporters of free trade, and opposed to the compulsory Socialist system of the economy. These demands were presented in the form of peasant risings in various districts in Siberia, Tambov, etc.[3] Things did not look so bad as the counter-revolutionary press tried to picture it, but these events were symptomatic. In their eyes, the political solution of the economic situation consists in the motto: 'For the Bolsheviks, and against the Communists!'

At first this appears quite absurd, but though it is cryptically formulated, this motto has an intelligent explanation. At the time of the October Revolution and previous to it, we were the party that told the peasant to kill the landowner and to take his land. The Bolsheviks were then thought to be capital fellows. They gave the peasants everything, and demanded nothing in return. But in the end we became the party which gave nothing and demanded everything from the peasants. They were consequently against the Communists, who were taking away their bread, and moreover preached absurd ideas of Communism, unsuitable to the peasants. The second watchword was free trade. The first watchword was: 'For non-party soviets, against the dictatorship of a party!' If there are even Communists who fail to understand that a class can only rule if it has a head, and the party is the head of the class, then we can easily understand the peasants failing to grasp that idea. Such is the intellectual atmosphere prevailing amongst the lower middle class and the peasantry.

The proletariat, too, insofar as it was declassed, of necessity shared the same views. In some places even metal workers took up the watchwords: 'Free trade against the Communists!', 'For class dictatorship, but against party dictatorship!' Thus the equilibrium between the proletariat and the peasantry was destroyed. A misunderstanding arose which threatened the whole system of the proletarian dictatorship. The crisis found its expression in the Kronstadt mutiny. The documents which have since been brought to light show clearly that the affair was instigated by purely White Guard centres,[4] but at the same time the Kronstadt mutiny was a petit-bourgeois rebellion against the Socialist system of economic compulsion. Sailors are mostly sons of peasants, especially Ukrainian peasants. The Ukraine is more petit-bourgeois than central Russia. The peasants there resemble more the German farmers than the Russian peasants. They are against Tsarism, but have little sympathy for Communism. The sailors were home on leave, and there became strongly infected with peasant ideas. This was the cause of the revolt.

The Principles of the New Policy

As is known, we acted with all speed; we mobilised and sent against Kronstadt one third of our party congress, we lost many comrades, but we quelled the rebellion. But victory could not solve the question. We had to take certain measures. Had there been a revolution in Germany, we could have brought workers from there and have made a surgical operation. But we have to act on our own. There was one principle which we had to maintain at all costs: the preservation of the dictatorship. We had the picture of the Hungarian affair before us.[5] It is true we should have come into power again after a few months or years, but the bourgeoisie would try its method of reorganisation, which costs something, and then we would again try ours. The disorganisation of national industry would be so terrible that no one can even guess whether any tolerable state of things could ever result from this chaos.

When the state apparatus is in our hands, we can guide it in any desired direction. But unless we are at the helm, we can give no direction at all. Consequently, we must seize power and keep it, and make no political concessions. But we may make many economic concessions. But the fact of the matter is we are making economic concessions in order to avoid making political concessions. We shall agree to no coalition government or anything like it, not even equal rights to peasants and workers. We cannot do that. The concessions do not in any way change the class character of the dictatorship. When a state makes concessions to another class, it does in no way alter its class character, no more than a factory owner, who makes concessions to his employees, becomes a worker. If we look at it from a social and political standpoint, the significance of the concessions lies in the pacification and neutralisation of the lower middle class. Our former investigations brought us to the conclusion that the economic difficulties consisted in the lack of an incentive to increase production. Now this incentive has been offered in the substitution of a tax in kind instead of requisitions. Now the peasant knows that he will have to give up more if he produces more, but he knows also that he will keep more. Experience has already shown that such are his calculations. As soon as we decided on this new system at our party congress, the area under cultivation increased at once to that of 1916, and even 1915.

Politically, a general pacification has set in. The guerrilla warfare in the Ukraine has lost its intensity. These political measures succeeded in putting an end to the Makhno gangs. Some will naturally doubt the wisdom of making these concessions to the petit-bourgeoisie. They may say that a period of accumulation, such as existed hitherto, has been inaugurated, and that usury will result that will transform itself into industrial capitalism. We are faced by the same danger as we were at the time of the Brest peace, when we stood in danger of being engulfed by German capitalism. However, such a state of things is only temporary. Our position now is that we want bread and a pacific peasantry, or else we shall go to the dogs. Even the worker will revolt against his own government if he has nothing to eat. Communism requires a certain time to mature, and this process under our conditions of life is more painful than it would otherwise be. We have in our hands large industry, the coal industry, transport, etc. A whole period of history is required to transform the peasant into a capitalist. Our view is that capitalism will rise slowly from below, but we will keep under our control the chief branches of industry. Once this is achieved, all the industrial processes will assume their normal course. The declassing of the proletariat will cease, we shall be able to invite in foreign workers, etc. We could then pass on to the technical revolution, and will be able to realise the electrification of Russia, which is now in an embryonic stage. If we succeed in realising even a part of our programme, then we shall get the better of the petit-bourgeois tendencies. If the peasant receives from us electric light and power, he will be transformed into a social functionary, and his proprietary instincts will not be offended.

If the tendencies of capitalist growth gain the upper hand over the tendencies to improve large industry, then we are doomed. But we hope the contrary will be the case — then we shall master all difficulties in the field of economics.

Paul Levi and all the opportunists of the world say: 'You see, the Bolsheviks are making concessions to the peasants and we make concessions to the masses.'[6] But this analogy is not correct. We make concessions to secure the equilibrium of the Soviet system, and he does not seem to notice this little difference. We might as well say that there is an army in France and there is an army here, a police system there and an Extraordinary Commission[7] here. The essential point is — what are the class functions of these institutions, and which class do they serve? Whoever makes an abstraction of the class lives in the skies, not on earth. And I think it would be better if our enemies remain in the skies and we remain on solid earth.

Notes

1. These extracts from a report delivered by Bukharin to the delegates of the Third Congress of the Communist International on 8 July 1921, appeared in Lenin, Bukharin and Rutgers, *The New Policies of Soviet Russia*, Chicago, 1921, pp41-61.
2. Blockades, trench warfare and sheer material destruction made the American Civil War (1861-65) exceptionally damaging to the economy of the USA.

3. The Siberian peasants expressed their opposition to the Soviet regime in an outbreak of banditry in early 1921. Major outbreaks of peasant unrest occurred in the Tambov region from the summer of 1920, and were not quelled by the Red Army until early 1921.
4. On this accusation of the Bolsheviks against the Kronstadt mutineers cf Ida Mett, *The Kronstadt Commune*, Solidarity (London) pamphlet no 27, 1967, pp15-7, 42-4.
5. The main cause of the overthrow of the Hungarian Communist regime led by Béla Kun in 1919 was its failure to grant land to the peasants in time.
6. For Paul Levi's remarks on the Russian peasantry, cf 'Introduction to Trotsky's *Lessons of October*', *Revolutionary History*, Volume 5, no 2, Spring 1994, p67.
7. The 'Extraordinary Commission' was the Cheka. Cf above, p81, n10.

Leon Trotsky
Theses on Industry[1]

1. The General Rôle of Industry in the Socialist Structure

THE MUTUAL relations which exist in our country between the working class and the peasantry rest in the last analysis on the mutual relations between industry and agriculture. In the last resort, the working class can retain and strengthen its rôle as leader, not through the state apparatus or the army, but by means of the industry which gives rise to the proletariat. The party, the trade unions, the youth associations, our schools, etc, have for their task the education and preparation of new generations of the working class. But all this work would prove as if built on sand did it not have for its basis a continually expanding industry. Only the development of industry creates the unshakeable basis for the dictatorship of the proletariat. At present agriculture is of primary importance in the economic life of Soviet Russia, although the technical level on which it stands is still very low.

Only in proportion as industry makes real progress and as the heavy industries — which form the only firm basis of the proletarian dictatorship — are restored, and in proportion as the work of electrification is completed, will it become both possible and, indeed, inevitable to alter the relative significance in our economic life of agriculture and industry, and to shift the centre of gravity from the former to the latter. The party must work systematically and perseveringly, whatever the sacrifice or labour, to accelerate this process, especially as regards the rapid restoration of heavy industry.

How long the period of the predominant importance of peasant economy in the economic system of our federation will last will depend not only upon our internal economic progress, which in view of the general conditions mentioned above can be but very gradual, but also upon the process of development taking place beyond the boundaries of Russia, that is, before all, upon the way the revolution in the West and in the East will proceed. The overthrow of the bourgeoisie in any one of the most advanced capitalist countries would very quickly make its impress upon the whole tempo of our economic development, as it would at once multiply the material and technical resources for Socialist construction. While never losing sight of this international perspective, our party must at the same time never for a moment forget or omit to keep in mind the predominant importance of the peasant economy, when it is estimating the consequences of any step it is on the point of taking.

Not only ignoring, but even paying insufficiently close attention to this circumstance, would involve incalculable dangers, both economic and political, since it would inevitably undermine or weaken the unity between the proletariat and peasantry — that feeling of trust of the peasantry towards the proletariat which during the present historical period of transition is one of the most fundamental supports of the proletarian dictatorship. The preservation and strengthening of this unity is a fundamental condition for the stability of the Soviet power, and consequently represents the most fundamental task of our party.

It is necessary to remember the resolutions passed by former party congresses, which very justly emphasised that the support of the peasants for Socialist methods of production can only be won by actual ocular demonstration, during a number of years, and that such methods are economically more advantageous, more rational, etc. In the domain of finance, the policy of economising on state resources, of a correct system of taxation, of a correctly constructed budget — which we have now adopted, and which must and shall be unflinchingly adhered to — will only achieve decisive results on the condition that the state industries show energetic development and substantial profits.

Owing to the extreme diminution of the army, now practically reduced to skeleton formations, and the consequent gradual transition to a militia system, the problem of national defence is reduced to a question of transport and war industries.

Consequently, the construction of our budget, the state credit policy, the measures taken with a view to the military protection of the state, in fact, all state activity in general, must bestow its first and greatest care upon the planned development of state industry.

In view of the general economic structure of our country, the restoration of state industry is narrowly bound up with the development of agriculture. The necessary means for circulation must be created by agriculture in the form of a surplus of agricultural products over and above the village consumption before industry will be able to make a decisive step forwards. But it is equally important for the state industry not to lag behind agriculture, otherwise private industry would be created on the basis of the latter, and this private industry would in the long run swallow up or absorb state industry.

Only such industry can prove victorious which renders more than it swallows up. Industry which lives at the expense of the budget, that is, at the expense of agriculture, could not possibly be a firm and lasting support for the dictatorship of the proletariat. The question of creating surplus value in state industry is the fateful question for the soviet power, that is, for the proletariat.

An expanded reproduction of state industry, which is unthinkable without the accumulation of surplus value by the state, forms in its turn the condition for the development of our agriculture in a Socialist, and not in a capitalist, direction.

It is therefore through state industry that the road lies which leads to the Socialist order of society.

2. Active and Passive in the First Period of the New Economic Policy

The healthy effect of the New Economic Policy on the economic life of the country is incontestable. It is expressed in the revival of industrial activity, in increased production in many important branches of industry, in the rise in the productivity of labour and in the quality of the products, in the indubitably very considerable improvement in the position of the workers, and, above all, in the much more correct approach to both fundamental and detailed economic problems.

And this latter is the basic condition for their effective solution in the future. Nevertheless, the actual position of industry remains very serious. The revival of light industry, which naturally finds its explanation in the fact of the restoration of the market in conjunction with the satisfactory harvest, is very far from implying that all enterprises and branches of light industry can be guaranteed a further healthy development. In spite of the fact that the prices of the products of light industry are extremely high, especially in comparison with the prices of agricultural products, these high prices are often far removed from the price of reproduction, that is to say, they do not guarantee the expansion of production. An increase in the activity of a whole number of trusts has been achieved at the expense of old stocks of raw materials, the replenishing of which is at the present time one of the most acute problems of state economic policy.

On the other hand, heavy industry has barely come into contact with the market. It depends essentially upon state orders, and needs for its restoration that the state should make large and well thought-out investments in it. This also applies to a considerable extent to railway and water transport.

Thus, as a result of the total economic conditions, a healthy regulation of prices in light industries remains as yet unattained. This and the backwardness of heavy industry in comparison with light industry represent the chief items on the debit side of the first period of the New Economic Policy. It is as much the result of the general economic conditions, existing before the New Economic Policy, as of the inevitable crippling of economic relations during the transition to the New Economic Policy.

The attainment of a price regulation, on the basis of the market, better corresponding with the needs of industrial development, the establishment of more normal correlations between the branches of the light industry and those branches of industry and agriculture which provide it with its raw materials, and finally the straightening out of the front of the heavy and light industry — these are the root problems of the state in the sphere of industrial activity in the second period of the New Economic Policy now beginning. These problems can only be solved by a correct correlation between the market and the state industrial plan.

3. The Problems and Methods of Planned Industrial Activity

In Soviet Russia, where the chief means of industry and transport belong to one owner, the state, the active interference of the latter in industry must of necessity take the form of a state industrial plan. In view of the predominating rôle of the state as an owner and a master, the principle of a uniform plan acquires at the very outset an exceptional importance.

The whole of previous experience has shown, however, that a plan of Socialist economy cannot be established a priori in a theoretical or bureaucratic manner. A real Socialist economic plan embracing all branches of industry in their relations to one another, and in the relation of industry as a whole to agriculture, is possible only as a result of a prolonged, preparatory economic experience on the basis of nationalisation, and as the result of continuous efforts to bring into practical accord the work of different branches of industry, and to estimate correctly the results achieved.

Thus for the coming period our task is to determine the general direction, and is, to a considerable extent, of a preparatory character. It cannot be defined by any single formula, but presupposes a constant and vigilant adaptation of the guiding economic apparatus, of its basic tasks, methods and practice to the phenomena and conditions of the market. Only at the final stage of their development can and must the methods of planned industry subordinate the market to themselves, and by this very fact abolish it.

Hence we can perceive quite clearly two dangers accompanying the application of state methods of planned industry during the present epoch, namely:

1. If we try to outstrip economic development by means of our planned interference, and to replace the regulating function of the market by administrative measures which have no basis in actual experience, then partial or general economic crises are inevitable, such as occurred in the epoch of Military Communism.[2]

2. If centralised regulation lags behind the clearly matured need for it, we shall have to solve economic questions by the wasteful methods of the market in cases where timely economic-administrative interference could obtain the same results in a shorter space of time and with a smaller expenditure of effort and resources.

Insofar as we have adopted market forms of economy, the state is bound to grant to individual enterprises the necessary freedom of economic activity in the market without trying to influence this free activity by administrative means. But if, on the one hand, each trust, in order to function successfully, must feel free to orient itself and be conscious of full responsibility for its work, the state, on the other hand, must regard the trusts and other associations as organs subordinate to it, by means of which it is able to sound the market as a whole, and thus render possible a number of practical measures which transcend the market orientation of individual enterprises and associations. A central economic organ may, for instance, come to the conclusion that it is necessary to liquidate a certain trust long before experience brings home to the latter the hopelessness of its position.

The question of the mutual relations between light and heavy industry can by no means be solved in accordance with supply and demand, since this would lead in a few years to a smashing up of heavy industry, with the prospect of its subsequent restoration as a result of market pressure, but, in that case, on the basis of private property.

Thus, in contradistinction to capitalist countries, in our country the principle plan is not confined to individual trusts and syndicates, but embraces industry as a whole; more than that, the state plan must cover the mutual relations of industry, on the one hand, with agriculture, finances, transport, trade (home and foreign), on the other.

In other words, insofar as the state remains not only the owner but the active master-spirit with regard to the majority of the productive forces of industry and transport, and with regard to the means of credit, the principle plan under the conditions of the New Economic Policy will remain much the same as obtained during the epoch of Military Communism, but it differs in the most radical manner in its methods. The administration of the chief committees is substituted for economic manoeuvring.

In its administrative application the campaign must develop in this sphere with extreme cautiousness, by way of a very careful sounding of the ground.

The preparation must be based on economic foresight and consist in conveying instructions to the corresponding economic organs with regard to various phenomena which will either inevitably or in all probability arise at such and such an economic juncture (in connection with the appearance of corn from the new harvest on the market, with the flow of money to the village, etc, etc), and in making such foresight as definite as possible in its application to individual branches of industry or to particular districts, in publishing model calendars supplying directions as to the necessary measures which are to be taken in order to make the best use of the expected situation.

It is quite evident that the fundamental planning of industry cannot be attained within the industry itself, that is, by way of strengthening its guiding administrative organ (the Supreme Council of the National Economy), but must form the task of a separate organisation which stands above the organisation of industry, and which connects the latter with finance, transport, etc. This is the function of the State Planning Commission.[3] It is necessary, however, to define more clearly its position, to organise it more strongly, to give it more definite and incontestable rights and, especially, duties. It ought to be established as an immovable principle that not a single economic question which concerns the state as a whole may be dealt with in the higher organs of the republic without consulting the State Planning Commission. This latter must in all cases, whether the initiative is taken by itself or by some other department, analyse the new question, form some project or proposition in connection with the whole of the remaining economic work, and by the means of this analysis define its specific gravity and its importance. It is necessary to take note in the most unflinching manner of the efforts of various departments and establishments, be it at the centre or in the provinces, to obtain this or that decision by a roundabout way under the pretext of urgency, of pressure of circumstances, of improvisation — considering such efforts as manifestations of lack of economic foresight, and as the most pernicious remnants of administrative partisanship.

In estimating the success of the work of each department, one must very largely take into consideration whether it presents its proposals in good time to the State Planning Commission for their detailed elaboration; the success of the work of the State Planning Commission itself must be estimated from the point of view of the timeliness with which it starts economic questions, of the correct foresight of what will take place tomorrow, and of how insistently it spurs other departments to a timely estimation of the forms of collaboration to be arranged between branches of their work.

It is necessary to fight by the means of the State Planning Commission against the creation of all sorts of temporary and casual commissions of inquiry, together with directive, advisory and provisional committees, which are the greatest evil of our state work. It is necessary to secure regular work through normal and permanent organs. Only thus the improvement of these organs and the development of the necessary suppleness becomes possible, by way of their many-sided adaptation to the tasks allotted to them on the basis of continuous experience.

Without deciding beforehand the question of whether it will be necessary to confer upon the State Planning Commission — the general staff of the state economy — this or that administrative right, it seems to be sufficient for the near future to lay it down that if compulsory force is necessary to exact conformity to the plan decided upon, the sanction for such compulsion must be obtained from the corresponding organs of the central power (from the individual economic commissariats: the Council of Labour and Defence, the Council of People's Commissars, the Presidium of the All-Russian Central Executive Committee).

4. The Trusts, Their Rôle, and the Necessary Reorganisation

The state is the owner of the basic means of production and transport. Individual economic departments, and inside these departments the separate organs, establishments and associations (the trusts), manage the sections of the state economy entrusted to them with that degree of independence which the requirements of management under present market conditions necessitate, and which is determined from above, that is, by the superior state organs.

The right of the state to dispose of the whole property of those trusts which are free from obligations and of the railways, etc, remains absolute. In practice the limit and form of state interference with the present work of the economic organs, and of these latter with the present work of the independent establishments of the trusts, etc, are determined exclusively from the point of view of economic expediency, and are regulated by corresponding statutes (or standing orders).

The greater part of state industry is organised in the shape of trusts, that is, as associations which are endowed with a wide measure of economic autonomy, and which appear on the market as free trading organisations. The fundamental problem of these economic organisations, as well as of the separate enterprises of which the former are composed, is the extraction and the realisation of surplus value for the purpose of state accumulation, which alone can guarantee the raising of the material level of the country and the Socialist reconstruction of its whole economy.

The state enterprises which work for the immediate satisfaction of the most important needs of the state, as, for instance, its military needs, must also be completely subordinated to the requirements of the increase of the productivity of labour and of the decrease of the cost on each unit of production.

In view of the fact that the transition itself from Military Communism to the New Economic Policy proceeded to a considerable extent by the methods of Military Communism, the grouping of the enterprises, their breaking up into trusts, the distribution of means among the trusts, possessed, and to a considerable extent possess even to the present day a provisional and bureaucratic character. From the point of view of economic work according to plan, these are but rough-draft essays, and it is not by speculative methods that they can and must be corrected and reshaped, but on the basis of examining them in the light of experience, in the light of the combined elements of commercial and administrative experience from day to day.

Complaints of the lack of means of circulation do but bear testimony to the fact that on the introduction of the New Economic Policy the state undertook the management of too great a number of industrial enterprises, so that its strength was overtaxed, enfeebled as it was by several years of civil war and blockade. As a consequence, there is the instability of the enterprises, the work going on by fits and starts, and, what is still more important, the freighting is insufficient, which in its turn leads to a great increase in the cost of production, and to the narrowing down of the market with all the economic difficulties ensuing therefrom.

The way out of the difficulty is a radical concentration of production on those enterprises which are technically the most perfect, and geographically the most conveniently situated. All sorts of indirect and secondary considerations put forward against it, however essential they may be in themselves, must be pushed aside in the face of the fundamental economic problem, namely, the providing of the state industry with the necessary circulating means, the lowering of the cost of production, the expansion of the market, and the extraction of profit.

The re-examination of the construction and composition of the trust, both from the purely productive and from the commercial points of view, must be perfectly free from the prejudices in favour of a bureaucratic uniformity in the work of combining the enterprises, either only according to the horizontal, or according to the vertical principle alone. We must be guided in our revision not by formal but by material considerations with regard to the connection and the mutual dependence of the enterprises upon one another, to their relative geographical situations, and with respect to transport and market (combinations, etc), and so on and so on. While sweeping aside departmental or local claims insofar as they come into conflict with the principle of a more advantageous and a more profitable organisation of production, it is necessary at the same time to take into careful consideration and listen attentively to the voice of the interested trusts and separate factories, insofar as their living experience has proved the necessity of withdrawing from some of our organisation projects.

The lowering of the cost of production must be aimed at, not for the sake of transient successes in the market, but with a view to the regeneration and the development of the economic power of the country.

A mode of calculation in which the prices of raw materials are falsified by being given according to out-of-date quotations, and nothing to do with the lowering of costs, must be severely punished as a dissipation of state property.

Equally wrong and ruinous would be a policy of temporarily lowering prices at the expense of causing a direct or indirect loss to heavy industry. Without the restoration of the latter, light industry, as well as the whole process of economic construction, would be deprived of its foundation. Coal, naphtha, metal — these are the branches of industry, the successful development of which will insure both the economic prosperity of the Republic and its external safety.

Only a firm and constant guidance of the trusts on the part of the Supreme Council of People's Economy, uniting — in the spirit of the above directive principles — all the basic elements of industry; foreseeing and preparing their necessary combinations; guaranteeing the timely, full, and proper use of all the factors of production at every stage (fuel, raw materials, semi-manufactured articles, machines, labour power, etc), will insure not only partial but general progress on the industrial front.

5. Industry and Trade

Without a properly organised sale, increased production will again lead to partial gluts, that is, to crises of trading helplessness, which cannot be justified even by the extremely limited market of the present day. The perfection of the lowest links of the trading apparatus, even though only capable of insuring the smallest number of genuine connections between industry and the peasant market, is of paramount importance. The formation of syndicates in the near future should be conducted with the greatest circumspection and with due consideration to the state of the market and the resources of the trusts. The transformation of the syndicates into trading 'chief committees' would only obstruct trading activity and swell the burden of additional expenses. Compulsory syndication must be economically prepared for and commercially justified.

The increased operative independence of the trusts and separate enterprises, the more flexible activity of the syndicates, and the whole position of our industry in general require an incomparably greater coordination as to the relations between the purely productive and the purely commercial spheres of activity. This applies both to home and to foreign trade. Without predetermining the forms of organisation that this coordination will take, it ought to be already established that the systematic study of the experience which is accumulating in this sphere and the elaboration of practical methods of coordinating industrial and commercial activity constitute a vital problem, the solution of which is possible only through the combined efforts of the Supreme Council of the People's Economy, the People's Commissariat of Foreign Trade, the Commissariat of Internal Trade, and with the active participation of the State Planning Commission under the general guidance of the Council of Labour and Defence.

6. The Factory

The root of success or failure in production is to be found in the basic industrial unit, that is, in the factory or mill. The question, therefore, of properly organising each separate enterprise, and that not only from the technical-productive, but also from the commercial point of view, is of decisive importance.

While retaining the general guidance of the enterprise in its hands and centralising those productive and commercial branches and operations which are ripe for it, the trust must at the same time avoid by all manner of means the sort of centralisation which strangles, which extinguishes initiative, and it must avoid mechanical invasions into the work of its enterprises.

The independent accounts of each factory must not only provide the means of determining its profits and its growth or decline, but must also serve as the general basis of a premium system strictly adjusted to the peculiarities of the enterprise.

7. Calculation, Balance and Control

Under the present conditions, material results form the only serious and reliable empirical verification of whether mutual relations between the enterprises, the trusts and the state are satisfactory, as well as providing the sole test of the success or otherwise of our methods of economic management as a whole. Only from the careful tabulation of **balance sheets** can we judge our commercial position, for without a system of correct book-keeping which embraces state economy from top to bottom, without scientific accounts to show the real cost of the products of state industry, there is no guarantee against the gradual dissipation or dilapidation of nationalised property, and the trusts in this case might but serve as channels for pumping state property into private hands.

To work out methods of uniform book-keeping, to see to it that it be really carried out and made more and more accurate, all this must constitute one of the more important problems of the leading economic establishments in general and of the State Planning Commission in particular, this work having for its aim the attaining of **a single real balance** from which can be estimated the position of state industry, and, later on, of the whole state economy in general.

The Council of Labour and Defence must organise a state audit of commercial and industrial accounts and balance sheets. The absence of a competent and skilled control on such lines makes all other kinds of economic inspection useless, and spreads a sense of irresponsibility incompatible with a properly organised economy.

8. Wages

The system of wages adopted during the period that has just expired has on the whole confirmed the soundness of the decisions of the Eleventh Party Congress and the Fifth Trade Union Congress,[4] as well as that of the conclusion of collective agreements between the trade unions and economic organisations.

During the year just elapsed, a considerable increase of wages for all categories of workers can be recorded, and this has resulted in a considerable increase of the productivity of labour.

The general wages policy must for the future be directed towards a greater or smaller levelling up of the average wage in all branches of production with the necessary modifications on the basis of the average skill in such a manner that workers of similar or equivalent skill should be drawing approximately equal remuneration in different branches of industry, and as far as possible independent of the fluctuations of the market; at the same time the individual wage in reality should be proportional to the actual output. The corresponding state organs must, hand in hand with the trade unions, direct their efforts towards coming to a more favourable agreement in a given branch of industry which will serve the interests of the workers not only of this or that branch, but also of those of the working class as a whole, by increasing the earnings in the backward branches and, above all, in heavy industry and transport.

While striving in every way to improve the condition of the working class, the state organs and the trade unions must at the same time remember that a continuous and all-embracing improvement is possible only on the basis of their own development as a profit-bearing industry. From this point of view measures which retain poorly-furnished enterprises in operation, or employ in a mill a number of workers not proportionate to the actual productivity of the enterprise, constitute the most expensive and irrational form of social insurance, and are therefore against the interests of the future of the working class.

The burdening of industrial enterprises with all sorts of additional expenses neither necessitated by production itself nor provided for by law are highly detrimental to the enterprises in question and to the state, however important the purpose for which they are incurred, for they undermine the possibility of an accurate mode of calculation, and impose upon the state in a semi-disguised manner an expenditure which under the present conditions is beyond its strength to bear. Arbitrary donations on the part of the trusts, that is, donations unauthorised and unregulated by the state, are nothing but a dissipation of state property, and as such must be punished by law.

It is necessary to undertake a close inquiry into the practical application under present conditions of the Labour Code and, in general, of all the statutes on labour power, wages, length of the working day for different categories, deductions for social insurance, cultural and educational needs, etc, etc, with a view, on the one hand, to satisfying the interests of the workers in the highest degree that is compatible with the present state of industry and, on the other hand, to setting aside or altering for the time being statutes which are manifestly unrealisable in existing circumstances. Industrial managers and trade unionists must cooperate in collecting, in the most objective manner, closely examined and well-sifted facts which would serve as a basis for the above-mentioned legislative alterations or administrative measures.

9. Finance, Credit, Customs Duties

A necessary condition for the restoration and development of industry, especially of heavy industry, is the proper drawing up of the state budget in the sense of bringing it into close correspondence with the real state resources and with their expenditure according to plan.

It is necessary to do away completely with that greatest of evils — forced upon us, it is true, to a considerable extent by objective conditions — namely, the lack of unity and the discrepancy between our productive schemes and those resources which were at our disposal for their realisation. This sort of scheming inevitably spelt chaos — industrial and financial — and badly shook the stability of the most important economic establishments.

Exactly the same consequence resulted from the practice of requisitioning the products of industry (chiefly of the mechanical, metallurgical and fuel industries) by the state — chiefly for the benefit of the military and the transport departments, either without any payment at all, or else at arbitrary prices which did not cover the cost of those products.

Should future discrepancies crop up between the incoming revenues and the estimated allocations, and should a necessity of curtailing expenditure result therefrom, the reductions should be effected not under some mask or other, but openly, by way of reconstructing the budget and reducing allowances for transport and industrial enterprises, the army, etc, always according to a definite plan.

The system of providing industrial credit constitutes not only a financial or banking problem, but the most important part of activity in the business of organising and guiding industry. It is necessary, therefore, that the business of financing the state industry should be as far as possible concentrated in one credit establishment which should be very closely connected with the Supreme Council of People's Economy.

The imposition of taxes and excise duties, in strict conformity to the ability of industry to pay and the capacity of the market, must be closely studied, while the effect which higher or lower duties on different imported articles may have on corresponding branches of home industry (from the point of view of protecting them) ought to be carefully considered.

Purchases and orders from abroad, even at prices which are lower than in the home market, must be unhesitatingly pushed aside in all those cases in which they are not absolutely necessary, for the placing of the order inside the country may serve as a considerable spur to the development of the corresponding branch of our state industry.

It is only a system of Socialist protectionism carried out in a consistent and determined manner that can insure at the present transitional period a real development of industry in our Soviet state, surrounded as it is by the capitalist world.

10. Foreign Capital

The experience of the past year has confirmed the fact that the process of state Socialist construction under the New Economic Policy is quite compatible (within certain by no means narrow limits) with the active participation of private — foreign as well as home — capital in the sphere of industry. Further systematic measures are necessary in order to attract foreign capital to industry in all those forms the expediency of which has already manifested itself up till now: concessions, mixed companies, leasing. A careful study of which domains of industry and which enterprises can be left to foreign capital and on what principles, with advantage to the general economic development of the country, is essential to the formulation of future plans by our leading economic organisations.

11. Managers, Their Position and Problems ; The Education of a New Generation of Technicians and Managers

The mutual relations between trade unions and administrative bodies defined by the resolutions of the Eleventh Congress of the party, the correctness of which is confirmed by the experience of last year, must continue to be developed and strengthened in the spirit of those resolutions.

The system of real unity of power must be carried through in the organisation of industry from top to bottom. The selection of workers and their transference or dismissal constitute in the hands of the leading administrative organs a necessary condition for the real guiding of industry and for enabling them to bear the responsibility for its fate. The recommendations and attestations of the trade unions must be fully and sympathetically taken into consideration, but they should under no circumstances release the corresponding administrative organs from their responsibility, as the existing statutes leave to the latter full freedom of selection and appointment.

Heaviness, immobility and lack of enterprising spirit form the weak side of the state industry and trade. The reason for it lies in the fact that the managing staffs are as yet very far from being the best fitted for their jobs, that they lack experience, and are not sufficiently interested in the progress of their own work. It is necessary to take regular and systematic measures towards improvement in all these directions. In particular, the remuneration of the managers of enterprises should be made to depend upon the credit or debit balance, as wages do upon output.

The work of leading administrative workers (trade corporation controllers, directors of mills and factories, chairmen and members of the boards of trusts), insofar as their task consists in lowering the expenses of production and in extracting profit, is beset with extremely great difficulties frequently resulting in conflicts, dismissals and transferences. Two dangers always confront an administrator:

1. That his strict demands will stir up against him the workers of the enterprise and their representative organs or the local party and soviet establishments.

2. That following the line of least resistance in questions of the productivity of labour, wages, etc, he will endanger the lucrativeness, and therefore the future, of the enterprise. It goes without saying that a director of a Soviet factory must

take into the most sympathetic consideration the material and spiritual interests of the workers, their feelings and frame of mind. But at the same time he must never forget that his highest duty to the working class as a whole consists in raising the productivity of labour, in lowering the costs of production, and in increasing the quantity of material products at the disposal of the working class state. It is the duty of the party and trade union workers to give the Soviet director their whole-hearted support in this respect. Attention, perseverance and economy are the necessary qualities of a Soviet administrative worker. His highest testimonial is to run the enterprise on a basis of soundly-balanced accounts.

It must be made plain to the mass of the workers that a director striving to make the enterprise profitable serves the interests of the working class just as much as a trade union worker who strives to raise the workman's standard of living and to safeguard his health.

The preparation of new administrative workers must assume a systematic and, at the same time, a highly specialised character. Summary methods, as when instruction was taken in a hurry merely by watching others at their duties, must be replaced by systematic training according to an exact plan, coupled with a definite period of experience. Workers placed at their posts in the first period and who have not yet had time to acquire the necessary knowledge must be given the opportunity of filling the more serious gaps.

Specialisation in different kinds of practical activity, however, ought to be closely connected with a raising of the theoretical and political level, and with a closer contact with the party; otherwise specialisation might prove injurious to the party, as a superficial knowledge of everything is detrimental to any economic enterprise.

The party and the trade unions must pay the most serious attention to the question of increasing the number of working-men managers of industry, and especially of Communists in managerial posts at all the stages in the economic hierarchy.

Technical training ought to be for the new generation not only a question of specialisation, but also one of a revolutionary duty. Under the conditions of a workers' state all the enthusiasm of the young working men which formerly used to be devoted to the revolutionary political struggle should now be directed towards the mastering of science and technical subjects. It is necessary that a student who neglects his studies should be treated in the same way as a deserter or blackleg was treated in the struggle against the bourgeoisie. The organisation of a Socialist economy is for the proletarian vanguard not a method of obtaining a career, but an heroic action.

12. Party Institutions and Economic Institutions

Without for one single moment forgetting its permanent revolutionary educational problems, the party must clearly realise that at the present constructive-economic period of the revolution, its most fundamental work lies in guiding economic activity in the basic points of the Soviet process of construction. The party will accomplish its historic mission only if the economic experience of the whole party grows together with the growth in size and complexity of the economic problems which the Soviet power has to face.

Therefore the Twelfth Congress is of the opinion that not only a proper distribution of workers, but also the function of supervising every important branch of economic administration, must be considered by the party as its bounden duty, especially in view of the New Economic Policy, which creates the danger of degeneration for a part of the managing staffs, and of perverting the proletarian line of policy in the process of economic reconstruction. Under no circumstances whatever should this guidance turn in practice and as a matter of course into frequent dismissals or transference of managers, into a meddling in the current everyday work of the administration, or into attempts at their direction.

Directions with regard to concrete questions imposed by party organisations upon administrative machinery are inevitable and indispensable under existing conditions, but it is necessary constantly to strive that such guidance should bear the stamp of a broad plan, which would eventually lead to an actual diminution of the number of cases where there would be any necessity for direct administrative interference in independent or specialised questions of current practice.

The more regularly the administrative and economic work of the state itself proceeds in the execution of the plans brought forward by the party, the more completely the leadership of the party will be safeguarded.

The Twelfth Congress confirms the resolutions of the Eleventh with regard to the necessity for a division of labour and a delimitation of the work in the economic sphere as between the party and the soviets, in particular, and insists that this resolution be carried out more completely and systematically both in the centre and locally. The Twelfth Congress especially calls to mind that in accordance with the resolution of the Eleventh Congress, the party organisations 'solve economic questions independently only in those cases and insofar as the questions imperatively demand a solution according to party principles'.

One of the important problems before the party is to give its support to an arrangement under which competent economic organisations would have not only a formal right, but a practical opportunity of gradually educating administrative workers and providing for their regular advancement in proportion as they gain in experience and develop their qualities.

This is only possible if workers are systematically selected according to their economic experience both in business and in skilled trades, and also if inside economic institutions the principles of discipline and of a corresponding system of coordination and subordination among the separate branches of the work and among the workers at the head of these branches are observed.

But in view of the particularly important and responsible work with which the administrative workers are charged at the present moment, the party as a whole and all its organisations must give them the most hearty support, and systematically take care to create such an atmosphere as would exclude the possibility of groups of administrative workers breaking away from the party.

13. The Printing Trade

The question of putting the printing trade on a sound basis is not only of economic but also of immense cultural importance.

The congress recognises the present state of the printing trade as unsatisfactory and considers it necessary to take decisive measures to improve it.

It is necessary first of all to raise the technique of those publications which are for a mass sale. The question of the organisation of the typographical trades must be solved as early as possible, and in such a way that the biggest and most important state publishing establishments should be able to put their work on a broad, regular and technically satisfactory basis.

Notes

1. Report presented by LD Trotsky to the Twelfth Congress of the Russian Communist Party, April 1923, reprinted from *Labour Monthly*, Volume 5, no 1, July 1923, pp19-29, and no 2, August 1923, pp94-104.
2. Military Communism, or as it is generally termed in English, War Communism, is the name given to the system of centralised state regulation of the economy to supply the needs of the army and country during the Civil War (1918-21).
3. The State Planning Commission (Gosplan) was a state planning agency set up in 1921 under the presidency of Gleb Krzhizhanovsky.
4. The Eleventh Party Congress was held in March 1922, and the Fifth Trade Union Congress in September 1922.

Leon Trotsky
Production and Revolution[1]

THE FIRST and the most elementary of the tasks of the NEP decided upon by our party has been to provide a boost to the productive forces. The second is to steer the forces of production in the direction of recovery, or whilst recovering, towards Socialism. These two questions must in no wise be confused.

The NEP has accomplished its first goal. Our statistics for 1913, 1921 and 1922, however inexact they may be, describe the movement of production quite well. In 1913 the total revenue of all branches of Russian industry and agriculture amounted to 11 000 million gold roubles. In 1921 it was less than 4500 million, and in 1922 it was 5300 million.

In 1913 agriculture furnished a yield of 6700 million. In 1921 it provided 3500, and in 1922, 4000 million. In 1913 the whole of industry produced 4400 million gold roubles, and in 1921, 929 million. In 1922 production surpassed 1300 million. But what concerns us most is nationalised heavy industry on the one side, and small workshop production on the other. In 1913 heavy and medium industry produced 3700 million, in 1921, 669 million, and in 1922, 954 million. In other words, in 1922 it achieved an increase of 43 per cent over 1921. But what did the small workshops produce? It was 730 million a year before the war. In 1921 it was 260 million, and in 1922, 435 million.

The Primitive Nature of Exchange with the Countryside

Exchange between town and country has likewise increased. It mainly manifests itself in consumer goods. The link with the countryside has thus gone through a basic stage, and we are only now approaching a second, in which the countryside will provide raw materials to the town and receive machinery from it.

The primitive character of our exchange with the countryside is conditioned by two factors: it is based upon consumer goods, and small handicraft production plays an enormous part in it. Let us recall that this production has gone up to four or five million gold roubles, whereas that of heavy and medium industry is only 954 million. The question is here posed sharply: is the exchange between town and country proceeding towards Socialism or towards capitalism? The NEP is a sphere legally recognised by us in which private capital is in competition with us.

Petty commodity production is the yeast of the culture in which capitalism has developed in Russia, otherwise introduced by foreign capital. Private capital has hardly penetrated our heavy and medium industry. The permitted enterprises only play a rôle of scant importance amongst us. But private ownership is predominant in trade. Petty commodity production and private trade form a hostile bloc of forces against us.

The Recovery of Production

Production has been revived. A little more has been produced, and a little better. The productivity of labour has increased, and wages along with it. Does this mean that the state is better off? In Germany the recovery of business meant the ruin of the country. But we do not pay reparations to anyone. We settled all our debts in October 1917,[2] and our prerogative remains intact. If our nationalised industry works at a loss, who can therefore grow wealthy, seeing that it is not foreigners?

Because this year our production taken as a whole has worked out at a loss. Some branches hoped to make profits. Production went up by 43 per cent. There was a very slight improvement in fuel. That of paper has gone up by 86 million gold roubles to 191, and that of wool from 72 to 137. Textiles are in the lead, and privately owned light industry is in front of that. Nationalised heavy industry is still in deficit.

This deficit can be compared with the effort of running a machine which has almost ceased to function, and which has completely ceased to function in some respects. In this case there is nothing upsetting about it, it was inevitable. Only it must not go on. The start that has been made must not be ruined. The conclusion to draw from this experience is that we are still in the basic stages of recovery. This recovery helps us, that is obvious. It means a gain, and the rise in wages is another. But if we ask ourselves for whom it has provided its first profits, we would do well to reply that it was to our competitor, the small producer. And it is necessary for us to admit that we have spent part of our capital in order to put our equipment back in working order. Rykov[3] has concluded this, and adds: 'It is necessary during the third year of the NEP for our industry and transport to make up their costs and produce.'

Improving the Condition of the Peasant and Exporting Grain

During the second stage of the NEP, our aim is that of uniting with the countryside. The peasant is confronted with the small producer and nationalised industry. Our Commission of Internal Trade points out that the peasant today is paying in grain for his manufactured goods, his coal and his petrol, etc, 2.75 times more than in 1913. Last August the prices of manufactured goods on our markets were less than those of 1913. They have not stopped rising since. At the same time the prices of agricultural goods were higher than those of 1913, and they have not stopped dropping since. This is the whole problem of our economic life and of our progress towards Socialism.

It is urgently necessary to bring closer the prices of rural production and of industrial production, without which no control of the frontiers will save us from the competition of the foreign market.

The prime question here is that of our grain exports. It would be of first rank importance if we sold them at a profit. But we are in a period of Fascism,[4] and blockades are possible. The Americans have so much grain that they are using it to feed to their pigs, and are even burning it: during the war America took over nine-tenths of our grain markets. Can we regain them? Without the slightest optimism we can reply in the affirmative: Europe, even a Fascist one, must eat our Soviet bread, and the profits from this export, profiting the peasants directly, will in the final analysis help revivify our industry again. But this is still not the solution. It is more a link between capitalist Europe and the Ukrainian countryside than between our proletariat and our peasantry.

Creating Accountability

We are too awkwardly equipped with regard to our competitor, the small producer. His equipment is rudimentary. Out of our vast industrial enterprises we are utilising only 17 to 20 per cent, 25 per cent at the most, and we are carrying the entire weight of the rest. Our enterprises remember with all too much respect the former partisan armies, who had 500 bayonets, three aeroplanes and two telegraph apparatuses in order to convey the impression of an army. It is thus necessary, with the greatest circumspection, to reorganise them, the party and the trade unions devoting all their attention to it.

We must put a stop to all useless work. It is better to feed the unemployed than to make useless machinery function, to centralise our enterprises rigorously, to reduce the secondary costs of production, whether those labelled as training or support to the Red Army, and even more so those of advertising. In this connection one fact must be mentioned: a great part of our press is kept going on the completely useless advertising of our industrial establishments.

Moreover, we need strict accountability, the absence of which encourages theft and waste. Where are we in our calculations? The Workers' Inspectorate[5] has learned that 80 per cent of our calculations are arbitrary — and we can assume that the others are worth absolutely nothing at all. The enterprises boasted of profits, and the Workers' Inspectorate proved to them that they were in deficit.

There is a whole lot of black and white magic with numbers, and we must finish with it. We have now experienced the period of 'requisitions' that justified everything, and then that of 'speculations', and I fear that we may now be in that of 'calculations'. We have to create accountability, accurate calculations, which will no longer disguise the pillaging, but will really allow us to carry on our business. Accountability is not an office requirement, a technical detail, it is the way to Socialism.

Regularising Wages

The Party Commission on Wages, presided over by Rykov, has taken some important decisions: obviously wages must rise at the same time as production, but they must not reflect the boosts of the latter. The profits of the textile industry, for example, must not be entirely absorbed by wage rises, but must partly contribute to the recovery of the whole of the nationalised industry.

Concentrating Credit

Financing an enterprise is three-quarters of controlling it. In our state the financial mechanism is more and more called upon to reactivate industry, in its broad lines, naturally, and not in its details. The People's Commissariat of the Economy would be impotent if it did not have the use of a good financial mechanism.

Financial control of production obviously must not draw its inspiration from the immediate fluctuations of the commercial market, and must not lose sight of the long-term perspective, examined by the principle services of the state and by the party. The only way of avoiding all dilettantism in this sphere is to concentrate credit.

The monopoly of foreign trade must not be put in question.[6] If we had to explain upon what our hopes for a Socialist future for Russia rested, we would reply:

1. Upon the political power of the party, supported by the Red Army.
2. Upon the nationalisation of production.
3. Upon the monopoly of foreign trade.

It would be sufficient to throw down one of these pillars for the building to fall.

Working in Conformity with a Rational Plan

I will now go on to a question that I regard as fundamental, that of coordinated economic work on a unified plan. What is this plan? In the capitalist system it is the free play of supply and demand, crises, etc, that regulate production. There is only a plan for private industries; it is only when they are monopolies that their combined activity extends to the world market. Under War Communism we had to substitute the calculations of our administration for the interaction of all the economic forces. We therefore succeeded for good or ill in feeding the army and the proletariat. But we have to admit that we were not able to control our industry in this way. And we called the market to our aid. Only we could not incautiously put our industry at the disposal of the market. The army is always one systematic economy that does not depend upon the market; our transport is entirely nationalised; and our heavy industry and our fuel industry mainly work for the army and for transport. There can be no question of putting them at the disposal of a market, no matter how insignificant. We are thus obliged to reconcile the projected, planned activity of the economic organs of the state with the mobility and flexibility of the market, and that calls for the necessity of a plan. In 1921 we had a fuel crisis. In 1922 it was a sales crisis. We now have a crisis of raw materials. With reference to the fuel crisis, Vladimir Ilyich told us in 1921: 'We are wrong in our forecasts.'[7] The crisis developed from our lack of a system, and the absence of a well-constructed plan. The sales crisis later was the result of our lack of commercial foresight; we had saturated the feeble internal market. The raw materials crisis has the same cause; products were brought out at a price not warranted by the supply of raw materials. Our crisis was caused by the insufficiency of our plans. By planning our work better we could foresee and neutralise the movements of the market to the extent of five to six-tenths.

Controlling economic life means foreseeing and planning it. But we must not confuse the general plan with the possibilities for manoeuvre and action allowed to isolated enterprises. These are different things and will remain so.

Drawing up and applying a plan means doing what Morgan[8] and his general staff do for their trust in America: coordinating leadership and administration. We must direct all our nationalised Russian production in the same way as they direct their trusts.

We thus move into agreement with the theses of the Central Committee on the necessity of having a great Economic Headquarters.

Overcoming the 'NEP'

We invoked the competition of the free market, and we must try our strength against it. We will persevere by a concerted effort, and our success will be indicated by the part in the reconstruction of the national wealth that will return to conscious control. The New Economic Policy is serious and long term, but in no way eternal. We have only created it so as to overcome it with the aid of the laws of the market, to utilise these laws for ourselves, introducing our powerful economic machine into it, whilst unceasingly extending into it the lever of work upon a unified plan.

The plan extended to the entire market will end by finishing it off. Is this victory possible? Obviously. Is it certain? No. Have we already begun it? In my opinion, no. We have only now been able to draw near to the positions upon which we can succeed. We have created the preliminary conditions for victory. What must we do to win?

Our Advantages

1. As opposed to the capitalist countries, knowing our capabilities and our needs, we can consciously control our economic life.

2. In its general interest we can to a certain extent proceed in the relations between agriculture and industry to displace certain forces, and make them pass over from one to the other.

3. We can consciously direct the resources of our state, supplying certain branches of production better, and suppressing those of which we have no need.

4. We can consciously allocate our resources between enterprises in industry, developing some and holding back others.

5. Infinitely better than in the capitalist system, we can coordinate the work of different enterprises.

6. Finally, the Russian working class can allow the state some credit on wages.

These are six of our main advantages. These I find enumerated in a pamphlet devoted to the Moscow mining region, whose author adds that if we are now in deficit, that is because we lack chiefs of industry, taking an interest in everything, dedicated to their work, who know it and dedicate their nights as well as their days to it. For the proletariat has only one means of realising Socialism, accumulating **profits**. Here the most simple rule is the best: saving the Soviet kopek will make the Soviet rouble.

At the Ninth Party Congress, Vladimir Ilyich made the selection of men the main question.[9] Comrade Kuibyshev's Commission[10] examined 28 firms, and concluded that they were as 'maladroit, imprudent and unsystematic as those who directed them', to the consequent scattering of accountability. It also proposed that henceforth the administration of the all-Russian enterprises must be appointed by the Supreme Economic Council along with the Central Committee of the party. Similarly, in the provinces, the provincial party committees should collaborate as regards recommendations with the provincial economic committees.

Primitive Socialist Accumulation

We are getting ready to leap over the stages of primitive Socialist accumulation. You should understand what primitive capitalist accumulation is according to Marx,[11] and what pressure of forces it presupposes for the small employer. This small exploiter works miracles, attains to a sort of heroism, sleeps only four hours out of 24, lives on black bread, exploits his wife and children, and cuts down the pennies. This is a disgusting spectacle, because it is a matter of an individual penny of a rapacious petit-bourgeois. But we need a strict economy ourselves, to which we must devote all our insight, all our energy, and all our will. We should throw out to the nation this slogan: Save the Soviet kopek. With the same devotion and attention that previously we used to put into clandestine revolutionary work, keeping the addresses of our comrades that must never be lost, and never be betrayed, we must henceforth defend steadfastly every little bit of the inheritance of our Socialist country.

Let us get to work, and we will bring this country out of misery and slavery. And we will not surrender in front of capital.

Notes

1. The English text of this piece first appeared in May-June 1991 under the title 'Socialism and the Market' in *Workers News*, the paper of the Workers International League, to whom we offer our thanks for giving us the permission to reproduce it here. It consists of a report on production made by Trotsky to the Twelfth Congress of the Communist Party of the Soviet Union on 10 April 1923, and subsequently reprinted in *Pravda* (88), 22 April 1923; *Ekonomicheskaya Zhizn* (88-90), 22-25 April 1923; and *Protokolui xii Sezd RKP (B)* (pp282-332). The speech as it appears here was translated by Richard Stephenson from the *Bulletin Communiste* of 10 May 1923 as reproduced in the *Cahiers de CERMTRI*, no 58, September 1990, pp4-6. We have restored the original title.
2. The sum of £6.6 million in gold marks was fixed in 1921 for the payment of reparations by Germany to the Entente powers under the terms of the Treaty of Versailles. But Russia repudiated all her foreign debts at the time of the October Revolution.
3. Alexei Ivanovich Rykov (1881-1938) was appointed President of the National Economic Council in 1918. He became a leader of the Right Opposition along with Bukharin, and was a defendant with him in the third Moscow Trial.
4. The first Fascist dictator, Benito Mussolini, seized power in October 1922 after the March on Rome.
5. The Workers and Peasants Inspectorate (Rabkrin) had been set up to control bureaucracy, inefficiency and mismanagement in the state institutions. Under the direction of Stalin (1919-22) it soon became deeply involved in promoting them.
6. In October 1922 the Central Committee adopted decisions weakening the state monopoly of foreign trade. Lenin and Trotsky formed an alliance, and had them reversed.
7. VI Lenin, 'Speech at a Meeting of Moscow Party Activists', 24 February 1921, *Collected Works*, Volume 42, Moscow, 1969, pp272-5.
8. John Pierpont Morgan (1867-1943) was head of an enormous American trust with investments in steel, railways and banking.
9. VI Lenin, 'Speech on the Immediate Tasks of Party Development', 24 September 1920, *Collected Works*, Volume 42, Moscow, 1969, pp207-12.
10. Valerian Vladimirovich Kuibyshev (1888-1935) was a member of the Presidium of the Supreme Economic Council, and Superintendent of the Central Electricity Administration.
11. Marx described the period of primitive accumulation in Part 8 of Volume 1 of *Capital* as one of acute distress and exploitation in the newly founded industries, in the driving of the peasantry off the land, and in the plundering of the colonies. For the theory of 'Primitive Socialist Accumulation', cf E Preobrazhensky, *The New Economics*, Oxford, 1965.

Book Six

Leon Trotsky and Grigory Zinoviev

State and Class

This last section looks forward to the main problem of the future of the Russian Revolution: the relationship between the workers and 'their' state.

By 1921 the Russian working class hardly existed any more. It had never amounted to any more than 10 per cent of the population to begin with, and the ruin of industry led to a return of the city proletariat to the countryside, and a swelling of the ranks of the peasants. Post-revolutionary Russia was even more of a peasant country than had been the Russia of the Tsars. The most active sections of the working class that had made the revolution of 1917 had either perished at the front, or been absorbed into the state apparatus. Trade unions, parties, factions, soviets and the state 'represented' a working class that to all intents and purposes no longer existed. The victory of the working class during the Civil War had ended in its annihilation, and the entire apparatus of society that claimed to speak for it hung suspended in mid-air.

Zinoviev's speech here looks both ways. On the one hand he makes a great deal of the dangers of bureaucratism, and on the other he hints at Trotsky as being a potential Bonaparte. The history of the English and French Revolutions shows that he was correct to look for the emergence of a Bonaparte when a revolution goes into reverse gear, but events were to prove that he was wrong in the direction in which he was looking.

Society as a whole had been completely militarised for some time. The Red Army had been the chief instrument of this state for four years of civil war, and such illusions had grown up with regard to this form of social organisation that labour armies had been planned to replace it in the reconstruction of the economy afterwards.

At the same time it has to be said that Trotsky's articles in this section show that he did nothing to allay the fears of the Bolsheviks. His suggestions for a way out of the impasse lend substance to the remarks in Lenin's *Testament* about his 'excessive preoccupation with the administrative side of the work'. After all, Stalin only took over the task of sending out personnel from the centre to reconstruct the Bolshevik party apparatus in the provinces relinquished by Trotsky's army at the end of the Civil War. Trotsky reasons in a formalistic way that because the USSR was a workers' state, the function of the trade unions as a defence for the working class was now largely redundant. He assumes that the trade unions should only assert any independence from the Soviet state when the state itself relinquishes its total control over the economy under the NEP. Nowhere does the real situation of social relations within the economy really break through, that in the absence of a working class in any meaningful sense at all, arguments as to whether state, party, trade unions, soviets or workers' committees represented it was a dispute whose unreality would have delighted the theologians of the Middle Ages.

Now that we stand at the end of the process that began during these debates, we can say that the exhaustion of the revolution, Lenin's increasing illness, and the defeat of the revolution in the advanced capitalist countries all formed the background for the rise of Stalinism, which after three-quarters of a century has destroyed the last vestiges of the Revolution of 1917.

Leon Trotsky

Trade Unions and Their Future Rôle[1]

$1.$ OUR trade unions are going through a very grave crisis which nearly all workers in the trade union movement, whether local, or central, feel, are aware of, and confirm. This crisis is due to many causes, and takes different forms in different unions. The trade union crisis is complicated by those unhealthy phenomena, the problems of 'tops' and 'lower ranks'. But it is necessary to stand aside from these conditions, hindrances and phenomena which characterise all the organisations and institutions of Soviet Russia, in order to clarify to oneself the exceptional, special character of the crisis being experienced by the trade unions as such.

2. The fundamental reason for the crisis is the indefiniteness and duality of the trade union's position and rôle in production. In the first period of Soviet power the unions tried to take direct control of the productive apparatus; but they proved inadequate for this. At this time they were still organised along the lines they had when the revolution took them unawares. A Soviet apparatus administering industry and other spheres of the economy began to take shape, parallel to the unions. Relying to a certain extent on the unions, this Soviet apparatus became, however, completely independent from them and concentrated the direction of the economy in its own hands.

Thus the union apparatus exists in parallel to the apparatus in charge of any given branch of industry. The self-reliance and closed character of the administrative-economic organs will develop still further, as will, consequently, their independence from the unions. In other words, the trade unions will become still further removed from real participation in economic life. They have been assigned a somewhat indefinite and in any case limited rôle in the nomination of candidates to economic posts and in the propaganda for production.

No future prospects lie ahead for the unions. Much better economic organs than trade unions can be found for discovering suitable candidates and for production propaganda. Many active union workers, disturbed by this position, are tending to give up union work. If the crisis continues in its present form, complete disintegration threatens the trade unions.

3. In the workers' state, the trade union is an organisation embracing the workers in a given branch of the economy aiming at the most correct and successful service of the interests of production itself, and, at the same time, raising the material and spiritual levels of the workers. A production union does not mean a union subservient to production but a union for production, that is, for multilateral participation in production, including its direction. Thus it is evident that the parallelism of productive organs and trade unions can be tolerated only as a temporary phenomenon, and not as a principle of the workers' state. The

thought and energy of the Communist Party, the production unions and the organs of the workers' state must aim, in the fairly near future, at the fusing of the economic organs with the unions so that all workers without exception in any given field of industry shall be included in a union, and so that the administrative-economic apparatus will be not other than the production arm of the unions, that is, their most important section, and after this will follow the organs of agitation and enlightenment, of supply, of discipline, etc.

4. Thus, for the working class that has come to power, the problem of trade unions presents itself in a dual form: on the one hand it is essential that the workers control production; on the other, the unions must be made capable of this, and not only of assisting in it.

Precisely this aim must be clearly and distinctly put before the trade unions. The production rôle of the trade unions in the workers' state is fundamentally different from their basically Syndicalist rôle in capitalist society. Meanwhile, with the preserved and fortified independence of the state-economic and union organs within the unions, **the attitude to the state as a contractual party** continues. This Syndicalist element, penetrating the psychology of many trade union workers as a result of the situation described above, is extremely dangerous for the trade unions, as for the economic organs; in other words, for the working class as a whole.

5. Having placed before itself and the unions the clear and distinct task of ensuring for the unions the leading rôle in our economic life, the party must place before itself and the unions the task of reorganising, reconstructing and re-educating the unions in **the name of this aim**.

We build, reorganise, break and build again economic-soviet organs, selecting and checking various workers for different posts. The unions are almost entirely excluded from this process. Meanwhile, it is quite evident that if we were and are going to set the unions in one, two or three years the task of administering production, then it is essential just now to get down to reorganising the unions, that is, above all to selecting leading cadres with the above task in mind.

6. It is quite evident that only the party, the All-Russian Central Council of the Trade Unions (VTsSPS) and the Soviet state are really capable of reorganising the unions into production unions, and of employing to this end the necessary conditions regarding personnel and materials (staff personnel, technical apparatus, etc). In one case (Tsektran) the organisational changes required to bring the unions closer to the production type were achieved only after extremely harsh and drastic organisational measures had been taken, necessitated by special conditions.[2]

If we define clearly and exactly the aim of the trade union organisation in the Soviet state and make this aim the property of all trade union workers, then the organisational measures for reconstructing the unions can have a more peaceful character, with a minimum of friction. But it is quite obvious that in this decisive problem on which depends the future fate of the unions (whether they disintegrate or rise to a higher historical level), the unions cannot be left to themselves, but must receive clear and distinct guidance from the party, and full organisational-material aid from the workers' state. In one case, such an organ of leadership and action could be a Politotdel (Glavpolitput)[3] [Chief Political Administration], in another, it would be a temporary commission of the VTsSPS with the participation of representatives of the party Central Committee, the Central Committee of the corresponding union and the Economic Central Board [of the industry].

7. From what has been said, it is clear how trivial is the accusation of Syndicalism against the point of view outlined above. By Syndicalism we understand the tendency for trade unions, that is, of worker's organisations in capitalist society, to take control of production without and apart from a proletarian party and proletarian state. The Marxist point of view on the problem says that only a proletarian party and a proletarian state can help the trade unions to reorganise themselves in such a way that they will be fully capable of taking control of production.

8. The reorganisation of the unions must consist of:

i. Giving them a broad aim in production (control of production), and this must be the basis of agitation and propaganda, organisation and selection of personnel.

ii. Immediately strengthening the unions with a significant number of workers whose qualities in economic and general organisational matters have been proven in various fields

iii. Providing the unions with the indispensable apparatus which can really take hold of the technical problems facing the unions.

9. The general situation in the country excludes the possibility of a once and for all uniform rise in the economy of the country, and at the same time makes impossible a once and for all uniform strengthening of all the trade unions; there would not be the resources nor the means for this. The principle of shock working inevitably stems from the present conditions, and by and large its inevitability is understood by the broad masses, including the trade union workers. Workers in those spheres of the economy and the unions which cannot at present claim exclusive attention, themselves apply the principle of shock working, in the sense that they choose a small number of enterprises and concentrate their energy on reviving them. To what extent the principle of shock working, in spite of all its negative sides, is acknowledged as an unavoidable method of reviving the economy is clear from the fact that at the present conference of trade unions a resolution was adopted on the report of the VTsSPS by an overwhelming majority in which the leading organ of the trade unions was reproached for an insufficiently significant application of shock working.

Only by getting solid results in production in this direction will the effective conditions be created for a significant levelling-up and by and large for a genuine improvement in the material position of the working masses.

10. Next we must consider the problem of strengthening in every way possible the Metal Workers Trade Union. It is essential to set up immediately a commission with the participation of representatives from the VTsSPS, the CC of the Metal Workers, and the CC of the party, and the Department of Metals for an all-sided clarification of the position of the Metal Workers Union, and for adopting the widest and most energetic measures for strengthening the Union in the centre and in the localities by energetic workers and organisers.[4]

11. A production union must include all workers necessary in a given field of the economy, from the labourer up to the most highly qualified engineer. The union must take stock of its members from a production point of view, always having a sufficiently full and exact idea of the productive aptitude of each worker.

The union must place definite union obligations on all workers who hold some administrative-technical post or other. **It is necessary that a worker from a union carry out this necessary obligatory work in addition to production work.**

It is necessary that the working masses be imbued with the consciousness that their interests are best defined by those workers who raise the productivity of labour, revive the economy, and increase the quantity of material benefits. It is necessary that such an organiser and administrator be elected to the leading organs of the unions beside the workers who continue to work at the bench, and alongside those who carry out specific trade union work.

12. In the unions, where internal improvement in labour development has been achieved by the revival of a given branch of industry, it is possible and necessary to apply '**the methods of workers democracy**' still more: systematic discussion at broad mass meeting of all economic-production measures, elections to a whole series of economic-administrative posts, coordination of these posts with definite positions within the production organisation, etc.

13. Definite difficulties arise with the problem of **specialists**, that is, the establishment of a correspondence between their positions in production and in the trade unions. However, even this problem can be resolved through persistence and systematic work.

14. All specialists without exception must pass through the filter of a trade union. Because of the condition of yesterday's still-unfinished civil war, specialists can be divided into three categories: i. probationary members (the recent followers of Kolchak, Wrangel, and so on); ii. candidate members; iii. full members.

Only specialists of the latter category can be nominated to responsible posts which have no commissar. Specialists of the second category can occupy responsible posts only under the supervision of commissars of the production unions. Specialists of the first category can only be assistants or consultants to administrators who are members of a union. In such a way the title of union member acquires a great weight in production, which is reflected in a singularly beneficial way in the consciousness of workers and specialists.

Between the principle of production democracy, the independent activity of the workers, the possibility of a wide application of elections, etc, and the principle of militarised labour and shock work (in the spirit of the resolution of the Ninth Party Congress) there is absolutely no contradiction. Militarised labour is an unavoidable method during the transition from a destroyed and ruined labour market to planned universal labour service — in the dire economic conditions of the country. But this militarisation, as the Ninth Party Congress made clear, can be realised only under the leadership of all conscious workers and revolutionary peasants, since the unavoidable means of coercion in the transitional period must be based on ever wider work in involving, organising, developing initiative, and raising the production and general cultural level of tens of millions of workers and peasants.

The naked counterposing of 'military' methods (order, penalties) to trade union methods (explanation, propaganda, independent action) is a manifestation of Kautskyite-Menshevik-SR prejudices. The militarisation of labour in a workers' state cannot be realised without the independent activity of hundreds and hundreds of thousands of workers and peasants, which will be transformed into the independent activity of millions and millions, gradually swallowing up and dissolving within itself the most severe methods and the method of compulsion.

The very counterposing of labour and military organisations in a workers' state is a shameful capitulation to Kautskyism. The Red Army is the fruit of the independent activity of the proletariat and the revolutionary peasantry. On the independent activity, in incessant agitation and propaganda among the backward layers of the peasantry is altogether founded the 'militarisation' of the Red Army itself, that is, its education in the spirit of fulfilment and selflessness in the struggle for the defence of the Soviet Republic.

15. Developing this system further, increasing gradually the application of elections from below upwards, linking more closely a responsible rôle in the union with a responsible rôle in production, we shall arrive in a more or less short interval to such a position that the union embracing a given branch of industry as a whole and in all its aspects will, by combining methods of election and selection, fashion from itself an entire administrative-economic apparatus under the general control and leadership of the workers' state which coordinates the work of all spheres of the economy.

Notes

1. This text consists of the first draft of Trotsky's theses on the trade union question submitted to the plenum of the Central Committee of the Russian Communist Party on 9 November 1920, translated by Tom Scott from the collection entitled *The Party and the Trade Unions* published in Petrograd in 1921. It was given by Louis Sinclair to Ken Tarbuck, who published it along with the following article in the pamphlet *Trade Unions and Their Future Rôle and the Rôle and Tasks of the Trade Unions* in 1994. We express our thanks for allowing us to reproduce them here.
2. Tsektran, or the Central Transport Commission, was the Central Committee of the Rail and Waterway Workers set up by Trotsky in August 1920. During the war with Poland, Trotsky, with the support of the Communist Party's Politbureau, dismissed the leadership of the railwayworkers' union after it objected to the militarisation of the railways, and brought in a new and compliant leadership.
3. Glavpolitput was the organisation set up by Trotsky to distribute cadres to organisations throughout the country.
4. Dissidence within the Metal Workers Union expressed itself in strikes and a repudiation of Communist domination in the soviets at the time. Two prominent Bolshevik metal workers, Lutovinov and Shliapnikov, later became leaders of the Workers Opposition in 1921. Cf above, p192.

Leon Trotsky
The Rôle and Tasks of the Trade Unions[1]

I. The Crisis in the Trade Union Organisations

1. OUR trade unions are passing through a severe crisis, expressed in the weakening of their contact with the masses, and the piling up of irritations and conflicts with the economic institutions and party organisation; they are not resolute in their tasks, and do not get on well. In consequence, there is such a disturbance of spirit that some trade unionists have arrived at a 'trade union' viewpoint which was exploded long ago by the party.

2. It is generally accepted that one principle source of the crisis of weakness and anaemia of the trade unions is attributable to the heavy responsibilities placed on them in the whole Civil War period. Also numerous active, initiative-taking elements were withdrawn from the trade unions and utilised in supply work and other areas of the Soviet work administration. This weakening of the leading circles must have left its mark on trade union work, on the relationship of the leading organs to the masses, etc.

3. To a still higher degree and in the same direction operated the circumstances that all the party attention and efforts were concentrated on the military fronts. Economic tasks, and with them the trade union questions, moved to the background.

The Civil War placed superhuman demands on the strength of the working class — so that a weakening of the inner life and independent activity of the workers' organisations, amongst them the trade unions, was unavoidable. The methods of workers' democracy (broad discussion, criticism, intellectual struggle, elections, etc) had to be unusually limited and narrowed.

4. The causes shown above, which operated for all working class organisations — party and soviet as well as trade union — **do not by any means account completely** for the special, specific characteristics of the trade union. This fact appears strongly at the present moment.

Whilst the transition to the methods of independent activity, electoralism, etc, are viewed by the whole party as self-evident — in the area of the trade union movement we encounter differing tendencies on the rôle and significance of the trade unions and their methods of work.

For the impending party congress there remains only **to establish the fact** that methods of workers' democracy are coming into broader application in all areas of our work and are striking ever deeper roots. The same party congress, however, will have to choose between two tendencies in the area of the trade union movement.

5. The principal cause of the crisis of the trade union movement is the disproportion between the tasks which objectively devolve upon the trade unions

at their present stage of development, and the customary thinking, methods and work procedures which reign as the inheritance of the past of the trade unions. This disproportion between the trade unions as they are now and as they should be has become the greatest internal contradiction of the worker's state. Until we overcome this contradiction, we shall not be able to make serious steps forward in the economic field.

II. The Condition of the Trade Unions — According to Our Programme and in Practice

6. Our party programme states on the question of the rôle and tasks of the trade union organisations:

'The organisational apparatus of the associated industries must rest above all on the trade unions. They must more and more free themselves from guild-like narrowness, and transform themselves into great production associations which encompass the majority and eventually the totality of the workers of the concerned industries.

'When the trade unions, by the laws of the Soviet Republic and indeed in practice, participate in all the local and central administrative organs of industry, **they must come to concentrate in their hands in actuality the general administration of the entire economy as a unity.**

'Thereby an unbreakable bond is forged between the central state administration, the political economy and the broad masses of activists, which forthwith from the trade unions must come to include in the broadest compass the work of economic management.

'**Participation in economic management** is for the trade unions, and through them for the broad masses, **the best weapon against bureaucratisation of the economic apparatus** of the Soviet power, and offers the possibility of introducing genuine popular control over the results of production.'

During the last period, we have in practice not approached the goal set out in the programme, we have deviated further from it. If this development should go to completion in the same direction, it would signify the greatest danger, not only for the trade unions, but for the economy.

7. In bourgeois society, the working class trade unions expressed the struggle for the improvement of workers' conditions, and also the struggle for the revolutionary elimination of capitalist production methods.

In the Kerensky epoch, the trade unions went over to the control of production, which represented a form of the class struggle of labour against capital.

After October, the working class — primarily with the help of the trade unions — formed from its midst primitive organs which made possible an actual disposition of the nationalised enterprises. This movement was designated, on an insufficient basis, 'elementary Syndicalism'. Basically, in the first period of the revolution, the workers, with exactly the same methods of semi-elemental mass executive power, undertook to shape the Soviet state organs, the democratic apparatus, the army, etc.

In the course of further development of the economic institutions, their perfection, specialisation, etc, occurs their disengagement from the trade unions. The growth of the independence of the economic organs must necessarily manifest itself in parallelism, competitive struggles, organisational friction and conflicts. The economic organs, and in a higher degree the Soviet power in general, orient themselves in the period of specialisation and separation of functions so as to bring the trade unions into a defined framework, and limit their intervention into economic life.

What made up the essence of the trade unions in bourgeois society was abolished; in the workers' state the trade unions could not conduct an economic class struggle. On the other hand, the participation of trade unions in economic construction was ever smaller, less systematic, more superficial the more the economic organs, having separated from the trade unions, developed and drew upon the necessary workforces, created new work methods and work habits, and carried out themselves the building and rebuilding of their apparatus. From just this sprang the deep-going crisis of the trade union movement.

8. The exclusion of the trade unions from the active, responsible work of construction promoted extraordinarily the development of a trade union conservatism in the leading circles of trade unionists.

In the three years which have elapsed since the start of the Soviet regime, the trade unions have to a significantly lesser degree than all other organisations altered their structure, their methods of work and the composition of their leading bodies. After the loss of their old basis of existence in the economic class struggle, the trade unions have not had the power, in altered circumstances, to assemble from their own ranks the necessary forces and methods which would enable them to solve the new task which the proletarian revolution lays upon them, and which is formulated in our programme: to organise production.

9. The present situation, in which the All-Russian Central Council of the Trade Unions and the central committees of individual production unions remain entirely outside any important economic work, is completely intolerable. It is a wholly abnormal system, whereby nearly every trade unionist who distinguishes himself by organisational, economic and administrative capabilities is automatically torn away from the union and wholly swallowed up by the production apparatus. Nevertheless, the fact that the Glavki[2] (leading administrative organisations of the branches of production) and the Commissariats separate themselves more and more from the production unions, isolate themselves from them, and to a degree monopolise in their hands the administration of the economy, may on no account be charged only against the economic organs. In order to create a healthier relationship, it is necessary that the trade unions have the will and capacity to participate immediately in the working out of the economic plans and their method of development. They must be entirely clear about this task.

In the workers' state there can be no organisational separation between specialists of the production organisation and specialists of the trade union movement. It must be recognised as a principle that whoever is needed for Socialist production is simultaneously needed for the trade unions, and vice-versa — each valuable trade unionist must be at the same time a participant in the organisation of production.

10. The concentration of the total productive forces in the hands of the trade unions, as our programme demands, signifies the systematic transformation of the trade unions into apparatuses of the workers' state, and the gradual growing

together of the trade unions and the economic organs. It is not a matter of formally proclaiming the trade unions as state organs, but of transforming them in actuality into production organisations which lay hold of each individual branch of production all-sidedly, and are responsible for the interests of production as well as the producers. This viewpoint, which was expressed in the resolution of the Ninth Party Conference, is formally, that is in words, acknowledged by the majority of the trade unionists. Thus did Comrade Tomsky[3] at the Ninth Congress of the RCP(B) take his distance from a counter-report, and joined with Comrade Bukharin, who represented the viewpoint of our programme.

11. A recent new edition of a brochure of the publishing house of the All-Russian Central Council of the Trade Unions characterised the rôle and condition of the trade unions in the workers' state in the following way:

'As a result of the indicated processes, the trade unions transform themselves unhesitatingly into organs of the Socialist state, in which all persons engaged in individual branches of production are under state obligation to be organised and to cooperate.

'The trade unions transform themselves from organs of the fight against capital into organs of Socialist construction, so that with the progressive development from capitalism to Communism, the main weight of trade union work passes over to the field of organisation of the economy. On the trade unions rests the main task of organising work and production, and the more the trade unions master their task, so much more do they coalesce with the economy and become its backbone.

'In the transitional epoch, the workers' councils and the trade unions form in common the organs of production administration (economic councils, chief committees for administering the nationalised enterprises, etc); with the advance of Socialism they themselves lose their specific characteristics: the joint work of the councils and trade unions is concentrated on the organisation of work and production; the productive functions alone remain, all else disappears. There takes place a fusion of the trade unions and the Soviet economic organs; there arises the unified trade union economic apparatus.' (S Lozovsky, *The Trade Unions in Soviet Russia*, Publishing House of the VTsSPS, 1920)[4]

12. Our task does not consist of revising the *Programmatic Theses on the Trade Union Question*, but of making real new steps towards the realisation of the principles acknowledged by the party and embodied in its programme. In the year gone by since the Ninth Party Congress, the economic organisations have made a significant step forward. In some areas real production results have been achieved. The question of unified economic plans takes on ever more concrete, practical forms. Meanwhile, the expression of all this work in the trade unions is as good as nothing. If it were not disputed amongst us that the general trend of development is for the trade union organs to coalesce with the production organs, it would be clear that each new stage in the economic field means at the same time a new stage in the process of the unification of the trade unions with the economic organs. As long as this is not achieved, the crisis will sharpen.

On the other hand, we observe that the more the economic tasks come to the foreground, numerous trade unionists turn more strongly and implacably against the perspective of 'growing together', and against the resulting practical deductions. Among these trade unionists we find Comrades Tomsky and Lozovsky.

Still further. Whilst many trade unionists take up arms against the new tasks and methods, at the same time a spirit of club-like exclusiveness develops in their midst, and a hostile relationship to the new forces which are called forth to work in a given economic area. Thereby they raise up in deed the outlived guild spirit in the midst of the organised union workers.

III. The Different Viewpoints on the Trade Union Question

13. If the question is posed correctly, the task of organisation of work in the workers' state can have its basis and goal only in production; in other words, the organisation of work and the organisation of production in general. Exactly here appears the gradual 'intertwining' of the trade unions and the economic apparatus. That is the viewpoint of the party programme, as we have seen.

14. The viewpoint of 'Soviet trade unionism' stands in opposition, represented in a more or less complete and open form in the ranks of our party by Comrade Riazanov (see for example his counter-report at the Ninth Congress of the party). Comrade Riazanov wants to retain the old status of the trade unions in the state, as an organisation uniting the workers for the protection and defence of their material and moral interests. Naturally, Comrade Riazanov abjures combat methods, that is, strikes, in the place of which he puts organised pressure and influence on the state power. But even in the bourgeois countries, especially the Anglo-Saxon, the leaders of the great 'trade unions' forswear combat methods against the bourgeoisie and the bourgeois state, and see their task in conceptual, parliamentary and other influence on the state. Fundamentally, Comrade Riazanov endeavours to hold the trade unions in the workers' state in the situation in which powerful, opportunist 'trade unions' find themselves in the capitalist state. Comrade Riazanov wants Comrade Tomsky to be the Gompers[5] of the workers' state.

· 15. We have seen that Comrade Tomsky formally associated himself with the report of Comrade Bukharin at the Ninth Party Congress, while Comrade Lozovsky rather sharply formulated his viewpoint on the 'intertwining' and 'fusing' of the trade union and economic organs. Meanwhile the contradiction between the old methods and usages, the old organisation of the trade unions and the principal new tasks (organisation of production) is so strong that almost automatically many trade union leaders shrink from the practical consequences of the viewpoint of our programme. The more Comrade Tomsky and his co-thinkers oppose their own viewpoint to the gradual intertwining and statification, so much the closer do they arrive at the 'Soviet Trade Unionism' of Comrade Riazanov.

16. Comrade Shliapnikov[6] and the group of his co-thinkers propose to hand over direction of the economy immediately and completely to the trade unions — to 'trade unionise' the state. Such a measure, which is dictated evidently by a Syndicalist tendency, appears very radical, but in fact lacks completely any real content. To hand over the direction of the economy to the trade unions means, in the present state of things, to hand over direction to the apparatus which is on hand at present; in other words it means to put the Presidium of the Central Committee of the Metal Workers in the place of the Board of the Metal Division, and also to carry out the corresponding local changes. The Central Committee of the Metal Workers does not have at its disposal the least apparatus for the exclusive direction of the metal industry. It must, therefore, after it has formally

trade-unionised the Metal Division, utilise the apparatus which has been formed in reality in the course of three years in the Metal Division under the participation of the Metal Workers Union.

Naturally, it can happen in the further course that the new Board of the Metal Division established by the union can reshape the organs of power, can entrust the leadership to a new person, to especially capable trade unionists or to others. Nevertheless, that would still not signify that the union is now in reality directing production; it would, indeed, come significantly closer to a fusion, which could hardly be considered as done correctly and systematically. For it has certainly not been demonstrated that, in the present state of the trade unions, the Presidium of the Central Committee of the Metal Workers has a higher capability of directing the metal industry than does the present Collegium of the Metal Division. But the attempt to override all difficulties by a mass attack on production, when there is on hand already a designated, non-accidental apparatus, without making preparations to qualify the trade unions to a higher degree to direct production — this attempt would only have as a consequence monstrous chaos for the organisation.

The seemingly radical viewpoint of Comrade Shliapnikov covers the outlook of the conservative trade unionist, because, in just the same way, he cannot see the main task; the necessity to regroup, reconstruct, and re-educate the trade unions in conformity with the tasks of organising production.

IV. Production Criteria and Production Education.

17. The transformation of the trade unions into production associations, not merely in name but in the specific content of their work, forms the most important task of the epoch we are entering. The trade unionist should feel himself, not as an agent of the needs and requirements of the workers, but as an organiser of work activity, appointed to lead production to an ever higher technical basis.

In the workers' state the significance of the trade unions extends insofar as they understand how to master production in actuality, to unite in their associations all workers on the individual branches of production, to improve the organisation of work, to increase its mechanisation and productivity, and on this foundation to improve the material conditions of the masses and to raise the level of their morale. The union must carry out any other work, be it in the area of production, of instruction, or in the military field, without losing the basis of its existence as a practical production organisation.

18. The production association must include all workers required in a particular branch of the economy, from unskilled workers to the most highly qualified engineers. The association must register its members from the viewpoint of production, and provide for a sufficient, complete and exact determination of the value of each individual worker for production. The association must place specific association responsibilities upon all workers who hold these or those administrative and technical positions.

Work for the association must form the necessary and indispensable supplement to administrative production work.

The working masses must be saturated with the consciousness that their interests will be served best by those who increase labour productivity, rebuild the economy, and increase the quality of material goods. Such organisers and administrators must be chosen for the leading organs of the associations, in addition to workers who pursue their work in the factory, and in addition to specialist trade unionists.

'All selections, the nominations of candidates, their support, etc, must take place not only from the angle of political experience, but also of economic capabilities, previous administrative career, organisational qualities, and a concern, demonstrated in deeds, for the material and moral interests of the workaday masses.

'The party is obliged to promote and educate with all means the new type of trade unionist, who is an energetic manager endowed with initiative, who looks at economic life not from the viewpoint of distribution and consumption, but from the angle of increasing production: and this is not with the eyes of a person who makes demands upon the Soviet power and concludes agreements with it, but with the eyes of an organiser who feels himself, so to speak, a leader and proprietor of an enterprise.' (Resolution of the Central Committee of the party, 7 December)

19. The new production education must, as is self-evident, be extended in the first instance to the trade unionists whose firmness must be strengthened and renewed by all means. The leading trade unionists in the centre and in the districts must endeavour to penetrate into purely economic questions, and in this way apply a production criterion to their own daily trade union work; on the other hand the leaders of the economic organs must learn to handle all production questions with growing understanding and solidarity, including purely technical ones, as questions primarily of the organisation of living labour power. Only this fructifying reciprocal relationship can create the necessary psychological foundation for the intertwining of the existing side-by-side parallel apparatuses into one single apparatus, which in equal proportions satisfies the overall interests of production and the immediate interests of the producers.

20. Production propaganda, as a component of production education, has the task of producing new reciprocal relations between the workers and production. If the critical thinking of workers in capitalist society develops only so far as to enable them to liberate themselves from the chains of wage slavery, so now must thought, criticism, initiative and workers' will be directed towards the organisation of production so as best to construct and use the appropriate instruments and machines, to mechanise and 'machine-ise' labour, and to organise it scientifically in the workplace, factory, economic district and the entire state.

This untiring agitation and propaganda, utilising ever new teachings, taking place primarily by deed and example, but also through the spoken and written word, must henceforth be the most important content of the life and work of the trade unions. One of the most important criteria of the vitality and worth of a trade union is the thoroughness and concreteness of its production propaganda. The workers must learn to scorn the external visible shapes, economically empty — the purely decorative forms of workers' democracy — if they lack all content useful for production.

The working class masses were awakened and taught by the Bolshevik strike-leaders and Bolshevik barricade-fighters, and followed them to storm the bourgeois state. They came to know this Bolshevik on the battlefield as commander and commissar, developed together with him, exerted their strength in common with him, and under his leadership gained a series of victories. Now the broadest and most backward masses must come to know yesterday's strike-leader, barricade-fighter and Red warrior as the production leader, the organiser, the people's economist, and renew and confirm their faith in him as a practical architect of the Communist society.

V. Workers' Democracy and Production, Military Method, Bureaucratisation, Specialist and 'Proletarianisation'

21. The attempt of some trade unionists to portray the present struggle of ideas on the trade union question as a struggle of 'democratic methods', of 'appointment managing', of 'commissarism' and 'ordering', creates a fundamentally false picture of the real content of the matter.

Appointism and commissarism in the field of the economy are only an unavoidable supplement to the weakness in production of an association, in its incapacity to solve urgent economic problems at a given moment. It is not enough to condemn appointism and commissarism in principle as extraordinary measures to which the Soviet power must have recourse in the most endangered sectors of the economic front. We must overcome in practice the need for extraordinary measures, through methods of production democracy. The trade unions must place both feet on the ground of the economy, and learn to solve, by their own methods, the most important tasks which heretofore were solved customarily without the associations.

22. In no way can the viewpoint of production be interpreted as opposed to the idea of workers' democracy. On the contrary, workers' democracy can blossom only as production democracy. Workers' democracy cannot develop under conditions of exhaustion and poverty. The self-activity of the masses can thrive only on the basis of growing material satisfaction. To concentrate all forces and attention on the economy must constitute the essence of the inner life of all organs and forms of workers' democracy.

As work in the trade unions unfolds more in the new direction, as it penetrates deeper into the masses and enlists their thinking toward production, the sooner will it be possible to apply democratic methods in the area of the economy, that is, not only to discuss the most important economic measures systematically in assemblies of the broad masses, but to extend the principle of eligibility to a whole range of posts of economic-administrative significance, in such a way that these posts will, at the same time, hold definite influence within the production organisation.

23. Workers' democracy must subordinate itself consciously to criteria of production. It is quite evident that meetings, proposals, discussions, criticism, propaganda and elections are necessary and admissible, insofar as they do not damage the course of production. How and to what extent democratic methods may be applied must be determined in dependence upon objective circumstances. To solve all questions from the angle of abstract — that is, empty — workers' democracy is basically upside-down.

A living illustration of formal democratic conduct relative to economic questions is shown in the bitter attacks by a section of the trade unionists relative to the activity of the Political Head Committee of Traffic[7] in the field of transportation. Notwithstanding that the party created the Political Head Committee of Traffic as a provisional organ in view of the extraordinarily difficult condition of the railways; notwithstanding that the Political Head Committee of Traffic solved the task set for it, that is, it contributed to bringing transport out of the condition which threatened the entire country with ruin — some trade unionists ignore completely the significance of this question for production, treat it under a formal democratic criterion, and condemn the Political Head Committee of Traffic, without questioning whether under the given conditions it would have been possible to achieve the required results with the help of the methods of trade union democracy. Here the standpoint of workers' democracy becomes formal, and therefore vulgar. Workers' democracy recognises no fetishes. It recognises only revolutionary suitability.

24. Between the principle of production democracy (self-activity of the masses, greatest possible extension of eligibility, etc) and the principle of the militarisation of labour and the system of economic shock groups (in the sense of the resolution of the Ninth Party Congress), there is absolutely no contradiction. The method of the militarisation of labour is inevitable during the transition from the annihilated and destroyed labour market to the systematic general work obligation — under the most difficult economic circumstances in the country. But this militarisation can be realised, as the Ninth Party Congress explained, only under the leadership of the trade unions, whereby the constraint measures, unavoidable in the transition period, must support the expanding work which aims at the mobilisation and organisation of uncounted millions of workers and peasants, aims at the development of their initiative, and which tries to elevate their producing level and general cultural level.

Not long ago, a measure of recognition towards military methods and labour organisation was accorded on the part of the conservative wing of the trade union organisation:

'The militarisation of labour during the dictatorship of the proletariat' — wrote Comrade Tomsky in October 1920 — 'is nothing other than the **distribution of labour according to a general state plan, and according to the flow of economic requirements, which takes place even against the will of individual groups of workers who at this or that moment are taken aback by these measures.**

'It must be understood at last and committed to memory that a battle is taking place on the labour front, just as difficult as on the war front. Each act of negligence, of slovenliness, of indifference in relation to economic activity, leads in consequence to need, cold and hunger for hundreds of thousands of active workers, and the inevitable accompaniment — epidemics and mortality. The same energy and determination as in the war are needed here. Weepy complaints about "the forced system" cannot prevent the working class and its organisations from applying immediate measures which promote the interests of the working class and its liberation from defeat, need, and sickness.

'No matter how much the representatives of petit-bourgeois Socialism, at present representing the old egoistic layer of the working class, may cry out, the trade unions are committed to and will carry through the militarisation of labour, supporting the interests of the working class as a whole, because it is one of the most necessary prerequisites for the victory of the Russian proletariat on the economic front.' (M Tomsky, *The Work Messenger*, monthly organ of the All-Russian Central Council of Trade Unions, October 1920, p24)

'The economic front' — writes Comrade Lozovsky — 'is the most important front of the Russian Revolution, and every citizen is obliged to work. Work deserters will receive no forbearance. That is the sense of the work duty, that is the sense of the militarisation of labour. Who can deny this right to the proletarian state in the period of the destruction of private property in the means of production and exchange? **Who can deny its duty to require of each person a certain sum of labour for the benefit of society?** No one, apart from miserable Philistines, complete ignoramuses, or demagogues without honour.' (S Lozovsky, *The Trade Unions in Soviet Russia*, 1920)

25. 'To work militarily' signifies for us not simply or primarily work under intimidation rather than conviction. Communist military work demands the highest devotion and heroic consciousness of duty, to carry out the assigned work, even at the cost of life. For this end, it must be joined with punctuality, exactness and a feeling of responsibility. We will solve the gigantic tasks now placed before us only on the condition that we lend to our economic work the same heroic character which was borne by our work at the front. In this sense, work in the military manner is the exact opposite of external discipline and government bureaucratism. It signifies not a renunciation of workers' democracy, but on the contrary, its highest heroic expression.

26. Production democracy means the conquest of **bureaucratism**. Our party programme speaks of this with exceeding penetration: precisely 'the participation of the trade unions in the conduct of the economy, and through them of the broad masses, is the best means of combating bureaucratism in the economic apparatus...'. From the standpoint of our programme, therefore, the fight against bureaucratism is not a special task in itself, to be solved with the help of special organisational methods, but is above all the main component of trade union work in the area of the production education of the masses and the actual disposition of production. Hereby it is seen that in the struggle against bureaucracy, the workers' state must not so much apply its strength to load up the control bodies, but rather to shape and improve the existing economic apparatus, which for this purpose must be united with the mass of production associations.

So far as the trade unions do not place themselves on the ground of creative production work, they do not avoid the stain; they ossify, they themselves experience all the disadvantages of bureaucratism.

27. The so-called proletarianisation of the Soviet organs — not in the sense of squeezing out the specialists and replacing them by incompetent workers, but in the sense of the organised proletariat systematically managing all branches of state activity — can be achieved in fullness on the basis of production democracy. Only through educating, selecting and utilising political economists and organisers, only by creating an atmosphere of production in the trade unions and the entire country, can the party and the trade unions, in the next period, obtain the necessary influx of fresh, creative forces. The upswing of the economy guarantees not only an upswing in spirit of the proletariat as a whole, but also shapes the conditions for the creative development of its most talented sons.

28. It may be objected that the coalescence of the trade unions and the economic organs cannot be hastened unduly, that the degree of consciousness of the masses must be taken into account, that the statification of the trade unions smoothes the ground for the Menshevik 'trade unionism' that is antagonistic to

the workers' state, etc, etc. But these objections do not hold up. The tempo of development can vary according to the basic established conditions under which our whole development during the next period will take place. But it is essential that the direction of development be clear to all trade unionists, and that each step forward be a definite one, modest as it may be.

In no case is it allowable to put off the statification of the trade unions until St Neversday, and make it a 'final goal' without influence on current practice; precisely in this sphere the 'trade unionist' tendency was born. Statification is a creative process carried out in stages. We must lay down these stages attentively and carefully, drawing into consideration the general level of the masses and the peculiarities of the individual branches of industry; we must also hold to the direction clearly, so as not to take steps backward when the circumstances demand decisive steps forward.

29. In any case, it turns the matter upside-down completely to ponder whether the working class masses may not understand the transformation of the trade unions into production associations, and may turn against it. 'Trade union' politics, namely external pressure on the state, does not now open the least perspective for the masses. In contrast, production politics improves the economy, and overcomes the needs of the masses. **The activists want economic successes above all; they will support every serious and reasonable effort in this direction.** Once the first economic successes are achieved palpably to the masses, they will develop the most powerful production enthusiasm. If anyone is standing up against the new production course in the trade unions, it is not in any event the masses, but rather the more conservative-minded section of the trade union bureaucracy.

VI. Practical Consequences

30. Proceeding from the considerations stated above, a series of organisational measures must be taken immediately which overcome the lazy, unyielding character of the trade unions; they must be led practically into the field of their new responsibilities, and their work must be harmonised with the work of the economic organs. The All-Russian Central Council of the Trade Unions and the Presidium of the Supreme Council for the National Economy must now display from one-third to one-half of their membership in common. This makes impossible a one-sided specialisation of the two most important production boards. In each will be found a portion of co-workers who will experience directly the influence of administrative and technical production requirements, and simultaneously will live in the atmosphere of the trade union organisation. At the same time there will be found in each board one-half to two-thirds of 'pure administrators and 'pure' trade unionists; in the transition period this guarantees adequately the necessary specialisation of work, as well as sufficient elasticity in the exchange relationships of the economic and trade union organisations.

Both boards, the All-Russian Central Council of the Trade Unions and the Supreme Council for the National Economy, must report periodically at common plenary sessions concerning their activity, and discuss and decide all the principal questions of the organisation of the economy, and thereby also the organisation of work.

The same arrangement of organisational exchange relationships, and the rule that one-third to one-half of the members should exist in common, who engage regularly in the work of both organisations, is also valid for the economic commissariats, chief committees and central committees of the appropriate production associations.

The same organisational principle will be applied to the lower sections of the economic and trade union organisations (provinces and districts, gubernia, economic districts and branches of industry, shops and factories, etc).

Under the requirement that the administrative-economic organ be built on the principle of personal management, it is necessary to enrol the responsible administrator in the appropriate trade union organisation with at least a consultative voice.

Insofar as it involves a work situation which has the full confidence of the trade union, it is desirable to admit the administrator into the trade union with voting rights, as the membership may decide from time to time.

If it has to do with a specialist whom the association for one reason or another considers impossible to take in as a member, then the membership of the association should designate a plenipotentiary (commissar) to exercise control over the specialist (factory manager) in the name of the trade union.

Note: The appointment of plenipotentiaries (with the rights of commissars) should be the exclusive right of the production associations, and is a means for realising the proletarian regime in the economic apparatus.

In the individual shops, mines, etc, the organisational fusion of the administrative and trade union organs and the fusion of the leading personnel will become easier as the trade unions drive through the production orientation with more determination, and as the production criterion penetrates deeper into the consciousness of the masses in all kinds of decisions.

It is quite expedient to appoint a member of the factory committee as a factory manager, provided that he is a qualified person. On the other hand, if the factory manager is appointed from outside and has earned the confidence of the workers through his work, the trade union organisation must make every effort to take him into membership.

31. The economic sections of the trade unions, strengthened by the best administrative and technical functionaries of the corresponding economic organs, must become the most powerful weapons for the improvement of the entire economic organisation, for the scientific arrangement of production, for the introduction of the Taylor System, etc.

The corresponding factory organisation must enter into a defined relationship with the work management, which is under an obligation to test carefully all technical and organisational proposals passed along through the support groups and other organisations; and within a specified time period must give an account, if possible before a general factory assembly, of carrying out the proposals brought forward.

32. The distribution of work forces and the regulation of tariffs will be turned over to the trade unions.

33. Conflicts between workers and the economic organs in the process of production will be settled exclusively through the trade unions, for which they will answer to the workers' and peasants' government.

34. The question of specialists presents certain difficulties from the viewpoint of factory democracy, that is, to bring their position in production into accord with

their position in the trade union. But this point, too, can be solved with complete success by a consistent and firm policy of the production association.

All specialists without exception must be passed through the filter of the trade union associations. In consideration of the entire past and of the recently concluded Civil War, the specialists must be divided roughly into three categories: i. those who must be tested (yesterday's Kolchak and Wrangel people); ii. candidates; iii. trade union members with full rights.

Only specialists of the last category can be placed in responsible posts without commissars. The specialists of the second category can take responsible posts only under the control of commissars of the production associations. The specialists of the first category can only be helpers or advisors of administrators who are members of the unions. In this way, the title 'members of the union' achieves a great weight in production, and in the same way carries over beneficially into the consciousness of the workers, as well as of the specialists.

35. The management of industrial enterprises by individual persons remains an unimpeachable rule for the whole transition period, despite the fact that production unions and economic organs exist side by side in parallel, up to a certain degree. The decision-making power belongs to the management, which is set up in the appropriate form. But the whole manner of designating the management, the preparation of the candidates and their relationship to the association, and the production atmosphere under which the management works, must be transformed more and more into functions of the economic administrative organs established for this purpose by the production associations. Under these conditions, the whole question of intervention or non-intervention by the association into the management of production falls away, for it is quite natural that the production propaganda section or the section for the improvement of workers' conditions cannot intervene into management work, which is handled specifically by the section set up for that purpose.

36. In order to reach complete agreement on the work of the production associations and the economic organs, the one as well as the other must pass the same muster in all relationships, in harmony with the structure and requirements of the appropriate branch of industry. In the transformation and reorganisation of the trade unions, their sectioning, etc, we must not let ourselves be influenced by the selfish requirements and necessities of the association apparatus, but by the deeper needs of the economy itself.

37. There is no ready-made organisational recipe, and there can be none, which encompasses all the instances of interchange-relationships between the economic and association organisations. In this relationship the creative gift is required; initiative and the combined personal-organisational touch which is adapted to the concrete situations. But all these practical experiences must be illuminated by the single task:

To educate and promote from the midst of the trade unionists political-economic functionaries;

To draw closer together and to fuse into each other the work of the associations and the economic apparatus;

To crystallise the common portion of their work, and to execute it in common:

To strive systematically towards the goal that the common portion of the work is more and more broadened, and eventually encompasses the entire work, that is, that the trade union and economic organs finally coalesce together.

38. If we develop this system all-sidedly, gradually apply more and more the principles of eligibility, and unite ever more closely the responsible rôles in the associations with those in production, then we will arrive sooner or later at the situation where the association (comprising wholly and all-sidedly the entire branch of production) will separate from its midst, on the path of combined methods of election and recall, the entire administrative and economic apparatus — under the general control and leadership of the workers' state, which harmonises the work of all the economic branches with each other.

39. The question of the tempo of development in the direction indicated cannot be solved beforehand precisely, since it depends for the most part on the international situation and the development of the world revolution; that is, to what degree we may encounter the possibility of concentrating all our forces and means on economic work. It is self-evident, however, that under favourable or unfavourable circumstances the tempo of development in different branches of the economy will vary according to the technical peculiarities of the respective branches of industry, and according to the level of the workers involved.

Doubtless the question of the reciprocal relations of the economic and trade union organs can be solved much more rapidly in the field of transport, especially the railways, and in the metal industry, than in the fields of textiles and the timber industries, or particularly in the field of agriculture, where the question has not yet unfolded to an extent worth mentioning.

In this relationship the policy of the All-Russian Central Council of Trade Unions must be flexible, must be conducted with an exact evaluation of the characteristics of each particular branch of the economy, and in no case should set a goal of mechanical fusion of all associations and economic branches according to a fixed average of organisational pattern, which would be too narrow for one, and two wide for another.

It would certainly not be a loss for the unity and solidarity of the working class, but a great gain for all, if the advanced industries outstripped the backward ones in Socialist structure, and thereby gave them an example and accelerated their development.

40. From all that has been said, it follows that the reorganisation of the associations should consist of the following:

Firstly, to give them a broad production goal (the management of production) which can stand on the basis of propaganda, organisation and selection of personnel;

Secondly, to strengthen the associations immediately with a significant number of functionaries whose economic and general organisational capabilities are proven;

Thirdly, to give the association the necessary apparatus able in fact to accomplish the tasks placed before it.

41. The general condition of the country precludes the possibility of a simultaneous and uniform up-swing of the economy, and therefore makes impossible the simultaneous and uniform strengthening of all the trade union associations: the forces and means are lacking.

In the area of **consumption**, that is, the personal requirements for existence of the workers, we must carry through unconditionally a line of equality. In the area of production, the shock troop system must be standard throughout for a long time: only after we have passed through the stage of a shock troop economy will we create the necessary proportional relationships in the main sectors of the economy.

The depth of penetration of these thoughts into the ranks of the trade unionists appears from the fact that: the last (fifth) congress of the trade union associations approved by an overwhelming majority the resolution on the report of the All-Russian Council of Trade Unions, in which the leading trade union organ was reproached for not having undertaken sufficiently energetic measures to carry out the shock troop methods.

42. At the present moment, the mine workers' and the metal workers' associations stand in the foreground in accordance with the general requirements of the economy. In order to strengthen them with all means, they must be the object of the special attention of the party and of the All-Russian Central Council of the Trade Unions.

43. Production education should not be limited to the walls of the factories and the clubs. The question of the personal existence and life of the workers must be the object of special attention for each production association. In spite of all the economic difficulties of our country, there are enough broad possibilities to better the housing, clothing and sustenance conditions of the workers, with the assistance of the local Soviet organs, with the initiative of the working men and working women themselves, and with the utilisation of the elements of collectivism for daily needs (house communes, peoples' kitchens, crèches, communal repair workshops, etc).

Every responsible trade union functionary is obliged to find ways and means for the improvement of the living conditions of the workers, and to communicate periodically to the higher association organs and to the association press regarding the measures taken by him, and the results achieved.

Notes

1. This is the final form of the theses submitted by Trotsky to the Tenth Congress of the Russian Communist Party on 25 December 1920. They appear here by kind consent of Ken Tarbuck (cf p221, n1).
2. Glavki is an acronym for glavnoe opravlenie, the chief administration, meaning the chief directories managing the different branches of industry.
3. Mikhail Tomsky (1886-1936) was leader of the trade unions and an old Bolshevik. He was later to become joint leader along with Bukharin and Rykov of the Right Opposition, and committed suicide before he could be purged.
4. Solomon Lozovsky (1878-1952) was head of the Red International of Trade Unions, and a supporter of Stalin.
5. Samuel Gompers (1850-1924) was President of the American Federation of Labor, and an ardent proponent of class collaboration.
6. Aleksandr Gavrilovich Shliapnikov (1883-1937?) was an old Bolshevik and a skilled engineering worker who was first Commissar for Labour under the Soviet government. He later played a prominent part in the Workers and Left (Trotskyist) Oppositions.
7. The Political Head Committee of Traffic was the Tsektran, the Central Transport Commission.

Leon Trotsky

The Trade Unions and the Soviet State[1]

COMRADES! THE resolution of the Tenth Congress on the trade unions did not last to the Eleventh Congress.[2] Some of us had predicted this. What in this resolution has not stood up? What has not stood up is the part characterising the interaction between the unions and the economic organs. What is still valid? The part characterising the general historic rôle of the unions as 'schools of Communism' throughout the various stages of historical development, beginning in bourgeois society, and extending through the various transitional forms of the dictatorship of the proletariat on the road to Communism. This part is maintained. But the part that dealt concretely with the present forms of economic life and characterised the interaction between the unions and the economic organs, and hence the Soviet state as such, merits radical revision.

During the discussion here we have heard two interpretations, two explanations, of this radical revision. (Unfortunately, I was unable to be present during the report of Comrade Tomsky,[3] having been compelled to direct my attention to obligations which could not wait.) But in the course of the discussion Comrade Lozovsky[4] spoke of a radical turn in the realm of our economic policy, a turn which requires and will ever more urgently require a radical turn in the realm of trade union policy in the broad sense of the term. Comrade Riazanov, who we heard from subsequently, claimed on the contrary that it was simply a matter of returning to the invariable principles which he had proclaimed in 1917, 1918 and subsequently, against the upholders of illusions and against ignorant people. (Comrade Riazanov does not spare the strong expressions.) We thus have two counterposed explanations of the party's new policy in the realm of the trade union movement. The first explanation: a return to the path of the absolute principles of Riazanov, 'absolute', not in the sense that we accept them philosophically, but in the practical sense, that is, permanently useful. The other explanation: a radical turn in the domain of economic life entails a radical turn in trade union policy. We must choose between these two explanations, not only for our own purposes, but also for Europe, because our experiences are instructive for Europe.

My opinion is that under the circumstances the position of Comrade Lozovsky — namely that the turn in economic policy requires another turn in trade union policy — is correct. Where did we begin? As was pointed out in the discussion yesterday, and as Comrade Lenin said in his report three days ago,[5] we began our economic policy with a radical and irreversible break with the bourgeois past. Before, there was the market; we abolished it. Free trade was abolished. Commercial calculation was abolished. And what did we put in their place? The Supreme Council of the National Economy (Vesenkha), supreme and sacred, which distributes everything, organises everything, and in the end takes care of everything — where the machines go, where the materials go, where the finished products go. On the basis of a single centre, it decides and apportions everything, through its responsible organs. We have now brought this experience to a close. Why? Because we had trouble carrying it out, or in other words, as Comrade Lenin put it, because our cultural level was too low. What if we had not called a halt? In other words, what if another working class, at another stage of its dictatorship, had had the possibility, because of its cultural preparation, of continuing this state-organised suppression and centralisation of the market, competition, and commercial calculation, of establishing a single economic plan taking account of everything and examining everything? In that case there surely could have been no room for any ambiguity between the trade union organs and the economic organs. In that case the statisation of the unions and the planned direction of the Socialist economy would have been nothing but two sides of one and the same process.

Where, then, was our error? Speaking from the economic point of view — and yesterday I tried to show that this was a revolutionary inevitability, in general and in particular — but looking solely at the economic side of the question, then the error was that the proletariat tried to reach beyond its strength as far as economic construction is concerned. Under the existing conditions in the country, and given the present state of its cultural, technical, productive and organisational capacities, the working class was unable to build Socialism in a centralised manner. But if it had done so, if it had advanced on this road, then even today I personally see no other road than the statisation of the trade unions. One thing flows from the other. The error was not in the need for statisation, but in the economic policy, which did not correspond to existing conditions.

And this is why in February 1920, on the eve of the Ninth Congress, when I proposed moving from rationing to money accounts in consumption and to contractual relations in production, winning four votes against 11 on the Central Committee on this point, after my proposal had been defeated,[6] I then concluded that it was necessary to make a turn towards abolishing the duality that existed in economic leadership, that is, to statising more energetically and rapidly the trade unions. And this was a correct conclusion. If we want to draw a conclusion for us and for Europe on the basis of the new policy, then this can in no case be done in the metaphysical spirit of the invariable trade union truths Comrade Riazanov lays down when he tells us that for 36 years, or anyway since 1918... [Interruption from Riazanov: 'It's what I've been repeating for just four years.'] Of course, you can keep repeating the same thing for four years, if the situation that corresponds to what you're saying does not change. But the essential point lies in what has changed, as Lozovsky said, in the sharp change in the methods of organisation of the Socialist economy. And the methods of trade union activity for the proletariat are linked to the methods of economic organisation. This is the essential point.

Riazanov's error lies in this, that a great turn has occurred during the past four years, although he has not noticed it, and brushes it aside. I would even go further: after we had taken this profound economic turn, from which the need to alter trade union policy resulted, the Central Committee, by the force of inertia, strove to maintain the old trade union policy. One has the feeling that we were on shaky ground economically. In the resolution on the trade unions passed at the Tenth Congress, the party formulated its thought this way: It is beyond the strength of the trade unions to direct the economy; but the economic foundations of this direction were not questioned. Centralised leadership through the unions is not possible, said the Congress, without affecting the leadership of the omnipotent Vesenkha. Hence the contradiction and ambiguity of the resolution of the Tenth Congress, which did not serve us for even a year. Out of inertia, the Central Committee did not link trade union policy to the organisation of the economy during the past year, when it was nevertheless already moving toward formulating the New Economic Policy. Take the decision of the Council of People's Commissars (Sovnarkom) of August last year. The Sovnarkom decision, published 11 August 1921, spoke of the New Economic Policy very clearly and precisely for the first time, formulating its principles — well, if you want, not exactly clearly and precisely, but at least more clearly and precisely than before. Point 2 of this decision said: 'During the application of the new course in economic policy it is indispensable to associate the unions, and through them the workers themselves, even more decisively, in the organisation of statised production, in decision making in the organisation of the management of the economy, labour, etc.' **Associate even more decisively.**

That was the error. Although in practice even the remuneration and regulation of labour were in fact and concretely passing into the hands of the leadership, we still said in this decision that it was necessary 'further to associate the trade unions' with the organisation of economic management under the conditions of the New Economic Policy. That was in August 1921. Some comrades have asked me how I can welcome the new theses now. But these theses flow entirely from my old position. I may remind you that I proposed the second thesis of the August decision when it was submitted to the Central Committee. 'Given that the new economic course consists of a return to commercial principles in a considerable number of enterprises and a re-establishment of the free market, within certain limits, the evolution of the trade unions toward statisation must not only be halted but even reversed' (8 August 1921). That is what I proposed. This was rejected by the Central Committee. I advance this important point in order to show that it is only in the concrete relations between trade union policy, the methods of trade union organisation, and the forms of the organisation of the economy that we can find the key to the question we are considering here, and not in general principles supposedly valid for all stages of economic growth. It is true that Larin[7] has said on this subject that the leasing of factories does not matter; the lease, the concession, and all that play no rôle, mainly because, according to him, they can be important only when we have to wage war against the bourgeoisie. But didn't Germany and England fight, and won't they aspire to fight again? And in the intervals between wars, when confiscation of enemy enterprises takes place, they still set up companies in each other's countries. The reformists used to tell us that the internationalisation of capital ruled wars out, that there would be no war, because English capital was investing in German factories, because French capital was investing in factories in England, and so on. And we revolutionaries said that this was an absurdity.

The internationalisation of capital postponed the war, that's true, but at the same time it sharpens the contradictions and gives wars a catastrophic character. The same thing is valid in the relations between bourgeois Europe and us. But Comrade Larin's fundamental error is different: even apart from the enterprises that are leased or are concessions, which are not very numerous, the New Economic Policy also entails market 'games' among the state enterprises themselves. In fact, if you take a look at page 4 of *Izvestia* you will see advertisements for Mastorg, Gum and other state enterprises. They trade with one another. All these are state advertisements, for there are practically no private ones. The advertisements reflect our economy. What does this mean? If we eliminated the fourth page of *Izvestia*, these enterprises would be linked together only through offices, as was the case in the past, and their mutual accounting would be settled by order and not by the flow of Soviet currency. It's as simple as that. Could this possibly be the correct way out? No, it would be fatal. For the moment, the question is not the leases (the proportions they will assume will depend on the march of development). The point is that the utopian idea of centralised statised orientation from the centre of general accounting systems, distribution, construction, supply, etc, has been postponed to a later period. The trust, the factory, the provincial Sovnarkhoz[8] will orient themselves: they will sniff around, see what exists in the Soviet state, buy; those who can buy will be the strongest. And it doesn't matter if the provincial Sovnarkhoz of Moscow and the one of Petrograd occupy the same position in the Soviet hierarchy; if today one has money and the other doesn't, then one will be supplied and the other won't be.

The orientation toward the market, the orientation toward commercial calculation and no longer toward centralised accounts — such is the absolute necessity of the transitional stage. But this absolute necessity of the transitional stage rules out the possibility of the unions' practically participating in the leadership of the enterprises. In the past, in the resolution of the Tenth Congress, we spoke not of leadership, but of informal participation, thus sowing confusion. Today we can no longer do this. Our task is to manoeuvre in the market. Since we tried to break directly and all at once with the market past, since we tried to embrace the entire economy in a centralised manner, no specialist could teach us these methods, because there is no specialist who knows them. Under these conditions we could build only through the unions. They did not know how to do this either, but the position of principle was clear for them, or at least for their leaders. But now, when we are venturing out into the market, we cannot 'allow' the unions into the management of production. Would Rockefeller[9] be so frightened if Tomsky was his competitor in a Russian trust, and wouldn't Rockefeller invest his capital in another trust? No, that's not the point. The reason is different. We are sure that Tomsky will do a good job defending the interests of the working class against Rockefeller, but we are also sure that in a contest over speculation and market manoeuvres, Rockefeller will make mincemeat out of Tomsky in five minutes, of this we have not the slightest doubt. Now, we have to learn from him, from Rockefeller. But this means manoeuvring on a daily basis, and that is absolutely incompatible not only with trade union leadership of the economy, but even with practical control by the trade unions over the continuing activities and practices of the economic organs. Naturally, control is possible through the general institutions of the state, control by the public opinion of the working class, but in practice the daily control of these market manipulations is not possible. That is the essence of the problem.

Comrade Riazanov's error is linked to this: what relation is there between the programmatic question concerning the unions and the little incident in the management of the Moscow waterworks, the conflict between a group of workers and a specialist? The specialist hanged himself, and the workers were hauled into court.[10] Their behaviour, Riazanov tells us, is only the fruit of your own errors.

This is quite possible. But it changes nothing in the substance of the affair. The arrest and the trial itself constitute a sharp call to order addressed to the working class as a whole by the vanguard of the class. This shows again that we are much too uncultivated — for that is what we believe the affair boils down to in the final analysis. That is, we were unable to construct a Socialist economy through the centralised path on the basis of our own Communist strength, and we are forced to assimilate capitalist methods of organisation, the path of calculation, competition, advertising in *Izvestia*, and so on. We are forced to learn from the bourgeoisie and the bourgeois specialists in this damnable sphere of commerce. And — it would be ridiculous to deny it — linked to this is an increase in the rôle and significance of bourgeois specialists in the present transitional epoch of our society. Of course, the specialist tries to increase his own importance, and naturally we will put him in his place in due time. And we must tell the most backward workers that the specialist is indispensable to us at the moment. Of course, without us he is lost; he is compelled to serve us, but we are compelled to place him in conditions such that he can serve us.

So, what is the meaning of what happened in the Moscow waterworks? Just this: not only did these comrades in this enterprise lack the minimum culture necessary to be able to take charge of the distribution of water, but they also lacked the cultural level that would have enabled them to say to themselves: 'I have enough strength to take power over the distribution of water, but not enough preparation and education to manage the distribution of water', not enough technical or commercial expertise, or however you want to put it. Naturally, this has less significance than managing the enterprise oneself, but it is already important for the workers to say to themselves consciously: 'I cannot do everything, so I will accept a specialist and place him in certain conditions.'

If not even this level has been reached, then things are even worse. And the party cries severely: 'Comrades, if during the retreat to new defence lines, where we have to hold the line shoulder to shoulder at the risk of falling under capitalist control again under the worst possible conditions — that is, under conditions of colonial subjugation — if during this move to the new defence lines you do not find within yourselves sufficient energy, comprehension, and political culture to make use of all the indispensable instruments and methods we need to maintain this line of defence, then we are lost.' Hence the severe judgement. In truth, didn't we act in this way during the time of the army's retreat, when we implacably shot disrupters? And who were they? Scoundrels? Not always; there were a lot of guys who just lost their way, who were on the wrong track. Shooting them was a cruel measure designed to warn the others. It is also indispensable to issue severe warnings in the economic domain. Not because foreign specialists will get scared and not come to work with us if we don't, as Riazanov claims, but because we disorganise ourselves and our own economy if we treat the specialists as though we could get along without them.

It is in this lack of understanding of the character of the present moment that the great misfortune of Comrade Riazanov lies. I don't know whether he deserved this sanction or a different one.[11] [Interruption by Riazanov: 'You were the ones who took it.'] I have neglected to mention many of your acts, probably highly laudable, in particular the details of the intervention for which you were sanctioned. It was only today that I heard the reading of your resolution from you, and I don't know if it was only because of it that you were sanctioned. I cannot guarantee the justice of the sanction, but I cannot take it upon myself to call it unjust. Your point of view is erroneous. You have written a very good little book, *Commentary on the Communist Manifesto*.[12] That's another thing. [Riazanov: 'Because I had some free time when I was thrown out of the trade union movement.'] If that's the way it is, then Riazanov is making the most self-destructive reply against himself, because none of us could have written the commentaries he wrote on the *Communist Manifesto*. I don't think there's a man who knows Marxist literature as profoundly as Riazanov does — I recognise your extraordinary erudition — but that does not mean that he applies it correctly in practice. [Riazanov : 'Like a Minister of War in the domain of political economy.'] It's possible that this Minister of War should not write theoretical works on political economy, and if he did so anyway we might punish him. We are not punishing you because of your useful commentaries, but because of your attempts to immortalise certain methods which you apply in the trade union movement, independent of the character of economic relations and the political period. That is your enormous error.

Notes

1. LD Trotsky, speech made at the Eleventh Congress of the Russian Communist Party, 30 March 1922, translated by Guy Desolre from the *Stenographic Report of the Eleventh Congress of the Russian Communist Party (Bolshevik)*, Moscow, 1922, pp269-75, and printed in *Inprecor*, new series, no 3, 31 March 1977, pp33-9. We are especially grateful to Comrade Desolre for permission to include this valuable item.
2. The Tenth Congress of the Russian Communist Party (8-16 March 1921) had made membership of the trade unions compulsory, and abolished the right to strike. The Eleventh Congress reversed this.
3. Tomsky, who had also been disciplined at the same time as Riazanov, defended the right to strike throughout.
4. Lozovsky was defending the position eventually adopted by the congress (cf n2, above).
5. VI Lenin, 'Political report of the Central Committee of the RCP(B)', 27 March 1922, *Collected Works*, Volume 33, Moscow, 1966, pp267-9.
6. Cf I Deutscher, *The Prophet Armed*, Oxford, 1954, pp496-7.
7. Mikhail Alexandrovich Larin (Lurye, 1882-1932) served on the Foreign Trade Monopoly and the State Planning Commission. He proposed to the Congress that it lift the ban upon Riazanov's trade union activity.
8. The Sovnarkhoz was the Council of People's Commissars, in this case at a provincial level (that is, local government).
9. John Davison Rockefeller Junior (1839-1937), President of Standard Oil of New Jersey, was one of the richest men in the world.
10. Oldenberger, the Chief Engineer of the Moscow waterworks, committed suicide as a result of repeated harassment by some of the Communists in his enterprise. The Supreme Court of the Central Executive Committee of the Moscow Soviet dealt with them with exceptional severity.
11. Riazanov had induced the Communist fraction inside the trade unions to pass a resolution affirming the principles of the Tenth Congress of the Bolshevik Party (that is, opposing the right to strike and calling for compulsory trade union membership) in May 1921. The Central Committee of the party intervened to annul it, and removed Riazanov from his functions within the trade union movement.
12. D Riazanov, *The Communist Manifesto: A Commentary*, translated from the Russian by Eden and Cedar Paul, London, 1929.

Grigory Zinoviev

The Future of the Russian Communist Party[1]

THE QUESTION of the line of demarcation between the Soviet government and the Communist Party is one which has already been under discussion, and is worthy of further attention.

It is no new problem, as may be seen by the clear-cut resolution passed at the Eighth Congress of the party,[2] which said:

'The mingling of party functions with the functions of state organs such as the soviets is under no circumstances permissible. Disastrous results, especially in military affairs, would accrue from any such mingling. It is the duty of the party to realise its decisions by means of the soviets within the Soviet constitution. The party endeavours to give a lead to the soviets, but not to supplant them.'

This resolution was passed in 1919, the year in which also the watchword was issued: 'Back to the Party!' That was a period when we had concentrated with too great impetuosity on the soviets, and the party became a mere appendage of the soviets, where bureaucracy began to take root. For this reason we issued the watchword: 'Back to the Party!' The party was thus enabled to combat, independently, these unhealthy traits of the Soviet power, and we gained certain results.

We have put into effect the lessons of this experience as far as trade unionism is concerned. Their field of activity is marked out exactly: trade unions will now be trade unions! Certain comrades have wanted to add that 'The party will now be a party!'

In what sense will the party be a party? What is the Communist Party in other countries? What were we prior to 1917? We were the party of agitation, and fulfilled the same functions as does our present section for agitation and propaganda. We agitated, carried on propaganda, organised strikes, and at best, when we were lucky, we organised revolts. That was what our party was hitherto, and that is what the party is in other countries. The party in this interpretation must concentrate on agitation and propaganda, and must on no account meddle with the work of our economic state machinery. But in broad outline we cannot accept without reservation the formula: 'The party must be a party!' Our party is a leading party, as a Menshevik said, whom I shall quote later. Our party has to undertake the guidance of economic activities. As regards the section for agitation and propaganda, it receives the utmost attention, but it cannot now be said that it should absorb nine-tenths of our work. Formerly that was the case, but it must not be so now. Hence we cannot accept the formula: 'The party must be a party!' On the contrary, the party must take the lead, it must be a party that guides the life and activity of the state.

Its most important duty is as follows: in view of the fact that it is incumbent upon us to direct the state, we should establish within our party such a division of labour as would free us from the necessity of directing political life by means of resolutions of the provincial party committees. We must divide up the live forces of our party in such a way that **they** themselves are enabled to guide the work. If the provincial party committee possesses such first-class material, and a full understanding of economic affairs, then they must be delegated to the various economic departments. In this way we shall make an economical division of our forces.

According to available figures, the number of members in the party who had joined before 1917 is but **two per cent** of the total — the remainder are more recent additions to the party. This circumstance is of great importance. For even the Mensheviks say that we are living on the dividends of our basic capital, that is, from that basic group which gained prominence because of the revolution, comrades who have been at work since 1917 being regarded as old comrades. This position is one of the most delicate in the whole party problem, and must be made clear. Comrades of long standing should certainly possess more tact than to maintain that they understand the work better because their 'party beards' are longer, and because they date from such and such a year.

The total membership of the party amounts to 486 000. Here we touch on another delicate question, namely, the relation of the members of the party in central Russia and in the border regions. Undoubtedly, the party membership in the latter is of very recent origin. We can rejoice that there are 25 000 members in Turkestan now, although for historical reasons there could be no such number of workers as in the proletarian centres of central Russia. But we must beware of allowing the appearance of even the least trace of what has been aptly nicknamed 'colonisation'. We must not regard the party members in the border regions as citizens of a second order, but prove the reality of our internationalism, allowing that the party membership there is of a special type, and requires special attention. The party in an immense country such as ours, which forms one-sixth of the whole globe, cannot be homogeneous. The new Executive Committee should pay particular regard to these differences in the social constitution of our party membership; types from Siberia, Turkestan and Bokhara, for instance, require in each case to be treated from a different point of view.

Let us next examine the statistics of the Red Army. From official figures, which Comrade Trotsky confirmed as regards essentials, it appears that there are from 90 000 to 100 000 Communists in the Red Army. In this figure the military youth organisation and the staff colleges are included. I must, however, make it clear that of these 100 000 Communists only about 40 per cent are workers, and the other 60 per cent are peasants. So far we have been accustomed to believe that in staff colleges workers were in a majority, but it appears that they all consist, to the extent of two-thirds, of peasants.

I consider this estimate of the number of Communists to be more or less correct. And if it were possible to make a distribution of the membership of the party according to a well thought out plan, I would estimate the number necessary for the army at 100 000; 25 000 to 50 000 for the government machine; 100 000 for the district and regional organs, and the balance for the factories and big undertakings. In my opinion, this is the first duty to be accomplished.

Hitherto the distribution of our forces has not been in keeping with our numbers. It is a fact that there are big districts, mines, etc, where there are from 10 000 to 12 000 workers, where we have only a party nucleus of six. With our present strength, a more correct distribution should now be possible. The proportion in the army is quite right; it might be possible to raise the number to 120 000, but it is important that the present figure is about right. Comrade Larin has written: 'How can a government party exist, if it removes its members from the state apparatus, and sends them into the factories and workshops?'[3] He is wrong. We are both a governing party and a workers' party, and should possess a percentage of Communists everywhere where there are workers. A revision on these lines is possible, and the party must carry it out.

A word may be said on the proportion of non-party members in the various executive committees. In the period 1920-21, taking 20 more or less arbitrarily selected provinces, the number of non-party members was doubled, and in many places reached 50 per cent of the total. Although I am a supporter of the view that the number of non-party workers could be increased, this number appears to me to be somewhat too great, and attention should be paid to it.

What is to be the future method of accepting members in the party? To me this is one of the most important questions before this congress, and our proposal is to adhere to the rules extant during the period in which the party was being purged of unsuitable elements.[4] In other words, it is our intention that any entrance to the party should be held over until the next congress.

Is there any necessity for such a decision? Certain derogatory comments have been made against it; Comrade Larin and some other comrades wrote that by these tactics we should be transformed into a mandarin sect. The reason why Comrade Larin should fear this is quite apparent to me; he anticipates a separation from the masses, from whom we are already partly separated. But such truisms as unity with the masses must not lead us astray; the party must be taken actually as it is, with its useful and good points, as it stands after the new registration, the expulsions in the year 1922, at the time of the New Economic Policy, etc, and in the light of that position we should examine whether there is actually a danger of our becoming a sect. I do not think any party but ours can show such an increase during the past four years, when its membership rose tenfold. There is no necessity for us now to put all our energy into increasing the party membership. Let us examine the present position. In the Putilov works we now have 60 members. If that 60 should be increased to 100 of the same standard, nothing would have been gained. Before the revolution there were 30 to 40 members of the party in the Putilov works, all chosen comrades, energetic men with wide-awake minds, a picked crew. Every non-party worker understood that every Communist towered above all the others. We must now make it our duty to see that the Communists tower over the others, that they attract attention, and that the masses regard the Communists as they used to do, as those who are the most far-sighted and clear-headed. It is this position that calls for the focusing of our attention, not on the increase of the membership, but on an earnest and energetic endeavour to improve the quality of the existing membership. We are more interested in quality than in quantity. A year or two ago this position was evident, but no steps could be taken to better matters because of the war and the absorption of all our forces by other duties.

Now, however, we can cover Russia with a network of schools. By one year's intensive work, the level of the average party member can be raised. The heroism and self-sacrifice displayed generally by the mass of the party members is well known; they saved the republic and the party, and the republic takes off its hat to these common soldiers of the party. But these comrades, because of their upbringing, and not through any fault of their own or yours, are in the ranks of the preparatory class, and it is questionable whether it is even the preparatory stage, for some comrades do not know the ABC of Communism. The party and this congress are their debtors. Hence we must devote this year, which to all appearances may permit of the quiet development of our economic life and that of our party, not to gaining new adherents, but to the improvement of the present membership. Let us shut our doors to all but those who would exercise a healthy influence on the party; to no others should we give admittance. The workers will understand. This will be no lasting regulation, but merely an episode in the life of a great party whose membership under the Tsar was but 5000, and afterwards suddenly jumped to 40 000, and then to 50 000. A year's interval is absolutely essential to enable the party to examine the hidden corners, to size up the position, and to help the mass of the members to become Communists in reality. To this work we should devote all our energies.

Something should be said also of some special activities. More attention must be paid to work among the youth. The Red Army is almost entirely a youth organisation. In 1921, in order to complete the army and navy cadres, 20 000 men were called up, and all these new recruits have to go through the youth organisation. Work among women is also of equal importance. Among women we have only 70 000 members of the party, representing some three million women workers.

In reviewing the progress of the party, it is important to consider existing dangers, and in this respect I should like to draw special attention to the opinions of our fairly far-sighted enemies, the Mensheviks. In a work devoted entirely to our party, the author writes:

'Why do we devote so much attention to the inner life of the Bolshevik party? By no means out of deference either for the party or its theory. During the past years, however, with their lack of any sort of public life, in the prevailing atmosphere of apathy and the general confusion, all other parties and organisations were helpless, and the Bolsheviks, together with the Red Army, have been the only organised social power. For this reason, the downfall of the Bolsheviks cannot be brought about in the same way as that of former governments. Revolt cannot avail; the period of revolts corresponds with revolutionary advance and the growth of revolutionary feeling. The fall of the revolution will be signified by quite different political upheavals, such as splits, plots, and **coups d'état**.

'There is the peasant element in the party without any special tendency, although firmly entrenched in the district and regional administrative bodies. The party possesses besides very important workers' groups, just beginning to awaken to their special interests within the party state. There are also large intellectual groups, partly of democratic views, and partly with desires for a "great power" state, as aimed at by the *Smena Vekh* (*Changed Signals*).[5] Finally, there are within the ranks of the party no small number of the new bourgeois elements. All these elements at present live alongside one another in the same party. When the appointed hour strikes, all these elements will come out of the common womb into the light of day, and their quarrel with each other will accomplish the task of political history.'

The author scorns our cleansing policy and declares:

'How childish are these attempts at frustrating the inexorable centrifugal forces by means of "party purification"! How it shows the bureaucratic arrogance and boundless vanity common to all conquerors! What was the outcome of this "party purification" which was planned to expel the bourgeois from within its ranks? Widespread discontent, the expulsion of both right and left elements, of pure and defiled, and in addition a few dozen anecdotes which are careering round the world. Such methods will not change or conquer the history of the world.'

And he concludes:

'This is the cause of the long drawn out delay in overthrowing the Bolsheviks; it is also the reason why Bolshevism can only be destroyed from within, by the decomposition and decay of the Russian Communist Party.'

These words, coming from one of our greatest enemies, should not be forgotten. Although this same writer foretold, a year ago, that the downfall of Bolshevik rule would happen thus :

'From their own ranks, from the ranks of the Red Army, there will spring up some commander or lieutenant who will become a miniature Napoleon.[6] And the sympathy for the government will dwindle to such an extent that Napoleon will one day march into the Kremlin, seize the reins of power, and scatter the Council of Commissars.'

His recent prognosis, on the other hand, counts on the decay of our party and the formation of internal divisions resulting in the total break-up of the party. There is an atom of truth in this statement. Our party is a party of monopoly, and because it is the only one active in public affairs, certain elements force their way into it which under other circumstances would belong to their parties. What a variety we have! The peasant element is a source of danger, so too the office workers, who are not from the ranks of the working class, and have joined us merely from self-interest. There is no denying the difficulties in our path. It is quite true that a molecular process is taking place within the party which reflects more than one struggle, which even reflects the class struggle.

We must think of the unity of the party. We dare not forget the Mensheviks' statement that they are waiting for the heterogeneous elements within the common womb to emerge and do the work of political history by fighting one another. It is on this card that the whole international counter-revolution, including the Second and Two-and-a-Half Internationals, put all their hope. It is not our intention to hush up the weaknesses of the party. We must go forward step by step, inch by inch. Many difficulties beset our path, but the thought that for us there is nothing dearer than our party should be ever present. Communists of the whole world admit that we guided the party on the right way during all the difficulties in those four years of revolution. We mean to continue to guide it in the same way.

Notes

1. GY Zinoviev, speech to the Eleventh Congress of the Communist Party, on the occasion of the Fifth Anniversary of the Russian Revolution, March 1922, *11 Syezd RKP (B)*, Moscow, 1922, pp408-13, translated in *Labour Monthly*, Volume 3, no 5, November 1922, pp281-8.
2. The Eighth Congress of the Communist Party was held in March 1919.
3. Larin, an ex Menshevik-Internationalist, was a member of Gosplan, and very much associated himself with the administrative personnel of the party.
4. The first party purge took place towards the end of 1921, removing some 170 000, or nearly 25 per cent of the party members.
5. *Smena Vekh* was a journal published in Paris between October 1921 and March 1922. It expressed the views of White emigré intellectuals, and some of the old bourgeois intelligentsia employed by the Soviet state during the NEP.
6. Napoleon Bonaparte (1769-1821) established himself as military dictator as a result of the exhaustion of the French Revolution by a coup d'état in November 1799. Zinoviev is making this reference as a hint in Trotsky's direction. Cf I Deutscher, *The Prophet Unarmed*, Oxford, 1959, p95, n1.

Appendix

Nikolai Bukharin

Lenin as a Marxist[1]

We have relegated this speech to an appendix, since although it relates closely to the material collected together in Book One above (pp76-81), it strictly falls outside our time span, having been produced in October 1925. It should also be read less closely, since the poor quality of the translation has made necessary considerable alterations, not only for stylistic reasons, but even to make it coherent in some places. However, we feel justified in including it, as its approach differs from that of Radek, and helps us to understand the range of opinions about what was the essence of Leninism within the Bolshevik leadership.

Like Zinoviev's speech above (pp243-8), it also looks to the future, and allows us an insight into the early stages of the formation of the Lenin cult, showing how the regime selected from Lenin's legacy those aspects that were appropriate to its needs. This is particularly the case when we read Bukharin's sections on the peasant and colonial questions, as the hope of European revolution faded into the background as the 1920s wore on. The hopes expressed here for a slow evolutionary development for the Soviet Union over a long period were soon to receive a rude shock in the chaos of the forced collectivisation, and the defeat of the Chinese Revolution was an equal setback for the colonial perspectives. And although Stalin is nowhere mentioned, Bukharin is already making ideological concessions to his power, since his remarks about the development of contradictory 'tendencies hostile to us' also reflect the increasingly bitter factional struggle that had already engulfed Trotsky, Radek, Zinoviev and Kamenev, and was shortly to swallow him up as well. Although this is not identical with Stalin's notorious anti-Marxist theory that the class struggle will sharpen under the dictatorship of the proletariat, it is already well on the way to it.

IT IS generally regarded as incontestable within the wide circles of our own party and outside its ranks that Vladimir Ilyich as a man of the practice of the labour movement was incomparable and a genius; appreciations of his theoretical work, however, are generally on a lower plane. In my opinion, the time has come when we should carry out a slight, or perhaps even a very considerable, revision on this point. I think that this inadequate appreciation of Comrade Lenin as a theoretician is due to a certain psychological aberration which we all develop. What Comrade Lenin has accomplished in theory has not been condensed, compiled and presented in a few handy volumes. Comrade Lenin's theoretical theses, formulae and generalisations were made to a considerable extent, in nine cases out of ten, when occasion required. They are scattered throughout the vast number of his works, and needless to say, just because of the fact that they are scattered and not presented to our reading public in a compact, finished and handy form, for this reason alone there are many people who consider that Lenin as a theoretician is far behind Lenin as a practician. But I think that in the near future this idea will be shattered, and in the more distant future Comrade Lenin will appear in his real stature, not only as a genius practitioner of the labour movement, but also as a genius theoretician.

I will just quote, if I may, one little example from my own work, from my own theoretical practice, if one may use such an expression. I once had occasion in one of my articles to deal in a fairly detailed manner with the question of the differences in principle which exist between the growth of the Socialist structure within the capitalist system and the growth of the capitalist system within feudal society. Afterwards, the corresponding theses, which I published in the periodical *Under the Banner of Marxism*, appeared more or less theoretically sharpened in a number of juridical, general-political and other works. But after having written this article, and after having sincerely believed that here in this modest theoretical scope, within definite limits, a new word was said, I recognised that all I had said was actually contained in four lines of a speech by Vladimir Ilyich at our Seventh Party Congress during the discussion on the Brest-Litovsk peace.[2] I believe that those of us who are engaged, and who in the future will be engaged, on theoretical work, and who will now read Lenin's works from a rather different aspect, will undoubtedly discover a whole number of new things in these works, things that we hitherto passed over, that we did not notice, and the great theoretical extent of which we had not previously understood. Lenin as a theoretician still awaits his systematiser, and in future when this work will be accomplished, and when everything new that Lenin gave us, scattered in endless quantities throughout his works, will be put in a systematic form — then Lenin will appear to us in his full gigantic height as a genius theoretician of the Communist workers' movement. The aim of my lectures is to indicate some of the lines which might serve as a guide for subsequent work in studying Vladimir Ilyich as a Marxist theoretician.

The Marxism of the Epoch of Marx and Engels

Marxism, just as any other doctrine, any other theoretical conception — both in the purely theoretical and in the applied-theoretical domain — is a certain live quantity which develops and changes. It may change in such a way that the quantitative aspect of these changes becomes qualitative, and like other doctrines it may degenerate under definite conditions — social conditions — but it never remains the same. I think that now in this period in which we are living, it has become clear that Marxism has passed through three main phases of historical development. These three phases of the historical development of Marxist ideology or Marxism correspond with the three great divisions in the history of the labour movement, which in turn are connected with the three great epochs in the development of human society in general, and primarily of European society. The first phase of Marxist development is Marxism as expressed and as formulated by the founders of scientific Communism themselves — Marx and Engels. This is the Marxism of Marx — in the true sense of the word. The social basis for this Marxism was by no means in the organic or the peaceful epoch of European development. It was in the epoch when Europe was experiencing a number of upheavals, an epoch which found its highest form of expression in the revolutions of 1848.

The chief material for theoretical generalisation which from the social stand-point gave an impetus to the revolutionary formulations was rooted in the catastrophic nature of European development. The epoch in which Marxism had its origin gave this great proletarian knowledge peculiar features of its own, which also left their trace on the logical construction of the Marxism of that epoch. We can follow quite easily the fundamental lines which, as I expressed it here, gave a revolutionary impetus to the Marxism of Marx and Engels. In the first place, there is the combination of the enormous forces of abstraction, of theoretical generalisation, with revolutionary practice. You know that at the highest stage of theoretical abstraction, Marx brought forward in his *Theses on Feuerbach* the statement with which we are all acquainted, that the philosophers up to now had explained the world, whereas it is really a question of changing the world.[3] It should be understood that this practical and real tendency in the Marxism of Marx and Engels had its social basis. Furthermore, the whole theory of Marx was of a sharply-expressed subversive character. It was thoroughly revolutionary in its very substance, from the upper rungs of its ideological structure down to its practical-political conclusions. The whole content of this Marxism was thor-oughly revolutionary, both in the domain of pure theory and of applied theory. You all know what Marx replied to the question of what composed the spirit of Marxian teachings, that this teaching does not consist of the theory of class struggle, since this was already known before his time, but that his teaching is that social development inevitably leads to the **dictatorship of the proletariat**.[4] Marx asserted this in contradiction to many others — and when I say many others, I even have in mind those who now think of themselves as Marxists. One might say that the formula generally applied to Marxism — that Marxism is the algebra of the revolution — was perfectly correct as a formula for the Marxism of the epoch of Marx and Engels. This was a wonderful machine which served as a most excellent weapon for the overthrow of the capitalist regime in all its theoretical branches and, I repeat, in all its branches of practical and political conclusions.

The Marxism of the Epigones

Such was the first phase of the development of Marxism, and, if one may say so, its first historical outlook. But you know perfectly well that later another epoch, and another Marxism, commence. This other Marxism might be termed the Marxism of the epigones, or the Marxism of the Second International. It stands to reason that the transition from that phase of Marxism to the Marxism of the epigones did not occur catastrophically. This was an evolutionary process, and this evolution in the ideology of the labour movement was based on that very evolution which firstly European capitalism, and then world capitalism, were passing through. I repeat, first and foremost, European capitalism. After the revolutions of 1848 a relative stability in the capitalist system was established, and a period of capitalist development commenced in which its most catastrophic peculiarities, together with its most striking contradictions, were transferred to the colonial sphere. In the basic links of the ever-growing large industries, there was a process of the organic growth of the productive forces, with a relative enlightenment of the working class. There was also a corresponding political superstructure on this socio-economic soil — the consolidated nation states — 'the fatherland'. The bourgeoisie sat quite firmly in the saddle. Imperialist policy commenced to make itself particularly apparent, for example, in the 1880s. On the basis of the rise in the standard of living of the working class, and the growth and rapid progress of the labour aristocracy, the working class organisations were internally and ideologically recast in the system of the general capitalist mechanism. This process thus served as a background, as soil for the reformulation of the dominating ideology of the labour movement. Ideology, as is known, lags behind practice. There is, therefore, a certain disharmony between the ideological development of Marxism and the development of Marxism in its purely practical sense.

Marxism in both of its basic forms began to be transformed. The Revisionist tendency within the German Social Democracy[5] gave the most striking expression to this tendency of alteration. Insofar as it is a question of exact theoretical formulae, we have no more classical examples in other countries, despite even more decisive remodellings. Owing to a series of historical conditions, which I cannot analyse here, this practice did not acquire in those countries a sufficiently clear and exact formulation such as it received in the most thinking country, if I may so term it. In Germany, the Revisionist currents already signalised perfectly clearly, and, what is more, completely expressed, the departure from the Marxism peculiar to Marx and Engels and the entire previous epoch. The departure from Marxism on the part of other groupings calling themselves radical or orthodox Marxists, headed by Kautsky, was much less clearly defined. I have already had occasion to refer to this elsewhere, and personally I consider the view that the decline of the German Social Democracy and Kautsky started in and dates from 1914 to be an incorrect one. It seems to me (and now we may confirm this) that a long way back we could quite clearly perceive the departure from real orthodox and real revolutionary Marxism, as formulated by Marx and Engels in the previous phase of the development of the ideology of the labour movement, on the part of those groupings among the German Social Democrats, who for a long time gave the lead to the whole international, although this was not so rapid as with the Revisionists.

At the commencement of this period, I repeat, there was a certain disharmony between theory and practice. The most thoroughgoing ideologists of the Revisionist type laid down the practice of the German Social Democrats, after having developed the **appropriate** theory. Another section of the Social Democrats still relied on their theoretical formulae, not being strong enough, and as a matter of fact not making much effort, to overcome these harmful tendencies in practice. This was the position that Kautsky's group took up. But at the end of this period, when history brought to the fore a number of questions of the greatest importance, both in principle and in their essentials — I am speaking of the commencement of the World War — it then became apparent that both practically and theoretically there was no difference between these two wings. In principle, both these two wings — Revisionism and Kautskyism — expressed exactly the same tendency of the **degeneration of Marxism**, the tendency of adaptation, in the worst sense of the word, to the new social conditions which had sprung up in Europe, and which were peculiar to this period of European development. They expressed exactly the same theoretical current that was leading away from

Marxism in its true and really revolutionary sense. Generally speaking, we might characterise this difference as follows: Revisionist 'Marxism' in its pure form — and this has become clearer and clearer during recent years — has acquired a sharply expressed fatalistic character with regard to state power, the capitalist regime, etc, whereas in Kautsky and his group we are faced with a Marxism that we might call democratic-pacifist.

This line of differentiation was conditional, and during recent years became more and more effaced as these two tendencies merged into one channel, deviating more and more decisively from Marxism. The substance of this process is a flight from the revolutionary content of Marxism — instead of the revolutionary theory of Marxism, revolutionary dialectics, revolutionary teaching on the dictatorship, etc, we had the **ordinary bourgeois democratic evolutionary doctrine**. We can demonstrate in detail as to how this deviation became very apparent in a number of theoretical problems. I have partly made this analysis in a speech devoted to the Programme of the Communist International at one of the international congresses.[6] We meet with this revisionist deviation when Kautsky absolutely falsifies the theory of the state and of state power; the same with Plekhanov, who was one of the 'most orthodox'. The existence of this revision in the theory of the state makes it quite clear why the Kautskyian wing also took up a bourgeois-pacifist position during the world imperialist war.

We are all acquainted with the real Marxist formula with respect to the theory of state power. We might express this teaching, for example, in this manner: During the Socialist revolution, the state apparatus of the bourgeoisie is destroyed, and a new dictatorship is created — 'anti-democratic' — and at the same time a proletarian-democratic state, having absolutely peculiar and specific forms of state power which afterwards begin to wither away. With Kautsky, however, you will not find anything of the sort on this point; both with Kautsky and with all the Social Democratic 'Marxists', this point is expounded so as to imply that state power is just something that is transferred from the hands of one class to the hands of another, just as a machine that has first been held by one class and then handed over to the other, without the new class taking all the nuts and bolts to pieces and then putting them together again. From this theoretically pure formula, and from this teaching, arises the attitude of national defence during wartime. When the war started, this kind of argument could be heard scores of times at specially organised patriotic meetings, and this exceedingly primitive argument has a certain amount of logic in its standpoint. It stands to reason that should the given bourgeois state be in our hands tomorrow, there is no use in destroying it; on the contrary, we must protect it, because tomorrow it will be ours. This problem was approached in a manner quite different from the way Marx dealt with it. If we must not destroy the state, because it will be in our hands tomorrow, then we must also not disorganise the army, because it is a component part of the state apparatus, we must not destroy any state discipline, and so forth. All this was very nicely laid down, and, needless to say, when these theoretical constructs were tested on the anvil of mutual struggle, then Kautskyism and German Social Democracy, in complete solidarity with their theoretical premises, drew the appropriate practical conclusions.

I repeat, it is incorrect to think that we have here some kind of instantaneous catastrophical transgression. Theoretically, it was all well founded. We simply did not notice this internal degeneration also within the so-called 'orthodox' wing, which had very little in common with real orthodoxy. We might say the same thing of the theory of the collapse of capitalist society, of the theory of emiseration, of the colonial and national questions, with regard to the teachings on democracy and dictatorship, with regard to tactical teachings such as the study of mass struggle, etc. From this point of view, I would recommend all comrades to read the well-known classical pamphlet by Kautsky — *The Social Revolution* — which we have already read once, but which we will now read from quite another aspect, because it is now quite easy for us to discover in this pamphlet a Mont Blanc of all possible distortions of Marxism and opportunistic formulae which are now perfectly clear to us. If these Marxist epigones took into account certain new changes in the domain of the capitalist order, of the interrelation between economics and politics, if they examined under their theoretical magnifying glass some new phenomena or other in the realm of current life — then they would on principle always take into consideration these new phenomena from one aspect, from the aspect of **the incorporation of the working class organisations into the general system of the mechanism of capitalism in an evolutionary manner.**

For instance, there came into being a new phenomenon, the limited company, and they immediately used this to explain that capitalism is becoming democratised. On the continent, improvements in the conditions of the working class occurred, whereupon conclusions were at once drawn that perhaps the revolution is also redundant, and that everything can be achieved in a peaceful way. Insofar as they referred to Marx, they at once seized on a number of quotations, separate theses and words, torn from their contexts. It is well known that Marx said with reference to Great Britain: 'In Great Britain things may happen even without bloodshed.'[7] This was quickly generalised by everyone. It is well known that Engels once made some not particularly favourable statements about fighting on the barricades.[8] Thus every possible conclusion was at once drawn with the necessary quotations; every phenomenon was considered from the aspect whereby the labour organisations were being generally absorbed by the capitalist system, the aspect of which we might agree to call the standpoint of class truce. Ultimately, the whole revolutionary substance of revolutionary Marxism began to melt away. Something had happened which very often occurs in history when we have exactly the same words, the same phrases, the same labels and the same symbolism, and, I repeat, when we have quite a different socio-political content. In German Social Democracy, which in this was a model, Marxist phraseology was still preserved, and also Marxist symbolism, the Marxist verbal husk, but there was absolutely no Marxist **substance**; there remained only the verbal cover from the teachings that had been developed in the epoch of the social upheavals of the middle of the last century. The revolutionary spirit had taken flight, and in fact we already had to deal with a teaching that corresponded with the **opportunist practice** of German Social Democracy and of the opportunist Labour parties, objectively reviving their respective national bourgeoisies, and being bought over by them. One might have even designed a kind of special socio-political map of the degrees of roguery of these 'Marxists'. The more the country became involved in the world market, the more powerful her position, the stronger and the more imperialist the policy of the given country and its national bourgeoisie, the larger and stronger the labour aristocracy, the stronger the chains that bound the working class of a given country to its own bourgeoisie and its state organisations — the more opportunist and the baser were the theoretical formulae, although they may have been covered by Marxist labels. I repeat, we might draw such a map as would illustrate exceedingly well the connection between socio-political development on the one hand, and the sphere of ideological development (in this case the ideology of the labour movement) on the other.

Such, comrades, was the **second** phase in the development of Marxism. The physiognomy of that Marxism was something quite different from the Marxism of Marx and Engels. As you perceive, we are dealing with quite a different socio-political ideology, because we have to a large degree a different foundation for this ideology. This foundation is the working class of the most predatory imperialist states, and of their labour aristocracy in particular. When this process acquired its most classical expression in the social realm, we then began to get the most classical formulae, **deviating from orthodox Marxism all along the line.**

The Marxism of Lenin

I will now come on to the question of Leninism. I have been told that on one of the flags of the Institute of Red Professors the following words were inscribed: 'Marxism in Science, Leninism in Tactics — Such is Our Banner.' It seems to me that such a distinction is highly inappropriate, and quite unworthy of 'the vanguard on the ideological front' (as our red professors style themselves), since it is absolutely impossible to separate the theory and practice of the class struggle. If Leninism in practice is not the same as Marxism, then we get precisely that separation of theory from practice which is specially harmful for such an institution as the Institute of Red Professors. It is clear that Leninist Marxism represents quite a particular form of ideological education, for the simple reason that it is itself a child of a somewhat different epoch. **It cannot be simply a repetition of the Marxism of Marx**, because the epoch in which we are living is not a simple repetition of the epoch in which Marx lived. There is just something in common between these two epochs; that epoch was not a stable epoch, while this epoch is in a lesser degree a stable epoch. The Marxism of Marx was a product of the revolutionary epoch. And Leninist Marxism, if we may thus put it, is a product of an unusually stormy and unusually revolutionary epoch. But it is a matter of course that there is so much **new** in the very process of social development, in the very empirical **material** which can be used as material for theoretical generalisations in those **tasks** which face the revolutionary proletariat, and, consequently, demand a corresponding response and a corresponding reaction, that our present day Marxism is not merely a repetition of the sum total of the ideas that Marx brought forward.

I will deal with this question at length so that there will be no misunderstanding with regard to **comparison**, for I by no means desire to contrast one teaching with the other. **One is the logical and historical completion and development of the other.** But I would first like to touch on those new facts of socio-economic politics which are the basis for Leninist Marxism. Indeed, how many new factors are we faced with in this domain — new in the sense that these phenomena were inaccessible to Marx because they simply did not exist at the time when Marx was alive? First of all, we have rather a new phase in the development of capitalist relations. Marx understood the epoch of mercantile capitalism which lay behind him. Marx likewise knew industrial capitalism. It might be said that the epoch of industrial capitalism was considered as a classic type of capitalism in general. You know very well that it was only at the time of Engels that such things as syndicates and trusts began to be formed. But of the entire new stage of capitalist development, with its great reorganisation of productive relations under capitalism — what Lenin designated as monopoly capitalism — it is obvious that Marx could not know about all these phenomena, since they were non-existent during his time, and it is just for that simple reason that he was unable to express and generalise them.

These new phenomena must be theoretically grasped, and once theoretically grasped they represent a further link in the old chain of theoretical discussions and theses. All these are phenomena arising from **finance capital**, and from the imperialist policy of this finance capital. The problem of forming and consolidating world economic organisations of capital and state and a number of other analogous problems arising from the specific structure of capitalism as expressed in the last years of the nineteenth century and the first decades of the twentieth, were all problems which were unknown to Marx, and which could not be subjected to theoretical analysis. The **second** group of problems consists in those connected with the World War, and with **the decline** of capitalist relations. But no matter how much I were to estimate the degree and profundity of the decline of capitalist relations, no matter what prognosis I were to state in this respect, no matter how much I estimate the present economic situation in Western Europe in particular, no matter what I might say as to the serious crisis or collapse, no matter what radical formula I might bring forward on the one hand or on the other — it nevertheless remains perfectly clear to you that conditions now exist such as did not exist before. During the days of the founders of scientific Communism, there was no state capitalism in its special form, or the phenomena connected with it — nor were there the phenomena of the decline and disorganisation of the capitalist mechanism with its quite specific social phenomena in the process of decline, starting from the productive basis and ending with the phenomena connected with the currency. These questions bring before us a number of most interesting and new theoretical problems, and naturally — together with these theoretical problems — the corresponding practical and political conclusions based on them and necessarily connected with them. These other kinds of phenomena are very extensive, since they constitute a whole epoch — in a certain sense — and these were phenomena unknown both to Marx and to Engels. Finally there are **a third series of factors** directly connected with **workers' risings** during the time of the collapse of capitalist relations, in the period resulting from the tremendous crash of these purely capitalistic bodies during the wars, which are nothing more or less than a peculiar form of their capitalist competition — these special formulae were unknown to the period and epoch in which Marx and his closest adherents lived and studied. At the present moment, these questions are directly connected with the process of the Socialist revolution. They represent an immense social phenomenon of quite an objective character which we must study theoretically, and which has its own peculiar laws, and which confronts us with a whole number of theoretical and practical-political problems. It is self-evident in Marx's time that only the most general formulae could be produced, whereas the present empirical material provides a huge quantity of all possible theses and phenomena which must be worked out theoretically. These are the third kind of phenomena, the problems connected with them and the practical-political conclusions connected with the solution of these problems. Such is the third class of problems — both theoretical and practical — which were unknown to Marx, since they were generally unknown until this epoch. Finally, there is yet a **fourth series** — an entire block of absolutely new problems. This is the series connected with the epoch, or with the **commencement of the epoch of working class rule.** How did Marx approach this question? Let me remind you of the Marxist formula which I have already quoted: 'My teaching and its substance do not amount to being a question of the class struggle, but to the fact that it inevitably leads to the dictatorship of the proletariat.' That was the boundary line. When this dictatorship of the proletariat is already a fact, then it becomes perfectly natural that in proceeding further we must cross this boundary. The substance of Marx's teachings is that there is an inevitable dictatorship of the proletariat, and it is only here that there can be a pause.[9] In that historical epoch it could not be otherwise, since the proletarian dictatorship was not presented as a real fact, and the phenomena accompanying it were not given as material for purely experimental use, and observations which might have been theoretically generalised and could serve as the object of theoretical analysis or of practical realisation. There was nothing of that kind. It therefore stands to reason that the whole cycle of these immense phenomena presents itself as something perfectly new, since we have already arrived at what Marx himself called the boundary line. Now we have a number of phenomena on the other side of the boundary line. The newer these phenomena are in principle, the more should they also be theoretically new in principle; consequently, the conception embracing the general examination of these phenomena — new in principle as regards all previous epochs — should also be more original. Such is the fourth group of socio-economic, political and all other kinds of phenomena, which must also serve as an object of theoretical examination and a theoretically systematised basis of conduct on the part of the working class. I have presented you with four distinct groups of events. Needless to say, they all represent not only a colossal epoch in the development of European capitalism, but also of human society in general. This epoch, with all its complications and concreteness, represents a colossal accumulation of every kind of problem both theoretical and practical, such a tremendous enormity of these problems that it is perfectly natural that the learned dialectician and practician who combines the working out of theoretical problems with practice on this empirical material already goes beyond the confines of Marxism in its old form.

There is one point I must touch on here so as to avoid misunderstandings. What might we understand by Marxism? By Marxism we might mean two things: it may be either methodological — the system of methods of investigating social phenomena — or else it is a definite sum of ideas, let us say, including the theory of historical materialism, the study of the development of capitalist relations, and so forth. We might also include in addition a number of concrete factors, that is, we will take Marxism not merely as a method or as theoretically formulated methodology, but we will take a number of concrete applications of this method, and the entirety of the ideas resulting from this application. From the latter point of view, it is quite clear that Leninist Marxism is a much wider field than the Marxism of Marx. This is obvious, because an immense quantity of new ideas connected with the analysis and the practice based on this analysis, of entirely new phenomena, and of quite new historical phases, has been added to all the ideas that then existed. Thus it is in this **restricted** sense of the word that the frontiers of Marxism have been crossed. But if we regard Marxism not as the entirety of ideas such as existed in the time of Marx, but as constituting the instrument and methodology of Marxism, then it becomes quite clear that Leninism is not something that modifies or revises the method of Marxist teaching. On the contrary, from this point of view Leninism is a complete **return** to the Marxism formulated by Marx and Engels themselves.

I think that we may thus solve the contradictions, which to a great extent are based on a confusion of terms, and on the fact that many terms are used for different meanings. If we now ask ourselves how we can characterise the history of this Leninist Marxism as a whole, then it seems to me that we may consider it as a combination, **as a synthesis of a threefold nature. Firstly**, it is a return to the Marxist epoch; only not an ordinary **return, but a return enriched with all that is new**, that is, a synthesis of the Marxism of Marx, with all the additions based on the application of Marxism; we may consider this as the Marxist analysis of the colossal amount of new phenomena given us by the new epoch. **Secondly**, it is the combination and **synthesis of the theory and practice of the struggling and conquering working class. Thirdly**, it is the synthesis of the **destructive and constructive** work of the working class, and, in my opinion, this latter circumstance is the most important of all.

Allow me to say a few words to explain this third conception. Orthodox Marxism, that is today revolutionary Marxism, or in other words, our Marxism, is naturally confronted by various practical tasks in different historical epochs, and accordingly there ensues a logical selection, because ultimately the practical tasks also determine our theoretical judgement and our ability to connect up the separate theoretical theses and links in this system into a theoretical chain.

When the working class and the revolutionary party take up their positions for the struggle for power, we must inevitably sharpen our activities and stress all definitely ideological work, specially analysing all contradictory factors. We must take note of all the basic disharmonies within capitalist society, and we must thoroughly mark, select and reform into theoretical order everything that disjoins the various elements of this society. And this is for the simple reason that what is of practical importance for us, in my opinion, is to drive into these clefts the sharpest and most pointed wedge. We are confronted with a destructive task, we have to overthrow the capitalist system, and therefore it is obvious that in the first instance the selection of all the theoretical theses and connecting links will be entirely along these lines. It is theoretically important for us to take note of all contradictions which are of practical importance, and to intensify them, so that from mere general theoretical ideas they would pass through periodical links and through our agitators, and then on further — for here we are faced with the basic destructive task of overthrow. The whole character of our theoretical work was constructed on this line. But when the working class is faced with power, it is confronted with the task of binding together various sections of a common whole under the definite hegemony of the working class. Practical interest presents quite a number of questions now which formerly were of no interest at all, and therefore much more thought must now be given to them. Now we must not destroy, but construct. This is a totally different aspect, and I think that any one of us who now reads a series of things, or even makes a number of observations on current life, will say that he sees under quite a different aspect the very same phenomena on which he formerly looked with different eyes, for the simple reason that formerly he had to destroy practically some definite complex or other, whereas now he must construct or make it cohere somehow or other. That is why I think that this current finds its corresponding theoretical reflection and theoretical expression in a number of questions related to these kind of problems. Formerly, during the epoch of the initial formulation of Marxist teaching, they did not bring to the fore the formulae that Marx himself made. In the epoch of the Second International, these formulae were regarded from the aspect of **absorption into the bourgeois state**. And since they were regarded from this aspect of absorption into the bourgeois state, that is since the Social Democratic opportunist parties made their task that of peaceful cultural construction, not that of the overthrow of the capitalist system, but of adaptation to and for a molecular evolutionary renewal of this capitalist system — it becomes clear that these beginnings of the theory of 'construction' met with a hostile reception from we revolutionary Marxists. For all this was generalised under the aspect of absorption into the capitalist state, and the absorption of the organisation into the mechanism of the capitalist regime, which we aimed at destroying. But the dialectics of history are such that when we came to power it became quite clear that we had need of a new aspect — both practically and theoretically. The point at issue is that on the one hand we must destroy, and on the other hand **construct**. We had to face a number of problems such as would give us a synthesis of this destruction of the old and the construction of the new, and a synthesis of these aspects in some united whole. Insofar as it is a question of theoretical generalisations, Vladimir Ilyich gave us this synthesis. It is exceedingly difficult for us to formulate here general basic conceptions in this direction, because we are here again faced with a large number of separate remarks scattered throughout all Lenin's works, and especially in his speeches, etc, but it is quite clear that this is absolutely the newest and the most important of what Leninism has given us as a theoretical system for the subsequent development of Marxism. Of course, I dare say a great deal has been done in the realm of theoretical selection as far as the destructive sphere is concerned. But in the constructive field, the former formulae of Marx gave us very little to go on. Here also things have to be constructed anew, and therefore it seems to me that the biggest and the greatest things that Lenin brought into the treasury of Marxism may be formulated thus: Marx provided in the main the **algebra** of capitalist development and revolutionary practice, while with Lenin there remains this same algebra, but in addition there is also the algebra of new phenomena, both of a destructive and of a positive character — and there is also their **arithmetic**, that is the deciphering of the algebraic formulae in a more concrete and more practical form.

Lenin's Theory and Practice

After these general remarks, I would like to draw your attention to quite a number of features and sketches, both of a theoretical and of a practical nature, which will illustrate the conceptions expounded above. It seems to me that the fact that Lenin had formulated his theoretical conceptions in a scattered fashion certainly arises from the most evident domination of practice in all the activities of Vladimir Ilyich, which in turn is related to our epoch, essentially an epoch of activity. We can act efficaciously when theory becomes a kind of instrument or weapon in our hands, which we can wield to perfection, and not something that weighs us down or dominates us. In a speech of mine — I don't remember which — I expressed this by saying that Vladimir Ilyich wields Marxism, but Marxism does not wield Vladimir Ilyich. By this I meant to say that one of the most characteristic features of Vladimir Ilyich, one of the most curious, was his **realisation of the practical implications of every theoretical construction and of any kind of theoretical conception.** I know it often happened that we even used to joke sometimes amongst ourselves at Vladimir Ilyich's over-practical attitude towards quite a number of theoretical problems. But, comrades, now when we have already become tempered on the revolutionary anvil after many years, and when we have been able to see and experience a great deal, it seems to me that our merriment should be turned against ourselves, because here again it was nothing more or less than an example of that very same habit of ours, the habit of intellectuals, of narrowly specialised journalists, writers or people more or less engaged on theory as their special profession. In exactly the same way as Vladimir Ilyich disliked any kind of verbal acrobatics and specific erudition — which sometimes also was not to our taste, and he jeered at us — in exactly the same way he could not bear anything superfluous, and approached theoretical conceptions and doctrines in a purely practical manner. Have they any other meaning besides the practical one? From the point of view of Marxism, it is clear that they have no other meaning whatsoever. But insofar as we had up to a certain degree been specialists, this dampened our ardour, and in this respect Lenin saw into the future to a much greater degree than any of we sinners, since what for him was organically disgusting had for us a certain attractive force. And I think that this well thought out realisation, this realisation of the practical application of any theoretical construction, no matter how advanced it might be, constitutes an extraordinarily valuable and positive feature of Leninist Marxism.

There is another curious feature connected with this, which could never be understood without the first. This feature might be termed 'de-fetishisation', or, in other words, the expulsion of any fetish-like cliché or dogma from any position, etc. At first, we were very often astonished at the unusual audacity with which Vladimir Ilyich tackled certain theoretical or practical problems. Remember such incidents as the Brest-Litovsk peace, when Vladimir Ilyich raised the question as to whether one might take arms from one foreign power for use against the other; this troubled our internationalist conscience to its very depths.[10] Meanwhile, our 'internationalism' was lulled by our theoretical ignorance as to the fact that when we took over power the whole landscape changed. Remember the slogan 'Learn to Trade', which offended the eye of many a good revolutionary, and also had a theoretical substratum, and which was connected with quite a number of theoretical conceptions. The only person capable of such theoretical audacity along with this practice is a person, an ideologist, a theoretician and a practician who himself wields the exceedingly sharp weapon of Marxism, but who at the same time never understood Marxism as some sort of lukewarm dogma, but as an instrument of orientation in definite surroundings, a man who thoroughly understood that every external correlation should inevitably be followed by some other reaction of conduct on the part of the workers' party and of the working class. Indeed, just see how Vladimir Ilyich formulated this conception in general. I do not wish to burden you with quotations, and have not brought any extracts with me, nor have I even worked on any; but I will remind you of a series of points and formulae which Vladimir Ilyich presented. One of his most common tactical formulae concerning experience reads: '**A very great many errors occur through slogans and measures, which were quite correct in a definite historical phase and in a definite state of affairs, being mechanically transferred to another historical setting, another correlation of forces and to other situations.**' That is one of his general tactical formulae. Let us examine the ideology of our opponents, let us take such a problem as democracy, for instance. We also were all democrats during a definite period, we all demanded the democratic republic and the Constituent Assembly only a few months before we overthrew it. That is quite natural. But, nevertheless, only those who understood the relative social rôle of these slogans, who understood that under the capitalist regime we cannot present demands to the capitalists, could adopt such an orientation. And, for this reason, freedom for our workers' organisations had inevitably to receive the formula: 'Freedom for All.' When we pass into another historical phase and situation, we must abandon this formula. Those who adhered to it, and made a fetish of it, did not keep up with the march of events, and were found on the other side of the barricades. This is but a minor example, but there is an endless quantity of such instances. Vladimir Ilyich stood out as having astonishing audacity in this respect.

Let us now take another question in its general formulation. I spoke here about the evolutionary aspect **after** we had carried through the revolution. Take for instance such slogans of Lenin's as 'Learn to Trade', or 'One Specialist is Better Than Such and Such a Number of Communists'. The practical sense of these slogans is now clear to us. They were quite correct, but in order to be able to say these things it is quite evident that some theoretical thinking was necessary. Insofar as the situation has changed, one must act in quite another manner. At the present time, the correlation between the ideology of our Communists and, on the other hand, the necessity to attract non-Communists is of such a nature that it was necessary here to carry out quite a new and peculiar policy of a **constructive** nature. If in former times such words as 'tradesmen', 'trade', 'bank' and so forth, sounded like words of insult for any revolutionary, now, in order to pass on to the slogan 'Learn to Trade', the most profound thinking was essential on a number of basic theoretical questions of great importance in principle. What for us is **only now** just a self-evident thing was thought out theoretically by Lenin down to the most minor detail. After all, it is only the vulgar superficial understanding of our opponents that represents Vladimir Ilyich as a man hewn out with an axe, after the manner of some statuette from the time of the Stone Age. As a matter of fact, this is absolutely untrue. If Comrade Lenin launched some simple slogans as 'Rob the Robbers', this sounded unusually terrible and barbaric for all our civilised opponents; whereas, as a matter of fact, this was but a result of profound theoretical thinking as to what slogan must now be issued, as to what is the mass psychology at the present moment, and as to what the masses will understand and will not understand.

Lenin always approached the question in such a way as to obtain an alliance with the greatest possible number of people who could play the rôle of known quantities of energy to hurl against the old regime. This demanded very elaborate theoretical thinking. But when Lenin said 'It is necessary to learn to trade', this sounded very paradoxical, although now it appears to us quite obvious. Every serious step that Vladimir Ilyich took, both in the theoretical and in the practical field, was in its own way a placing in position of Columbus' egg. When

Columbus' egg was put in position, it appeared to everyone that it could only be made to stand up in that manner. And here you have this slogan 'Learn to Trade', which is dependent upon a number of theoretical calculations and solutions of theoretical problems, the problem of the correlation between town and village, the problem of the rôle of the currency process — and in general the problem as to the rôle of the trading apparatus in this currency process. This was not merely a slogan taken down from the shelf, it was simply a practical watchword formulation of quite a number of theoretical conceptions which had been thought out step by step. Only when you begin to read the thoughts of Vladimir Ilyich volume by volume, and combine the different sectors of his thinking, will you be presented with a clear picture of the ideological path which Vladimir Ilyich trod when working out these problems. Lenin was only able to carry out all these big moves so successfully as a strategist because he was a very strong theorist, who was able quite clearly to analyse the given combination of class forces, take proper stock of them, make theoretical generalisations, and from these theoretical generalisations draw the corresponding practical-political conclusions. What lay at the bottom of all this was the fact that Lenin wielded the Marxist weapon in a masterly way. Lenin never allowed it to get cool, or to remain motionless. It was always a really powerful instrument which in Lenin's hands was turned round to one side or the other according to the demands of **practical actuality**. It is Marxism which, vulgarly speaking, held nothing sacred except the interests of the social revolution. It is an ideological instrument of such a type that knows no fetishes whatsoever, and which understands to a nicety the significance of any theoretical doctrine, of any move, and of any separate theoretical conception, and is foreign to anything lukewarm.

How did Vladimir Ilyich approach a number of problems? When within the party or outside its ranks there arose among us some kind of theoretical digression from Marxism, he at once approached this with a definite practical gauge, because he bound up theory with practice so excellently, and excellently deciphered any verbal superficiality. I said above that if Marx possessed the algebra of revolution, Lenin had both the algebra of the new period, and, I repeat, the arithmetic. But I will cite you one example which I will also have to touch on later in another branch of logical thought. The analysis of Marx's *Capital* is done in such a manner that the peasantry is to a considerable extent eliminated, since it is not a specific class in capitalist society. That is the most advanced algebra of all. But it is obvious that for arithmetical action we need quite other things. So now you see what it is that distinguished Lenin. It is the combination of algebra, at a much higher degree of generalisation (which in mathematics corresponds with the general theory of numbers, or the theory of many variants) with arithmetic, that is, the arithmetical solution of algebraic formulae, the combination of the large with the small. It means being concerned about something or other in the practical field — being concerned about electrification, or about saving some little nail or other, and on the other hand it also means taking care of the theoretical field — being engaged on the most serious of theoretical problems, commencing with philosophical problems, and at the same time tracking down and fishing out every incorrect theoretically formulated detail which might be dangerous in its further development.

This **ability to survey an epoch, and to observe even the smallest detail in it**, this ability to analyse and examine such questions as that of 'the thing in itself', and at the same time to understand the theoretical significance of any formula whatsoever in any given resolution (you all remember that Lenin wrote a number of pages as to how one should not write a resolution in his pamphlet on the 'Two Tactics'[11]) this immense ability to see everything in such proportions that both the very great things and the most minor details are all centred on a little chess-board of political strategy and theory, in just those places where they should be centred from the point of view of the interests of the working class, and from the point of view of practical political action — this ability, I repeat, found its expression in a remarkable synthesis combining theory with practice.

The Problem of Imperialism

Now, comrades, I will proceed to touch on a few points in a more concrete manner, points which are significant mainly from the point of view of **what is new** in all that Vladimir Ilyich brought in here. The most fundamental of all problems is the problem of **imperialism**. The question of imperialism has been formulated by Vladimir Ilyich in his well-known work,[12] and it is quite unnecessary for me to give either a sketch of this, or to give an abridged survey of its contents here. But, comrades, I would like to draw your attention to the fact that you will not be able to name me any one theoretical work concerning imperialism which is so realistic as the work of Vladimir Ilyich, because in his work any theoretical conceptions you may choose, and any statistical illustrations of these theoretical conceptions, are connected with those practical political conclusions which Vladimir Ilyich deduces from them.

It is not just a simple analysis, the theoretical analysis of a particular epoch. It is this analysis taken from such an aspect whereby the path immediately becomes clear upon which the working class must proceed in connection with the development of the ruling class, and in connection with the analysis of imperialism. There is also one more problem which is most important for our epoch that has not yet been resolved in any theoretical work whatsoever. **This is the national problem, and the problem of the colonies — the colonial question.** It seems to me that we might remark here that Vladimir Ilyich produced work that was theoretically enormous. I repeat, there is no such book where everything is collected together and systematised. But in quite a number of his works there is an absolutely correct diagnosis of both the national and the colonial questions, a diagnosis that has been fully proved by our own practice. Here, indeed, Vladimir Ilyich has created an entire school. The substance of the matter is that Marx's degree of abstraction in many problems was so great that it was necessary to establish a whole series of interrelated logical links in order to arrive at direct practical conclusions. I have already indicated that in *Capital* there is an analysis of three classes. Here we do not meet our peasants; here capitalist society is taken in the abstract; its problems are not connected with such things as the world economy, the clash of various capitalist bodies, the problem of the state insofar as it remains in the hands of our enemy, or the question of the rôle of the state in the economic life of the country: that is to say, a number of problems of a more concrete character are not analysed in *Capital*. In order to turn this theoretical system into practical action, and particularly so in our epoch, we had to form a number of interrelated logical links which **in themselves represent very big theoretical problems.**

Those who dealt with the problems of colonial policy in the epoch of opportunism belonged with but a few exceptions to the most out-and-out Revisionists, and were mainly engaged in apologising for the 'civilised' rule of capitalism in the colonies. Marx made quite a number of references to Ireland, and a number of generalisations; but at that time Marx was unable to deal with the question to its fullest extent, because in those days the problem had not acquired such a degree of acuteness as it received afterwards, and the epigones could not do this because of the very nature of the question. It was the Holy of Holies of bourgeois policy of the time, and one dare not lay a desecrating finger on the matter. Gentlemen such as Hilferding entered the arena, and developed all kinds of 'Marxist' theories concerning the colonies in order to justify the policies of the capitalist state.[13] In this respect Lenin's school, which was then being formed, made a complete revolution. The practical significance of this is now perfectly clear. It may be that this Leninist teaching on the national and colonial problems was not always understood by everyone in the initial stages of its development, but now his ideas have become clear. We are concretely faced with a world war and states which have entered a period of decline, and which, according to the Nietzschean law, must be thrust further downwards.[14] In order to expedite this, all the elements in the decline of these bodies must be encouraged, including the separatism of the colonial and national movements, that is, all the destructive forces which objectively weaken the might of the great iron state — this state that is the most potentially powerful force of the bourgeoisie. Therein lies the source of those things that many of us did not understand, both in the field of pure theory, and in that of the practical slogan: the right of nations to self-determination.

In the field of pure theory, the prognosis that in the coming epoch there will be a number of periodical revolutions, colonial risings and nationalist wars, and struggles on the part of some nation or another for freedom against a great power, and similar theoretical prognoses which correspond with a number of periodical stages in the process of the general decline of capitalist relations — all these are prognoses which are based on very well thought out theoretical conceptions. Vladimir Ilyich presented these. I advise all those who are interested in this side of the question to read Vladimir Ilyich's polemical article against Rosa Luxemburg, which was written at the time of the world war.[15] You will be amazed at how the most subtle points of transition, which the overwhelming majority of us (if not all of us) only recognised later when they became facts, had already been theoretically foreseen by Vladimir Ilyich. Why was this? It was because he was a deft tactician and strategist, and the reason for this was because he relied on a tremendous theoretical foresight, which in its turn resulted from an unusually well thought out analysis of existing capitalist relations in all their intricacies and concreteness. This is quite clear to us now.

It is exactly the same with the next period of development, where the working class has already taken power and carries on the struggle with the great powers. Everything possible had to be done for the proper understanding of all that we inherited from the decline of the old imperialist property relations, of the historical forces of their inertia, and also for a theoretical understanding of what had to be preserved of them so as to destroy them at some time in the future — the basis of all these problems had been entirely neglected. The solution to these problems is scattered throughout a number of Vladimir Ilyich's articles, so that we are now able to understand his ideas, and to form out of these ideas a battering ram against bourgeois society on the one hand, and on the other, by means of the lever of the proletarian state, to construct new political institutions, the greatest of which is our Soviet Union. Thus we have here a combination of theory with practice on the basis of new phenomena, which are a result of decline on the one hand, and of new construction on the other.

All of this is summed up in a definite theoretical system. This was no small task, and it will serve us through many decades in the future as one of our most important theoretical and practical weapons. If we remember what rôle colonial risings and national wars have still to play in the general process of the decline of the present capitalist relations, if we continue to review the process of revolution on other continents in a well-reasoned manner, starting with Western Europe, we shall then realise what a mighty weapon the theoretical system of Vladimir Ilyich represents in this sphere. We will also realise what enormous power and method of organising the masses and leading them in struggle is represented by the teaching which Vladimir Ilyich developed in the field of national and colonial problems.

Lenin on the State

I think that the next theoretical problem to which we should devote our attention is the question of **the state in the period of Socialist revolution.** Here it is quite self-evident that there was nothing new in principle in Comrade Lenin's conceptions, but the services he rendered were immense; on the one hand he rehabilitated the genuine teaching of Marx with respect to the state and its rôle in the period of the social revolution — I have in mind here the theory of the destruction of the state power and the objective historical necessity for the collapse of state control — and on the other hand he gave a concretisation, or, as one might say, a deciphering of the problem of the proletarian dictatorship, that is, the teaching as to soviet power being the **form** of the workers' dictatorship.

This side of the matter seems so clear to us today that one might think that there was no need to utter another word about it. It appears thrice clearly to us, since we ourselves built up a state on a new class basis, and according to a new principle of construction — with our own hands. But we must remember the past, and place all that is self-evident and all that appears so clear to us now in a given historical context, and amongst certain historical developments. If we take the old 'Marxist' literature on these problems we will perceive in them a completely mystifying distortion of Marxist teachings. We would not only fail to find in them a single thought that could be called a development of the Marxist theory of state power, or of the Marxist theory of law, or of the problem concerning the changes in these categories during the period of transition, but we would also not find even a single word about the process of the Socialist revolution itself, or about the state of affairs after the revolution. The main task of working class ideology was to restore the genuine Marxist doctrine, and to concretise this very same doctrine, in other words, to give it a definite form in the teaching on the dictatorship of the working class; and this, it stands to reason, was because the problem of our relation towards the state power was, and is now, the main problem — the problem of problems.

Our relation to the class that is hostile to us — the revolutionary relationship to this hostile class — is in the first instance our relation to the most centralised and most rationally constructed organisation of this dominant class, which consists of its state power. It should be quite clear to anyone on the other hand that the most important lever for constructing a society on some new principles of dynamic force, to rearrange the existing productive relations, is the new state power set up and organised by the victorious working class. We have here a number of both theoretical and practical problems of an auxiliary nature. These are set out in their entirety in Vladimir Ilyich's well-known book *State and Revolution*.[16] But this teaching developed by Vladimir Ilyich is not simply a return to the point of view which Marx developed himself. It is a synthesis of the old orthodox Marxist viewpoint with the theoretical generalisation of quite a number of new facts, together with an anticipation of what Marx could not yet have foreseen at the time when he was alive and wrote his works. This problem, as I have already stated, is the key problem of the revolutionary workers' movement, the central question of modern times, and one must not at any price underestimate this theoretical work of Vladimir Ilyich.

It stands to reason that the problem of democracy was also solved — a problem that the epigones of Marxism, the Marxists of the Social Democratic and Second International type, had made quite a fetish of and transformed into a blind dogma quite unrelated to its historical basis, which had therefore led to absolutely incorrect and historically reactionary practical and political conclusions.

Soviet power is something that is being recognised de jure by our greatest and most bitter enemies in the bourgeois camp. The theoretical and practical significance of this idea and teaching about soviet power is really tremendous. If we take the countless number of slogans that are now in circulation in all parts of the globe, there is not the slightest doubt that the most popular of these slogans — out of all those that seize hold of, attract and organise the greatest number of people — **is the slogan for soviet power.** You will recall how when Vladimir Ilyich first returned to us in Russia after many years of absence in exile, we welcomed the famous *April Theses* of Vladimir Ilyich, and that a part of our own party — no small part of the party, as a matter of fact — saw in this practically a betrayal of the usual Marxist ideology.[17] But it is as clear as daylight that no contradiction of Marxism existed here at all. On the contrary, it is quite clear to us now that this was a development of Marxist teaching, of orthodox Marxist teachings about the proletarian dictatorship.

It is now quite clear that soviet power is the most vital form of the existence of the workers' dictatorship, which has a whole number of enormous practical advantages for the victorious working class. But if we at the same time compare this general acknowledgement with the reception that Lenin's first formulae met with even in the ranks of our own party, not to speak of in the ranks of our opponents, then we can realise what an immense practical and theoretical statement was made by Lenin on this occasion. It often happens in the hectic scurry of life that a great deal of what is new to us soon becomes self-evident. But when we begin to carry out an historical survey of these new factors, we have to forget that we have merely become used to them; we have to remember what went on before the present, we have to remember how this theoretical concept was received, and also how we took on board the practical conclusions arising from it. I repeat that not only were they not received with general recognition, but that they were on the contrary the target of bitter attacks. Now they do enjoy full recognition, and this is proof that something really colossal had been achieved here, both from the point of view of the theoretical contemplation of the problems of the proletarian dictatorship and of the theory of state power, as well as from the practical point of view. Bear in mind that this is not only a practical problem, although I did say that the only thing that is decisive for us in the long run is practice. It is a tremendous theoretical problem, because the study of the forms of class rule is both a theoretical and a practical problem for the bourgeoisie also. The question of the forms of its rule is of outstanding interest in exactly the same way as it is for the working class, the only difference being that for the working class it is of much more interest and involves much more difficulty, since different varieties of the state power of the bourgeoisie have historically succeeded each other, whereas the proletariat had never yet enjoyed this power.

Bourgeois states were founded a very long time ago. Various changes in their structure and the reorganisation of the state apparatus are based on immense and long traditions. The various forms of the state regime were established, enormous experience was acquired, etc, etc. The working class has to do everything new without any previous experiments. It has not had the uninterrupted existence of its state, and consequently has not had the existence of a series of the forms of this state. Here it had to build everything anew. And the fact that a concrete form of the proletarian dictatorship had been discovered, a form that was both vital and excellent in its stability, and which revealed the ability to resist all hostile influences and attacks — all this goes to show the immensity of the theoretical services and the practical conclusions from these theoretical premises which ought to be ascribed to Lenin, insofar as he is the theoretician of the workers' state.

Lenin and the Peasantry

Finally, in proceeding further, it is important that we should approach the question of **the working class and the peasantry**. I need not enlarge upon the rôle which this problem plays in our practical politics. But the further we proceed with the development of the revolution in other countries, the more we see that this problem has not only a significance for Russia, but that this problem also has an enormous significance for quite a number of other countries, and one might almost say that the countries in which this problem has no great significance are exceptions to the rule. You can count on your fingers the countries where the peasant problem, combined with the problem of the revolution, does not play the most outstanding rôle. Of course, the basis for the solution of this problem was laid down in general Marxist theory, and it goes without saying that the methodology for the solution of this problem is also contained in the general concepts of Marxism. We all know Marx's formulae with regard to Germany, in which he talks about which combination of forces would be most desirable from a point of view of a successful workers' revolution, when a proletarian revolution would coincide with a peasants' war.[18] Marx foresaw what would be the most favourable circumstances from the point of view of the development of a successful workers' revolution. But the particular working out of this problem, which is the main problem from the point of view of the strategy and tactics of the class struggle, is the work of Lenin alone. Of course, much may be explained here by the fact that Vladimir Ilyich was born, grew up and worked above all in a country where on account of its socio-economic structure the peasant problem could not avoid attracting great attention. But we should bear in mind that here it was not just a question of asserting this fact, but of an exceedingly extensive actual working out of this problem, starting from the most fundamental and deep theoretical problems, and ending with practical political conclusions.

It seems to me that Vladimir Ilyich was the most outstanding **agrarian theoretician** to exist among Marxists. The agrarian problem is the question to which the best pages of his works were devoted. From the very beginning of his conscious activities as an economist and statistician, Vladimir Ilyich began to take up the agrarian problem along with a number of problems of a more abstract nature, such as those of 'the diminishing fertility of the soil', of absolute rent, etc, ending with questions of a practical nature, all bearing on the relations between the working class and the peasantry. All these problems were worked out and developed by Vladimir Ilyich in the most detailed fashion. I do not believe that anyone did so much that was essentially important in the field of the agrarian problem as Vladimir Ilyich did. Furthermore, if it had been dealt with on another level of abstraction, we might then have restricted ourselves to analyses of abstract capitalist society where such remnants of feudal relations as the peasantry played no essential rôle, and could be discarded from the analysis. But no sooner is it a question of commencing to decipher algebraic formulae into arithmetical formulae, or into formulae of a certain type that we might reasonably represent as occupying a particular intermediate position between algebra and arithmetic, then you at once begin to grapple with this question.

The recognition of the fact that during the period of the Socialist revolution the working class must have on its side some ally as representative of the great mass of the people, led to the analysis of the agrarian question. And Lenin's teachings about the alliance between the working class and the peasantry and of the relations between these two classes is one of the corner stones of all that is specific in Vladimir Ilyich's additions to general Marxist theory.

At this point it is interesting to remark that this teaching was developed in a struggle on two fronts; it developed on the one hand in the struggle against the Narodniki,[19] and on the other in the struggle against what we might describe as liberal Marxism. Vladimir Ilyich fought on these two fronts both theoretically and practically, and this struggle is quite adequately and clearly explained from the political point of view, as well as from the viewpoint of revolutionary practice, by the fact that it was solving the problem of finding an ally for the working class; from the point of view of a working class aiming at the successful accomplishment of a Socialist revolution, this problem was connected with yet another deep-rooted problem which had to be come to terms with both theoretically and practically — that of the **hegemony of the proletariat**. It was necessary to explore theoretically such a policy as would make it possible to liberate the peasantry from the influence of the liberals, or of any other bourgeois influence, and unite them with the working class: the most serious practical difference between us and the Mensheviks and SRs was over whether the working class should ally itself with the liberal bourgeoisie or go along with the peasantry, or should the peasantry stand apart from all other groups. The group of the radical Narodniks always put the peasantry first. The liberal Narodniks always stood for an alliance with the liberal bourgeoisie, which was to have hegemony over the peasantry. The Menshevik formula was for the working class to support the liberal bourgeoisie.

It is obvious that out of all these combinations, the only correct one was an alliance of the working class with the peasantry in such a way as would allow the working class to lead the peasantry. This was the practical basis for a number of theoretical problems. From this viewpoint, Lenin examined all the problems under the common heading of 'The Agrarian Question' in their entirety, in their extensive historical scope, and with all the details and subsidiary problems arising from them. We should also remark in this connection that in the future this problem is still bound to play a colossal rôle. This is because whilst on the one side it is bound up with the problem of the hegemony of the proletariat, on the other side it is connected with the national and colonial questions.

If we raise ourselves above our planet today and survey the entire process on an international plane, looking at the whole of Europe and the industrialised parts of America as one entity, comparing Western Europe with the colonies, with China, India and the other colonial dependencies, we shall then see quite clearly that the national revolutionary movement and the colonial movement, or rather a combination of these two, represent but another form of the problem of the relations between the working class and the peasantry. For if Western Europe in the setting of the world economy as a whole represents a great collective town, the colonial dependencies of the capitalist countries represent a huge village. And insofar as the proletariat of the industrialised countries combines its forces for an attack upon the capitalist system and leads into battle millions and yet more millions of colonial slaves, for that reason these slaves are no more nor less than the great peasant reservoir for the international revolution. So the problem with regard to the relations of the working class with the peasantry leads on to yet another problem to which I have already made allusion — that of nationalism, national wars and colonial uprisings.

Thus this problem, comrades, still has to play an important rôle. Here also the basic words were spoken in the school of Lenin. The development of this problem, the foundations of the theoretical concept and the basic line we can observe here have been indubitably provided by Lenin. I think it would be superfluous to talk here about the hegemony of the proletariat and the leading rôle of the working class, because this is a theoretical point with which we are already acquainted, and which needs no comment here. Such in the main are the theoretical problems, along with their practical conclusions, which were stated and resolved by Vladimir Ilyich, and from which general practical conclusions have been drawn. The general edifice has already been constructed; we must now finish it off and work it all out in detail, whilst of course taking into consideration the new factors that will develop in the years to come.

The Theoretical Problems Awaiting Us

In making a general review of the problem, we find about five fundamental theoretical problems that Vladimir Ilyich outlined, and which it is necessary for us to work out. Firstly, there is the study, or rather the course of study, that we have to make of the **transition to Socialism after the successful workers' revolution.** This term 'transition to Socialism' was generally highly distasteful to us. It was repellent because it was a term used by Revisionist teachings, the teachings of the epigones of Marxism, or if you like the betrayers of Marxism, who elaborated an entire theoretical construction according to which the revolution was unnecessary. According to them, it in no way arose out of the objective process of historical development; the working class, they said, can get on excellently without revolution, since capitalism will organically assume such forms as will ultimately correspond with Socialist forms, without catastrophes and by reason of the inherent conditions of the development of capitalism itself. So the working class is continually putting out 'feelers' in various directions, both in the economic sphere and in the realm of state administration, and in this way the working class will occupy strategic positions, both within the state apparatus and in the field of economic management, without the need for any revolution or any dictatorship of the proletariat.

You are all well acquainted with this teaching, and this is what the label 'the transition to Socialism' meant. But comrades, it is immediately **after** the dictatorship of the proletariat that the period of organic development **commences**. If you already have the dictatorship achieved by the workers, it then becomes very clear that the very basis of this problem changes radically, and in principle, just like so many other problems. So if we want to ask ourselves the question as to what should happen after the conquest of power by the working class (naturally insofar as we are referring to one isolated country), it is then a question of the further development towards Socialism in this country proceeding along an evolutionary path, and it cannot be otherwise; in other words, after the conquest of power by the working class, the real transition to Socialism begins.

Vladimir Ilyich did not formulate this in an exact manner. But an endless number of examples can be quoted from Lenin's works to illustrate the idea. He says quite definitely in his later articles, particularly, for example, in the article 'On Cooperation',[20] that whereas during the former period of historical development the hub of our endeavours was a revolutionary policy, now during the present period of construction the hub of our policy is peaceful organisational work. He states exactly what I have just been saying in his formulae, but it should be understood that this must be worked out and reasoned out in its various aspects, for here is an endless number of problems.

It is a question of the evolutionary struggle of economic forms; then of a definite process, firstly of an increase in state power, and then a decrease by an evolutionary path. We must first reinforce and strengthen the ruling organisation of the proletariat; we must strengthen the proletarian dictatorship; then the state organisation will begin to wither away in the same evolutionary manner. There can be no question of any third revolution here, and on the other hand any sudden attack against the system of proletarian dictatorship objectively amounts to nothing more or less than counter-revolution. For this reason, a workers' state is a state of a peculiar type in just the same way as our army, which contains the germ of its own evolutionary destruction, and it is for this very reason that the whole order of development was arranged in its original evolutionary sequence. In fact, the transition to Socialism only begins after the period of the conquest of power and the beginning of the dictatorship of the proletariat. Needless to say, special laws should be applied here, and the elimination of contradictions during this period should be sharply distinguished from the elimination of contradictions during the period of capitalism.

This is for a simple reason. If the development of capitalism is no more than an extended reproduction of its contradictions, which disappear at one period only to reappear at another, and where every successive group or cycle is accompanied by a sharpening of them, ending in the collapse of the entire system, in the new sequence of development starting off from the workers' dictatorship (I am not speaking here of the possibility of destroying a workers' dictatorship from outside, as in Finland[21]) we are faced with a natural sequence, where the development of contradictions begins to be eliminated. I mean to say by this that we will not be faced with the extended reproduction of the contradictions of our system, but with a continual decrease in their reproduction, and this reproduction of the system will be transformed along evolutionary lines into the development of Communism. The whole nature of the development acquires quite another character, quite different in principle than under capitalism. Certain places in Lenin's works can be indicated where this conception is confirmed. This is a new kind of sphere in the construction of theory, where new laws are formulated that are different from those that existed during the period of the development of capitalism. This is new: but it is quite clear that it also has its practical and political conclusions.

If from the situation of Russia today we take the perfectly concrete problems of the New Economic Policy, it is quite evident that we must draw a number of conclusions from these theoretical premises. We shall not overcome the NEP by smashing up all the shops in Moscow and the provinces, but by eliminating it by means of the growth and competition of our state industry and state organisations. I am only giving a small example, but you will see that within it lies the substance of a number of theoretical and practical problems of quite another order, which we had not formerly approached, because in those days our social position was that of destroyers. We were the most decisive, courageous and consistent destroyers of one system, but now we are the most consistent constructors of another system. Its nature is different, and the total sum of the practical and theoretical problems is also different. But it is quite clear that there is here no break whatsoever with traditional Marxism, since it is a matter of continuing and adapting the methods of Marxism under completely new conditions that were quite unknown to both Marx and Engels in their concrete forms, for the simple reason that there were no empirical data that would allow any generalisations to be made.

In connection with this there is one question, which in my opinion acquires very great importance. This question has still to be developed from the theoretical point of view; it is the question of the **problem of culture** during the period of transition. I think that this is a question on which there are many theses scattered throughout a number of Lenin's works. To these we should add his speech at the Youth Congress concerning the rôle and use of specialists,[22] and his speech and theses on Communist education,[23] as well as the question of combining so-called 'proletarian culture' with the old culture, and the way in which this should be done. All these questions together must also be subjected to theoretical analysis. They also represent one of the most important problems of modern times, and I think that we may even say that some of the fundamentals of it can be found in the theoretical concepts of Vladimir Ilyich. We must continue this work. This question is again quite new. No one could have or had broached it during the previous phase of historical development. It did not exist with the most revolutionary of Marxists, or with Marx himself. It is a new task — our future task.

Now we come to the third question, which I might call the question of **various types of Socialism**. In our country, Socialism came down to earth from the clouds, or at any rate nearly so. This is the question of the moment. How did we go about the question of Socialism previously, and how did Marx approach it? Marx put it in this way in one of his letters: 'We know the starting point, and the tendency of development.' This is a thoroughly unmistakable and correct formula. Now taking Lenin's last article 'On Cooperation', let us unravel the concepts he develops. In analysing the old views about cooperation, Vladimir Ilyich states that at the present time, when power has been transferred into the hands of the working class, the approach to this question has changed in principle, and that if we were to lead the peasants to cooperation under the leadership of the working class, it would mean the realisation of Socialism. But this formula would be of no use at that stage in a Soviet Britain. And Vladimir Ilyich frequently emphasised in private conversations, speeches, articles, documents and his works, that we must be very careful when drafting such formulae for other countries.

Maybe the type of Socialism being constructed here shows great originality, arising from the fact that Socialism is being built with existing material. It is as clear as daylight that whilst the capitalist system, standing on the verge of collapse, has its general laws of capitalist development, there also is no doubt that (if we take the general trend of capitalism in the various countries) just as capitalism in one country has its specific form of organisation, it is of quite a different form in another. If capitalism has preserved its existing peculiar characteristics in the various countries, even during the period of its decline, when its development has already gone on for some hundreds of years, and when it is confronted with the terrible force of levelling tendencies, it is self-evident that basic peculiarities will also remain during the period of the construction of Socialism, since the starting point of this development is none other than capitalism.

Revolution in various countries also has its original features, and in the same way the construction of Socialism must also inevitably have its original features. If the peasantry plays such a tremendous rôle in our country, the same cannot be said for Britain, because capitalism in our country was quite different, the socio-economic structure was quite different, the relations between the classes were also of a different nature, and our muzhik was also quite different; for all these reasons it is quite natural that the starting point for the development of Socialism is different. There is also a difference in the intermediate forms through which the development of Socialism passes right up to the time when it is transformed into the universal world Communist system; in fact, these forms will show an extraordinary difference. So you will see that this problem must be theoretically worked out, forming as it does the basis on which practical conclusions must be drawn.

When Vladimir Ilyich worked in the Communist International, one of his warnings to those of us who were working there was that we should on no account lose sight of originality in development, that we should not look at things in a stereotyped manner, that we must be able to distinguish and simultaneously perceive both the general and the minor particularities that sometimes play a decisive rôle in the subsequent transition on the road to Communism. This is the third sequence of problems outlined by Vladimir Ilyich, which has in the main been solved, and which we must now develop and concretise.

In connection with the question of the peasantry and the working class, a most original problem crops up which must be subjected to theoretical analysis. In one of the colleges where I studied, one of the comrades there, Comrade Rozit,[24] brought up this problem, and I think that when this question is presented it requires theoretical attention, and in precisely this context Vladimir Ilyich did a great deal. It is the question of the **theoretical analysis of a two-class society during a workers' dictatorship.** By this we mean the working class and the peasantry. Whereas the capitalist regime was mainly occupied with the problem of analysing a three-class society — the working class, the bourgeoisie and the landowners (which was, after all, simply an abstract analysis) — it would be extremely interesting for us theoretically to approach the problem of the two classes, the working class and the peasantry, following the abolition of landed property and the expropriation of the bourgeoisie. Of course, as we approach nearer to a concrete application, a whole number of very significant modifications will arise, which might radically alter the appearance of our picture, both theoretically and practically. But this problem proceeds along the same lines as the problem of the alliance between the working class and the peasantry, because in substance these classes are none other than the class bearers of particular economic forms.

It cannot be said that these are simply social forces, and nothing more. Each class bears its own economic forms. When we take it as a social class category when speaking of the peasantry, we must not forget that this peasantry bears a definite form of productive units which might overcome us, and which might develop along a course undesirable for us, but which might also take the path along which we **wish** to guide it. As a result, the social class viewpoint here has a purely economic basis and significance, and the question of the relationship between the classes is at the same time also a question of the relationship of economic forms. The question of the hegemony of the proletariat over the peasantry is at the same time also a question of the relationship between Socialist industry and the peasant economy. The whole importance of this question is quite self-evident, and I think that the presentation of the questions that I have here spoken about deserves very great attention.

Finally, there is one more sequence of problems also dealt with by Vladimir Ilyich which has tremendous significance for all of us, for our party and for the working class. For example, there is the problem of the various **contradictions** that have emerged in the process of our present social development under the proletarian dictatorship, and the problem of **tendencies hostile to us, developed by these contradictions.** If under the workers' dictatorship things will proceed on the whole in such a way as to amount to an evolutionary sequence, it by no means follows from this that there will not be extremely great contradictions, which might even **increase** during certain periods of development, particularly during the **first** phase of the dictatorship of the working class. When speaking of the general possibilities of the disappearance of these contradictions, and even going as far as the coming of Communism, this means I am looking at things in the long term. We should not draw the conclusion from this that during certain particular historical periods there will be no increase in contradictions, especially at the beginning of this development.

For instance, with regard to this, there is the question of the so-called **regeneration** of the working class. This question is extremely important for us politically. Vladimir Ilyich brought it up at the Metal Workers Congress,[25] and in fact posed it quite frequently at quite a number of our meetings. He was the first to speak of the possibility of an uncultured proletariat being overcome by a more cultured bourgeoisie, who might beat us by virtue of its cultural training. He made no bones about this danger, which has indeed enormous significance for us. This danger is incorporated into the contradictory tendencies of our development and the contradictory position of the working class itself, which on the one hand stands at the bottom of the social pyramid, and on the other stands on top of it. This contradictory position of the working class causes in turn a number of other contradictions, which can be resolved and removed only after very many years, and during entire historical epochs.

Vladimir Ilyich posed these questions, and solved them in principle. We must now continue to resolve them, drawing the appropriate practical conclusions. All these problems, of the nature of every revolution, of the workers being a culturally oppressed class, and of the danger of the internal degeneration of every revolution, must and will be overcome by analysing antagonistic tendencies, both harmful and useful in their mutual struggle and in the mechanics of their interaction, which could not even be concretely posed in the middle of the last century, or even at the beginning of this one. But they could and had to be posed when a definite amount of material had been accumulated that would allow us to assess these dangers concretely, and the tendencies which we must support and strengthen in order to overcome them.

I am not able to touch on a number of questions of secondary importance, and for the same reason I cannot deal with the question of the general formulation of working class tactics and strategy, since this field of application has its own generalisations; there is in the field of applied Marxism, that is, in the field of applied theory, a peculiar type of law, such as in applied mechanics, for example. Vladimir Ilyich did stupendous things in this respect, but there is no single book where all this is written out, split into paragraphs and presented to you. Lenin's book *Left Wing Communism, An Infantile Disorder*[26] is an attempt to sketch out this general teaching about strategy and tactics, and we now read this book with different eyes than we did formerly. I should say that the reason for this is because we have here an embryo or rough sketch, or rather a general rough draft, of applied Marxism during the epoch of revolution. In this remarkable work are provided all the milestones whereby we may formulate the strategy and tactics of the working class struggle, and which we can use like a syllabus for the study of the strategy and tactics of the working class.

Lenin also takes the palm in this field, since he had such colossal experience gleaned from various situations. He had, for example, the experience of our party when it was a small group of a few people, when it entered the political arena as a semi-legal party in 1905, when it began operating as an underground party but with legal feelers, when it was completely illegal, when it was attacked and had to retreat, etc, etc, and when it finally became a ruling party. Nowhere else was there such experience as this, such a variegated play of different forces, positions and situations, with the completely different types of activity rising from them, and nowhere else was there such an understanding of particular forms, or such a keen search for different paths of orientation. You will not find a single statesman with this experience, either in the bourgeois camp, or with Marx himself. There can be absolutely no question of this.

One of the components of this general totality of the problems of applied Marxism that can be brought together is that group of questions of an organisational and inner party nature. In exactly the same way in this respect we find in

Lenin's works on the organisational question, on the structure of the party, on the relations between the party, the class, the masses and the leaders, etc, incomparable models which have now been verified by the experience of several revolutions, which have now to a considerable degree penetrated the consciousness of very wide masses, which may be regarded as firm gains during the epoch of class struggle, and will become unnecessary only when the class struggle ceases. We have nothing better, and there will be nothing better, in this connection and in these fields — the field of applied Marxism, the field of the organisational structure of the party, the field of the relation of the party organisations with all other organisations, with the non-party masses and even across class boundaries, because here we have entered a fundamentally new epoch with the mechanism of the victorious revolution of the workers.

We conclude that in this respect we will not be able to think out anything better than Lenin, though obviously Leninist ways will continue to be applied to concrete circumstances. Nothing would be more repulsive to Lenin than the transformation of Leninism into a dogma. He had a very low opinion of those 'Old Bolsheviks' (in the bad sense of the word) who were only able to repeat parrot-fashion all that had been written a few years ago. In private conversation he called them 'old fools'. But he did not resort to this hardly academic formula in print, and in all his concepts he firmly demanded both from himself and others that the original thesis be taken into consideration side by side with a definite methodological content.

Anyone who does not take the march of events into consideration, and does not consider the original thesis, will create nothing correct, either in theory or practice. We cannot take up a position during new events without perceiving the growth of new forms, because life is eternally moving, continually producing these new forms, and creating new situations and relations. It is the bounden duty of every theoretician and man of practice, the duty of every Marxist, to sense all these factors more than anyone else. Lenin sensed the new more than anyone else. If we examine his activity, both the theoretical formulae and the practical slogans he produced, we see an absolute fearlessness, an audacity and a quick sense of perception, hitherto unequalled, with regard to what is new. The great changes of course in our party policy, and the corresponding critical formulations that either preceded or coincided with these changes, represent the supreme example of revolutionary Marxist dialectics, which fears no changes of any sort, at every stage in the objective sphere corresponding with the essential changes, and adapting the strategy and tactics of the proletarian party to what is new.

It very often happens that Marx is compared with Lenin, and the question arises as to who was the greater, Marx or Lenin. Usually the reply to this is that Lenin was the greater in practice, and Marx in theory. In my opinion there are no scales by which we might weigh such great figures, for the simple reason that we can neither place together nor measure up the greatness of characters of such different types, who have grown up under different conditions, and have played different rôles. No, we cannot do this. Such a presentation of the question is basically erroneous. But what we can say quite unmistakably is that these two names will determine the future of the working class for as long as the working class really exists as such. This is quite clear, and after Lenin's death we may console ourselves with the thought that we have lived, struggled, fought and conquered under the permanent leadership of our great teacher.

Notes

1. This is an amended version of the text as it appears in the pamphlet published as no 2 in the Lenin Library series by the Communist Party of Great Britain in October 1925. Corrections have been made to the style, as well as to where the printed text was completely impervious to understanding. We are much indebted to Raymond Challinor for the original of this item.

2. VI Lenin, 'Political Report of the Central Committee to the Extraordinary Seventh Congress of the RCP(B)', 7 March 1918, *Collected Works*, Volume 27, Moscow, 1965, p89.

3. Marx's eleventh thesis on Feuerbach: 'The philosophers have only **interpreted** the world, in various ways; the point is to **change** it.' (K Marx: *Early Writings*, Harmondsworth, 1975, p423)

4. 'And now as to myself, no credit is due to me for discovering the existence of classes in modern society nor yet the struggle between them. Long before me bourgeois historians had described the historical development of this class struggle and bourgeois economists the economic anatomy of the classes. What I did that was new was to prove: i. that the **existence of classes** is only bound up with **particular, historic phases in the development of production**; ii. that the class struggle necessarily leads to the **dictatorship of the proletariat**...' (Karl Marx, Letter to Weydemeyer, 5 March 1852, K Marx F Engels, *Correspondence*, London, 1934, p57)

5. The Revisionist controversy, a major questioning of the class theory of the state, was begun by an article entitled 'Probleme des Sozialismus' by Eduard Bernstein (1850-1932), published in *Die Neue Zeit* in October 1896.

6. Nikolai Bukharin, Report on Parliamentarism to the Second Congress of the Comintern, 2 August 1920, in John Riddel (ed), *Workers of the World and Oppressed Peoples, Unite!, Proceedings and Documents of the Second Congress*, Volume 1, New York, 1991, pp421-31.

7. 'In England, for instance, the way to show political power lies open to the working class. Insurrection would be madness where peaceful agitation would more swiftly do the work.' ('The Curtain Raised', interview with Marx in *Woodhull and Caflin's Weekly*, 12 August 1871, Phillip S Foner (ed), *Karl Marx Remembered*, San Francisco, 1983, p245)

8. 'Rebellion in the old style, street fighting with barricades, which decided the issue everywhere up to 1848, was to a considerable extent obsolete... since 1848 the newly built quarters of the big cities have been laid out in long, straight, broad streets, as though made to give full effect to the new cannon and rifles.' (Friedrich Engels, Preface to K Marx, *The Class Struggles in France*, 6 March 1895, Moscow, 1975, pp18-21)

9. The Paris Commune was simply a hint which for Marx served as the basis for a number of brilliant prophecies. But Marx was certainly not in a position to **work out** the problem. [Author's note]

10. VI Lenin, 'The Itch', 22 February 1918, *Collected Works*, Volume 27, Moscow, 1965, pp36-9.

11. VI Lenin, 'Two Tactics of Social Democracy in the Democratic Revolution', July 1905, *Collected Works*, Volume 9, Moscow, 1977, pp13-140.

12. VI Lenin, 'Imperialism, The Highest Stage of Capitalism', June 1916, *Collected Works*, Volume 22, Moscow, 1964, pp185-304.

13. Rudolf Hilferding, *Das Finanzkapital: Eine Studie über die jüngtse Entwicklung des Kapitalismus*, Vienna, 1910; English translation by Sam Gordon, *Finance Capital*, London, 1981.

14. Friedrich Nietzsche (1844-1900) was a German philosopher who believed that superior human beings emerged out of struggle. He believed that it was necessary for the weak and the effete to be forced downwards.

15. VI Lenin, 'The Right of Nations to Self-Determination', May 1914, *Collected Works*, Volume 20, Moscow, 1964, pp393-454.

16. VI Lenin, 'The State and Revolution', September 1917, *Collected Works*, Volume 25, Moscow, 1964, pp 381-492.

17. VI Lenin, 'The Tasks of the Proletariat in the Present Revolution' (the 'April Theses'), 7 April 1917, *Collected Works*, Volume 24, Moscow, 1964, pp19-26. When Lenin returned from Switzerland there was great resistance when he presented these theses, because Stalin and Kamenev had brought over the St Petersburg Committee of the Bolsheviks to support for the Provisional Government in March 1917. There was considerable conflict within the party before they were accepted.

18. 'The whole thing in Germany will depend on the possibility of covering the rear of the proletarian revolution by a second edition of the Peasants' War. Then the affair will be splendid.' (Karl Marx, Letter to Engels, 16 April 1856, K Marx and F Engels, *Correspondence*, London, 1934, p87)

19. Narodniks is the term generally used to identify the supporters of the party of the People's Will (Narodnaya Volya), the Russian peasant-populists.

20. VI Lenin, 'On Cooperation', 4-6 January 1923, *Collected Works*, Volume 33, Moscow, 1966, pp467-75.
21. A general strike in Finland, followed by a premature uprising on 27 January 1918, was smashed by Marshal Mannerheim with the assistance of German troops.
22. VI Lenin, 'The Tasks of the Youth Leagues', 2 October 1920, *Collected Works*, Volume 31, Moscow, 1966, pp283-99.
23. VI Lenin, 'Speech Delivered at an All-Russian Conference of Political Education Workers of Gubernia and Uyezd Education Departments', 3 November 1920, and 'On Proletarian Culture', 8 October 1920, *Collected Works*, Volume 31, Moscow, 1966, pp363-73, 316-7.
24. DP Rozit was one of Bukharin's circle of 'Red Professors', and a member of the Central Control Commission of the CPSU.
25. VI Lenin, 'Speech Delivered at an Enlarged Conference of Moscow Metalworkers', 4 February 1921, *Collected Works*, Volume 32, Moscow, 1965, pp108-11.
26. VI Lenin, '"Left-Wing" Communism: An Infantile Disorder', June 1920, *Collected Works*, Volume 31, Moscow, 1966, pp19-118.

Index

Become a Friend of Porcupine Press

We live in an intellectually mean-spirited age, where horizons are narrow and aspirations low, and where the dominant mood is one of cynicism and despair. Capitalism is as mired as ever in its own contradictions, yet any talk of an alternative society is dismissed with either a sneer or a snarl. Too many radicals and critics have lost their sense of direction and their identity, and wallow in confusion and shallowness as they reject fundamental tenets and values as 'old fashioned'.

We at Porcupine Press consider this to be a mistaken course. We see the present era as a time of opportunity, with the chance to help with the rebirth of radical thought, based unequivocally upon the concept of self-emancipation. Marxism is a rich and broad tradition, centred on human freedom, and it is upon this richness and breadth that we wish to grow. We intend to publish original and provocative new material, as well as translating and republishing material of proven value in the areas of political thought, philosophy, history, cultural theory and economics.

If you are impressed by this book, then why not become a Friend of Porcupine Press, and help us produce more exciting material? Just send us £100 now, and we will send you the next 10 books **absolutely free** as soon as they are published. Details of some of these books can be found on the following pages.

Enquiries should be sent to **Porcupine Press, 10 Woburn Walk, London WC1H 0JL**

Coming soon from Porcupine Press

The Ideas of Leon Trotsky

Edited by Hillel Ticktin (Glasgow University) and Michael Cox (Queen's University, Belfast)

This volume will discuss Trotsky's thought in relation to the major themes of his life: his analysis of the Soviet Union, his understanding of capitalism, and his concept of revolutionary politics.

This collection of essays from the journal *Critique*, with a new introduction, plus some previously unpublished pieces by Trotsky, is not a hagiographic exercise, but is a contribution to the process of critically assessing Trotsky's thought.

Contributors include Hillel Ticktin, Michael Cox, Suzi Weissman (St Mary's College, California), Stephen Dabydeen, Antonio Carlo (University of Cagliari), David Law (University of Keele), Richard Day (Toronto University), Loren Gouldner (Harvard University) and Alan Wald (University of Michigan).

Coming soon from Porcupine Press

A Life-Long Apprenticeship

Bill Hunter

This is the first part of the autobiography of a working class militant who became a leading partisan of the British Trotskyist movement. It covers Bill Hunter's life from his early years growing up in a miner's family in the harsh conditions of the Durham coalfield before the Second World War, through to the founding of the Socialist Labour League in 1959. In it Bill Hunter recounts his introduction to Trotskyism through meeting the group led by Harry Wicks and Hugo Dewar, his experiences as a shop stewards' convenor in an aviation factory during the Second World War, his activities in the Revolutionary Communist Party, which he joined in 1944, his role as a delegate to two congresses of the Fourth International, his editorship of *Socialist Outlook*, and his struggles in the trade unions and the Labour Party.

Coming soon from Porcupine Press

The Political Economy of the 'New' South African Capitalism

Hillel Ticktin

The end of apartheid in South Africa was the cause for much celebration across the world, but it is already clear that there are substantial, perhaps insurmountable, problems confronting the new regime, and it appears to be far from obvious that the entrenched socio-economic inequalities will be overcome.

This book develops a Marxist explanation of the dynamic forces behind the 'end' of apartheid, and of the obstacles and grave difficulties barring the road towards the much-vaunted 'New South Africa' of Nelson Mandela and the ANC government.

Coming soon from Porcupine Press

Marxist Political Economy: Essays in Retrieval

Geoff Pilling

This book consists of a series of essays written over the last 30 years, together with some new material. Most of the essays that have previously been published appear here in a substantially revised form. The underlying conception of the book is the need to rescue the heritage of Marxism from the distortions to which it has been subjected for the last 50 years or more.

The book is in three sections. The first investigates a series of issues in the history of economics, including chapters on the relationship of Ricardo and Marx, the place of Keynes in the history of economic thought and policy, and a survey of the current crisis in bourgeois economics.

The second section is concerned with the contemporary crisis of capitalism, and is focused around an analysis of the monetary relations established after the Second World War and their eventual breakdown.

The third section considers some problems in respect of the notion of the productive forces in the light of the theory of imperialism.

Coming soon from Porcupine Press

The Theory of Revolution in the Young Marx

Michael Löwy

Debates over the nature of the thought of the 'young' or 'early' Marx have been central to the development of Marxism in the postwar world, and there have been many who have sought to counterpose the 'early humanistic' Marx with the 'later scientific' Marx. There have, however, been few detailed and rigorous attempts to trace and explain exactly how Marx came to develop Marxism in the historical and intellectual context he inhabited. This is what Michael Löwy, a distinguished cultural and political critic, offers in this work.

This book seeks to illuminate Marx's philosophical and political trajectory from 1842 to 1848 through a consideration of his relationships with the Young Hegelians, the French socialist workers' movement, and the revolutionary wave of 1848. Demonstrating how Marx constantly sought to unite theory and practice, and how his politics and philosophy mutually informed each other, Löwy also draws out the broader implications for the nature of Marxism through a consideration of such figures as Lenin, Luxemburg, Gramsci, Lukács and Trotsky. This book will be crucial in the restoration of the emancipatory core of Marxism.

Coming soon from Porcupine Press

The Communist Left in Russia, 1918-1938

Ian Hebbes

This pioneering work is a documentary history of the little-known left communist groups, including the Left Communist fraction, the Democratic Centralists, the Communist Workers Group, the Sapronov group and the Workers Truth group. It traces the evolution of this tendency from its origins in the First World War to its physical liquidation in the mid-1930s, as well as its relationship to the more widely known Workers Opposition and the United and Left Oppositions.

Ian Hebbes follows the development and continuity of the communist left in terms of its political positions and social practice, and here presents many rare texts of the period, including many that have never before appeared in the English language. This book will be an essential resource and stimulant to thought for scholars and militants alike.

Coming soon from Porcupine Press

Karl Marx

Karl Korsch

Karl Korsch is widely recognised, along with Georg Lukács and Antonio Gramsci, as one of the founders of 'Western Marxism', yet his biography and study of Marx has not been republished for over 30 years. Acclaimed by academics and activists alike as a classic of its genre, Korsch's *Karl Marx* succeeds in being both a popular introduction to Marx's thought and a stimulating account from a particular philosophical perspective.

Coming soon from Porcupine Press

Every Cook Shall Govern: Soviets Versus Parliament, Echoes From the 1920s

Edited and Introduced by Sebastian Budgen

Socialism is best described as the self-emancipation of the working class, and the Marxist tradition has a rich and partially obscured body of theoretical discussion and debate on the best institutional form for such a socialism.

This anthology presents a broad range of debate on the question of workers' councils (soviets) and parliament in the 1920s, focusing especially on the three main centres of postwar revolutionary activity: Russia 1917-23, Germany 1918-23, and Italy 1919-20. It will bring to the English-speaking audience for the first time many texts from the Austro-Marxists Otto Bauer, Max Adler and Karl Renner, the debate between Antonio Gramsci and Amadeo Bordiga, Karl Korsch's theoretical work on socialisation, writings by the council communists Anton Pannekoek and Hermann Gorter, plus extracts from the debates amongst the rank and file of the factory committee and räte movement.